THE HANDBOOK OF SCHOLARLY WRITING AND PUBLISHING

THE HANDBOOK OF SCHOLARLY WRITING AND PUBLISHING

Tonette S. Rocco and Tim Hatcher, Editors

Foreword by John W. Creswell

JOSSEY-BASS
A Wiley Imprint
www.josseybass.com

Published by Jossey-Bass
A Wiley Imprint
One Montgomery Street, Suite 1200, San Francisco, CA 9104-4594—www.josseybass.com

Jossey-Bass books and products are available through most bookstores. To contact Jossey-Bass directly call our Customer Care Department within the U.S. at 800-956-7739, outside the U.S. at 317-572-3986, or fax 317-572-4002.

Jossey-Bass also publishes its books in a variety of electronic formats. Some content that appears in print may not be available in electronic books.

Library of Congress Cataloging-in-Publication Data
Rocco, Tonette S., 1954-
   The Handbook of Scholarly Writing and Publishing/Tonette S. Rocco and Tim Hatcher, Editors; Foreword by John W. Creswell. — First edition.
      p. cm. — (The Jossey-Bass Higher and Adult Education Series)
   Includes bibliographical references and index.
   ISBN 978-0-470-39335-2 (pbk.)
   ISBN 978-0-470-94918-4 (ebk)
   ISBN 978-0-470-94919-1 (ebk)
   ISBN 978-0-470-94921-4 (ebk)
      1. Authorship.   2. Academic writing.   3. Scholarly publishing.   I. Hatcher, Tim (Tim Gary), 1950-   II. Title.   III. Series.
   PN146.R63   2011
   808'.02—dc22
                                                                                    2010048703

Printed in the United States of America
FIRST EDITION
HB Printing   10 9 8 7 6

THE JOSSEY-BASS HIGHER AND ADULT
EDUCATION SERIES

CONTENTS

For our graduate students, emerging scholars, and colleagues, who have challenged us on our journey to demystify the writing and publishing process

◆ ◆ ◆

For my husband, Maurice T. Madry, who was there at the beginning of my journey to learn to write—Tonette Rocco

◆ ◆ ◆

For our families who should be in a "Family and Significant Other Hall of Fame" for putting up with both of us for the many years it took us to finally birth this book. I thank Linda Hatcher, my wife and partner of many years, for her patience, understanding, and love.
—Tim Hatcher

FOREWORD

The sign of a good book, whether it is a book of poetry, a novella, or an academic text, is that it draws readers in and causes them to reflect on their own experiences. This book, edited by Tonette Rocco and Tim Hatcher, had this effect on me. I thought about my own scholarly writing approach, my publications in academic journals, the reasons that I have embraced writing, the scholarly voice I write in, my collaborations, and my mentoring of students as writers. These are a few of the diverse topics that you will encounter in the twenty-one chapters of this book. These chapters fold into four well-organized parts: becoming a published scholar, improving writing techniques, preparing scholarly manuscripts, and reflecting on the writing and publishing process. Topics such as these are seldom discussed in the research literature; putting them together in one book provides an original contribution to the entire process of scholarly writing. In addition, we readers are treated to an array of discipline perspectives by chapter authors coming from such diverse fields as management, research methods, special education, higher education, educational administration, adult education, communication, curriculum and instruction, and comparative education. So often we expect faculty, students, and practitioners to know how to engage in scholarly writing. But that is not a given. Academics need a skill set for understanding the scholarly writing process just as they do to become good teachers.

I cannot explore here all of the topics raised in this book, but I applaud the advice to consider the skill of academic writing as more than grammar and punctuation. It also involves giving and receiving meaningful constructive criticism, finding time to write, and overcoming writer's block and voice issues. Audience is also important, as I learned during my undergraduate years when one of my professors told me that I needed help learning to write. My parents hired a tutor to work with me. Through many arduous sessions, I learned to write for others rather than for myself.

I appreciated in this book reference to the reality of writing: that scholarly writing emerges from rough beginnings and then smoothes out through revising and editing. I often bring to my research methods classes initial drafts of my books or articles and compare them with the final version. This approach is what the chapter authors underscore: that research is a process that unfolds over time.

Advice is plentiful in this book. How does a scholarly writer find voice? How does an author make sense of feedback from reviewers? How should a person write to be sensitive to cultural issues? I especially liked the triad of chapters about preparing (and the differences among) research articles that might be qualitative, quantitative, or mixed in their methodological orientation.

As a former editor of an international journal, I appreciated the advice for prospective authors—advice that fills in the blanks of somewhat general author guidelines typically found on Web sites or as statements in the front of journal issues. We learn about the emotional devastation resulting from unfair or unreasonable criticism and what the recovery period looks like, reasons for rejection, and how to prioritize the comments received.

You can see that this book not only takes you into an engaging portrait of scholarly writing; it also draws you in and causes personal reflection. Your experiences may certainly differ from mine, but I daresay that you will be a more reflective writer and more aware of scholarly writing by the end of this book.

◆ ◆ ◆

JOHN W. CRESWELL
UNIVERSITY OF NEBRASKA-LINCOLN

PREFACE

This book is intended to enable emerging scholars and anyone else wishing to improve their writing skills to better understand the parts of a manuscript and how they fit together and support each other to create a quality publication. Our goal is to fill a conceptual and practical gap within the literature by bringing together in one book different perspectives and providing information about different types of manuscripts that a scholarly writer is likely to encounter.

The Handbook of Scholarly Writing and Publishing is unique in that it brings together the wisdom of scholars from different professions (education, business, communications), disciplines (adult education, comparative education, educational leadership, higher education, human resource development, management, research methods, special education, teacher preparation), and countries (Australia, Canada, China, India, Netherlands, Russia, United Kingdom, the United States) who share their insights into specific aspects of scholarly writing and publishing. The chapter authors represent a wide range of experience and expertise, from doctoral students to established and prolific authors (including a few who have written books on writing for publication). Many have won awards for their writing, and most have been editors of journals or reviewers of manuscripts, or both.

Content Overview

The book is divided into four parts. Part One, "Becoming a Published Scholar," contains six chapters. The first chapter provides an overview of the reasons to write, creating writing opportunities, learning to write, writing tips, and helping others to write. The second chapter presents information on publishing in peer-reviewed academic journals and nonrefereed professional journals. Three doctoral candidates share their insights in Chapter Three on organizing materials for a writing project, overcoming writer's block, and techniques for working with coauthors. Chapter Four presents techniques for reading critically to improve scholarly writing. The last two chapters in Part One deal with the tensions of writing a dissertation and publishing (Chapter Five) and with designing a dissertation project to yield multiple publications (Chapter Six). Graduate students and their advisors are the primary audience for the chapters in Part One. More experienced authors may learn new ways to organize notes, critically read and write, and simply overcome writer's block.

The four chapters in Part Two, "Improving Writing Techniques," provide insights for authors on writing concisely (Chapter Seven), developing a scholarly voice (Chapter Eight), understanding common problems with manuscripts (Chapter Nine), and crafting a problem and purpose statement (Chapter Ten). A problem for journal editors is that manuscripts written in a clear and concise style with a well-defined and well-articulated problem and purpose statement are not the norm. This means that anyone who writes for publication can benefit from the insights provided in these chapters.

The six chapters in Part Three, "Preparing Scholarly Manuscripts," offer useful information for all scholars. They provide guidance on developing specific types of manuscripts such as literature reviews (Chapter Eleven); qualitative (Chapter Twelve), quantitative (Chapter Thirteen), and mixed methods (Chapter Fourteen) reports; conceptual or position pieces (Chapter Fifteen); and book reviews, editorials, and essays (Chapter Sixteen).

The five chapters in Part Four, "Reflecting on the Writing and Publishing Process," cover topics such as becoming a reviewer (Chapter Seventeen), addressing feedback (Chapter Eighteen), dilemmas international authors face (Chapter Nineteen), working with coauthors (Chapter Twenty), and mentoring (Chapter Twenty-One). The book ends with a section of resources for further reading on scholarly writing, highly useful to anyone developing a manuscript or thinking about developing one.

Audience

The Handbook of Scholarly Writing and Publishing is for anyone interested in improving their writing skills and better understanding the processes behind developing and publishing scholarship. Although the focus is primarily on helping graduate students and emerging scholars, those in midcareer and even more established scholars may find helpful insights as well. Emerging scholars (graduate students, scholar-practitioners, and new faculty) are given specific guidelines on how to craft scholarly papers and other writing suitable for submission to academic journals and other ventures within their respective fields of study. They will also gain information on how to follow through with editors, how to handle rejection, and advice on rewrites and resubmittals. Another audience is instructors who teach writing for publication and who mentor colleagues and graduate students through the practice of writing and publishing. Professors who teach advanced doctoral students dissertation writing and instructors who teach research methods may also find the book useful. Finally, since much of the book is about the publishing process, we hope journal editors will find the book a useful reference in their work with authors.

Acknowledgments

We have many people to acknowledge and thank. First, we extend our sincere and heartfelt thanks to our contributing authors, without whom this book would not have been possible and whose intellect, expertise, experience, time, energy, and patience are without equal. Next, we are forever grateful to our editor, David Brightman, who believed in this project from its inception. His feedback and insights have been invaluable to this process. We would be remiss if we did not acknowledge the many students and colleagues who challenged us and gave both of us ample opportunities to learn about the contributions of scholarly writing.

TONETTE S. ROCCO
TIM HATCHER

ABOUT THE EDITORS

TONETTE S. ROCCO is associate professor in the Adult Education and Human Resource Development Program at Florida International University in Miami. She has published four books and coedited a special issue of *Advances in Developing Human Resources*. *Challenging the Parameters of Adult Education: John Ohliger and the Quest for Social Democracy* (with André Grace, 2009) received the 2009 University Continuing Education Association Frandson Book Award. She received the Elwood F. Holton III Research Excellence Award 2008 from *Human Resource Development Review* and a Cyril O. Houle Fellowship funded by the Kellogg Foundation. Her university awarded her the 2010 Excellence in Mentorship award. She has over one hundred publications in journals, books, and proceedings. She is coeditor of *New Horizons in Adult Education and Human Resource Development*, assistant editor for *Human Resource Development Quarterly*, and qualitative methods editor for *Human Resource Development International*. She is a founding board member for the *Journal of Mixed Methods Research* and serves on several boards.

TIM HATCHER is associate professor of human resource development and adult education at North Carolina State University in Raleigh. He joined academe in 1991 after twenty years of working in international business and industry where he was primary author of several hundred procedures, specifications, and manuals. Since 1991, he has published over one hundred book chapters, research articles, concept articles, editorials, books, white papers, conference proceedings, and other scholarly writing. His book *Ethics and HRD: A New Approach to Responsible Organizations* was awarded the Academy of Human Resource Development 2002 Outstanding Book Award. For eight years as associate editor (2002–2005) and then editor (2006–2009) of the *Human Resource Development Quarterly,* he managed the blind review, editing, and publication of several hundred research manuscripts. He has been or is on the editorial board of five international journals.

ABOUT THE AUTHORS

CLAIRE AITCHISON is a senior lecturer (postgraduate literacies) in the Learning Skills Unit at the University of Western Sydney, Australia, where she coordinates writing development for higher-degree research students. Her research interests are pedagogies for doctoral education and doctoral writing, including writing for publication and thesis writing. Her recent publications include *Publishing Pedagogies for the Doctorate and Beyond* (2010) with Barbara Kamler and Alison Lee; "Writing Groups for Doctoral Education," *Studies in Higher Education* (2009); and, with A. Lee, "Writing In, Writing Out: Doctoral Writing as Peer Work," in M. Walker and P. Thomson (Eds.), *The Routledge Doctoral Supervisor's Companion* (2010). She has a Citation for Outstanding Contribution to Student Learning in postgraduate writing from the Australian Learning and Teaching Council (2008) and is an editor for the *Journal of Academic Language and Learning*.

RALPH G. BROCKETT is professor in the Department of Educational Psychology and Counseling at the University of Tennessee, Knoxville, where he teaches graduate courses in adult education and adult learning. He has served as coeditor of *Adult Learning* and editor-in-chief of the New Directions for Adult and Continuing Education series. He has also served on the editorial boards of four other periodicals, including *Adult Education Quarterly* and the *International Journal of Self-Directed Learning*. He is coauthor, editor, or coeditor of ten books, including *The Profession and Practice of Adult Education* (with Sharan B. Merriam), which received the

Cyril O. Houle Award for Outstanding Literature in Adult Education, and *Toward Ethical Practice* (with Roger Hiemstra). In 2005, he was inducted into the International Adult and Continuing Education Hall of Fame.

STEPHEN D. BROOKFIELD is Distinguished University Professor of the University of St. Thomas in Minneapolis-St. Paul, where in 2008 he won the university's Diversity in Teaching and Research Award and the John Ireland Teaching and Scholarship Award. He has written and edited thirteen books on adult learning, teaching, leadership, and critical thinking, four of which have won the Cyril O. Houle World Award for Literature in Adult Education (in 1986, 1989, 1996, and 2005). He also won the 1986 Imogene Okes Award for Outstanding Research in Adult Education. He has authored over seventy-five chapters in edited books, published over seventy articles in refereed journals, and delivered over forty papers that were published in juried conference proceedings. His work has been translated into German, Finnish, Korean, and Chinese.

RONALD M. CERVERO is associate dean for outreach and engagement in the College of Education and codirector of the Institute for Evidence-Based Health Professions Education at the University of Georgia. He is also a professor in the Department of Lifelong Education, Administration, and Policy. Of his six books, three have won national awards, including the 1989 Cyril O. Houle World Award for Literature in Adult Education. He has received the Imogene Okes Award for Research three times from the American Association for Adult and Continuing Education for his research into the politics of education. He has served in a variety of leadership positions in adult education, including as editor of *Adult Education Quarterly*.

BRADLEY C. COURTENAY is professor emeritus in the Adult Education Program at the University of Georgia, having retired in 2007. He was rehired as a part-time professor a month after retirement to coordinate a distance education doctoral program and coordinate training and development grants. He continues scholarly activities in advising doctoral students, writing for publication, and serving on editorial boards. Results of his research have been published in *Adult Education Quarterly*, *International Journal of Lifelong Education*, and *Journal of Adult Development*. He is a coeditor of *Global Issues in Adult Education: Perspectives from Southern Africa, Latin America, and the United States* and an active reviewer for *Adult Education Quarterly*, *International Journal of Lifelong Learning*, and *Journal of Research and Reflection in Education*.

JOHN M. DIRKX, is professor of higher, adult and lifelong education at Michigan State University. He is also the editor of *Adult Learning and the Emotional Self* and a coauthor of *A Guide to Planning and Implementing Instruction for Adults: A Theme-Based Approach,* both published by Jossey-Bass. He is the author of numerous book chapters and journal articles. He is a former editor of *Adult Education Quarterly* and current editor of the *Journal of Transformative Education.* He serves on the editorial boards of several journals, including *Adult Education Quarterly, Adult Basic Education,* and *Human Resource Development Review.* In addition, he has served as a guest reviewer for *Human Resource Development Quarterly* and *American Educational Research Journal.*

ROBERT DONMOYER is professor of leadership studies at the University of San Diego (USD), California. He has been the editor of the journal *Theory into Practice* and the American Educational Research Association journal *Educational Researcher.* He has published three books and over one hundred papers in a wide range of publications, including *Daedalus: The Journal of the American Academy of Arts and Sciences,* the *International Journal of Qualitative Research in Education, Nonprofit and Voluntary Sector Quarterly,* and *Educational Administration Quarterly.* In 2008, he received the USD University Professorship Award given to faculty who have exhibited a sustained record of excellence in teaching, research, and service.

ANDREA D. ELLINGER is a professor in the Department of Human Resource Development and Technology in the College of Business and Technology at the University of Texas at Tyler. She was the recipient of the 1998 Malcolm S. Knowles Dissertation of the Year and the 2003 and 2005 Richard A. Swanson Research Excellence Award presented by the Academy of Human Resource Development and was also awarded a Cyril O. Houle Fellowship funded by the Kellogg Foundation. She was recently awarded an Outstanding Paper Award from the Emerald Literati Network 2009 Awards for Excellence. She is the associate editor of *Human Resource Development Quarterly* and is a series coeditor for the American Management Association's Innovations in Adult Learning: Theory into Practice book series sponsored and published by AMACOM.

ERWIN H. EPSTEIN is director of the Center for Comparative Education at Loyola University Chicago. He was for ten years editor of *Comparative Education Review* and currently serves on the International Advisory Board of the British journal *Comparative Education.* He has served on editorial boards of a variety of journals, including the *American Journal of Education* and the Spanish-language edition of *Educational Policy Archives.* He has taught a course on writing and editing at the Ohio State University, as well as at Loyola University Chicago, and has lectured on writing and editing at Harvard University, Florida International University, Tel Aviv University in Israel, and the World Bank. He currently serves as historian of the Comparative and International Education Society.

JESUS FERNANDEZ is the associate provost for curriculum for DeVry University and a doctoral candidate at Florida International University's College of Education in the adult education and human resource development program. Prior to his work in higher education administration, he held several senior management human resource positions in the financial services industry. He has presented at the Florida Educational Research Association Annual Conference, the Academy of Human Resource Development Annual International Conference, and the Association of Hispanics in Higher Education Conference. He is a member of the academic editorial board for the *Business Journal of Hispanic Research* and has served as a manuscript reviewer for the journal.

ROGER HIEMSTRA is professor emeritus, Syracuse University, and adjunct professor at Le Moyne College and the University of Tennessee. He is the coeditor of the *International Journal of Self-Directed Learning* and editorial review member of *Perspectives: The New York Journal of Adult Learning*. An inductee of the International Adult and Continuing Education Hall of Fame, he is coauthor of *Professional Writing: Processes, Strategies, and Tips for Publishing in Education Journals*. He developed the Internet-based "APA Primer," which provides hints on using the sixth edition of the American Psychological Association–sanctioned stylistic guidelines.

SUSAN IMEL has been either editor in chief or co-editor in chief of New Directions for Adult and Continuing Education since 1996. From 1981 through 2003, she managed the major publications program for the ERIC Clearinghouse on Adult, Career, and Vocational Education and also wrote many ERIC synthesis publications. She is on the editorial boards of *Adult Education Quarterly* and *New Horizons in Adult Education and Human Resource Development*. She has also authored a number of book chapters; most recently, she coauthored, with K. Duckett, the chapter "Libraries and Lifelong Learning" in the *Routledge International Handbook of Lifelong Learning* (2009), edited by Peter Jarvis. For many years, she taught a course on developing literature reviews.

RONALD L. JACOBS, is professor of human resource development in the Workforce Development and Education section at the Ohio State University. He has written over one hundred journal articles and book chapters, and six books on different areas of human resource development, workplace learning, and the research process. He has been an invited professor at the University of Utrecht, the Netherlands; the Shaw Distinguished Professor at Nanyang University, Singapore; and an adjunct professor of human resource development at East China Normal University, Shanghai. In 1994, he received the instructional technology research award from ASTD and in 1995 was recognized for his scholarly contributions to the field by the Academy of Human Resource Development. From 1998 to 2001, Jacobs served as the editor of the *Human Resource Development Quarterly* and has served on the editorial boards of several HRD-related journals.

ALISON LEE is professor of education and director of the Centre for Research in Learning and Change at the University of Technology, Sydney, Australia. She has researched and published extensively in higher and professional education, with a particular focus on doctoral education, doctoral supervision, and doctoral writing and publishing. She is coeditor (with Claire Aitchison and Barbara Kamler) of *Publishing Pedagogies for the Doctorate and Beyond* (2010) and of *Literacy and Numeracy Studies: An International Journal in the Education and Training of Adults.*

MONICA LEE is a visiting professor at Northumbria University, and a life member of Lancaster University in the United Kingdom. She is a chartered psychologist, a fellow of the Chartered Institute of Personnel and Development, and associate fellow of British Psychological Society. She is founding editor in chief of *Human Resource Development International* (1998–2002), editor of the Routledge monograph series Studies in HRD, and executive secretary to the University Forum for HRD. She came to academe from the business world, where she was managing director of a development consultancy. She has worked extensively in Central Europe, the Commonwealth of Independent States, and the United States coordinating and collaborating in research and teaching initiatives. Her publications include articles in *Human Relations, Human Resource Development International,* and *Management Learning and Personnel Review* and books such as *HRD in a Complex World* (2003).

KIMBERLY S. MCDONALD is a professor and chair of the Division of Organizational Leadership and Supervision at Indiana University-Purdue University in Fort Wayne. Her research focus is on career development issues, ethics in human resource development (HRD), and diversity education. She has published over fifty articles, chapters, and proceedings in several HRD- and career-related journals and has served as an issue coeditor for *Advances in Developing Human Resources* and the *Journal of Management Development.* Two of her conference papers have won awards from the Academy for Human Resource Development and the Institute of Behavioral and Applied Management. She is the associate editor in chief for *Advances in Developing Human Resources.*

GARY N. MCLEAN is senior professor and executive director of international human resource development programs at Texas A&M University and former professor and coordinator of human resource development and adult education at the University of Minnesota, St. Paul. He has served as president of the Academy of Human Resource Development (AHRD) and the International Management Development Association. He is installed in the Scholar Hall of Fame of the AHRD and in the International Adult and Continuing Education Hall of Fame. He recently received an honorary Ph.D. from the National Institute for Development Administration, Bangkok, Thailand. He has published widely and received the AHRD Outstanding Book of the Year Award. As an organizational development practitioner in McLean Global Consulting, he works globally.

SUNNY L. MUNN is a Ph.D. candidate in workforce development and education at Ohio State University. She teaches in the Corporate Training and Development undergraduate program and also served as a graduate admissions advisor. She received the Best Policy Paper award for her master's thesis on child support, visitation, and the rights of never-married fathers in her master's of public administration program. Sunny has published over ten articles, chapters, reviews, and proceedings. She has published in the *Journal of Public Policy and Management, Advances in Developing Human Resources,* and *New Horizons in Adult Education and Human Resource Development.* She serves as a peer reviewer for several conferences and journals in addition to presenting and publishing research at numerous academic conferences each year.

CLAIRE KOSTOPULOS NACKONEY is a lead learning and development consultant for a Fortune 500 insurance company. She has worked professionally in the field of human resource development for over twenty years and is a doctoral candidate at Florida International University's College of Education in the adult education and human resource development program. She is a reviewer for *Human Resource Development Quarterly.* She has written book reviews that have been published in *Human Resource Development Quarterly, Adult Education Quarterly,* and *New Horizons in Adult Education and Human Resource Development.* She has also presented papers at Academy of Human Resource Development and the Adult Education Research conferences that have been published in conference proceedings

ANN I. NEVIN is former visiting professor at Florida International University, an adjunct professor at Chapman University, Orange, California, and professor emerita at Arizona State University. Having authored or coauthored over a dozen books, more than seventy-five refereed research articles, and a score of chapters in edited books, she is recognized for her scholarship and dedication to providing mentoring and coaching to colleagues and students who want to publish their work. She is associate editor of the *Journal of Educational and Psychological Consultation.* She has codeveloped innovative teacher education programs, including the Vermont Consulting Teacher Program, Collaborative Consultation

Project Re-Tool sponsored by the Council for Exceptional Children, the Arizona State University program for special educators in infusing self-determination skills throughout the curriculum, and the Florida International University Urban Special Education Academic Leaders doctoral program.

CAROLE NEWMAN is a professor emeritus at the University of Akron, College of Education, where she received teaching and research awards as a teacher educator in the Department of Curricular and Instructional Studies. Currently she is an adjunct professor in teacher education at Florida International University and an educational consultant focusing on professional development. During her career, she has authored or coauthored more than one hundred refereed articles and presentations, and five chapters and books focusing on research and educational practice. She also served as a reviewer for three journals and a number of regional and national organizations. In addition, she has received over $6 million in federal and state grants and serves as a grant evaluator.

DAVID NEWMAN is the data manager for Reading First Ohio, a multimillion-dollar, multiyear No Child Left Behind federal grant. Among his major grant responsibilities are data analysis and program evaluation. He has taught research methods and statistical analyses at the University of Akron and has served as an evaluator on state and federal grants, focusing on educational and medical research. He is recognized for his methodological expertise in cutting-edge quantitative methods, such as HLM and multivariate analysis, and has a strong background in qualitative methods. These skills afford him a unique perspective on mixed-methods research. Because of his background and experience, he has been a reviewer for national and regional organizations, has consulted on more than sixty dissertations, and is highly sought after as a research and design methodologist. He is also chair of the AERA Multiple Linear Regression/General Linear Model Special Interest Group.

ISADORE NEWMAN is the visiting director of research and graduate studies for the College of Education at Florida International University. He is a Distinguished Professor Emeritus at the University of Akron, publishing over one hundred refereed articles, over three hundred refereed presentations, and approximately fourteen books, chapters, and monographs. He was honored by the University of Akron with the establishment of the Isadore Newman Endowed Research Fellow for the Center for Urban and Higher Education. He is a founding editor of *MidWestern Educational Research Journal* and was editor of the *Ohio Journal of Science;* he was also editor of *Multiple Linear Regression Viewpoints Journal* for nineteen years and served on many editorial boards. He received the University of Akron

Outstanding Teaching Award, Outstanding Researcher, and Service awards. He also received the Outstanding Alumni Award from Southern Illinois University, the Outstanding Evaluator Award from the State of Ohio (sponsored by State of Ohio Department of Mental Health), an award for dedicated service and contributions to multiple linear regression from the Special Interest Group of the American Educational Research Association, and an Outstanding Reviewer Award from the American Educational Research Association.

ANTHONY H. NORMORE is associate professor and program development coordinator of the doctorate in educational leadership at the California State University-Dominguez Hills in Los Angeles. His books include *Leadership for Social Justice: Promoting Equity and Excellence Through Inquiry and Reflective Practice* (2008); *Leadership and Intercultural Dynamics,* coauthored with John Collard (2009); and *Educational Leadership Preparation: Innovation and Interdisciplinary Approaches to the Ed.D. and Graduate Education,* coauthored with Gaetane Jean-Marie (2010). Normore is the book series editor for Advances in Educational Administration (Emerald Publishing, UK) and associate editor for *Asia Pacific Education Review* (Seoul National University, Korea) and *Journal of School Leadership* (University of Missouri-Columbia). He has published over one hundred articles, reviews, reports, and proceedings.

AAHAD M. OSMAN-GANI is a senior professor of business administration at the International University Malaysia in Kuala Lumpur, Malaysia. He is the editor (Asia) of *International Journal of Training and Development,* managing board member of *Human Resource Development International,* and editorial board member of several international journals. He was recognized as the Outstanding Human Resource Development Scholar 2009 by the Academy of Human Resource Development for his distinguished record. He has received several best paper awards from reputed journals and conferences and other recognitions from professional societies and academic institutions. He has written extensively in the areas of cross-cultural management and international human resource development, and published more than 150 journal articles, conference papers, book chapters, case studies, and research monographs. A prominent international scholar, he has been the keynote speaker and conference chair of many scholarly and professional conferences held across several countries in Asia, North America, and Europe.

MARIA S. PLAKHOTNIK earned a doctorate in adult education and human resource development from Florida International University, Miami. She has presented at several international, national, and local conferences and authored and coauthored publications that have appeared in the *Human Resource Development Quarterly, Adult Education Quarterly, New Horizons in Adult Education and Human Resource Development,*

New Directions in Adult and Continuing Education, and *Race, Gender, and Class.* From 2005 to 2009, she served as the managing editor of an open source peer-reviewed journal, *New Horizons in Adult Education and Human Resource Development.* In 2010, she was awarded a Dissertation Year Fellowship at Florida International University.

ROB F. POELL is professor of human resource development (HRD) in the Department of Human Resource Studies at Tilburg University, the Netherlands. He is currently editor in chief of *Human Resource Development International* and previously served as editor of several Dutch-language HRD journals for some ten years. He has published 150 articles and chapters in English and Dutch, four books, forty special issues in Dutch, and nine coedited books in English. Two recent books in his key area of expertise, workplace learning, which he coedited with Marianne Van Woerkom were published in 2010: *Workplace Learning* (Routledge) and *Supporting Workplace Learning* (Springer). Two of his papers have won conference awards, and he is the recipient of the Malcolm S. Knowles Dissertation of the Year 1998 Award of the Academy of Human Resource Development.

M. BRAD SHUCK earned his doctorate in education in adult education and human resource development from Florida International University in Miami. Shuck has held several leadership positions in both private and public organizations overseeing large-scale human resource and organizational development initiatives centered on employee engagement and employee wellbeing. His work has been published in *Human Resource Development Review,* the *International Journal of Small Business,* the *Journal of Genetic Psychology,* and *New Horizons in Adult Education and Human Resource Development.* Shuck currently serves as co-chair for publications for the Academy of Human Resource Development's Scholar-Practitioner SIG and has been a manuscript and conference proceedings reviewer for *Human Resource Development Review,* the *Academy of Human Resource Development,* and *New Horizons in Adult Education and Human Resource Development* for the past four years.

GARY J. SKOLITS directs the evaluation, statistics, and measurement doctoral program at the University of Tennessee, where he teaches evaluation theory, methods, and practice. He has published articles in the leading evaluation journals in the United States and Canada, as well as research studies in education journals encompassing K–12 and higher education content areas. He has also written and published over ninety evaluation studies in his role as the director of the University of Tennessee's Institute for Assessment and Evaluation.

JACQUELINE S. THOUSAND is a professor in the College of Education at California State University, San Marcos, where she co-coordinates the special education professional preparation and master's programs. Previously she directed inclusion facilitator and early childhood special education graduate and postgraduate professional preparation programs at the University of Vermont. She is a nationally known teacher, author, systems change consultant, and advocate for disability rights and inclusive education. She has authored numerous books, research articles, and chapters on issues related to inclusive schooling, organizational change, differentiated instruction and universal design, cooperative group learning, creative problem solving, and co-teaching and collaborative planning. She is actively involved in international teacher education endeavors and serves on the editorial boards of several national and international journals.

RICHARD A. VILLA has worked with thousands of teachers and administrators throughout North America. In addition, he has provided technical assistance to the United States, Canadian, Vietnamese, Laotian, British, and Honduran departments of education. His primary field of expertise is the development of administrative and instructional support systems for educating all students within general education settings. He has authored or coauthored numerous articles and book chapters on inclusive education, differentiated instruction, collaborative planning and teaching, and school restructuring. The professional development activities he has created and offered range from short-term keynote addresses and papers presented at national and international conferences, two-day workshops with guided practice for school teams, three- to five-day programs, three-week intensive workshops, and semester-long programs offered through universities.

MIKE WALLACE is a professor of public management at Cardiff Business School, Cardiff University, United Kingdom, where he researches the management of public service change. He is also interested in professional development for social science researchers, serving as the U.K. Economic and Social Research Council's strategic advisor for researcher development. His research training activity includes workshops on key writing tasks, such as critical reviewing of literature and developing research proposals. He is coauthor with Alison Wray of *Critical Reading and Writing for Postgraduates* (2006). He has published over eighty articles, chapters, and reports and nine books reporting his own and related research. He has also developed e-learning materials on study skills for postgraduates and published three edited textbooks on critical reading.

ALISON WRAY is a research professor in language and communication at Cardiff University, United Kingdom. She is an international research expert on formulaic language, with applications in language learning, language disorders, and evolution of language. She has a strong interest in researcher development, including research coaching, and is lead author of *Projects in Linguistics* (2006), an undergraduate textbook on research methods, and coauthor with Mike Wallace of *Critical Reading and Writing for Postgraduates* (2006). She has authored three major research monographs and edited two others. Her 2002 book, *Formulaic Language and the Lexicon,* won the annual book prize of the British Association for Applied Linguistics. She has published over seventy papers, including a number on her subsidiary area of interest: historically authentic pronunciation for early vocal music.

BAIYIN YANG is professor and chair of the Department of Human Resources and Organizational Behavior, School of Economics and Management, Tsinghua University, China. He received a Distinguished Young Scholars award from the National Natural Science Foundation of China and an Outstanding Scholar Award from the Academy of Human Resource Development. His research articles have been recognized by *Human Resource Development Review* and the Academy of Human Resource Development Annual Conferences. He is the editor of *Human Resource Development Quarterly.* He has published over forty articles and chapters, over fifty conference proceedings, and one book.

THE HANDBOOK OF SCHOLARLY
WRITING AND PUBLISHING

PART ONE

BECOMING A PUBLISHED SCHOLAR

CHAPTER 1

REASONS TO WRITE, WRITING OPPORTUNITIES, AND OTHER CONSIDERATIONS

Tonette S. Rocco

Neither my life experiences nor my academic experiences prepared me for scholarly writing and publication. When as a doctoral student I asked faculty how to write for publication, the response was vague. This set me on a path to learn how to write and publish. I continue to improve my writing by learning about writing and publishing. I do this by observing good writers, listening to authors talk about how they write, and finding colleagues to write with who are good at the craft. In this chapter, I discuss reasons to write, creating writing opportunities, learning to write, writing tips, and helping others write.

Reasons to Write

Writing can be a miserable chore, a difficult undertaking, and a challenge that produces growth and satisfaction—all at the same time. Hours, days, and sometimes months are spent just getting started. Scholars write for different professional and personal reasons, such as financial rewards, advancement, and joy. New assistant professors work at writing to keep their positions, to earn promotions, and sometimes to receive merit increases based on productivity. This might translate into the type of profit suggested in this quotation that a doctoral student shared with me (Nielson & Rocco, 2002): "An article published in a major journal early in a career could be worth about $25,000 in pay and benefits. A quality article in an important journal can mean a better job, higher pay over a long career with increased retirement and other benefits. . . . In hard cash, the average scholarly publication could be worth about $200 a year for every year you work" (Phillips, 1982, p. 95). Although I question whether an article is worth this now or whether one publication—even in a significant journal—is sufficient for an increase in salary, a consistent publication record does have rewards. A well-placed and well-received article can generate other opportunities with a financial benefit, such as being invited to speak at a conference or other professional event, expenses paid.

An example of a publication providing monetary awards occurred with two students who were taking an adult learning course with me as an elective in their health education master's program. This course has an assignment to write a paper following the guidelines for a local conference in hopes that students may want to submit the paper after they complete the course. My feedback on these papers is extensive and designed to increase the publishability of the paper. This pair of students revised the paper using my feedback, submitted it to the conference, and, using feedback from the discussion at the conference, revised the manuscript and submitted it to a professional journal. The paper was published and won the journal's award for best paper. At a professional conference they attended, they were greeted as celebrities and offered positions as instructors for continuing education courses on weekends around the country. They made good extra money doing this and got a weekend getaway too. They have continued writing for publication. One of them successfully competed for a slot as a plenary speaker and an all-expenses-paid trip to a health conference in South Africa. They do not have doctorates. They teach at a community college, work in a health profession, and have become scholar practitioners. Students at all academic levels should be exposed to the techniques useful for publishing work so that they can contribute in their own way to their professions and society.

For me, the purpose of writing was first to secure a faculty position, then tenure, and then promotion. After that was accomplished, I engaged in writing projects to clarify ideas, explore areas, and contribute to the profession. While financial reward and professional advancement are reasons to write, most write to join the professional conversation (Rankin, 2001); others write because they "enjoy the power they derive from writing and the power derived from subsequent publication" (Henson, 1995, p. 3) to clarify ideas, explore new areas, contribute to the knowledge base, and foster professional relationships. While I can imagine some writers feel a sense of power or increased self-importance after publishing, there is also a sense of sheer joy and awe at seeing their name in print. Money, power, and joy are simply the emotional end products after the task of writing is completed.

Many people have something to contribute to the knowledge base, professional practice, or some insight others would benefit from knowing. Knowledge is lost because potential authors do not know how to join the conversation, do not know the rules for writing, and may be intimidated by the process.

Creating Writing Opportunities

Often writers write or otherwise create alone. I prefer to write with others; an opportunity to work with other scholars or practitioner scholars and learn from them or stretch myself because of the partnership is an important reason to write. Opportunities to write with others have to be created, developed, and sustained.

As a graduate student, I knew publishing was important, but I had no idea how one went about doing this. So I made it known to the faculty members in my program area that I wanted to learn how to write for publication. During my second year as a doctoral student, a professor invited me and another student to join him in an investigation of older adults and volunteering (Boggs, Rocco, & Spangler, 1995). This paper was presented at a conference where participants encouraged us to write about the unusual data collection method we used (Rocco, Spangler, & Boggs, 1998). These two articles set the stage for future opportunities to write with other faculty about older workers while still a student (Stein, Rocco, & Goldenetz, 2000) and collaborations with others later.

Faculty members are busy with many competing demands, such as writing and research projects, teaching responsibilities, service commitments, and work and advisement of other students. Creating writing opportunities as a graduate student is not as simple as just making it known to faculty and colleagues that writing for publication is important to you. Students should meet with potential collaborators to discuss ideas, share rough drafts, and invite participation, or ask to assist a faculty member with a project. Once a faculty member extends an invitation, the student needs to persist and in many cases proactively set up meetings to discuss the progress of the paper, come to the meetings with an agenda, and take notes. If the notes and agenda are filled with details in addition to keeping the project participants on track, they can become useful in preparing the outline, keeping track of research design, and becoming an initial draft of the manuscript.

Writing opportunities can be created by listening to speakers and making connections. Phyllis Cunningham, a matriarch of adult education, sat on a stage and told the audience loudly that white men needed to deconstruct their privilege. This statement resonated with me and with another student, and we began to contemplate privilege beyond race and gender. This resulted in a writing project that won the best graduate student paper award at a conference and was published as an article (Rocco & West, 1998).

Networking at conferences is another way to identify and create writing opportunities. Networking can occur in regular sessions, in the hallways, or in special sessions such as a preconference, a small, often intimate gathering of scholars meeting to discuss a single topic for an extended period of time. The nature of a preconference creates an atmosphere where collegial relationships and, in time, real friendships and writing partnerships can develop. Sometimes engaging a colleague on an issue in a paper he or she wrote is a way of forming a writing partnership to work on another paper where that issue becomes the focal point. Jasper van Loo, an economist, and I met at a preconference on continuing professional education (CPE). He was using human capital theory to understand CPE; during the discussion, I maintained that CPE and training are different and that I thought that human capital theory was being used inappropriately (van Loo & Rocco, 2006). This discussion resulted in our first coauthored article, a friendship, and other collaborations.

Other opportunities come in the form of a call for papers for special issues of journals or books. A call contains information about the project's purpose and what manuscripts should address in order to fit the purpose and be considered. Calls have due dates, and although the manuscript may go through a peer review process, acceptance rates for authors who produce a well-written manuscript that fits the purpose and is accepted for review are higher than for manuscripts submitted for consideration in a regular issue of a journal. The length of time to publication is generally shorter too.

Opportunities can come from having a manuscript rejected. If an author lets his or her ego get in the way, becomes angry, and sets the manuscript aside, the rejected manuscript may never be published. However, after the author overcomes his or her emotional reaction to the decision, careful consideration of the feedback can improve the manuscript. And the manuscript can be revised for submission to another journal or to fit a call for papers for a special issue of a journal or book. Sometimes, though, the original authors may need fresh eyes to revise the manuscript and invite a colleague to join the project. If a colleague is invited to assist with revising a manuscript, the same considerations that need to be made before starting a new project need to be discussed in this situation as well, such as author order, a work plan, and where the manuscript will be submitted.

Learning to Write

For most authors, writing is a process that is never perfected and never ends. Authors should strive to produce their best work, even though revisiting a manuscript after a period of time will always produce areas of improvement. If you accept this, then you can work to improve your writing and produce manuscripts that require fewer and fewer revisions. Learning to write involves reading about writing, critically reflecting on what you read, discussing writing with others, and listening to authors talk about the writing process. Reading about writing can include books on writing for publication (Casanave & Vandrick, 2003; Huff, 1998; Kupfersmid & Wonderly, 1994) or about a specific part of a paper such as a litera- ture review (Hart, 1998; Pan, 2004). Style guides such as the *Publication Manual of the American Psychological Association* (American Psychological Association, 2010) are rich with information on the technical aspects of writing. Articles and books read for content can also be read for style. The way authors organize text, sen- tence structure, and paragraph flow and develop an argument should be exam- ined. If you find an author's work compelling or distracting to read, critically reflect on the style and techniques used to produce both good and bad work. Think about using the techniques of the good paper and eliminate the tech- niques of the bad paper from your own writing.

Writing discussions can occur when working on a project with a colleague as a natural part of the work. Discussions can also occur when people intentionally come together to discuss writing (Rankin, 2001). For several years, I have facilitated a discussion group at my university. Speakers engage the group on some aspect of writing, such as how to get publications from the dissertation (see Chapters Two, Three, and Six), how to write meaningful titles, finding voice (see Chapter Eight), or how to deal with rejection (see Chapter Eighteen). Group members also submit manuscripts to the group to review and discuss. No matter what field members come from, they can read for clarity, focus, and organization. Also, many useful suggestions for articles and books that could enhance a manuscript have been shared by colleagues from other fields. Anyone can start such a group, and anyone can benefit from the discussion. Making space to discuss writing can be as simple as a regular breakfast or lunch meeting with a colleague or two.

Listening to authors discuss writing can be done through a writing group on scholarly writing issues. Other sources are listening to interviews of best-selling fiction writers such as John Grisham or Stephen King, who talk freely about their writing habits, problems, and difficulties getting published. Both have shared that they have regular writing times and places where they like to write, one in an office at 4:00 A.M. and the other in a coffee shop. Others talk about how they conduct research, work out difficult plot lines, and create conceptual maps to keep the story moving. These skills are useful for improving any kind of writing, including scholarly nonfiction writing.

Working with coauthors, I have learned tips on using computer programs or tools on standard programs more efficiently. One learning experience came when a senior scholar asked two junior faculty to join her in responding to a call for a special issue on inclusive education (Landorf, Rocco, & Nevin, 2007) because we were all concerned with social justice but from different perspectives. During the first meeting, we discussed the call for submissions, specifically what the editors meant by the language in the call and how we would address what the editors were looking for in a novel way. One coauthor captured as much of the discussion as she could by typing quickly on the computer. The document was almost ten pages when she sent it to us for comments. As it happened, we all opened our e-mail at different times during the day. The author who started work early in the morning inserted a purpose, advance organizer, and headings and added text using track changes. The next author built on the first revised manuscript, and the next author worked on the revision. Each draft was named using the date and version number. This pattern continued until the manuscript was finished in a month. We met together two other times to read through a version or discuss specific issues. The editors accepted the manuscript and requested very few revisions.

Writing Tips

Writing opportunities do not become publications without follow-through and a commitment to the project. Often deadlines are difficult to meet because of all the competing demands on our time. For example, communicating with coauthors and editors when there is a problem or providing regular updates on progress is time-consuming but required and appreciated by authors. Being on time is an even more appreciated behavior. Try to keep your commitments.

To-do lists are one way to organize projects and prioritize. My to-do list is now on an Excel spreadsheet with different pages representing long-term projects. For instance, one sheet contains information on each chapter of this book. Another contains all of the chapters, manuscripts, and conference papers I am working on under different category headings, such as "in process," "in review," "revise and resubmit," "accepted with revisions," and "in press." As projects move through these stages, I move them into the different categories. I keep track of coauthors, who is doing what, when the project will require my attention, where we plan to submit, and due dates if there are any. I keep track of all the manuscripts I am asked to review on another sheet.

When I was starting out as a graduate student and later as an assistant professor, I used to keep an idea list using the outline function in Microsoft Word and could store much information about the idea in one place. Often we get good ideas but do not write them up or file them away when we get them. Some writers carry an idea notebook with them everywhere, and when an idea comes, they write as much as they can in the notebook. A lot of time is wasted trying to remember that brilliant idea you failed to write down. Organizing your work and your ideas by having a system saves time and energy. A system where projects are organized provides information when making decisions about additional projects or when updating colleagues.

Once an idea has been generated and development has started, identify at least one journal to submit it. Thoroughly read the guidelines for submission and the information for authors sections, which are frequently published on the back pages of the journal or on the journal's Web site. Then search the journal for articles already published that are relevant to the manuscript you will submit. Review these articles for content that informs your work, and incorporate meaningful material into your manuscript, citing and quoting material appropriately. Also review these articles for style. For example, do the authors place the purpose of the article in the first paragraph or on the second page at the conclusion of a problem statement? Does the literature supporting the study come after the purpose or somewhere else? Do the articles use a lot of figures or tables? How is the research design described? Are the headings used traditional ones, such as "Findings," or more descriptive and related to the purpose and title? If you are concerned about inconsistencies in the flow and organization of the articles, ask the journal editor what article he or she considers excellent or which won an award.

If a journal rejects your manuscript, this does not have to be the end of the project. Incorporate the reviewers' and editors' feedback into the next draft. Often one of the reviewers will suggest another journal to consider submitting the manuscript to. Do not let your emotional response to being rejected stop your progress. Examine the suggested journal, read the guidelines for authors, and locate relevant articles to incorporate in your next draft. Every chapter author in this book has had a manuscript rejected, and most of us have revised that manuscript, publishing it in another journal or as a chapter in a book. Never discard or forget about a reviewed and rejected manuscript.

The organization and flow of a manuscript are enhanced when the title mirrors the purpose, and important concepts from the manuscript are used as headings. Headings should guide readers through the argument or keep them focused on the purpose. Sometimes I begin a writing project with an outline or by taking notes while I read, and other times I pull the headings out of the manuscript and put them in a document to ensure proper heading level (refer to the guidelines for manuscript submission and the style guide used by the intended journal on levels of headings), good organization and flow, and that they are worded in a parallel manner. Authors need to pay attention to the organization and flow of the manuscript. Returning to a manuscript after it is finished to ensure that the text flows from one sentence to the next, that paragraphs build on each other and move readers forward, and that there are no puzzling sentences will improve the odds of acceptance for publication.

Crafting a manuscript takes time and patience. Slapping something together and calling it done increases the odds of a rejection decision and lengthens the time to publication. After several drafts and getting the manuscript to the point that I think it is done, I set it aside for a time and work on something else to clear my head. If I am writing alone, I read the manuscript page by page slowly and out loud. When I do this, I am paying attention to word choice, the relationship of words, and whether the words used are all necessary and add value. Reading aloud carefully can take an hour to read a few pages. When I have made fewer than a dozen minor revisions to a draft, I consider it ready to send to readers. I often send a manuscript to three people for feedback when I am writing alone. Different people who read my work catch different things.

When I write with colleagues, we come together when the draft is finished and take turns reading the paper out loud. We stop each other when something does not sound right. This can take twelve or more hours to do. Once we are done with the editing, the lead author usually checks the citations in text against the reference list and then the reference list against the citations in text. Another author then does the same check. At the end of this process, the manuscript is likely ready to submit, though sometimes we send it to a friendly reader. Reviewers can devote more time to providing feedback on substantive issues that improves the quality of the manuscript when they do not have to take time to provide feedback on technical issues such as a lack of focus, organization, and grammatical errors. The more polished the manuscript is when submitted, the more likely the authors are to receive a revise-and-resubmit decision or even an acceptance after the first review.

The review and publication process is naturally a long one. The only way to shorten the time to publication is to submit a manuscript that is well done. Although I always strive to submit a professional manuscript, reviewers nevertheless find areas that lack clarity, terms that should be defined, and connections that were not sufficiently developed. A revise-and-resubmit is good news. And time should be set aside to address the feedback from the editors and reviewers quickly.

Concluding Remarks

Writing projects are not just about reporting empirical research; some projects grow out of a commitment to a field or to help others. This book project began for me when I was a graduate student trying to learn how to write and out of a desire to teach students this skill. When Tim and I got together, it was because of a problem in our field with the quality of manuscript submissions from novice scholars. We found that some programs were insisting on a manuscript submission from a dissertation, yet it was obvious that committee members had not provided feedback or guidance on the manuscript. Or the author took whole chunks from the dissertation or a class paper without any attention to the journal submission guidelines or what the journal published. Many journal editors in different fields share this concern with manuscript submissions that lack focus, attention to detail, adequate research design descriptions, and meaningful problem statements. We do not want to discourage such submissions; we simply want to improve the quality.

The goal of this book is to assist students, practitioner scholars, and all other scholars in improving their writing. If the quality of the manuscripts submitted to journals is improved, then editors and reviewers can focus on substantive issues in a manuscript, which can help raise the standards for all authors. Poorly constructed and executed manuscripts put additional stress on the system, making the submission-to-publication time line longer, hastening burnout of editors and reviewers, and perpetuating the inaccurate assumption that journal editors publish only well-known scholars.

References

American Psychological Association. (2010). *Publication manual of the American Psychological Association* (6th ed.). Washington, DC: American Psychological Association.

Boggs, D. L., Rocco, T. S., & Spangler, S. (1995). A framework for understanding older adults' civic behavior. *Educational Gerontology: An International Journal, 21*(5), 449–465.

Casanave, C., & Vandrick, S. (Eds.). (2003). *Writing for scholarly publication: Behind the scenes in language education.* Mahwah, NJ: Erlbaum.

Hart, C. (1998). *Doing a literature review: Releasing the social science research imagination.* Thousand Oaks, CA: Sage.

Henson, K. T. (1995). *The art of writing for publication.* Needham Heights, MA: Allyn & Bacon.

Huff, A. S. (1998). *Writing for scholarly publication.* Thousand Oaks, CA: Sage.

Kupfersmid, J., & Wonderly, D. M. (1994). *An author's guide to publishing better articles in better journals in the behavioral sciences.* Hoboken, NJ: Wiley.

Landorf, H., Rocco, T., & Nevin, A. (2007). Creating permeable boundaries: Teaching and learning for social justice in a global society. In R. L. Quezada & P. Cordeiro (Eds.), *Teacher Education Quarterly, 34*(1), 41–56.

Nielsen, S., & Rocco, T. S. (2002, May). Joining the conversation: Graduate students' perceptions of writing for publication. In J. M. Pettitt (Ed.), *Proceedings of the 43rd Adult Education Research Conference* (pp. 309–314). Raleigh: North Carolina State University. (ED471830)

Pan, M. L. (2004). *Preparing literature reviews: Qualitative and quantitative approaches* (2nd ed.). Glendale, CA: Pyrczak Publishing.

Phillips, G. M. (1982). Publishing in speech communication. In S. Judy (Ed.), *Publishing in English education* (pp. 95–111). Portsmouth, NH: Boynton/Cook.

Rankin, E. (2001). *The work of writing: Insights and strategies for academics and professionals.* San Francisco: Jossey-Bass.

Rocco, T. S., Spangler, S., & Boggs, D. L. (1998). Methodological considerations for comparing the experiences of literary, historical and living adults as data sources. *Educational Gerontology: An International Journal, 24*(6), 567–583.

Rocco, T. S., & West, G. W. (1998). Deconstructing privilege: An examination of privilege in adult education. *Adult Education Quarterly, 48*(3), 171–184.

Stein, D., Rocco, T. S., & Goldenetz, K. A. (2000). Age and the university workplace: A case study of remaining, retiring, or retaining older workers. *Human Resource Development Quarterly, 11*(1), 61–80.

van Loo, J., & Rocco, T. S. (2006). Differentiating CPE from training: Reconsidering terms, boundaries, and economic factors. *Human Resource Development Review, 5*(2), 202–227.

CHAPTER 2

PUBLISHING IN PEER-REVIEWED AND NONREFEREED JOURNALS

Processes, Strategies, and Tips

Gary J. Skolits, Ralph G. Brockett, Roger Hiemstra

Throughout most of the academic world, publish or perish is a given. Within larger universities and, increasingly, in smaller institutions, publication record is clearly linked to decisions about promotion, tenure, and merit. Furthermore, there is often a hierarchy in terms of the most valued publication types. Although this hierarchy can differ across disciplines, in academia, the peer-reviewed, or refereed, article tops the list. Because refereed articles undergo peer review, they are often perceived to have a higher degree of credibility and are weighted more heavily than other types of publications in faculty promotion and tenure procedures.

This chapter offers strategies and tips about the process of publishing in peer-reviewed academic and nonrefereed practitioner journals. Unlike peer reviewed articles, nonrefereed articles, where publication decisions are made by one or more editors without using a blind review process, are important because they fill an important niche in practice-oriented fields like education, nursing, and business. They often serve to help new writers make their first contributions to the literature. In this chapter, we examine the following topics: (1) searching and selecting topics for articles, (2) writing and revising, (3) mechanics of manu-script preparation, (4) deciding where to submit the manuscript, (5) working with editors, (6) seeking feedback from others, and (7) building momentum by getting multiple articles from a single idea.

Before moving into the major discussion, we offer a few more comments about the two article types. Peer-reviewed, or refereed, articles undergo a blind review, where neither the authors nor reviewers know each other's identity. This process is designed to ensure that a manuscript has been reviewed and accepted in an ethical and unbiased manner by experts from the applicable field of study. Nonrefereed articles are not blind-reviewed but are instead reviewed by the editor or members of an editorial staff. Although refereed articles are often considered the gold standard in faculty promotion and tenure deliberations, nonrefereed articles nevertheless play an important role within most academic disciplines. Practitioner journals are targeted toward practitioners and deal with problems and issues tied directly to practice. Thus, an article appearing in a practitioner journal could receive wider circulation and visibility than one published in a respected academic journal that is narrowly targeted toward a more limited audience. In this chapter, we consider both types of articles but place more emphasis on refereed publications because of their special importance in scholarly publishing.

Searching for and Selecting Topics

Researchers and writers confront two challenges when contemplating scholarship that will lead to subsequent publication. The first is to find potential topics of interest that have initial publication potential. The second is to screen these topics and select one with the highest potential for a completed, publishable manuscript. This section addresses both challenges by introducing several sources of article ideas and offering some basic criteria for selecting a topic with high publishing potential.

Sources of Ideas

Article ideas can come from an unlimited number of sources that are either internal, emanating from within the writer's thoughts and interests, or external, coming from outside sources such as current events or personal experiences with specific programs or practices. The more experience an individual has as a scholar or practitioner, the more likely that personal professional experiences and reflections will help generate researchable topics. For example, a writer might convert a conference presentation not fully developed or even a pilot study into a complete article for publication. Similarly, one might be invited to submit an article by an editor who has seen the author present or is familiar with the author's areas of interest. However, external sources can also be helpful, especially to less experienced writers. Since the focus of this chapter is on developing writers, this section focuses on such external sources. Underlying this discussion is an assumption that potential writers have access to the Internet, are familiar with online search engines, and have access to a large community or university lending library.

Although there are an unlimited number of potentially fruitful sources for article ideas, this discussion focuses on scholarly based literature and nonscholarly based sources such as popular literature and media, professional association materials, dialogues with colleagues, and government and foundation grant programs. Of these, our primary focus is on scholarly literature, both peer reviewed and nonrefereed.

Scholarly Literature

Although there are many potential idea sources, the most obvious and promising source is the existing scholarly literature. For example, the research literature in a field of study offers a wealth of information on topics that researchers and journal editors deemed worthy of publication. Scholarly literature includes peer-reviewed articles reporting on original concepts or research (or both), literature review articles that analyze and report on previous publications on a topic, and theoretical articles covering concepts and topics from a broader perspective.

Peer-reviewed articles are generally considered the most authoritative source on researchable topics, whether they present original research, literature reviews, or theoretical examinations. Almost any section of an article can suggest a topic, beginning with the abstract. An abstract summarizes an article by briefly identifying the purpose, research methods, results, and implications. Other sections of articles can also be mined for topics. For example, an introduction offers background information on the problem or topic being investigated. Literature reviews, such as those found in the *Review of Educational Research*, can be rich sources as they tend to be well crafted and tightly focused, introducing and discussing previously published resources and books relevant to the topic. Bibliographical references can help readers locate this literature. The design, findings, and discussion sections can also suggest worthwhile topics. In many articles, the writer suggests specific topics for future research. Articles usually include contact information for the author, providing access for further inquiry regarding potential topics. Many scholarly writers are responsive to e-mail inquiries about their work. An added benefit of reviewing articles is that they expose readers to research topics, approaches, and methodologies in the literature, as well as particular journals that tend to address specific topics.

Writers can generate topics by reviewing non-peer-reviewed articles, doctoral dissertations, scholarly books, published conference proceedings, and technical research reports. A simple Web search can reveal many sources that are unpublished or have appeared in non-peer-reviewed publications such as specialized magazines and practitioner journals whose readers are more interested in the application of results than the research process that led to the findings. For example, the Education Resources Information Center (ERIC) clearinghouse on education contains thousands of practitioner-oriented papers in an easily accessible database, most of which have not been published elsewhere. Many domestic and international organizations, such as state governments or the United Nations Educational, Scientific and Cultural Organization (UNESCO), sponsor occasional papers and white papers on particular topics, and sometimes access is provided on the Web. For example, on UNESCO's Web site (http://www.unesco .org), several documents, books, and other documents are available to read or download. Similarly, ProQuest (UMI Dissertation Publishing, 2009), an online dissertation search program, can play a valuable role in helping writers seek out previous research on a topic, identify gaps in knowledge, and provide suggestions for future research.

Beyond non-peer-reviewed periodicals, a library search for books can provide access to longer scholarly works on a particular subject brimming with potential ideas. Even unpublished technical research reports on grant projects available through a search of various databases are idea sources. Search engines (such as Google Scholar, http://scholar.google.com/) can be very helpful with such sources. However, since they are not subject to rigorous peer review, it is usually a good idea to corroborate information from Internet searches with sources from the mainstream scholarly literature.

Nonscholarly Literature

Although starting with scholarly literature is preferred, nonacademic sources such as trade books and popular magazines and journals can also provide article ideas. Popular press items, including articles in magazines, newspapers, and newsletters, as well as broadcast media programming (for example, radio and television programming), can generate ideas on current topics. Nonrefereed professional conference materials and publications such as a list of papers presented and published proceedings offer a wealth of potential topics. Federal, state, and nongovernmental grant programs regularly issue requests for proposals (RFP) on many different topics. Such RFPs specify the topics of highest relevance for funding. An added benefit in studying RFPs is that they can help the researcher become aware of future funding opportunities related to possible topics. Even daily shop talk among colleagues who share common interests can be a source of topics. Many researchers in disciplines such as education and business are especially interested in topics that shed light on current problems and opportunities, and regular dialogue with colleagues is often relevant and helpful.

Screening Article Ideas

Once potential article ideas have been identified, the next step is to narrow the focus to a topic that is manageable and worthwhile to the author. Since there are many topic sources available, generating potential article ideas should not prove too challenging if a focused effort is made. The bigger challenge is what to do with all the potential topics. Once a research topic has been identified, it must be narrowed in light of the highest publishing potential. While numerous strategies could be used, the three criteria of relevance, capability, and marketability provide insight into publishable topics. These criteria can be expressed as questions:

- What is my level of interest in this particular topic? (*relevance*)
- Given the research design most appropriate for examining this topic, is it within my skill set? (*capability*)
- Can examination of this topic lead to a published article? (*marketability*)

The relevancy criterion focuses on the importance of the idea to the writer and the discipline. Although one could address many fruitful topics, not all topics are likely to be of equal interest to different audiences. Topics that have little intrinsic value to the writer should be avoided. The capability criterion addresses the writer's skills, including the ability and expertise needed to address a particular topic. For example, no matter how well prepared or knowledgeable a writer is when undertaking a research study, his or her background and training are typically more suited to specific types of research designs or practices. Finally, marketability considers the likelihood that a research topic is of interest to the profession, discipline, or field of study and may appeal to journal editors. This last criterion is especially important because despite the writer's passion for a topic, if the editor and reviewers do not consider it to be viable or significant to the field of study, it is unlikely they will accept the manuscript. Thus, a topic that successfully addresses these three criteria has the strongest chances for being published in scholarly outlets.

Writing and Revising the Manuscript

Once a topic has been identified and the research or background literature search is complete, the next step is the writing phase. Since the actual writing process is discussed in other chapters, we will not address it here except to say that it is important to recognize that different writers have different work habits. You should determine what works best for you and not try to follow someone else's guidelines. As an example, the second and third authors of this chapter have written together extensively over the years. Ralph finds he writes best at night, with music in the background and frequent stretch breaks. Roger is an early-morning person who prefers a quiet environment where he is able to work for long, uninterrupted stretches of time. However, when we come together to work side-by-side on a writing project, we are able to blend the best of our practices in a way that creates a synergy not possible when we work alone.

The initial manuscript assembly phase occurs when the writer consolidates or creates all elements of the manuscript into a basic draft. The specific elements of the manuscript vary based on the type of article (research or conceptual) and specifications of the targeted publication. Nevertheless, every article should include a clear statement of purpose and a logical flow of ideas that lead to results, recommendations, or conclusions (or all of these). When previously written work becomes part of a manuscript, the initial writing process involves assembling and connecting various pieces of writing. Typically the researcher then prepares the remaining manuscript elements, such as the abstract, research findings (if the article is based on research), findings and conclusions, and implications for practice or further research.

Once the initial draft is developed, the manuscript revision phase begins. Here, the writer begins to ensure that elements of the manuscript are brought together in a unified, coherent, and tightly focused manner. The revision process has several aspects. The first changes are the author's revisions to the initial assembled manuscript. Writers vary considerably in terms of the number of drafts they must write in order for the manuscript to be ready for submission. Some writers need only two or three drafts, while others may take five or more drafts to get the manuscript ready for submission.

The second set of changes may occur as a response to reviews of the manuscript by respected colleagues and associates prior to submittal to a journal editor. This second element usually results from sharing the paper with professional colleagues, who are asked to focus on content, and possibly more general editorial reviewers, who focus more on grammar, syntax, and stylistic considerations. The pros and cons of asking others to review a manuscript before submission are discussed later in this chapter.

Final revisions are typically made in response to comments from manuscript reviewers assigned by the applicable journal editor as appropriate. It is not uncommon to have a manuscript conditionally accepted, necessitating certain revisions prior to resubmitting. Sometimes it seems as if the review and revision process never ends, but each effort usually leads to a more polished and focused manuscript. Since writers are very close to their research and writing, they may be unable to review their own work critically. This brings the writer to a consideration of the specific mechanics of manuscript preparation.

Mechanics of Manuscript Preparation

Careful manuscript preparation should meet the purpose and stylistic expectations of the targeted periodical or journal. After determining that a journal or magazine is optimal, the writer must ensure careful adherence to its stylistic guidelines. Most periodicals describe their guidelines clearly or refer to existing guidelines such as the most current edition of the *Publication Manual of the American Psychological Association.*

If specific guidelines are not available, we recommend creating your own by studying several articles within one or more issues of the targeted periodical. This informal analysis helps to identify features used or expectations journal editors have, such as seriation style, heading levels, quoting protocols, referencing styles, the proper use of tables or figures, research methods used, and the range of topics covered. Such study can also establish an average number of words per article, which is critical in order to avoid submitting a manuscript that is way under or over the average acceptable word count. Inattention to important stylistic expectations can lead to outright rejection or unnecessary resubmission requests.

Another important consideration is the readability of the manuscript. If the publisher does not provide such information, you can calculate a readability score based on the targeted journal's previously published articles. A readability score is an estimation of a manuscript's comprehension difficulty, often associated with the approximate level of education required by readers in order to fully understand the manuscript. Microsoft Word, for example, provides the Flesch-Kincaid grade level (My Byline Media, 2009) when doing a grammar check. This procedure examines the average number of words in a sentence and an average number of syllables per word. A formula then determines the score for the material examined. Thus, if a periodical does not suggest a readability score, you can extract a random selection from one or more published articles and calculate the readability scores. Then, as an author you can raise or lower your own score by addressing the number of words used and whether harder or easier words are required. The Fog Index is another readability index (Hiemstra & Brier, 1994).

Another reason for the focus on stylistic expectations is to gain an understanding of a periodical's more technical requirements, such as font size, margin widths, spacing, and manner of manuscript submission. There also may be specific expectations regarding issues such as copyright regulations, how the journal expects permissions for use of copyrighted material to be handled, and whether a signed statement assigning first publication rights and guaranteeing the work is original material is required. Increasingly, journals and magazines prefer or even require electronic submissions, so a manuscript submitted in hard copy could either be returned or not even examined.

There may be times when the initial draft of the manuscript is considerably longer than what is allowed. This requires a tight edit of the final revision, eliminating some references, quoted material, and even entire sections. In their book *Professional Writing: Processes, Strategies, and Tips for Publishing in Educational Journals,* Hiemstra and Brier (1994) describe ways to reduce the number of words by establishing elimination quotas per page and keeping a tally of success while working through the manuscript. Appendix C in their book provides twenty-two strategies for shortening a manuscript.

Deciding Where to Submit the Manuscript

Determining where to submit a manuscript for publication is a critical decision. Most often, a manuscript will be more relevant and appropriate for a limited number of publications in the field of study. Submitting an article that is not a good fit for a targeted publication is not only less likely to result in a publication, but it can waste valuable time of the writer, journal editors, and manuscript reviewers. Good editors quickly recognize the lack of a good fit and immediately reject an article without fit. In other cases, this lack of a good fit occurs many months down the road after much time and effort has been expended by the reviewers. Targeting a manuscript to a journal and its audience is a worthwhile effort and can increase the chances of a manuscript's eventual publication.

Publications suitable for a scholarly article based on original research or practice include research journals, practitioner journals, other scholarly publications, professional association publications, technical reports, and book chapters, as well as the popular press and media. The number of research and practitioner journals is substantial. There are national, regional, and state journals, as well as online journals that are becoming increasingly popular. A careful review of these publications to determine where a manuscript is most likely to fit will greatly increase chances of acceptance. Other factors such as the prestige of the publication or its circulation can greatly influence decisions about where to submit a manuscript. Because the first step in determining potential journals is so important, the process of searching for a topic and conducting a literature review should highlight many journals related to the topic. The journals that appear most often in the literature review should be targeted first. The second step is to select two or three targeted journals and read recent issues to become familiar with manuscript approaches and stylistic formats. A good practice is to target one of these journals for submission of the manuscript and the remaining two as backups. It is also helpful to obtain information about the journal's manuscript acceptance rates, which can be obtained from the journal's Web page or editors.

Beyond the journals that are likely to be interested in a topic, the writer needs to understand and target specific audiences. Some journals focus on readers who are primarily researchers. Reviewers for this journal will be researchers, often with experience on the manuscript's topic or specific research methods. Other journals focus on the needs of practitioners who are seeking more practical knowledge. These reviewers are likely to be practitioner oriented. Journals can also have a sharper focus. For example, those primarily interested in research methodologies are likely to publish works that depict the effective application of the targeted methodology regardless of topic. Another example consists of journals that seek to influence policymakers on a specific topic or problem of concern. A policymaker may be less interested in a method's sophistication and more interested in implications of the findings for policy consideration. The key purpose of knowing the journal's audience is not only to determine which journal to target, but also how to focus writing to a specific audience. Ultimately successful articles are those that effectively meet the needs and interests of targeted audiences.

Another consideration in deciding where to submit a manuscript concerns answers to the question: "Do I send my manuscript to one of the leading, and more competitive, journals in the field, or do I opt for a journal that is newer or less well known, such as a state or regional publication, where there is a greater likelihood of acceptance?" There is always a trade-off between journals with higher status and visibility, with a lower acceptance rate, and journals that may be relatively new and actively seeking manuscripts. The latter may be a better option for authors hoping to get something in print soon; the manuscript is a pilot study or a preliminary report of findings, or the conclusions are tentative; and the manuscript's topic is directly tied to a journal's focus. Nevertheless, we recommend that you not be too quick to dismiss the possibility of submitting to a recognized top-tier journal. Sometimes less experienced authors have a topic that the journal editors have been hoping to cover, or new scholars may have a new or different perspective on a familiar topic.

There is no clear rule of thumb about where to submit a manuscript, but in general we suggest that more tentative or exploratory manuscripts be sent to second-tier journals (publications that are new, have a higher acceptance rate, or have a smaller circulation than top-tier journals), while original research studies or those with new theoretical or conceptual perspectives might be sent first to a top-tier journal. Authors are encouraged to query a journal editor about whether there might be an interest in the manuscript's topic or approach; however, it may be more common to just send the manuscript to the editor.

Working with Editors

When a manuscript is received by a peer-reviewed journal, the editor or managing editor typically acknowledges receipt and offers tentative information to the author about when a decision about acceptance might be made. In addition, the editor will likely review the manuscript to make sure it conforms to publication guidelines and is within the journal's scope. If it is, the editor sends the manuscript to a specified number of reviewers. These reviewers may comprise the editorial board of a journal or be approved reviewers. Sometimes they solicit reviews from non–editorial board members and even their own reviewers when the topic is outside the expertise of current members. Names and other identifying information are removed from the manuscript so that reviewers do not know the author's identity.

The review period varies from journal to journal, but typically reviews should be completed within three to four months. After reviewers have submitted their comments and recommendation about whether the manuscript should be published, the editor synthesizes the reviewers' information and makes a final determination about the manuscript's status. The most common outcomes are (1) accept with no revisions; (2) conditional acceptance, based on minor revisions; (3) reject (or not acceptable for publication) with a recommendation that the author consider a rewrite and resubmission; and (4) outright reject. It is not uncommon to have disagreement among reviewers. In these cases, the editor may adjudicate by making a decision based on information presented by the reviewers and his or her own assessment, or may send the manuscript to additional reviewers. Once the editor has concluded the review process, he or she sends a final decision letter along with the anonymous reviewers' comments to the author.

With many journals, when an accepted manuscript goes into production, authors are sent page proofs, a nearly final version of what the manuscript will look like in print. It is important to review these proofs carefully to make sure there are no misspelled words or sections of text that have been inadvertently dropped or omitted in the production process. This is also the author's final chance to ensure that tables and references have been presented correctly. In our experience, reviewing page proofs can also represent a time to make minor changes. Over the years, the three of us have found such errors as misspelling of our names, references that did not follow publication guidelines, and places where editors have inadvertently changed the meaning of a statement through the editing process. For the most part, we have appreciated the efforts of our editors, because their purpose is to strengthen our writing. But like all of us, they too can make errors or omissions. What is most important is that when the article appears in print, it is as correct as possible and adequately conveys the author's intent.

There may be times in the review process when an author needs to communicate with the editor, such as finding out about the current review status. There are no clear guidelines for whether this should be done. Much depends on the editor's style; some editors welcome such inquiries, while others may be less receptive. This is probably less of a concern today since much communication is over the Internet rather than by phone or postal mail. In any case, we believe it is reasonable for an author to make an inquiry if no decision has been received within four to six months. This should give the editor sufficient time to reach a decision, even if it is necessary to send the manuscript to additional reviewers.

Seeking Feedback: Pro and Con

Asking for feedback from one or more colleagues is helpful. The editorial guidelines of many periodicals actually recommend it. For the most part, we support this suggestion because it gives the author a chance to step back and review comments from others who may be familiar with the topic or the journal to which the manuscript will be submitted. This is a dry run for the review process and has the potential to strengthen the manuscript before it is sent to the journal.

Selecting colleagues to review manuscripts can sometimes be tricky. In our experience, it is important to select reviewers who will provide honest, constructive feedback and will do it in a way that does not leave the author feeling attacked. It is possible to give feedback in a way that openly addresses any problems or errors that may appear in the manuscript, but in a way that is respectful of the author's effort by avoiding sarcasm, insult, or condescension. Also, we recommend giving careful consideration before asking personal friends or family members to provide feedback. On more than one occasion, we have witnessed situations where personal relationships have been strained because an author and a reviewer with good intentions did not have a clear understanding of each other's informal expectations. So our recommendation is to seek feedback from people who can provide honest comments in a respectful way.

Building Momentum: Multiple Publications from a Single Idea

We have discussed at length the processes and mechanics involved in publishing scholarly articles. We now turn to ideas on how to obtain multiple publications from an idea or research project. This does not mean that we recommend simultaneously sending the same basic manuscript to several publications. Rather, we mean recasting a manuscript for different audiences, journals, and even message goals.

Targeting a specific journal or audience is often a critical decision in the manuscript conceptualization process. This step provides necessary submission information and motivation to move forward. However, we recommend that the success of that first publication be turned into momentum for one or more additional publications. In addition to examining the research effort for its potential breadth, any feedback from colleagues and even a journal's reviewers may provide information and incentive to recast the work for a different journal.

For example, with a research project involving intensive study of subjects on a particular area of interest, look for multiple ways of examining the results. The primary article could describe the basic study analyses and findings and be aimed at a research journal. A second article for another research journal or a practitioner's magazine could provide information specifically about gender differences in the findings and tie the discussion to implications for practice. A third article could provide several policy implications related to the findings and be aimed at a journal or online report that focuses on policy about specific issues. In other words, we recommend that you glean data for multiple ideas. This multiplies scholarly efforts by not putting everything discovered into one article.

Hiemstra and Brier (1994) talk about this momentum in terms of a three-by-three rule. For example, they suggest that any good idea, research project, or personal interest topic has at least three different ways it can be approached (rule 1). Rule 2 refers to the minimum number of times they recommend the author attempt to have a single article published based on prior rejections. Rule 3 is based on the notion that there are at least three periodicals that have potential interest in the manuscript.

What this means is not to give up on an article if it is rejected by the first journal. Rejection happens, and publishing competition can be fierce, especially within certain specialties or disciplines. We suggest not giving up on a manuscript until it has been rejected three times. Obviously resubmitting to a second or third periodical requires the manuscript to be recast each time according to new stylistic requirements and even considering feedback received from previous reviewers. The main idea, though, is to use your writing efforts as momentum for additional success.

Summary and Conclusion

In this chapter, we have examined several aspects of the processes and strategies of writing and offered tips that can assist writers in their efforts to become published. We discussed searching and selecting research topics, phases of the manuscript preparation process, mechanics of manuscript preparation, deciding where to submit the manuscript, working with editors, seeking feedback from others, and building momentum by generating multiple articles from a single idea. In each of these discussions, we shared the knowledge gained from our personal experiences with publishing.

We conclude with four takeaway messages that represent common themes within this chapter. First, remain strategic, and always understand what you are trying to accomplish in each step toward publication. Second, be realistic, and acknowledge that it is sometimes better to start publishing in journals that are less prestigious and more receptive to new writers. With experience, you can target efforts toward more competitive journals. Third, pay strict attention to details, especially manuscript mechanics and submission guidelines. Fourth, use editorial feedback to improve your efforts; even the most highly published researchers and scholarly writers have encountered rejections along the way. Remain positive, and the likelihood is high that you will be published.

References

Hiemstra, R., & Brier, E. M. (1994). *Professional writing: Processes, strategies, and tips for publishing in educational journals.* Malabar, FL: Krieger.

My Byline Media. (2009). *The Flesch grade level readability formula.* ReadabilityFormulas.com. Retrieved July 21, 2009, from http://www.readabilityformulas.com/flesch-grade-level-readability-formula.php

UMI Dissertation Publishing. (2009). *Proquest UMI dissertation publishing.* ProQuest.com. Retrieved July 21, 2009, from http://www.proquest.com/en-US/products/dissertations/

CHAPTER 3

LEARNING TO WRITE

Wisdom from Emerging Scholars

Claire Kostopulos Nackoney,
Sunny L. Munn, Jesus Fernandez

As emerging scholars, we have found that good writers have a variety of valuable tools and skills in their professional toolboxes. A critical tool is the ability to write effectively. Becoming a technically competent writer, mastering writing styles, and being able to communicate are important aspects of scholarly writing. Other tools are learning to make meaningful connections between concepts and data, developing informed opinions, and being willing to engage in dialogue with other scholars.

In this chapter, we share the toolboxes we have built over the years. Our toolboxes include insights we have garnered as emerging scholars who have presented and published as graduate students. We begin with our writing experiences and reflect on the importance of scholarly writing and then share techniques for organizing and starting the writing process. We reflect on the importance of establishing mentoring relationships, building scholarly networks, and collaborating with others. We discuss issues that can hamper effective writing and provide suggestions to resolve them. The chapter concludes with recommendations for taking the plunge and becoming published authors before graduating.

Our Scholarly Writing Experiences

Our experiences with scholarly writing vary. Claire, a doctoral candidate and a learning and development consultant for a Fortune 500 insurance company, has presented and published papers at conferences, reviewed conference and journal manuscripts, and published book reviews (Nackoney, 2006; Nackoney & Pane, 2006; Nackoney, Rajbansee, Rocco, & Gallagher, 2005; Nackoney & Rocco, 2005). She has written alone, with other colleagues, and with her doctoral advisor. In her professional work, she facilitates business grammar and writing courses.

Sunny, a doctoral candidate and a university admissions advisor, has written and presented on her own, with faculty, and with colleagues. She has presented and published articles (Munn & Rocco, 2008, 2010; Hornsby & Munn, 2009; Nackony, Munn, & Gallagher, 2007; Stein, Rocco, Munn, Ginn, & Antolino, 2006), published book reviews (Munn, 2009a, 2009b), and reviewed manuscripts. She also actively mentors, facilitates informal peer groups, encourages an exchange of constructive criticism, and promotes authorship and conference participation among her peers.

Jesus, a doctoral candidate and an academic administrator at a university, has written alone and with associates. He has published a book chapter (Melamed, Robbins, & Fernandez, 1981), presented and published papers at conferences, and reviewed manuscripts. He is a member of the executive editorial board of the *Business Journal of Hispanic Research.*

Appreciating the Importance of Scholarly Writing

Within the academy, scholarly writing and publishing are a measure of career success. Writing facilitates entry into the scholarly community, providing students interested in academic and research-oriented careers with a required skill set and an understanding of career expectations (Austin, 2002). Early exposure to scholarly writing can better prepare doctoral students for writing their dissertations, while also introducing master's and undergraduate students to the demands of advanced writing.

Scholarly writing has content "grounded in literature and/or empirical research" and goes through peer review and an iterative revision process (Caffarella & Barnett, 2000, p. 41). Through scholarly writing, the existing knowledge base is replenished with new insights, ideas, models, and theories. This process facilitates further dialogue and serves as a springboard for future research (Nackoney, Munn, & Gallagher, 2007).

Writing for a public audience can help emerging scholars grow intellectually and professionally through what should be a critical and reflective process (Casanave & Vandrick, 2003). Doctoral students are expected to become more critically reflective and master the complexities of scholarly writing as they approach the task of writing their dissertations (Nackoney et al., 2007). However, despite the amount of writing doctoral students do over the course of their studies, many begin their dissertations with limited scholarly writing experience (Caffarella & Barnett, 2000; Nackoney et al., 2007; Nielsen & Rocco, 2002).

Getting Started

Getting started on a writing project is often the most difficult step. We have used a number of tools to help us get started on writing projects. But no tool is perfect. Each project requires adjusting your practices in moving through the writing process.

Develop a Research Agenda

Some individuals know early in their graduate studies what they want to research and can benefit from establishing a formal research agenda—a plan for what they will write about and develop expertise in their disciplines. This plan can be organized as a time line for completing research projects, or it can be a working list of research ideas and questions kept in a notebook, computer file, or personal digital assistant.

Initial writing assignments from course work might spark research interests. Some students might be invited to collaborate with a professor on a project. Others, like us, have research agendas driven by professional interests, goals, organizational needs, and the desire to find answers to questions we have encountered through personal experiences.

Organize the Literature

Graduate students read and collect volumes of literature related to topics of interest. Organizing this collection in a way that allows information to be found quickly helps to write more efficiently. Organizing research articles might help in identifying gaps in the literature, resulting in future research questions and possible manuscripts. One of us prints articles she finds interesting and organizes them by topic in three-ring binders. All of us keep electronic copies of articles we have downloaded from library databases, creating electronic file folders by subject and then saving individual articles by title or by author and year.

Software like EndNote and Excel spreadsheets is useful to catalogue and save collected literature, such as journal articles and book information. We have used either the reference feature in EndNote or Microsoft Word to create a database of reference citations. Figure 3.1 illustrates the use of EndNote software to organize collected literature and reference citations. In this EndNote database, the user

FIGURE 3.1. EXAMPLE OF GROUPINGS OF LITERATURE BY TOPIC, REFERENCE, AND CITATION.

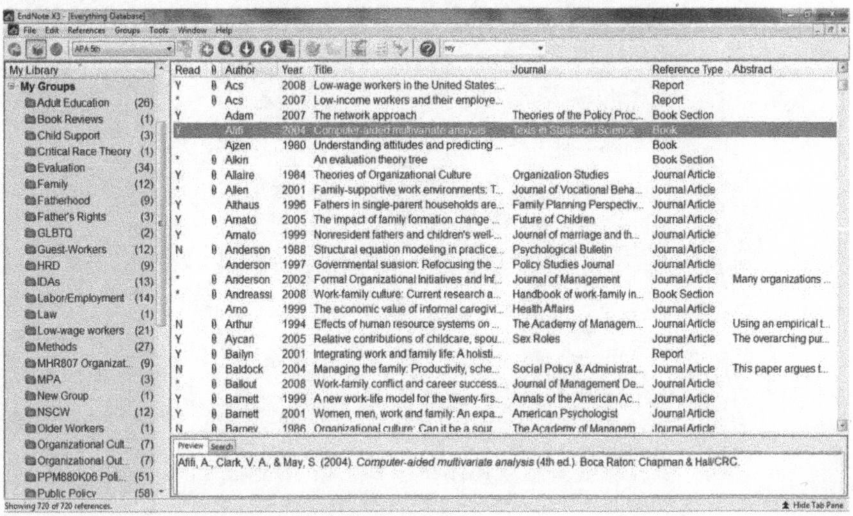

created several groups showing that the literature can be grouped and sorted by topic, on the left. The right pane shows a selected book and the citation below it.

Take Critically Reflective Notes

When you are ready to read articles, use a method that works best for you to capture key points. You might choose to print the articles and write in the margins, or you might read the article on a computer using a software program like Adobe Acrobat or Microsoft OneNote. Include not only bulleted clips of points of interest but also your critique and interpretation of what you read. If you see connections or disconnections between what you are reading and other articles, capture this too. Remember that being a scholar involves looking at a topic from all angles and developing a logical argument. In addition to or in place of taking notes in the document, creating a spreadsheet or table for capturing key concepts—for example, the purpose, research method, and results—is useful. Remember that the point of taking notes is not just to summarize but to critically reflect on what you have read.

Microsoft OneNote notebooks, Excel spreadsheets, and Word tables can be used to record key information about articles. Figure 3.2 depicts use of Microsoft

FIGURE 3.2. EXAMPLE OF ELECTRONIC NOTE TAKING.

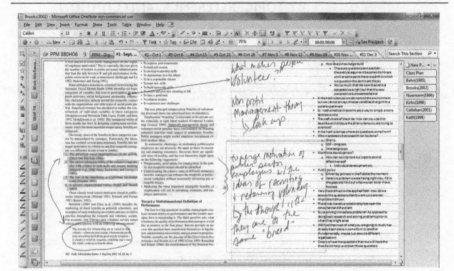

OneNote on a tablet PC where notes were written in the margins of an electronic copy and items organized as if in a binder.

In this example, Microsoft OneNote is used to divide a course by date or class session along the top and individual articles along the right. In addition to typing notes on the document, using a Tablet PC allows highlighting and hand-written notes on the document.

Microsoft Word tables and Excel spreadsheets can be used to organize notes, depending on your preferences. For example, we have used this method to organize comprehensive exam and dissertation notes (see Figures 3.3 and 3.4).

In the example in Figure 3.3, a Microsoft Word table is used to record key information such as the citation, key words, and main points of articles reviewed for a writing project.

In the example in Figure 3.4, a detailed Microsoft Excel spreadsheet is used to record key information about articles. A spreadsheet captures information in a single document or organizes notes by creating multiple sheets within a single workbook.

Freewrite

Freewriting is writing about a topic without attending to grammar or stylistic rules. The idea is to write anything that comes to mind without evaluating content

FIGURE 3.3. EXAMPLE OF A SPREADSHEET USED TO ORGANIZE COMPREHENSIVE EXAMINATION INFORMATION.

	ARTICLE CITATION	KEYWORDS	MAIN POINTS
1.	*Ambrose, D. (1997). Healing the downsized organization: What every employee needs to know about today's new workplace.* New York: Three Rivers Press.	Manager's dual role Managers as privileged	Managers caught in the middle; they are expected to coach, mentor, guide, instruct and create high-performing teams. Yet the manager in the context of downsizing may be seen as the enemy in the eyes of employees who see the manager as part of an elite group that makes decisions about who stays and who goes.
		Reduced risk taking/risk-averse culture	Downsizing can create a risk-averse workforce; also, when costs are cut, tools required to stimulate creativity and innovation are often cut in the proccess along with jobs.
		Paradoxes; the saying/doing gap	Organizational paradoxes Ambrose identifies organizational paradoxes expressed during her leadership seminars that points to a saying/doing gap or what Schein refers to as espoused theories and theories in use.

Used with permission from Microsoft.

FIGURE 3.4. EXAMPLE OF SPREADSHEET USED TO RECORD KEY INFORMATION.

	A	B	C	D	E	F	G	H	I	J	K	L
1	Citation	Summary of Main Points/ Keywords	Application/ Critical Comments	Research Questions	Research Type	Analysis Method	Population	Dataset	Sample Size	Dependent Variables	Independent Variables	Control Variables
2												
3												
4												

or worrying about grammar, overall coherence, or flow (Elbow, 1998). Editing, adding citations, and polishing the writing so that it conforms to scholarly norms can be done after freewriting. Freewriting can be a structured activity where specific time is set aside to freewrite, or it can be an unstructured activity where you write whenever you have something to write about. As a structured activity, you can freewrite after reading one or more articles by writing about what struck you and about ideas you questioned in the articles. We have freewritten on the computer, in notebooks, on sticky notes, and on napkins. Whether you use information immediately or save it for future use, this technique is an effective way to start the writing process.

Use an Interviewing Approach

Imagine that you are going to be interviewed about your topic. To prepare for the interview, think about the questions you might be asked. List the questions and answers to each. Include questions requiring critical reflection on the topic, and remember to include the important, "So what?" question: Why should others be interested in this topic?

When answering the questions, resist the temptation to quote someone else; instead, write in your own words, and answer the questions aloud to hear how the content sounds. After answering the questions, build your manuscript.

Develop Research and Writing Strategies

Each of us approaches research and writing in our own way (Torrance, Thomas, & Robinson, 1994). Some writers use a "think-then write" (Roberts, 2004, p. 390) strategy, planning content and reviewing the literature before starting the actual writing process. This might include developing a content outline to establish the flow of the manuscript before writing. Other writers move back and forth between thinking, reading, and writing, using a "think-while-you-write" strategy (Torrance et al., 1994, p. 390). In this case, a linear outline or creative brainstorm of ideas for the paper might gradually emerge throughout this iterative process of thinking, reading, and writing. First, you might think and read and then begin to outline content. Then you might return to thinking and reading, followed by adding more to the outline.

We have used mind mapping, a creative brainstorming technique, to help us think about what we might want to include in a writing project. Mind maps use radiant thinking: "associative thought processes that proceed from or connect to a central point" (Buzan & Buzan, 1994, p. 57). Mind maps can be developed using words, shapes, and even pictures. The idea is to brainstorm main ideas related to your central topic and then to brainstorm additional ideas associated with the main ideas. The process continues until you have exhausted all possible ideas. At that point, clusters of related ideas can be developed into a more structured outline, or the mind map can guide manuscript development.

Figure 3.5 depicts a high-level outline representing this chapter. Additional subtopics could be added for more detail. Figure 3.6 shows the same chapter mind-mapped. Details are added by expanding on the ideas presented.

Outlines and mind maps serve as flexible guides to help develop the manuscript; they are not meant to dictate the process of writing. The best place to

FIGURE 3.5. EXAMPLE OF A HIGH-LEVEL OUTLINE.

Learning to Write: Wisdom from Emerging Scholars

1. Introduction

    1.1 Reflections on Scholarly Writing
    1.2 Advanced Organizer

2. Our Scholarly Writing Experiences

    2.1 Doctoral Candidates
    2.2 Employment
    2.3 Varied Experiences with Scholarly Writing

3. Appreciating the Importance of Writing

    3.1 To Academics
    3.2 To Graduate Students

4. Getting Started

    3.1 Develop a Research Agenda
    3.2 Organize Your Literature
    3.3 Take Critically Reflective Notes
    3.4 Freewrite
    3.5 Use an Interviewing Approach
    3.6 Develop Research and Writing Strategies

5. Building Relationships

    5.1 Establishing Mentoring Relationships
    5.2 Building a Scholarly Network
    5.3 Collaborating with Others

6. Building Writing Skills

    6.1 Giving and Receiving Constructive Criticism
    6.2 Finding Time to Write
    6.3 Managing Writer's Block
    6.4 Talking Out Loud
    6.5 Expressing Your Scholarly Voice

7. Taking the Plunge

    7.1 Converting Papers into Manuscripts
    7.2 Volunteering to Peer Review
    7.3 Organizing Your Research
    7.4 Presenting at Conferences
    7.5 Reviewing Scholarly Books
    7.6 Submitting to a Journal

FIGURE 3.6. MIND-MAPPING EXAMPLE.

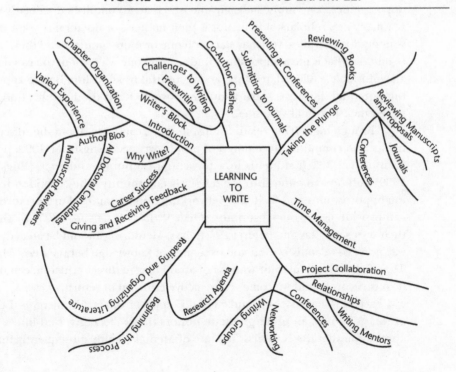

begin writing from an outline or mind map is wherever it feels comfortable. If you are writing a formal research paper and have drafted an outline or mind map, no rule says that you must write the introduction before the literature review or method. The objective is just to write. Remember that your outline or mind map is not carved in stone; as the manuscript develops, you might add, move, or delete items.

Building Relationships

Entering the scholarly community requires establishing and nurturing relationships with peers, faculty, and practitioners. Some of these individuals might become mentors, part of a scholarly network, and future writing collaborators. In this section, we share our experiences building relationships with other writers.

Establish Mentoring Relationships

Mentoring relationships can enhance the ability to pursue scholarly writing opportunities. A mentor can be anyone who is an accomplished scholarly writer. For many new scholars, the mentor is their master's or doctoral advisor. During your graduate studies, you may start with one or more mentors and then change to others. What is most important is finding someone with whom you can develop a comfortable, collegial, trusting, and respectful relationship. Before approaching potential mentors, learn about their work. Read their publications, and review their personal Web sites.

Through mentoring relationships, students can learn about the "discipline, habits, and commitment required of prolific writers" (Engstrom, 1999, p. 270). Mentors can teach students how to write for a public audience (Engstrom, 1999) and how to enter into the scholarly community. They can identify writing opportunities and facilitate networking opportunities. Furthermore, they can provide psychosocial support (Ortiz-Walters & Gilson, 2005) by sharing their own successes and failures as scholars. Mentoring should be an active two-way process—a conversation and exchange of knowledge between two scholars. Therefore, select a mentor who is not afraid to give direct criticism, can deliver it constructively, and welcomes constructive criticism in return.

Each of us has received guidance and support from faculty mentors. Because of this guidance, an undergraduate honors thesis was converted into a grant application that the National Institute of Mental Health subsequently funded.

As a master's student, one of us developed an award-winning thesis into a conference paper and presentation. Before officially entering the doctoral program, one of us was invited by a professor, who became her doctoral advisor, to attend a scholarly conference and presented a paper at that conference the following year. Tonette Rocco, a coeditor of this book, has also regularly championed us as we presented conference papers, wrote book reviews, and even wrote this chapter.

Build a Scholarly Network

Once you have established a research agenda and found a mentor, actively build your scholarly network. Attending professional and academic conferences is one strategy. These events provide opportunities to develop relationships with other scholars. In addition to the main program, many conferences offer preconferences on specific topics. Preconferences are usually more casual, fostering open dialogue and relationship building among students and academics with similar interests. Sometimes conferences host workshops and events to help aspiring scholars learn how to conduct research and to write.

We have also participated in a writing group facilitated by Tonette Rocco. Writing groups provide a venue to meet established and aspiring scholars who want to improve their writing. In a writing group, members constructively critique each other's manuscripts (Rankin, 2001). Some groups might invite faculty to share their writing experiences with them. If your program or university does not offer a writing group, consider creating your own group with your peers, and invite faculty to participate.

Collaborate

Students can collaborate with peers, colleagues, or established scholars. If someone is working on a project that interests you, ask if you can collaborate. Also, ask others to collaborate on your projects if you know they have similar interests. Collaborating allows scholars to tap into each other's expertise, illuminate multiple perspectives, and facilitate scholarly discussion. This can lead to further clarification of your thoughts, better expression of ideas, and deeper meaning making. Still, collaborating can be challenging. As the manuscript develops, authors might disagree with each other's feedback. Reaching agreement on feedback and joining voices to create a comprehensive and understandable manuscript, however, are critical to collaborative writing. Disagreement over feedback can lead to further discussion with alternative methods of addressing issues emerging, leading to more effective resolution of manuscript-related issues.

Technology has made it easier for people to collaborate from a distance. The three of us live in different states and attend different institutions. We have used e-mail, online interactive discussion groups, and conference calls to collaborate. In our conference calls, we have used Google Docs, an online collaboration tool, to view and edit our document live.

While finding people who have expertise related to your topic and method is essential, including people who share a similar work ethic and are committed to following through is also important. Decide on the rules of engagement from the start of the project. Delineate areas of individual responsibility, and jointly determine milestone dates for key activities (drafts, revisions, and final product, for example) to help ensure the process runs as smoothly as possible. Also, having one person serve as project manager to follow up with coauthors and with the editor is useful.

Although most of our collaborative experiences have been fruitful, some have not. If it appears that a collaborator is not meeting commitments, you can ask the person to leave or allow the project to proceed as planned and simply learn from the experience. If a collaborator has contributed content and leaves the project voluntarily or involuntarily, this can present potential ethical issues around authorship. A decision should be made about how to handle these matters. Every situation must be considered on its own merit. Remember that collaboration is rarely an equal process and requires flexibility. You cannot predict life events that might happen, requiring a renegotiation of the project plan.

Building Writing Skills

Good writing is not an innate skill. Building writing skills is a multifaceted process that requires practice and dedication and goes beyond learning correct grammar and punctuation. It includes giving and receiving meaningful constructive criticism, finding time to write, and overcoming obstacles that may prevent you from writing effectively (for example, writer's block and voice issues).

Give and Receive Constructive Criticism

Writing is an iterative process requiring many drafts, reviews, and revisions. Allowing yourself to fully engage in giving and receiving constructive feedback can strengthen your writing (Nielsen & Rocco, 2002). Formal and informal peer reviews are a collaborative process (Reither & Vipond, 1989) in which writers receive constructive criticism from their peers. The intent of constructive criticism is to illuminate unclear areas, provide alternative viewpoints, and offer suggestions for improvement. Being critiqued, however, can be intimidating because writing is such a personal activity (Nackoney et al., 2007; Nielsen & Rocco, 2002). Despite the anguish that some writers experience through peer review, a group of doctoral students taking a scholarly writing class cited constructive criticism "as the most influential element in helping them to understand the scholarly writing process and [produce] a scholarly product" (Caffarella & Barnett, 2000, p. 48).

When providing constructive criticism, students often focus on technical issues such as grammar and punctuation flaws (Rocco, Parsons, Bernier, & Batist, 2003). Although this feedback is helpful, peer review should also provide a thoughtful critique of content and offer insightful examples. The goal should be to help the author improve. Some people are more skilled at providing feedback than others. Therefore, when you are receiving constructive criticism, remember that the reviewer's comments are not meant to be a personal attack. Also, just because the reviewer offers feedback does not mean you must act on it. Critically reflect on the reviewer's comments and incorporate feedback into your writing as you see fit. However, if criticism is from conference or journal reviewers, be sure to explain in the letter to the editor why you did not incorporate suggestions if you chose not to. Also, remember that if more than one person offers similar criticism, chances are that something in the manuscript is unclear and needs to be revised.

Establishing your own peer group to review each other's manuscripts is a good way to improve feedback skills. As a master's student, one of us and two of her peers began an informal writing group for reviewing each other's research papers, becoming more proficient with this process. She continues this process today even though all three are in different fields at different universities.

Find Time to Write

In an ideal world, we would prefer to have large blocks of time to work on projects. However, this is not always possible. We therefore have to look for pockets of time to write. You can be structured or unstructured with your time. Sometimes the most opportune times are the easiest to overlook, such as using commuting time to write, read, take notes, and edit manuscripts. Some people find small pockets of time ineffective for productive writing and use them for relaxing and processing thoughts.

Creating a broad or narrow plan for completing writing projects is also an effective tool to stay motivated and focused. Sometimes, however, creating and perfecting the plan can inhibit your actual progress. In other words, you can become so fixated on the plan that you fail to write. Even the best plan cannot always resolve competing priorities. So if writing is a priority, something you may find helpful is scheduling writing time as you would schedule other appointments and meetings and then honoring your commitment to write.

Manage Writer's Block

An Internet search of educational Web sites using the keywords "writer's block" produced over fifty-two thousand entries. All writers at one time or another become blocked. Over half of all doctoral candidates end up ABD (all but dissertation) largely because of writer's block (Flaherty, 2004).

Preparing a scholarly manuscript is somewhat like putting together a jigsaw puzzle. A few pieces might easily snap into place. However, when your manuscript does not take shape quickly, you may become overwhelmed, frustrated, and blocked. The more you try, the more difficult it becomes, creating confusion, anxiety, and self-doubt.

It is a good idea at that point to set a troublesome project aside. Relaxing or changing direction sometimes allows you to gain perspective on that manuscript. Unexpectedly, another piece might snap into place, and you resume writing. More blocked moments may occur in the weeks that come, but with patience and persistence, you complete the manuscript. As for those extra pieces, they provide the stimulus for another manuscript.

Sometimes writer's block occurs because we are burned out or have read too much and experience information overload. Another common cause of writer's block is the inner critic (Boice, 1993). Each of us has an inner critic ready to criticize every word or sentence. If we give in, a block is likely to follow. Other common causes of writer's block are low self-confidence (Roberts, 2004), fear of failure or rejection (Boice, 1993), and perfectionism (Boice, 1993; Roberts, 2004).

Mind mapping (Germov, 2000) and freewriting (Elbow, 1998; Wahlstrom, 2006) are helpful for eliminating writer's block because they allow you to write in a nonjudgmental, natural way. Elbow and Wahlstrom both recommended freewriting in fifteen-minute slots to overcome writer's block. It does not matter what you write; what matters is that you are writing. This daily exercise often results in breakthroughs and movement toward finishing the manuscript.

Another helpful technique is talking through your ideas aloud. Conversing with others can help overcome your feeling of being incapable of thinking of anything meaningful to write. A recorder can be used to capture your thoughts in a manner similar to freewriting. This material can then be incorporated into the manuscript.

Writer's block also occurs when we are stressed and tired and when our goals or expectations are unrealistic (Boice, 1993; Roberts, 2004). You might intend to spend two or three hours at night writing, but after a ten-hour workday, this may be unrealistic. It is important to nourish your mind and body through sleep, exercise, and healthy eating. Write when you are most alert and can think clearly. One of us writes more clearly first thing in the morning and programs half an hour to write before heading to the office.

Express Your Scholarly Voice

Students often mimic academic writers rather than express their own voices (Rocco et al., 2003). *Voice* refers to the way we reveal ourselves to others when we write (Richards & Miller, 2005). Difficulties expressing one's voice are evident in manuscripts where the author has used direct quotes excessively or has excessively paraphrased others' work (Rankin, 2001; Roberts, 2004) without critically reflecting on content or developing a solid argument that will add something new to the knowledge base.

As emerging scholars, we might fall victim to the impostor phenomenon. Originally used to describe feelings of inadequacy in high-achieving women (Clance & Imes, 1978), this phenomenon also describes the fear of failure that many emerging scholars wrestle with that can sabotage their success. The inner critic that contributes to writer's block can incapacitate us to the point where we convince ourselves that we are not worthy, experienced, or knowledgeable enough to participate in scholarly conversations. If we give in, we might find ourselves sitting on the sidelines, watching and listening, but not fully engaging with other scholars (Nackoney et al., 2007). Becoming scholars, however, requires that we exorcise the graduate student within each of us, "the self-assured yet hesitant, assertive yet deferential and conflicted self that emerges whenever we find ourselves paying less attention to what we're saying than to how it will be received" (Rankin, 2001, p. 61). As emerging scholars, we must trust ourselves and believe that we are capable and worthy of participating in scholarly conversations (Richards & Miller, 2005; Rocco et al., 2003).

Being scholars means approaching everything with curiosity, continuously questioning what we read, making new connections, and looking for gaps in the knowledge base. If what has already been written and published could never be challenged, eventually the scholarly flame would be extinguished.

Taking the Plunge

Throughout this chapter, we have shared strategies and techniques that have helped us in our ongoing transition from students to scholars. While this process might seem somewhat confusing or intimidating, we have also found it very rewarding. Scholarly writing has allowed our voices to be heard and our insights to be added to the knowledge base. Here are some closing suggestions, in no particular order, for taking the initial plunge and getting published.

- *Although you might feel that you do not have anything to submit to a conference or journal, this is likely not the case.* If you have conducted research for course papers or to fulfill program requirements, you have material that can be developed into a manuscript. While this is a good starting point, remember that the audience for a conference paper or journal manuscript is different from classmates or professors being the audience. Just because the professor liked your paper does not mean the paper is ready for submission to a conference or journal. Instead, it might mean that it is a good piece to develop into a manuscript.

- *If you are in the dissertation stage of your doctoral studies, look for opportunities to create publishable manuscripts from your dissertation.* These manuscripts can be submitted first to a conference and then developed into a journal manuscript. This can help develop your reputation as an expert. Presenting conference papers developed from your unfinished dissertation or in-process writing projects is useful to obtain feedback that can be incorporated into the final dissertation or manuscript.

- *Volunteering to peer-review manuscripts and proposals will help you learn about the components of a good research paper or scholarly article.* Reviewing manuscripts provides several positive benefits. First, you will see what is being written in your field. Second, you will be exposed to a variety of writing styles and methods. You will soon be able to identify strong writing and learn from others' mistakes. Beginning writers often find it easier to critique others' writing and gain confidence in their own abilities.

- *For many students, presenting at a conference is their entry point.* Obtain a copy of the call for proposals or papers, and carefully review requirements. Explicitly follow submission guidelines to better ensure that your proposal or paper is accepted. Some conference proposals undergo a strict review process similar to a journal manuscript. Often a conference proposal, especially if it will be published in conference proceedings, will be accepted conditionally, pending the author's addressing reviewers' feedback. Receiving a revise-and-resubmit decision is common and not something to be upset about. Do your best to address reviewer comments. If you feel you cannot adequately do so or feel that some changes are unnecessary, justify your reasoning. If the conference rejects your proposal, use feedback provided to refine the proposal so you can resubmit the following year to the same conference or perhaps to another.

- *Writing a critical book review is also a good entry point.* Select scholarly or practitioner-based journals that fit your research interests or apply to your job. Start by reading recent book reviews in selected publications to understand what the editor expects in a review. Look for the journal's call, and review what you need to provide. Finally, contact the book review editor and let him or her know that you are interested in reviewing a book.

- *Select a journal that you are interested in, and submit a manuscript for publication.* Manuscripts can report on research or be a venue for you to propose a new theory or model or to write a structured literature review.

In any discipline, standard conventions exist that must be followed. Therefore, before submitting a manuscript to a journal, ensure that you have met all required formatting instructions and are familiar with work regularly published. Investigate the journal's publishing focus (for example, conceptual, qualitative, quantitative, or mixed methods), the preferred citation style, the preferred writing style (more formal or more casual), and the standard submission length. Follow guidelines and criteria explicitly.

Being published in a journal as an emerging scholar is typically more difficult than having a paper accepted for conference presentation or publication in conference proceedings. The exception might be if you are collaborating with seasoned scholars who have already published in a particular journal. Also, journal articles are rarely accepted on first submission. It is perfectly normal to receive a revise-and-resubmit decision. Do not allow this to discourage you. This is actually a positive response. Think of it as the editor's providing you with constructive criticism to improve the manuscript before accepting it for publication. Similarly, if the editor rejects your manuscript, use feedback provided to redevelop the manuscript into a better submission for another journal.

References

Austin, A. E. (2002). Preparing the next generation of faculty: Graduate school as socialization to the academic career. *Journal of Higher Education, 73*(1), 94–122.

Boice, R. (1993). Writing blocks and tacit knowledge. *Journal of Higher Education, 64*(1), 19–54.

Buzan, T., & Buzan, B. (1994). *The mind map book: How to use radiant thinking to maximize your brain's untapped potential.* New York: Dutton.

Caffarella, R. S., & Barnett, B. G. (2000). Teaching doctoral students to become scholarly writers: The importance of giving and receiving critiques. *Studies in Higher Education, 25*(1), 39–52.

Casanave, C. P., & Vandrick, S. (2003). Introduction: Issues in writing for publication. In C. Pearson Casanave & S. Vandrick (Eds.), *Writing for scholarly publication* (pp. 1–13). Mahwah, NJ: Erlbaum.

Clance, P. R., & Imes, S. (1978). The imposter phenomenon in high achieving women: Dynamics and therapeutic intervention. *Psychotherapy Theory, Research and Practice, 15*(3), 241–247.

Elbow, P. (1998). *Writing with power: Techniques for mastering the writing process* (2nd ed.). New York: Oxford University Press.

Engstrom, C. M. (1999). Promoting the scholarly writing of female doctoral students in higher education and student affairs graduate programs. *NAPSA Journal, 36*(4), 264–277.

Flaherty, A. W. (2004). *The midnight disease: The drive to write, writer's block, and the creative brain.* Boston: Mariner Books.

Germov, J. (2000). *Get great marks for your essay* (2nd ed.). Crown Nest, Australia: Allen & Unwin.

Hornsby, E., & Munn, S. (2009). University work-life benefits and same-sex couples. *Advances in Developing Human Resources, 11*(1), 67–81.

Melamed, B. G., Robbins, R. L., & Fernandez, J. (1981). Factors to be considered in preparation of children for hospitalization and surgery. In M. Wolraich & D. Routh (Eds.), *Advances in behavioral pediatrics* (pp. 217–243). Stamford, CT: JAI Press.

Munn, S. L. (2009a). Relationships between work-life benefits, organizational culture and organizational performance. In T. Chermack, J. Storberg-Walker, & C. M. Graham (Eds.), *Proceedings of the Academy of Human Resources and Development Conference* (pp. 3040–3069). Washington, DC: Academy of Human Resources and Development.

Munn, S. L. (2009b). [Review of *Work-life policies* and *Working after welfare: How women balance jobs and family in the wake of welfare reform*]. *Journal of Policy Analysis and Management, 28*(4), 760–763.

Munn, S. L., & Rocco, T. (2008). Towards a practical model: theory of margin and work-life balance of single parents. In *Proceedings of the 27th Midwest Research-to-Practice Conference in Adult, Continuing, and Community Education* (pp. 159–164). Bowling Green, KY.

Munn, S. L., & Rocco, T. S. (2010). Organizational policy and discretionary decisions: The issue of traditional versus non-traditional family structures. In S. Schmidt (Ed.), *Case studies and activities in adult education and human resource development.* Charlotte, NC: Information Age Publishing.

Nackoney, C. K. (2006). [Review of *Trust and betrayal in the workplace: Building effective relationships in your organization*]. *New Horizons in Adult Education and Human Resource Development, 20*(2), 60–63.

Nackoney, C. K., Munn, S. L., & Gallagher, S. J. (2007). Becoming scholarly writers: An autoethnography of three emerging scholars. In L. Servage & T. Fenwick (Eds.), *Proceedings of the 48th Adult Education Research Conference* (pp. 445–450). Halifax, Nova Scotia: Mount St. Vincent University.

Nackoney, C. K., & Pane, D. M. (2006). [Review of *Auto/biography and auto/ethnography: Praxis of research method*]. *New Horizons in Adult Education and Human Resource Development, 20*(3), 47–50.

Nackoney, C. K., Rajbansee, V., Rocco, T. S., & Gallagher, S. (2005). [Review of *The power of critical theory*]. *Adult Education Quarterly, 56*(1), 66–68.

Nackoney, C. K., & Rocco, T. S. (2005). [Review of *Strategic HRD*]. *Human Resource Development Quarterly, 16*(2), 293–295.

Nielsen, S., & Rocco, T. S. (2002, April). Joining the conversation: Graduate students' perceptions of writing for publication. In S. Neilsen & T. S. Rocco (Eds.), *Appreciating scholarship: Proceedings of the First Annual College of Education Conference* (pp. 75–80). Miami: Florida International University.

Ortiz-Walters, R., & Gilson, L. L. (2005). Mentoring in academia: An examination of the experiences of protégés of color. *Journal of Vocational Behavior, 67*(3), 459–475.

Rankin, E. (2001). *The work of writing: Insights and strategies for academics and professionals.* San Francisco: Jossey-Bass.

Reither, J. A., & Vipond, D. (1989). Writing as collaboration. *College English, 51*(8), 855–867.

Richards, J. C., & Miller, S. K. (2005). *Doing academic writing in education: Connecting the personal and the professional.* Mahwah, NJ: Erlbaum.

Roberts, C. M. (2004). *The dissertation journey: A practical and comprehensive guide to planning, writing, and defending your dissertation.* Thousand Oaks, CA: Sage.

Rocco, T. S., Parsons, M., Bernier, J. D., & Batist, C. (2003, October). Guiding the work of writing: Reflections on the writing process. In T. Ferro & G. Dean (Eds.), *Proceedings of the Midwest Research-to-Practice Conference in Adult, Continuing, and Community Education* (pp. 174–180). Columbus: Ohio State University.

Stein, D., Rocco, T., Munn, S., Ginn, G., & Antolino, L. (2006). Aging workers: An evolving framework for policy development. In T. Rocco & J. Thijssen (Eds.), *Older workers, new directions* (pp. 27–40). Miami: Center for Labor Research Studies, Florida International University.

Torrance, M., Thomas, G. V., & Robinson, E. J. (1994). The writing strategies of graduate research students in the social sciences. *Higher Education, 27*(3), 379–392.

Wahlstrom, R. L. (2006). *The tao of writing. Imagine. Create. Flow.* Avon, MA: Adams Media.

CHAPTER 4

SCHOLARLY READING AS A MODEL FOR SCHOLARLY WRITING

Mike Wallace, Alison Wray

You are no doubt familiar with the question, "Which came first, the chicken or the egg?" The answer is *neither* and *both*! The same applies to the question, "Which comes first, scholarly reading or scholarly writing?" That is why we are highlighting reading in a book about writing.

Reading is the first step toward writing. Scholarly writing would hardly count as scholarly if it ignored what other scholars had written on the topic. Scholarly writing usually includes an account that synthesizes and challenges previous research and puts forward new ideas. When reading, you need to pay attention to at least three different things. One is the topic matter, of course: the basic information contained in the text. The second is the quality of the claims made about that information. The third is the manner in which the claims are presented. Where authors create a clear and convincing account, you can apply the same techniques to improve your own writing.

You are no doubt aware how reading and writing proceeds in cycles. You read relevant literature to inform your writing—whether a dissertation, research paper, or funding proposal—and your writing becomes reading matter for others. The process often does not end there: another cycle may be triggered. You read feedback from tutors or reviewers and revise your writing in response. And so on.

Given this cyclic flow, reading and writing can be viewed as integral components of the two-way process of scholarly discourse. Mastery of these complementary activities results in more effective writing, which helps ensure that your contribution to new knowledge or practice is recognized and valued. Some scholarly discourse takes place face-to-face. But most takes place through the written word. Through Internet communication and electronic searching and downloading, readers can engage with the works of many writers from every part of the world. Yet the scholarly discourse community remains united in the purpose of exploring and evaluating others' work and presenting new evidence and interpretations for others to evaluate.

In this chapter, we explain how to develop scholarly discourse by integrating reading and writing. We show what it means to be constructively critical as a reader and how this skill can be applied to become self-critical as a writer. The key is recognizing that an argument has two components: a claim and its warranting based on evidence justifying the claim. We consider what an inadequate argument looks like and how the reader (and self-critical writer) can spot it. Then we examine two key dimensions of an argument that can often be challenged: whether the level of certainty about a claim is appropriate for the evidence, and how generalized this claim is, and should be. Finally, we consider the skill of writing for critical readers such as assessors and reviewers.

So this chapter shows how an accomplished writer benefits from critical reading skills. First, the quality of your account of others' work will be more sophisticated. Second, critically reading your own work will reveal any potential weaknesses in the arguments, so redrafting can be done before any critical reader sees it. We begin by considering what our purpose as scholarly readers and writers is: what we are doing when we engage in scholarly discourse.

Integrating Reading and Writing

Whether you are working on your first graduate assignment or aiming to get your first paper accepted in a top academic journal, the global scholarly community expects critical engagement with others' work. Everyone in this community has two complementary roles: as constructively critical reader and as self-critical writer. How can you learn to integrate the two roles as effectively as possible? To help you understand our approach, try answering the following questions:

Orientation Questions

- What is the best scholarly text you've ever read?
- Can you explain what the authors did in writing it that enabled you to learn so much about the topic?
- What is the worst scholarly text you've ever read?

- What did the authors do wrong, so that you were inhibited from learning as much as you had hoped about the topic?
- Can you see ways in which you could learn about how to write well from scrutinizing texts that you have found particularly effective and ineffective in conveying ideas?

We hope your answer to the last question is yes and that you want to accelerate your learning as a self-critical writer by being a constructively critical reader. In the next section we explore key aspects of that process.

Being Constructively Critical as a Reader and Self-Critical as a Writer

We emphasize being constructively critical because we value scholarly discourse as a way of pursuing worthwhile purposes: inquiring about what the social world is like, determining how it should be, and supporting each other's scholarly learning. We reject destructive purposes such as trying to show that people are foolish because of their views.

Being critical is often associated with being negative—trying to find fault. But being constructively critical is more positive. You aim to respect other scholars as potential contributors to your knowledge. But you adopt a skeptical stance toward what they have to say. There are two key reasons that a skeptical stance is necessary. First, anyone can make a mistake, overinterpret or misinterpret the information they are dealing with, or fail to take into account other relevant information, published elsewhere. As a critical reader, you work out whether to accept the authors' claims by drawing on your accumulated knowledge and experience and by looking for any logical flaws or inconsistencies.

Second, you may well find that different authors make incompatible claims about the same topic, backed by contrasting evidence. Can they both be right? Going beyond merely describing their opposing arguments, to judge which is more convincing and why, means engaging critically with the nature of their claims and the strength of any supporting evidence. Then you will be in a position to make novel and significant claims of your own, which reach beyond what others have already argued.

So, in reading, you remain open-minded and ready in principle to accept the authors' views—but only if you find them convincing. You make judgments about how far you agree and why. You also consider how well the authors have communicated their views through the structure of their account and the language used. If you cannot understand what they are trying to convey, you are likely to remain unconvinced. It would be unwise to take their claims on trust when you cannot follow their reasoning: weak evidence could be disguised in complicated language. Successful communication is an essential goal for all writers who wish to convince readers of the validity of their ideas.

When you come to write, informed by your reading, you can ensure you write effectively by being self-critical. You apply to your own work the lessons learned from your constructively critical reading of others' writing. You have judged how well others communicated with and convinced you. Now you have to communicate with, and convince, the critical readers of your work. You do that by emulating the good scholarly writing practice you have observed. Equally, you identify and avoid the pitfalls of bad practice.

Getting into an Argument

The term *argument* here does not mean a heated disagreement. Rather, an argument is a claim backed up (warranted) by evidence. In this section, we introduce these concepts and explain how they are relevant to critical reading.

Scholarly discourse entails finding something out and then demonstrating to others why it is significant. It is also about evaluating others' claims to have found things out. The discourse that scholars produce in the course of inquiry into the social world is rather like detective work. Detectives try to solve mysteries by uncovering evidence about what has happened. They convince others of what they have discovered and why it is significant by showing them this evidence. In a similar way, scholars are following a trail toward explaining what some aspect of the world is like. They seek clues by asking well-informed questions and designing literature-based and empirical investigations to answer them. As with detectives, the process of finding out is not enough. The discoveries must be followed up with a convincing presentation of the evidence. This evidence must provide support for the claims being made as answers to the questions posed. Were academic writers just to make claims about their discoveries, and not present evidence to justify the claims, their readers would rightly query how they could be so sure they were right.

You may be a more expert scholarly detective than you realize. Suppose we asked you, "How critical a reader and self-critical a writer are you already?" You might look for clues to the answer by reflecting on your recent experiences of scholarly reading and writing. Perhaps you would check through notes you have made while reading and look at the feedback you have received on your written work. Now suppose we said, "Actually, we already know. You're overly critical as a reader, and totally unself-critical as a writer!" How would you respond? You might ask, "Why do you say that? Give me an example to show me what gave you that idea." Next, you might start to cite counterexamples as evidence to back your view that we were being unfair. But suppose we quoted examples that you had to admit did give evidence of your being undercritical about your own writing. You might try to weigh up the evidence from both sides: from the experiences you remembered and the examples we highlighted. On the basis of all the evidence, you would come to a conclusion about how far you tend to be insufficiently self-critical toward what you have written. Suppose we then challenged your conclusion by scrutinizing how you judged the relative importance of the evidence from the experiences you remembered and from our examples. If we were unable to back up our challenge to your conclusion with evidence, you would be able to set our challenge aside as invalid. To convince us, you would have to give us your reasoning. And so on.

There is thus more to scholarly discourse than simply a flow of claims and counterclaims. If scholarship were only about claims, there would be nothing to debate. Readers and writers would merely indulge in games of, "Oh, yes it is," and, "Oh, no it isn't." Scholarship evaluates: it makes judgments about the acceptability of claims on the basis of an appropriate form of evidence. In other words, at the heart of scholarly discourse is the detective work of putting forward your own, and evaluating others', arguments.

Argument = Conclusion (Containing Claims) + Warranting (Based on Evidence)

An argument consists of two parts: the conclusion—one or more claims that something is, or should be, the case—and the warranting. The warranting is the justification that makes the conclusion convincing. The evidence offered in the warranting is adequate if it sufficiently supports the claims in the conclusion. This conception of argument is admittedly simpler than that used by philosophers (Toulmin, 1958). But for the purposes of this chapter, our definition is not only adequate but highly practical. You can apply it to any length of text, from a sentence to the whole of a dissertation or book. You can use it to identify and evaluate the arguments you read in other authors' texts and to construct arguments in your own scholarly writing.

To see how the argument is constructed, consider how Coleman (2003), exploring leadership and management styles of female secondary head teachers, presents the case that there was perceived to be "male resentment of female leadership" (pp. 114–115). She begins the section of that title with the claim, "Over half the surveyed heads reported experiencing sexist attitudes from their male colleagues" (p. 114). The claim is that such attitudes were experienced, and it is warranted by her evidence that over half the heads reported it. Later, exploring the nature of these attitudes, she makes the claim, "There was . . . an expectation that females would manage in a certain way" (p. 115). This claim is then warranted by a quotation from one of the heads surveyed: "The assumption was that you will be a female stereotype—keep changing one's mind, can't handle difficult male pupils etc."

To summarize, in learning to become an expert scholarly writer, you have two tasks: to evaluate others' arguments and to develop your own adequately warranted argument. Scholarly discourse is a two-way constructively critical process. As a constructively critical reader, you evaluate the conclusion and warranting of others' arguments as they attempt to communicate with and convince their target audience. As a self-critical writer, you develop your own argument, making it as clearly expressed and as well warranted as possible so as to communicate with and convince your target audience.

Often, constructing a strong argument in your writing will flow directly from your critical reading of others' work. Where you find others' arguments convincing, you may cite their findings, prescriptions, or theories as part of the supporting evidence that warrants the claims in your own argument. Where others' arguments are unconvincing, you may distance yourself from their claims and highlight the flaws or limitations in their arguments as evidence that warrants your claim that their evidence is inadequate.

When Is an Argument Not Really an Argument?

Not everything that looks like an argument actually is one, so we must be alert. Fairly easy to spot are cases where one of the necessary elements is missing. When there are just claims, with no warranting, then the author has simply offered an opinion. For example, "The earlier workers are trained to be leaders, the better," is, as framed here, simply an opinion. Even if you agree with it, you should not be satisfied to accept it without warranting. Ask, "How do you know?" The reason for caution is that sometimes popular beliefs turn out to be untrue. Once everyone believed the world was flat. But when sufficient evidence was examined, this belief was discovered to be an unwarranted claim. It is fine for authors to have opinions, but if they want to persuade their readers to agree, they must provide convincing reasons for why the claims should be accepted.

Alternatively, there might be warranting but no conclusion—a collection of statements amounting to a description that leaves readers asking, "So, what follows from this?" For example, a researcher reports, "The study revealed that 77 percent of those judged by others as good leaders had undergone leadership training at least five years before they took on a leadership role." This observation could be evidence used to warrant a claim—but no claim is made. A critical reader would ask, "So, what do you believe this means?" In fact, this statement would match rather well the claim we previously said needed warranting, and together, they could offer a sound argument: "The study revealed that 77 percent of those judged by others as good leaders had undergone leadership training at least five years before they took on a leadership role *[the warranting]*. This evidence suggests that the earlier workers are trained to be leaders, the better *[the claim]*." The reason for saying "suggests that," and not "proves," will be explained later.

The warranting-without-conclusion pattern just illustrated is an easy trap to fall into as a writer, particularly when the literature review is extensive. It is easy to provide a series of descriptive summaries of other people's claims and forget that they need to lead somewhere. Descriptions can certainly be used as evidence to warrant an argument, but similarities and differences among the claims must be identified so as to develop a case for why some should be preferred to others.

Some problems with arguments are more subtle and relate to what readers make of the conclusion and the warranting. There is nothing wrong with the structure of the argument, "The moon is made of green cheese, because my mother told me so," but you still might not be comfortable accepting the assertion as fact. The conclusion (the claim that the moon is made of green cheese) and the warranting (the evidence of my mother telling me so, and implicitly that whatever she said is true) are both there. But is the warranting adequate to render the conclusion convincing? The warranting must not only be present but also of sufficient quality to make the conclusion acceptable. In the next section, we consider what makes evidence convincing.

What Counts as Convincing Evidence?

Sources of appropriate evidence depend on what is being claimed. In the social sciences, researchers may refer to empirical evidence—the findings from their own or others' investigations—to warrant claims about how an aspect of the social world works. Scholar-practitioners may refer to the empirical evidence of their professional experience to warrant claims about how the social world does or should work. Theorists making claims about how the workings of the social world can be explained may warrant them by referring to the conceptual evidence afforded by a particular definition of a key idea.

So not just any old evidence will do. There must be a sufficient amount of evidence of sufficient relevance to make it appropriate for justifying the claims made. In other words, an argument must be adequately warranted if it is to convince others. We can extend our earlier definition by indicating what makes an argument convincing

Common Flaws in Arguments

To summarize the points so far, Table 4.1 illustrates common flaws in arguments that you may come across in your reading. The examples are at the level of a sentence, but they can occur at the level of the overall argument in an entire

Convincing Argument = Conclusion (Containing Claims) + Adequate Warranting (Based on Sufficient Appropriate Evidence)

What counts as adequate warranting to make an argument convincing obviously depends on the nature of the claims being made in the conclusion. But it also depends in part on the judgment of the individual writers and readers who engage together in scholarly discourse. As a critical reader, you evaluate the author's argument in each text you read. You scrutinize whatever evidence the author offers to support the claims and make your own judgment about how far the warranting is adequate—and why—for you to find the claims in the conclusion convincing. Even if the author was satisfied that the warranting he or she provided was adequate, it may not be enough to convince you. Disagreement between authors and readers about the adequacy of warranting is common. All individuals involved in scholarly discourse draw on a unique personal blend of knowledge, beliefs, experiences, reading of other literature, and judgments of their collective significance for the argument at hand. A person's basis for judging the adequacy of warranting will reflect factors not fully shared by others.

Similarly, as a self-critical writer, you scrutinize the argument you have developed in your text. You may judge that the warranting for your conclusion is adequate. Yet critical readers of your work may not be as convinced as you are. In evaluating your argument, they draw on their personal background, which will not be identical to yours. Often their feedback will direct you to information you were ignorant of, increasing your knowledge. Yet you need not fear coming to the wrong conclusion as long as you have attempted to warrant your argument adequately. You cannot guarantee that what counts as adequate for you will be judged the same way by the critical readers of your text. But you can maximize the chances of your argument being accepted as convincing if you make a conscious effort to provide what you judge to be sufficient evidence to warrant adequately the claims in your conclusion.

assignment, dissertation, or article. Even a long text is structured around a question, an answer to that question (the conclusion), and evidence justifying the answer (the warranting). We have included useful critical questions in the table that you can ask to tease apart the argument, once it has been found potentially unconvincing.

You could refer to Table 4.1 during your reading to help you evaluate how well the authors of a text have constructed their argument and how convincing it is. You could also use it for your writing to check that you have avoided these flaws in developing your own argument.

TABLE 4.1. FLAWS IN ARGUMENTS AND CRITICAL QUESTIONS THAT INDICATE THEM.

Type of Flaw in an Argument	Example (at the Level of a Few Sentences)	Critical Questions as a Reader, Suggesting There May Be a Flaw
Conclusion without warranting	Good footballers make bad coaches.	Why do you think that? How do you know?
Potential warranting without a conclusion	In his book, Wallace claims that there is no substitute for experience on the job if one wants to learn how to be a successful leader. I did a leadership course years ago, but now I've forgotten nearly everything I learned!	So what? What do these different pieces of evidence together imply?
Warranting leading to an illogical conclusion	A higher proportion of second marriages end in divorce than first marriages. So divorcees from a first marriage are likely to be incapable of making a marriage work, and they shouldn't attempt to remarry.	Does this reasoning add up? Aren't there other more plausible conclusions?
Conclusion not explicitly linked to warranting	Statistics show strong evidence that speeding drivers cause many unnecessary deaths on our roads. Powerful cars should not be sold to anyone under thirty years old.	What causal relationship between the factors are you meaning to suggest?
Conclusion with inadequate warranting	Students learn to write more effectively when they are praised than when their efforts are criticized. In an experiment, the ten students who received praise in their tutorials achieved, on average, better marks for their assignments than the ten who received criticism from their tutor.	Is the evidence adequate to justify the extent of the claim? Is the evidence appropriately interpreted?

Warranting the Degree of Certainty and Generalization of Claims

In this section we examine two key dimensions of claims that commonly affect their validity. Both relate to the last flaw described in Table 4.1, where there is warranting, and it is appropriate for supporting the claims in the conclusion, but it is not sufficiently convincing to a critical reader. An inadequately warranted claim may fail to convince because it is based on insufficiently extensive and robust evidence to support the degree of certainty with which this claim is made; the evidence does not justify the degree to which the claim is generalized beyond its immediate context; or both.

Let us first examine how the claims in a conclusion can be made with varying degrees of certainty. Often the degree of certainty is implicit, as with the inadequately warranted conclusion we saw in Table 4.1: "Students learn to write more effectively when they are praised than when their efforts are criticized." The authors here imply that praise definitely does help students more than criticizing their efforts—not that it might do or that it might do under certain circumstances. You may sometimes come across highly speculative claims made with a level of certainty that is unwarranted. Such claims are vulnerable when you scrutinize the match between the warranting and the certainty with which they are asserted. The more confident the claim is, the stronger the evidence needed adequately to warrant it. The more tentative the claim is, the less the evidence required, because not much is being claimed. As a self-critical writer, you can help to make your argument as convincing as possible by checking the match between the degree of certainty of your claims and the strength of the evidence you can offer to warrant them.

In the example just given, the certainty of the claim could be justified if the researcher had studied a very large number of students and always got this result. Some kinds of claims are compatible with strong certainty. For instance, "The earth is round," could be backed up by the evidence that every time you sail west for long enough, you end up in the east and that satellite photographs of the earth show its curvature. However, little in the social scientific world is likely to be that certain, which is why social science researchers typically avoid saying that their evidence proves a claim. It is almost always better to say the evidence suggests or is consistent with a claim. The level of certainty can be fine-tuned by saying "may suggest" or "strongly suggests."

Next, let us consider how the claims in a conclusion can be made with varying degrees of generalization. Typically generalization is concerned with the extent to which authors claim that the empirical findings from the particular context studied also apply to other contexts. As a critical reader, you can check the level of similarity between the study context and other contexts to which the claim is generalized. The conclusion with inadequate warranting in Table 4.1 is not only presented with high certainty (as discussed) but is also implicitly highly generalized. The claim that "students learn to write more effectively when they are praised than when their efforts are criticized" appears to have universal applicability because it is not delimited in any way. Praise is held to work for all students everywhere—not just some students in some contexts or in certain circumstances. If, as a critical reader, you scrutinize the evidence offered to warrant this claim, you are likely to find it unconvincing, since the evidence offered derives from only twenty students in one test setting.

When claims are generalized to many or all contexts, they are likely to be made at a *high level of abstraction*. The authors abstract—or zoom out—from the details of the context studied to capture something common to a much wider range of contexts. Generalized abstract claims must assume that the detailed factors differentiating each context are of no significance. As a critical reader evaluating such claims, you have to judge how far that assumption is warranted by the evidence offered. (You will take into account the entirety of the evidence offered by the authors, which may include both their own empirical findings and accounts of other relevant literature—which means you may need to evaluate the effectiveness of their critical reading.) The claim that "students learn to write more effectively when they are praised than when their efforts are criticized" glosses over the possibility that contextual differences (such as students' age, previous experience of studying, or cultural background) might significantly affect whether praise works better than criticism. The claim implies further that different kinds and amounts of praise and criticism, or the balance between them, have no significant effect either. The degree of abstraction entailed in this highly generalized claim leaves it vulnerable because the authors have not demonstrated that detailed contextual differences have no significance. (Contextual differences do tend to be very important in determining the findings of social science research, and two different researchers, dealing with different contexts, could easily get different results on that account. If both generalized their claims too far, the critical reader might find that each had predicted incorrectly what the other would find.)

The more generalized the claim is, the more warranting is required. Conversely the more specific the claim is, the less warranting is required. It follows that in your role as a self-critical writer, you should check the match between the degree of generalization in your claims and the extent of your supporting evidence.

Let us see how the degree of certainty and generalization of claims interact by examining Figure 4.1. Both operate along a continuum: from low to high

FIGURE 4.1. DIMENSIONS OF CLAIMS AND THEIR VULNERABILITY TO REJECTION.

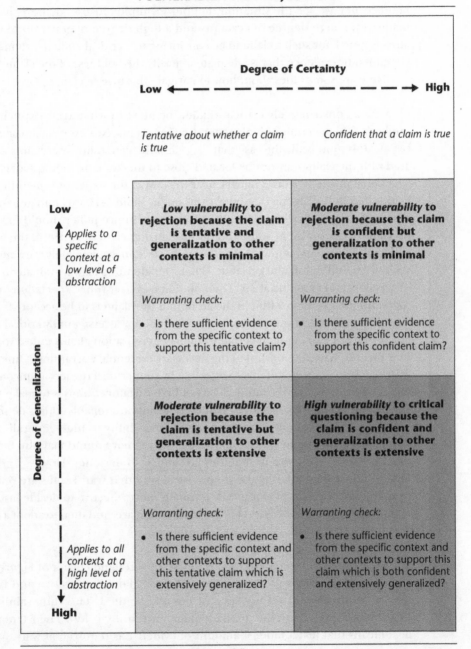

Source: Based on Wallace and Wray (2011, p. 86).

certainty and from low to high generalization. They are independent of each other, so it is feasible to have any combination. Beginning in the bottom right-hand corner, we see the situation that our example illustrated above: a claim made with a high degree of certainty and a high degree of generalization. As already noted, for such a claim to be convincing to a critical audience, it must be warranted by evidence that is adequate to justify the boldness of the claim.

Here are some clues about how to navigate this type of claim:

• As a constructively critical reader, be alert to what are—explicitly or implicitly—high-certainty, high-generalization claims. Not every such claim will begin, "It is universally the case that . . . ," and the generality or certainty associated with the claim may not be located close to the key concluding statements. The signal might be a brief remark near the end of the paper or something said or not said in the abstract. Subtler cases might build certainty and generalization into a new claim—for example, "Therefore, future policy should focus on promoting the praise of students and minimizing criticism." Here, the policy proposal is sweeping, implying that the study's evidence adequately warrants that level of generalization and certainty. When you identify a claim, evaluate its level of certainty and generalization. Then on that basis, set your expectations about the warranting you must find in the account if the claim is to be accepted.

• As a self-critical writer when you are writing for assessment by critical readers, be wary of making high-certainty, high-generalization claims unless you are sure that you have demonstrated the necessary evidential warranting. Otherwise your claim becomes vulnerable to rejection by your critical readers as unconvincing. A way of reducing the vulnerability of high-certainty claims is to make them conditional, as in, "To the extent that these results are reliable, this is definitely the case." A parallel way of reducing the vulnerability of high-generalization claims also makes them conditional, as in, "What I have found may also hold in other contexts to the extent that they are similar to this one." However, critical readers might then ask why you do not seem sure that your results are reliable or that your context is like others. It is usually more effective to decide just how reliable and generalizable you believe your findings are, and then to adopt a clear and appropriate position along each continuum.

The opposite extreme position is in the top left-hand corner of Figure 4.1: low certainty and low generalization, where a claim is tentative and is not held to apply far beyond the specific context studied. The vulnerability of such claims to rejection due to inadequate warranting is low. Their tentativeness means that just a modest amount of evidence is required as warranting.

Since the claims are not generalized to other contexts, evidence need come only from the context studied.

However, a low-certainty, low-generalization claim is safe from the criticism of being overly ambitious only because it lacks ambition. A claim that is both tentative and confined to a specific context is likely to be of little use—and thus of little interest—to most readers. In scholarly discourse, claiming that something may possibly be true in this particular setting will not attract much lasting attention from other scholars. How do readers and writers handle claims in this domain, then?

- As a constructively critical reader, be alert to low-certainty, low-generalization claims. Tell-tale signs are qualifiers like, "It may possibly be the case that . . . ," or, "It might be applicable only to this context," but authors may be more subtle. Sometimes only the absence of a more confident or generalized claim indicates how limited particular claims must be. Even when the claims are of low vulnerability, they still need checking for adequacy. Occasionally you might judge that the authors have been more modest than necessary. Perhaps you know from your reading of the literature that evidence from other studies matches their findings. Collectively that information may enable you, when you come to write, to express a greater level of certainty and generalization than they did. More often you find that the warranting the authors provide does match their tentativeness and caution about generalizing. When making notes on texts, it is worth recording not only authors' claims but also their level of certainty and generalization. Then when you write, you can ensure you avoid implying that the text attracts a higher level of certainty or generalization than it does or deserves.

- As a self-critical writer developing your argument, be wary of playing too safe. Critical readers are likely to be most interested in claims that are of wide significance for the field of inquiry. If you are writing a dissertation, your assessors may expect you to demonstrate significant new knowledge. If you are writing for publication in an academic journal, your reviewers may expect you to demonstrate robust claims to new knowledge of international importance. So your claims need to be as certain and generalized as you can adequately warrant using the evidence you can produce in support from both your own investigation and other literature. Obtaining that evidence, of course, entails conducting a robust study designed and planned to take into account the need, in the end, to make claims with a high degree of certainty and generalization (but that's another story).

Since the two dimensions depicted in Figure 4.1 vary independently, a claim could be of low certainty and high generalization ("may be the case and apply universally"), or high certainty and low generalization ("is the case in this context but its wider applicability has not been demonstrated"). Such claims have moderate vulnerability to rejection because they play safe with one dimension and are ambitious with the other. It is worth reflecting on how the results in studies that you can imagine carrying out in your own area of inquiry might attract that sort of framing. Keep in mind that the level of vulnerability can be predetermined to some extent by careful choices in the way claims are worded, since the degree of vulnerability also changes as one moves along the continuum in each dimension.

Writing for Critical Readers

Finally, we consider how mastering the skill of critical reading results in effective writing. Many students and not a few academics become so focused on developing their understanding and conveying their own ideas that they lose sight of the two-way nature of scholarly discourse. Here are some suggestions:

- When reading, keep in mind that the text was written by particular authors, for a particular purpose, to communicate with and persuade a target audience to accept their argument. This envisaged audience may or may not include you.
- When you are writing a text for others to read—and especially when it will be assessed—keep in mind your target readers and the likelihood that they will be constructively critical in scrutinizing your argument. Consciously craft your writing to ensure it communicates well, and develop a strong argument that is capable of convincing your target readers through the adequacy of evidence-based warranting.

Does a writer need to be a mind reader to know what will satisfy a critical audience? Not really. You can never be sure what readers will judge as adequate evidence for a claim. But you can ensure that they easily find the evidence and that they understand your view about its certainty and generalizability. When writing for assessment, find out in advance what your readers have been asked to look for. Their set of evaluation criteria for judging work may be publicly available. Whether for graduate student work or academic publication, the criteria are likely to include the importance of presenting a convincing argument. Try to anticipate the expectations and potential criticisms of your projected audience by becoming familiar with all the criteria and meeting them in your writing as fully as you can.

To help you employ scholarly reading consciously as a model for scholarly writing, we conclude this chapter with an exercise highlighting the link between the two. In Exhibit 4.1, we invite you to consider how far the approach you adopt as a reader is matched by the one you adopt as a writer.

EXHIBIT 4.1. LINKING A CRITICAL APPROACH TO YOUR READING WITH A SELF-CRITICAL APPROACH TO YOUR WRITING.

Here is how to determine how constructively critical a reader and self-critical a writer you are:

1. Check each element of critical reading that you already employ when you read scholarly literature.

2. Check each element of self-critical writing that you already employ in your scholarly writing for assessment. You may find it helpful to look at assessors' comments on your past work, to see what they have praised and criticized.

3. Add up the number of checks for each column, and consider your response to our questions at the end of the exercise.

Element of Constructively Critical Reading		Element of Self-Critical Writing	
When I read an academic text, I usually	✓	*When I write an academic, text I usually*	✓
1. Try to work out what the authors are aiming to achieve		1. State clearly what I am trying to achieve	
2. Try to work out the structure of the argument		2. Create a logical structure for my account to help me develop my argument and help the reader to follow it	
3. Try to identify the main claims made		3. Clearly state my main claims	
4. Adopt a skeptical stance toward the authors' claims, checking that they are supported by appropriate evidence		4. Support my claims with appropriate evidence, so that a critical reader will be convinced	
5. Assess the backing for any generalizations made		5. Avoid making sweeping generalizations that I cannot adequately warrant	
6. Check how the authors define their key terms and whether they are consistent in using them		6. Define the key terms employed in my account, and use the terms consistently	
7. Consider what underlying values may be guiding the authors and influencing their claims		7. Make clear what my values are that underpin what I write	

(Continued)

EXHIBIT 4.1. (CONTINUED)

Element of Constructively Critical Reading	Element of Self-Critical Writing	
8. Keep an open mind, willing to be convinced	8. Assume that my readers can be convinced, provided I can adequately warrant my claims	
9. Look out for instances of irrelevant or distracting material and for the absence of necessary material	9. Sustain focus throughout my account, avoid irrelevancies and digressions, and include everything that is relevant	
10. Identify any literature sources to which the authors refer that I may need to follow up	10. Ensure that my referencing in the text and the reference list is complete and accurate, so that my readers are in a position to check my sources	
Total number of checks	Total number of checks	

The more checks you have for both columns, the further you have progressed in becoming a constructively critical reader and self-critical writer.

Now examine the two totals and the distribution of checks. What do they tell you about your approach to scholarly reading and writing? For example, if you have more checks under writing than reading, does it mean you are a strong writer and weak reader? Might it mean that, by paying more attention to the detail of how other authors present their work, you can further develop the depth and effectiveness of your existing strengths in writing?

Look back at any boxes that you have not checked. Consider how you might incorporate these elements of critical reading and self-critical writing into your habitual approach to study.

Source: Based on Wallace and Wray (2011).

This exercise can raise your awareness of the many parallels between reading and writing and suggest possibilities for strengthening your approach to reading as a model for self-critical writing. You may find it useful to refer back to the exercise occasionally in the future to check your progress in becoming an expert writer. For a more detailed account of how one's reading and writing can be effectively shaped by applying the principles of constructively critical evaluation and skepticism, see Wallace and Wray (2011).

Conclusion

If you maximize your learning from the content and structure of arguments in what you read, bear your readers' evaluatory criteria in mind, and develop adequately warranted arguments in your writing, you will have a good chance of convincing your readers. You will then be well on your way to achieving a good grade for your assignment, passing your dissertation, or having your academic paper accepted for publication.

References

Coleman, M. (2003). The female secondary headteacher: Leadership and management styles. In L. Kydd, L. Anderson, & W. Newton (Eds.), *Leading people and teams in education* (pp. 103–120). Thousand Oaks, CA: Sage.

Toulmin, S. (1958). *The uses of argument.* Cambridge: Cambridge University Press.

Wallace, M., & Wray, A. (2011). *Critical reading and writing for postgraduates* (2nd ed.). Thousand Oaks, CA: Sage.

CHAPTER 5

WORKING WITH TENSIONS

Writing for Publication During Your Doctorate

Alison Lee, Claire Aitchison

This chapter outlines a set of tensions and dilemmas that we think are central to the concerns of graduate students setting out to publish from their doctoral research. We believe that getting published is not just a matter of practical know-how and skill but is more fundamentally a matter of clarifying and working through a subtle, perhaps less obvious, set of issues. Doctoral students undertaking writing for publication face issues such as a sense of insufficient understanding of the field of study, feelings of uncertainty as novice researchers and writers, and concerns about balancing out time to write the dissertation and other publications. Our research has demonstrated that behind these lie other sets of tensions that revolve around the risks and rewards of publishing during the time of writing the dissertation. We recognize the interplay of a complex range of professional and personal factors that give rise to questions such as, "Who are we?" and, "Who do we wish to become as published authors?" "How do we write with the right kind of authority?" and "What scholarly and professional communities do we seek to join?"

Our discussion in this chapter has grown out of many years of experience as graduate supervisors, writing teachers, and researchers of the doctoral writing process, as well as having ourselves been students. Our research on doctoral writing has been published in a variety of forums (Aitchison & Lee, 2006; Lee & Aitchison, 2009; Aitchison, Kamler, & Lee, 2010). We have witnessed the pain as well the pleasure that writing is for individual students, and we believe that the emotional dimensions of writing are central to the doctoral experience.

We have also seen the changes in the ways in which graduate study is conceived and managed in universities in response to increasing pressures from governments for timely completion of the doctoral dissertation at the same time as the increasing pressure to publish during and after the period of doctoral study. On the other side of the process, as reviewers and journal editors, we have received increasing numbers of manuscripts that often appear to be from inexperienced writers. And we also see a lack of good debate in the literature about the different purposes of writing from the doctorate and about how graduate students can find out what they need to know to move from a more personal to a more public mode of writing.

We present here a realistic account of the experiences of beginning to write for publication that students face. We do not seek to resolve the issues and dilemmas once and for all, since they are complex and must be experienced as part of the process of moving from student to scholar.

In this chapter, we present key issues for doctoral students to be thinking about as they work through the more practical guidelines in the remaining chapters of this book. We begin with an overview of the changing nature of the doctorate itself and the increasing pressures to publish both within and beyond it. Then we present a series of stories drawn from our research into doctoral writing and publishing that illustrate these tensions and dilemmas. Our purpose is to render visible struggles over one's changing identity as a writer; the personal risks, challenges, and benefits of deciding to publish one's own research; and the uncertainties that accompany these issues, the impact of which is generally unrecognized in the literature.

Our particular focus is on the issue of publishing research as a student, as we are aware that it suggests a specific set of issues that are not commonly addressed in dissertation development guidebooks. It is often assumed in these books that students do their research and then write it up. This assumes a linear process, where publication after the research is simply a matter of skill and know-how. Our experience, and the changing nature of the doctorate itself, teaches us that there are increasing pressures on doctoral students to present and publish their research during their course of study.

The Changing Doctorate

The doctorate is currently undergoing a rapid process of change worldwide, and we are seeing the effects of globalization in the increasing numbers of graduate students, greater movement of students between universities and countries, and a fascinating change in the nature and purpose of doctoral work (Walker, Golde,

Jones, & Bueschel, 2007; Boud & Lee, 2009). Some of these changes involve challenges to the disciplines and the rise of interdisciplinary research, the growth of professional doctorates with a focus on researching professional practice, and growth and diversification of kinds of doctoral awards, including doctoral degrees by publication, that is, where the thesis is a series of articles (Park, 2007).

There are important debates about whether the purpose of the doctorate is to produce a major piece of original research or to produce a researcher—someone who is educated and skilled to undertake further research in whatever career he or she pursues. Research in the United States and elsewhere tells us that fewer than half of today's doctoral graduates pursue a career as an academic (Wulff and Associates, 2004; Gilbert, 2009), and yet much of the work of supervision and course work is conducted as though all doctoral students desire to follow the academic path (Boud & Lee, 2009). The goals and aspirations of graduate students have a big impact on what kind of writers they may seek to become and where and how they might publish their research.

One important development is the growing role of published work as part of the doctorate rather than being separate from or an afterthought. In Europe, the United Kingdom, and Australia, awards such as the Ph.D. by publication use published work rather than a traditional dissertation as the major avenue through which doctoral research is reported and disseminated (Boud & Lee, 2009; Aitchison et al., 2010). A typical approach is where doctoral candidates design a series of interrelated smaller research studies, each of which is written and published as a journal article, and presented for examination with an exegesis explaining the coherence of the body of work and the developmental process across the course of study (Green & Powell, 2005).

At the same time that the nature of graduate study is changing, recent research has shown an overall low publication rate based on doctoral work (McGrail, Rickard, & Jones, 2006; Kamler, 2008), though there are important disciplinary differences. For example, Barbara Kamler (2008) has identified a clear distinction between hard science and social science disciplines in terms of when, how much, and with whom doctoral students publish. Science students who copublish with their supervisors or other members of research teams publish earlier and more often than students in disciplines where the research is more an individual matter and attitudes about coauthoring are more cautious (Kamler, 2008).

So the scene is changing, giving rise to some of the tensions we explore in this chapter. There is more pressure to publish, yet students are often left to their own devices when it comes to publishing from their doctoral research (Paré, Starke-Meyerring, & McAlpine, 2009). Dinham and Scott (2001) have surveyed graduate students' experiences of disseminating their research through publication and confirmed the importance of publishing support to increasing actual publication rates. The research demonstrates clearly that students who received assistance from supervisors or attended an institution with a coherent policy on publication of doctoral research were more likely to publish than those who did not. Clearly, explicit targeted support is important for graduate student publication outcomes.

Stories of Tensions for Doctoral Students

In this section, we sketch three stories that illustrate dilemmas or tensions for doctoral students. We have constructed these stories as representations of events or stories brought to our attention through our work with doctoral students who are engaging in publication. Around these stories, we explore different sets of questions in order to explore the kinds of practical and emotional issues and dilemmas faced.

A Story of Becoming: Who Am I Now? Who Do I Want to Become?

These questions go to the heart of the goals, purposes, positions, roles, and responsibilities of doctoral students and to the processes of personal and intellectual transformation involved in doctoral work. Doctoral students at times find themselves torn between these different roles of struggling to maintain progress on their research, keep writing their dissertation, and also writing conference papers and articles for academic journals. They may also be in paid employment within the university or elsewhere—not to mention maintaining their other identities as parents, partners, community members, and so on.

In many ways they are in transit: on the way to becoming researchers, producing new knowledge that contributes to a field of scholarly inquiry. In this process, the writing they produce must move from writing for self and advisor and panel, to writing for peers and other scholars in the discipline.

Our focus on research writing allows us to surface these conflicting and interacting questions of identity and their impact on a student's experience as a research candidate. In many ways, student writing is the place where the question, "Who am I?" is played out, as is illustrated in the following narrative in which a graduate student we call Maria reflects on her doctoral experience:

> I used to feel that I didn't have anything to say to the big wide world of experts out there. I felt like, I am a student and I am still learning. To be honest, I feel like a fraud sometimes when I put on this voice of authority—like when I say, "The literature clearly demonstrates a lack of attention to . . ." I mean, who

am I to say? And I often don't really know. The more I read, the bigger the map I am drawing and the more gaps and vague bits there are. But I have had a go at writing papers for conferences now. I know that I have done some work that adds some information and maybe offers some insight into my topic. But I have to become that person who talks—and writes—as though I am in control of it all. It feels like papering over the holes. But it's great, too. The more I do it, the more I enjoy it.

For Maria, the question, "Who am I?" reflects her position as a relative new-comer in a community of scholars. The question expresses the self-doubt that she feels, positioned as a learner and a student, defined by what she does not yet know but aware that she must shift from this student identity to take on the identity of a knowledgeable and trustworthy insider. This self-doubt, sometimes referred to as the impostor syndrome, is especially common among older students who have not undertaken formal study for a long period (Martins & Anthony, 2007). As graduate courses continue to attract a diverse range of students, many will be likely to experience a sense of disorientation or lack of confidence. It is not surprising—indeed it is important—that new researchers feel humbled as they come to find out about the wealth of existing knowledge in their field. At the end of the day, however, new doctoral research is judged for its contribution to knowledge, and this requires not only competence but also confidence for the researcher to move from student to scholar and peer.

The course of a doctorate can be seen as a process of becoming a certain kind of academic "through a gradual passage to full participation" (Pare et al., 2009). For some students from a particular class, linguistic, or racial background, for example, becoming acculturated into an academic context may bring with it a sense of disconnection and even loss as they feel the need to take on an identity foreign to them (Ivanic, 1998). In the excerpt, Maria is in the process of becoming this knowledgeable insider, and she recognizes the need to talk and write like one.

In particular, Maria recognizes that this shift encompasses becoming knowledgeable, that is, really learning and understanding information specific to her research endeavor, and then learning to write with the authority of this knowledgeable insider. This move requires her to engage in complex cognitive, emotive, and discursive changes that are not always explicit and certainly not easy to achieve. It is no wonder that at different times, she reports feeling overwhelmed, anxious, and uncertain.

Students learn a lot about both their topic and the kind of identity and authority that they wish to convey through writing. Often students in the early stages of their doctoral studies are writing largely to find out what they know or to explore the connections among ideas; that is, they write to learn, not simply to record their knowledge. On the way, they commonly write according to discussions with their supervisor, they engage the literature, they practice theory, they interpret data, and eventually they draft chapters.

When we work with new ideas and vocabularies, we experiment also with ways of writing, with discursive and rhetorical strategies common to scholarly writing in a discipline. Doctoral students often mirror the ways of talking and writing of their supervisor or of the readings that they have been immersed in. During this period, student writing is often tentative, perhaps even naive, and is characterized by a fluidity of voice reflecting their struggle to come to know their subject and then to present this in an appropriate and credible way to a particular audience. When writing for themselves or for their supervisor for the purposes of developing thinking, novice researchers can have greater freedom to be creative and even bold. As they gain expertise and confidence, they develop an authorial voice that reflects knowledge also of the discursive practices of their academic community (Kamler & Thomson, 2006).

In the example, Maria articulates her fears and anxieties, but also the pleasure of moving from a student identity to that of public author. She has "had a go" at taking on the identity of an expert knower who can claim that "the literature clearly demonstrates . . . ," and she has even begun to test out her new identity in public.

In the next two sections we look more closely at some of the conflicts and challenges students grapple with as they balance out attending to the writing of the dissertation and at the same time writing for a broader audience by writing for publication.

A Story of a Ph.D. by Publication: Can Publishing Be the Main Game?

In this narrative. Anna, a doctoral student from Sweden who is just completing a Ph.D. by publication, reflects on her experience:

> When I was writing journal articles for my doctorate by publication, I noticed that in my third and fourth article, my writing was different—more mature. . . . Also I used concepts differently. I do feel funny that my first one, I can't change it. I guess this shows the process and my development. For my friends who are writing a traditional dissertation, they have that too, but in the end they fix the whole thing up, they rewrite it in the last few months as one whole story, so you can't see their early thinking and writing so clearly.
>
> Also, the process of contributing to the international scholarly community through publication means I got used to being criticized and having a critical audience, which I know my friends never had. When they do their presentations

in the seminars, maybe they are not as used to being criticized as I am, and they feel more protective and precious about their writing than I do [laughs]. It's kind of like, someone said, "You're used to having walnuts thrown at you for all those articles you wrote, but we just get hit with coconuts at the end."

Anna's story is useful as a way to think through a set of questions about publishing during doctoral study. Her story of undertaking a Ph.D. by publication involves the development of a set of articles that report on a series of interrelated research studies. These are written together by means of a cover story at the end of the process that reflects on the coherence and nature of the contribution of the body of work, together with commentary on the developmental process. This is still an unusual mode of undertaking a doctorate in the social sciences, though it is becoming more common in Europe, the United Kingdom, and Australia. This process is structurally supported and normalized within the department at Anna's university. What can we take from her story to illuminate a set of issues facing students who do publish as part of the progression of their Ph.D.? How can this help doctoral students to envisage ways for achieving this?

Anna's ability to learn by critique and review is expanded beyond the more common private student-supervisor relationship. Unlike students who write only for their supervisors and other institutional colleagues, she gained feedback from an international readership from an early stage in her Ph.D. In this way, she has had direct experience of the complex discursive practices of her discipline; she learned how to position herself as a participant within her field of expertise; she could check her claims for new knowledge on the international sphere and gain an understanding of academic publishing practices. One effect of this is that for better or worse, the process of identity formation as a scholar and participant in her scholarly community is accelerated.

For Anna, writing for publication was a normal aspect of her program rather than an add-on. She was able to benefit from the experience of participating in academic publishing because this endeavor was supported by her supervisors and with strong institutional backup. In one sense, the expectation that students publish as a normal part of their program of study resolves some of the dilemmas others face in deciding whether or when they will write for publication. A strategy of building writing for publication as part of the research process is one method of improving the publication rate from doctoral research. It also means that for these students, the tensions about sequencing these tasks are removed, since students are expected to write for publication as their doctoral assignment.

Some doctoral students, however, write for publication as an additional, non-compulsory, perhaps even unsupported experience. For students working in some science disciplines, there will be an expectation to publish with the supervisor or other team members undertaking the research. In such cases, the tensions around writing for publication can be considerable. Certainly for students under pressure to complete their doctoral studies in a timely fashion and produce a dissertation as well as publications en route, there are very real challenges concerning how to manage writing multiple related texts.

Anna explains her concern that her early publication was less mature in writing style and even in the development of her ideas. Like her nonpublishing student colleagues, Anna's ideas altered over the years, but unlike them, her early thinking remains in the public domain as a published article, whereas typically a doctoral dissertation is completely revised at the end of the research process. In many respects, this kind of change and development mirrors the path of any published scholar, since evolution and even radical changes in thinking are part of normal scholarship. However, it is potentially a risky matter—for example, where future research funding is involved.

Those who are considering writing for publication during their Ph.D., and especially if this is not expected and supported within their institution, may want to consider some of the following questions:

- Will writing journal articles and conference papers take me away from my dissertation?
- How can I think about my research if I have to write for publication before I've finished the dissertation?
- If I spend time writing articles, won't that just delay my Ph.D. completion?
- How can I manage so many different writing tasks?
- How can writing for publication benefit me?
- Are there aspects of Anna's approach that I could adopt?

A Story of Unsupported Publication: What Kind of Problems Can I Avoid?

Our third scenario explores more closely some of the tensions that can arise for students who write for publication while writing their dissertation. Our intention is to offer for discussion some of the less palatable, even negative, aspects that can go along with publishing: What can go wrong when students write for publication? As we thought about the tensions and dilemmas students face, we posed the following questions: What are the risks of students' going public with their work before they have completed their dissertation? How do they know what their audience needs to know: Will they "look stupid" telling audiences the obvious or stupid to presume they already know?

In the excerpt that follows, we present a reviewer comment on a manuscript that was submitted for publication by a doctoral student, whom we will call Eric. The reviewer response represents the kind of feedback that we have often witnessed returned to novice researchers, and it prompted us to reflect on the thinking and the processes students engaged in prior to submitting articles for publication:

> Unfortunately this paper fails to situate the research in a broader context which would allow the reader to understand the importance of the work and the relationship of this paper to some larger project. The title and introductory statement are misleading in that they indicate that this paper reports on research findings, and yet its focus is a discussion of the methodological approach adopted for conducting research into middle school curriculum developments. The author seems unclear about their purpose. The paper makes claims that are not met, for example, "makes a contribution to our knowledge about middle school curriculum changes arising from policy alterations." The paper reads like an early draft of a chapter of a research dissertation, referring to other parts of large document and even referring to itself as a chapter.

We can see from this review how Eric does not yet appear to have understood some of the more implicit scholarly and discursive practices that accompany academic publication. He has made the kinds of cultural and linguistic errors that an insider practitioner would have avoided intuitively. So how is it that he gets it so wrong? Why has he aimed to publish so early in his career, well before learning the ground rules? Is it simply a matter of not knowing what he does not know, or poor or rushed editing? Is it an outcome of inadequate supervisory practice? What is motivating Eric to submit this paper for publication?

It is not uncommon for doctoral researchers in their early stages, and in their early experiences of writing about their research, to fail to adequately contextualize what it is they have to say. Such a lack of awareness can occur when students are deeply immersed in their research, but the range of aspects of their knowledge need to be made explicit to readers, as they move to go public with their work (Aitchison, 2009). In the case of Eric's submitted manuscript, he seemed to have written as an insider for other insiders, unaware of what a different kind of reader needed to know in order to understand the contribution. His inexperience with regard to the discursive practices associated with presenting research to a broader readership implies that his immediate community of practice is narrow and has had only limited opportunities to participate in publication-oriented scholarly communities.

This reviewer comment also highlights the different kinds of writing required in a traditional dissertation, compared to the much shorter, more targeted kind of writing that characterizes academic journal articles. A traditional dissertation requires significantly more meta discoursal writing, that is, writing that helps the reader navigate around the text, than does a shorter journal article (Swales & Feak, 2000). The greater the size of the document, the greater will be the need for this kind of writing. Any one chapter within a dissertation needs to make reference to other parts of the dissertation, reminding the reader of what has already been discussed and where or what will be taken up elsewhere. The article Eric submitted for review retained some of the dissertation's meta discourse, "even referring to itself as a chapter." Unlike a dissertation, a journal article requires a more economical use of words; the writer needs to quickly establish the article's scope and purpose and then maintain that focus.

The review illustrates the complex intertextual relationships between the dissertation and related texts. *Intertextuality* refers to the relationship one piece of writing or text has to others. Any individual text always bears an intertextual relationship to other pieces of writing by virtue of how it takes up the words of others, how it positions itself in respect to other words, and how it may come to contribute subsequently to other texts (Bazerman & Prior, 2004). Academic research writing is saturated with explicit references to other texts. It is clear from the reviewer's comments that Eric's article bears a relationship to another document, as it refers to itself as a "chapter" and to "other parts of a larger document," and as we have seen, this almost certainly means his dissertation. In our example, this intertextual reference has been handled inappropriately, resulting in a negative criticism.

But there is another way in which Eric's article should relate to other texts. Researchers need to locate their work within existing scholarly contexts by reference to relevant literature to justify their research (often in terms of a gap in knowledge) and in order to make claims that are justified against current knowledge. The reviewer refers to the broader context within which this particular piece needs to be located, indicating a lack of explicit intertextuality through a failure to reference existing sources, thus failing to tell the reader what work has already been undertaken and what is already known in this field.

In a traditional social sciences dissertation, a significant proportion of the whole manuscript is devoted to positioning the research against this literature. Documenting one's understanding of the literature is a relatively easy first step for a doctoral researcher. However, over the course of the research project, often this initial interpretation of the literature changes in the light of new data or sources of information, and with a growing appreciation of the field and the research endeavor itself. The way in which early researchers position themselves and their projects against the literature very often changes, sometimes quite radically, over a number of years.

It would seem that Eric is at an early stage in the development of his thinking and has yet to have reached the stage where he can represent what is familiar to him in a way that is appropriate to a wider audience. It seems that he has not had much prior exposure to external review and critique or to the practices of academic publishing. But perhaps not all students have ready access to opportunities to practice contextualizing research for other readers. Nor can we assume that writing a publication is necessarily and universally beneficial to everyone. For some students faced with the question of whether to publish during the course of their research, the following range of questions may be central:

- What if I don't want to be a professor? Should I publish?
- I know my department wants me to publish, but I am doing my Ph.D. only to get a promotion at work, or for my own interest, so how will publishing help me?
- It's so much work writing for journals, and the reviewers always want me to do so much more. Is it worth it?
- How can I connect my writing for conferences and journals effectively with completing my dissertation?

Conclusion: Working with the Tensions

Our intention in this chapter has been to raise and problematize those aspects of the writing and publishing process that are not frequently acknowledged. In order to contextualize some of the challenges and dilemmas facing emerging scholars, we have presented a series of true-to-life vignettes that illustrate some of the challenges doctoral students face.

Each student reading this chapter will have her or his own unique personal, institutional, disciplinary, and professional circumstances that will have an impact on her or his decision making and experiences of writing and publishing. Our perspective on writing is that we all learn to write in a particular way and become particular kinds of writers according to our social context, our discipline, our goals, and our purposes and talents. Thus, each student's circumstances within a particular supervisory relationship mediated by existing disciplinary practices and by course and institutional norms and structures will affect how, when, and what this doctoral student writes.

We began with an overview of some of the pressures that are affecting research students and doctoral practices in universities around the world. As teachers and researchers who are intimately engaged with student writing, we see writing as "laminations of activity" (Prior, 1998) where the interface of the individual, institutional, and even global forces is played out. We see that for individual students, these changing practices and expectations can sometimes create difficulties that will not be resolved simply by learning the rules of the game. Thus, we have avoided the temptation to offer simple solutions or a balance sheet listing the advantages and disadvantages of publishing during research studies. Rather we hope that as doctoral students consider publishing, they will take account of the personal and professional rewards made evident in this discussion. At the same time, perhaps our chapter can help students take steps to avoid potential hazards of seeking to publish too early and without adequate support. It is our hope that despite the different circumstances that readers face, our discussion of the tensions around doctoral publication will allow doctoral students to explore ways to work with and manage those tensions and dilemmas productively.

References

Aitchison, C. (2009). Research writing groups and successful thesis writing. In J. Higgs, D. Horsfall, & S. Grace (Eds.), *Writing qualitative research on practice*. Rotterdam, Netherlands: SensePublishers.

Aitchison, C., & Lee, A. (2006). Research writing: Problems and pedagogies. *Teaching in Higher Education, 11*, 265–278.

Aitchison, C., Kamler, B., & Lee, A. (Eds.). (2010). *Publishing pedagogies for the doctorate and beyond*. London: Routledge.

Bazerman, C., & Prior, P. (Eds.). (2004). *What writing does and how it does it: An introduction to analyzing texts and textual practices*. Mahwah, NJ: Erlbaum.

Boud, D., & Lee, A. (2009). *Changing practices of doctoral education*. London: Routledge.

Dinham, S., & Scott, C. (2001). The experience of disseminating the results of doctoral research. *Journal of Further and Higher Education, 25*(1), 45–55.

Gilbert, R. (2009). The doctorate as curriculum: A perspective on goals and outcomes of doctoral education. In D. Boud & A. Lee (Eds.), *Changing practices of doctoral education* (pp. 54–68). London: Routledge.

Green, H., & Powell, S. (2005). *Doctoral study in contemporary higher education*. Bristol, PA: Open University Press.

Ivanic, R. (1998). *Writing and identity: The discoursal construction of identity in academic writing*. Amsterdam: Benjamins.

Kamler, B. (2008). Rethinking doctoral publication practices: Writing from and beyond the thesis. *Studies in Higher Education, 33*(3), 283–229.

Kamler, B., & Thomson, P. (2006). *Helping doctoral students write: Pedagogies for supervision*. London: Routledge.

Lee, A., & Aitchison, C. (2009). Writing for the doctorate and beyond. In D. Boud & A. Lee (Eds.), *Changing practices of doctoral education* (pp. 147–164). London: Routledge.

Martins, R., & Anthony, L. (2007). The imposter syndrome: "What if they find out I don't belong here?" In R. Cantwell & J. Scevak (Eds.), *Stepping stones: A guide for mature aged students at university*. Camberwell, Victoria: ACER Press.

McGrail, M., Rickard, C., & Jones, R. (2006). Publish or perish: A systematic review of interventions to increase academic publication rates. *Higher Education Research and Development, 25*(1), 19–35.

Paré, A., Starke-Meyerring, D., & McAlpine, L. (2009). The dissertation as multi-genre: Many readers, many readings In C. Bazerman, D. Figueiredo, & A. Bonini (Eds.), *Genre in a changing world.* West Lafayette, IN: Parlor Press and WAC Clearinghouse. Available at http://wac.colostate.edu/books/genre/

Park, C. (2007). *Redefining the doctorate.* London: Higher Education Academy.

Prior, P. (1998). *Writing/disciplinarity: A sociohistoric account of literate activity in the academy.* Mahwah, NJ: Erlbaum

Swales, J. M., & Feak, C. B. (2000). *English in today's research world: A writing guide.* Ann Arbor: University of Michigan Press.

Walker, G. E., Golde, C. M., Jones, L., & Bueschel, P. (2007). *The formation of scholars: Rethinking doctoral education for the twenty-first century.* San Francisco: Jossey-Bass.

Wulff, D. H., & Associates. (2004). *Paths to the professoriate: Strategies for enriching the preparation of future faculty.* San Francisco: Jossey-Bass.

CHAPTER 6

THE PROCESS OF TRANSFORMING THE DISSERTATION OR THESIS INTO PUBLICATION

Anthony H. Normore

Recent doctoral and master's graduates, junior faculty, and professionals who primarily engage in practice often find the prospect of academic writing daunting and mysterious. Although the process may seem daunting, publishing articles from a dissertation or thesis is possible if planned well from the outset (Cone & Foster, 1993). Many of the problems associated with transforming graduate work into scholarly publications could be solved with a better understanding of the rationale for publishing scholarly work and if graduate students and junior faculty did not feel so helpless when engaged in the paring-down process of condensing the content of the original dissertation without losing its meaning. Furthermore, practitioners might be more supportive of the process if they saw the potential applicability of their published work to improving their professional practice (Becker, 1986; Day, 1994; Pollard, 2005).

Inexperienced writers, their mentors, and anyone who needs some added structure or confidence in putting pen to paper may benefit from following effective methods in the planning and writing process (Bolker, 1998; Harman, 2003; Pollard, 2005; Skinner & Policoff, 1994). By successfully publishing their first article from the dissertation, graduate students and junior faculty can overcome procrastination and become hooked on becoming an occasional or even frequent contributor to the academic literature (Clay, 2007; Witt, 1995). For many, the most readily available avenue for taking that first step is to plan and adapt their thesis or dissertation for publication. Good dissertation planning teaches doctoral candidates to assimilate their research, communicate succinctly, and write for people other than dissertation committees (Azar, 2006).

This chapter is intended to motivate graduate students and junior faculty who struggle with achieving and maintaining the confidence and momentum necessary for writing and publishing articles from their dissertations. A discussion ensues on how to craft manuscripts for publications prior to completing the dissertation and after the dissertation is completed. The focus is on the planning process for paring down the dissertation, targeting articles toward a broad audience, and potentially mining more than one publication from the dissertation. The balance of this chapter is organized around a rationale for publishing dissertation work, understanding the journal publishing process, and paring down the dissertation during the writing process. Within these broader issues, a litany of subissues is presented.

Rationale for Publishing the Dissertation

Most faculty members would agree that publishing the dissertation is a great kickoff for an academic career and good experience for breaking into journal publishing. Certainly some new scholars are eager to publish their dissertations, while others shelve their dissertations. Although many reasons exist that explain why graduate students make this decision, many researchers and faculty members assert that the prominent reason is the fear of transforming a traditional dissertation, averaging in the vicinity of two hundred or so pages, to a lean thirty to forty pages or fewer required by journals (Bolker, 1998; Chamberlain, 1999; Pollard, 2005). Revisiting the dissertation seems anticlimactic, and the amount of conversion can seem overwhelming. Converting and editing a dissertation is a challenging but not impossible feat if it is broken down into components.

Transforming a dissertation into a publishable article can be a major undertaking because student manuscripts are very different from the articles published in scholarly journals that have a different purpose, audience, and style. The real contribution of most dissertations is that they lead to conferral of the degree, open up new career options, help a graduate student to mature as a scholar, and socialize that student into the scholarly norms of the chosen field. As a result many see the dissertation for what Jalongo (n.d.) claims is "an unwieldy task, completed under less than ideal conditions by an inexperienced researcher working to a deadline" and simulates what graduate students are expected to do as scholars when their work is "subjected to the anonymous peer review process of scholarly publications" (para. 21).

During my years as a graduate student, I realized early on that I would be responsible for deciding whether the completion of my dissertation would be merely one last major hurdle until the Ph.D. was conferred. I made the decision that it would become the beginning of what I hoped would be a potentially scholarly life. As a graduate student, a novice researcher—and potentially a soon-to-be new faculty member—I had the fortune of having a supervisor who taught me how to assimilate my research, communicate succinctly, and write for people other than dissertation committees or professors—skills that he and I recognized I would need throughout my career. Furthermore, I learned early in the process that whether it made a large or small contribution to the field, my dissertation would become a contribution to the field. Consequently I began my dissertation project with an eye toward attending national conferences and publishing in a peer-reviewed journal. With the support of a powerful dissertation committee, I was determined to convince future reviewers that my contribution was useful, substantial, balanced, and fully reliable and a contribution to the knowledge in the field (Harman, 2003; Jalongo, n.d.).

Building the Knowledge Base

According to Witt (1995), a growing profession depends on an ever-increasing knowledge base to form the basis of practice. Knowledge base in any discipline will advance only if theory is continuously updated, extended, and refined. Therefore, building on a knowledge base provides the evidence and outlet for attempts to develop and refine theory and improve the application of theory to practice. Transforming a dissertation into publishable research has a powerful rationale beyond what is often known in academe as perish avoidance—a process intended to more than build a vita and ensure continued employment (Azar, 2006; Clay, 2007). Professions can benefit from the potential wisdom, expertise, and abilities of the largest number of graduate students and faculty in their fields. These individuals have too much collected knowledge and have (or could easily develop) the ability to put that knowledge in a useful form for utilization.

Scholarship of Research and Teaching: Making Connections

Developing an in-depth understanding of the background literature in a given area while simultaneously developing or refining theory provides a means for strengthening one's own understanding and knowledge of the particular topic (Harman, 2003; Muirhead, n.d.; Pollard, 2005). The systematic nature of the steps required to develop an intelligible piece, or several pieces from the dissertation, that makes a contribution to the literature will simultaneously "help the researcher keep current with the growing knowledge base and assess gaps in existing knowledge" (Witt, 1995, para. 10). Witt asserts that "the act of developing a manuscript will force the writer to seek a deeper understanding of the topic area and better ways to transmit ideas to students or practitioners" (para. 12). Essentially, "participating in the process of research and writing often has as much value as the actual published product itself . . . and in many cases, the best researchers are also the best teachers" (para. 12).

Fostering Critical Thinking Skills

Writing a dissertation with plans to publish maintains and extends critical thinking skills (Witt, 1995). While development of a good classroom lecture or professional presentation "forces the individual to organize ideas, ferret out complex relationships, and understand theory and/or its relationship to practice," the act of constructing ideas in a well-organized and systematic fashion "pushes the author to fully and cogently express these ideas for critical evaluation by others" (para. 14). The process of connecting prior literature, developing theory, or explaining complex interrelationships encourages a level of thinking that lecturing often cannot achieve. Through undertaking several drafts of a dissertation manuscript and revisions based on peer review, the author sharpens ideas and the ability to explain relationships (Muirhead, n.d.). The carry-over to other academic responsibilities is obvious. Thus, besides the contribution of the dissertation itself, "the writing process has the potential to make one a better teacher, researcher and consultant" (Witt, 1995, para. 13).

Shortcuts to the Publishing World

Graduate work usually provides a graduate-educated professional with her first intensive experience in academic writing (Azar, 2006; Clay, 2007; Pollard, 2005; Pyrczak & Bruce, 2005). For the most part, academic writing is quite unlike writing a dissertation (Pollard, 2005). Pollard emphasizes that while many graduates are encouraged by their dissertation committees to publish their work, the distractions and challenges that arise in fellowships or professional employment typically prevent graduates from doing so. The challenges of transforming a dissertation of hundreds of pages to a journal manuscript of two or three dozen can feel insurmountable. Pollard reiterates that "while the dissertations are highlighted in *Dissertation Abstracts International* it is likely that in most cases, these dissertations will not lead to wider scientific exposure" (para. 2). Consequently, the wider scientific community would not benefit from the important work that doctoral students often produce (Pollard, 2005; Pyrczak & Bruce, 2005).

Too often young professionals underestimate the value of their dissertation research and reflections on innovative or insightful clinical practice. Although the dissertation research is considered a worthy contribution to the field, the challenge is how to pare down the dissertation and transform it into "a svelte, pithy, and publishable manuscript" (Pollard, 2005, para. 5). It requires more than simply removing sufficient content to meet the maximum word count or page limits of a journal. More often than not, the organization and thrust of the dissertation will need to be reconceptualized in order for it to be considered for publication in a journal. The upside to this process is that all the information is readily available in the dissertation with a possible exception of a need to add newly published literature on the topic since the completion of the dissertation. However, if the graduate student chooses to publish throughout the development of the dissertation, then in all likelihood the literature is current.

The Publishing Process

Graduate students and junior faculty should initially have a good idea of how the review process of a journal works (Pollard, 2005). The first step in deciding where to submit a manuscript is to consider as many fields of study that might pertain to the planned article. Pollard encourages us to think broadly at this point by creating a short list of disciplines that overlap with the dissertation or proposed manuscript's content. The journal choices can be further narrowed at a later time.

Identifying an Appropriate Outlet: Knowing Your Audience

Brogan and Brewer's (2003) *Writer's Market* examines potential publications offering practical advice and contact information for writers who are investigating places to submit their work. Before making a final decision on the dissertation component and place of submission (Ray, 2002), graduate students and junior faculty need to devote time to studying various publications. For example, my dissertation topic focused on the recruitment, selection, and socialization processes of urban school leaders and accountability. The research design was a cross-case analysis of two large urban school districts. From the number of theoretical constructs in this study, it became apparent that several possible manuscripts could have ultimately emerged—both theoretical and empirical. Once I entered the professoriate, a natural extension of this research emerged that resulted in a research agenda focused on leadership development and preparation of urban pre-K–12 school leaders in the context of ethics and social justice. However, I submitted manuscripts to publication outlets whose main scope was beyond the practices and behaviors of school-site principals and assistant principals. There are times when something I have written might be of interest to a wider audience, although the content of the article happens to be about leadership.

New authors are encouraged to consult with the references list in the dissertation, which provides clues to journals in similar fields of study. Once they identify possible journals, the next step is to check out the characteristics of these journals—for example:

- Who is the intended audience: practitioners versus researchers versus educational leaders versus teachers versus consumers specialists versus generalists?
- How competitive is the journal?
- What are the submission-to-acceptance ratio, the turnaround time, and the publication lag time?
- How often do articles from that journal appear in the Social Sciences Citation Index? What type of article is most suitable for a journal: empirical versus theoretical versus ethnography or case study versus narrative?
- What is the typical article length?
- What is the subscription volume and breadth: top tier, popular, obscure, state, national, international?

Cabells Directory provides information on publishing opportunities that cover the fields of education. Included are more than seven hundred journals in education, the name of the journal, address, contact information, circulation figures, topics, scope and aim of the journals, guidelines for submitting manuscripts, reviewing process, and acceptance rates when available. The index in each directory is by subject emphasis of the journal and type of reviewing process.

The advice given to me was to aim for the top journals in my field and to write subsequently for journals that have a large readership but may not be considered a top journal. I aimed for both. The importance is in matching the manuscript optimally to the goals and characteristics of the journal and, as in my case, whether the manuscript is written for clinical practitioners (teachers, school leaders, district office personnel) or policymakers, researchers, unions, students, and so forth.

Once the actually transformation and writing process begins, what is most important to keep in mind is the readers' needs. When it comes to academic writing, one size does not fit all. Like most other graduate students, I did not receive any training in writing. It was just assumed that I knew how to write innately as part of my graduate student genes. That is simply not true. I learned how to write from books, my mentor, writing groups, critical friends, quality circles, brown bag luncheon discussions, and collaborative research with colleagues.

I was aware that few people were ever going to read my dissertation or my master's thesis. If I wanted to share my work I would need to break the project down into smaller tasks and set a deadline for each step—and have mercy on myself and the readers by writing concisely and resisting the urge to cram everything into the manuscript. As expected, it was too difficult for me to let go of material that I spent endless hours generating. Having an objective pair of eyes read my materials, such as the writing groups I joined, was enormously helpful. Other people can see where to cut because they are not personally involved in it (Chamberlain, 1999; Clay, 2007; Fisk & Fog, 1990; Harman, 2003; Henson, 1999; McGuire, 1986; Selvin & Wilson, 1984; Strunk, 1999).

Understanding the Editorial Process: Developing Good Relationships with Editors

According to Witt (1995, para. 14), "The first step in getting published is to identify an appropriate journal as a potential publication outlet." While I was paring down my dissertation, I would occasionally e-mail the editor to discuss the nature of the intended submission and whether the journal was appropriate. I would also include a brief abstract, as I now do with manuscripts. Pollard (2005) asserts that "editors are proud of their journals and, in some sense, are like talent scouts in that they are always on the lookout for appropriate, quality submissions, especially from new authors. Most will give generously of their time and advise or guide in this matter" (para. 15). In this section, I share my professional experiences as a manuscript reviewer for several peer-reviewed journals and as a member of three editorial boards for journals in my field: book review editor for the *Journal of Educational Administration,* regional editor for *International Electronic Journal of Leadership for Learning,* and associate editor for *Journal of School Leadership.*

The editorial process is similar in all three journals. If a manuscript falls within the general area of interest for the journal and is prepared in the correct style, it is then ready to be sent out for a blind review. The editors for these journals, as in most other journals (see Witt, 1995), act as the major gatekeeper for what is submitted. The editor is usually supported by a group of associate editors, an editorial advisory board, and a slate of reviewers. When a manuscript arrives, the editor checks the manuscript to ascertain if it is of sufficient quality to merit further review by the associate editors or reviewers. At this stage, the editor assesses the appropriateness of the manuscript for the specific journal, looks for a minimum level of readability, and checks the appropriateness of methods used. My three journals print submission guidelines on Web sites for authors that specify a writing style that a manuscript must follow. According to Witt (1995), these guidelines "should not be taken lightly as most journals will reject a manuscript or send it back without review if basic style considerations are not followed" (para. 16).

If the manuscript is unacceptable or does not seem appropriate for the journal, the editor returns it to the author with advice on how to alter the manuscript so that it would be more appropriate or suggest an alternative journal that would be more suitable. If the manuscript is appropriate for the journal, the editor or an associate editor evaluates the manuscript in more detail with a particular focus on significance, timeliness, rationale, review of literature, theoretical framework, methodological rigor, organization of content, implications for the field, conclusions, and clarity and consistency of writing. In most cases, the editor sends the manuscript for blind review to two to four reviewers. When reviews are received, the editor and associate editors combine the various reviews into a recommendation, and generally the editor will inform the authors of the disposition of the manuscript: accept, accept with revisions, revise and resubmit, or reject. Few manuscripts, whether from a dissertation, thesis, or otherwise, are published as originally submitted. Most require some degree of revision, and if these revisions are substantial, a second round of reviews may be necessary.

Graduate students and junior faculty ought to recognize the importance of appreciating feedback. Initially I struggled with the first one or two rejected manuscripts. Although the rejections were frustrating, they brought excellent feedback that served as learning points and ultimately improved my work. It became very important for me, as a graduate student and as a faculty member, to understand the realities of peer-reviewed journals. My suggestion to those who choose to transform their dissertations into published articles is to pay close attention to reviewers' suggested revisions because they may be substantial. I quickly learned how important it was (and still is) to keep emotional reactions in check and take full advantage of the comments. I gained publishing experience that was quite helpful the next time I submitted. The process was daunting, especially when it came on the heels of my dissertation defense. Nonetheless, with the support of my supervisor, I had the opportunity to start learning about publishing.

During my initial years as a junior faculty member, I recognized how essential it was to cultivate good relationships with journal editors by learning to be attentive to the publishing process. I recall an occasion when a journal editor informed me that, as a writer, I too was an editor and expected to provide updates on my progress on an article that required revisions in order to be accepted for publication in that journal. I soon discovered that potential authors were known to miss promised deadlines and then decide not to revise the manuscript without informing the editor. According to Muirhead (n.d.), "Unfortunately, some writers can operate in a manner that undermines their relationships with editors and it can diminish the possibility of having future writing opportunities" (para. 11).

Ray (2002) corroborated this point: "While editors may assign an article based on a query and subsequent exchanges, they may choose not to work with you again if you became lazy midway through a project, didn't respect their time, were difficult or time-consuming to communicate with, or didn't follow through on what was promised" (final paragraph).

As a result of that newly garnered knowledge, I made a serious effort to stay abreast of review processes and stayed in touch with editors as my manuscripts underwent the review-and-revision process for publication. In my current editorial and reviewer roles, I recognize that editors are always looking for significant, timely, and innovative manuscripts that will meet the needs of diverse readers. We must continue to strive to develop positive communication patterns with journal editors by submitting quality work, meeting promised deadlines, and responding promptly to their e-mail or telephone messages. Writing for publication, whether it is transforming dissertation research into publications or creating whole new research agendas, represents an opportunity to interact with others and make a positive contribution to the academic community.

The Writing Process: Paring Down the Dissertation

Understanding why and how publishing from the dissertation is useful will be motivating. However, bad habits or memories of tortuous writing experiences are so ingrained there may be little impetus for involving oneself in the process. Fear of failure, plus feeling that the odds of acceptance are low or that one does not possess the skills to develop an acceptable manuscript, all can add up to never taking the plunge (Pollard, 2005). The writing process can be helped along if students think about publishing before they even start writing their dissertations (Azar, 2006). They should keep publishing in mind so that the transformation from a dissertation format to a publishable article is not a huge rewrite but a modest set of revisions. The dissertation is a symbol of competence to work as an independent scholar. If even after going through the process of preparing a dissertation for publication, it is not accepted, this is just part of the learning process. The important thing is not to lose heart and to listen to what the editors and reviewers are saying in order to get it right the next time. Even if students write their dissertation with publication in mind, they will still need to make revisions to trim content and appeal to a broader audience other than doctoral committees.

Interdisciplinary writing groups provide a chance to get nonthreatening feedback and constructive criticism on everything from ideas to finished drafts from peers with fresh perspectives. Humility can go a long way when learning about ways to improve manuscripts. To reiterate an earlier point, commitment to sharing work also keeps writers on track. Without deadlines, putting writing on the back burner is too easy.

The Conundrum of Authorship and Coauthorship

Authorship can be a complicated part of the publication process. When a writer is collaborating with the dissertation advisor or with others during the paring-down process, deciding who is an author of the manuscript can be an important and sometimes messy decision, complicated by the fact that the authors have to do the choosing. Student advisors can hold students to a certain standard to get them involved in research and exposition of their work. Often both a student and faculty advisor contribute significantly to the research, so it is important to determine who will be listed as the first author if the work is published as coauthored work. According to Chamberlain (1999), "APA's ethics code states that students are usually listed as the first author on articles that are based on their dissertations. . . . Faculty and students must thoroughly discuss the meaning of authorship and how decisions are made to determine what contributions will be expected for a given level of authorship credit" (para. 18). In some fields, the tendency is to add coauthors generously. While seemingly nice, this makes it difficult to judge the role authors have played in manuscript development and can sometimes make who you know or where you are more important than what you know.

Coauthors are those who play a significant role in designing the research and conducting the writing of the manuscript (American Psychological Association, 2004; Chamberlain, 1999). If it is a dissertation manuscript, then according to the American Psychological Association requirement, the lead author will be the student who conducted the main research and wrote up its initial design and findings. The lead author assumes primary responsibility for organizing the work plan, outlining the content, keeping in touch with coauthors and contributors, adhering to time frames, receiving and organizing all text for submission of the final manuscript, writing a significant portion of the core text, and taking charge of all correspondence with the editor. The role of the second and subsequent authors is to assist with the research and the write-up of the completed text.

Another task to be determined is the role of any contributors to the research write-up. A contributor serves as a resource for original material, contributes one or more quotations, provides expert advice and counsel, and acts as an information resource for preparation of written text. Hence, contributors should be acknowledged in the manuscript. Finally, a fourth factor to be considered is the role of honoraria. The *honoraria* might be individuals who collected data, provided material or financial support, or reviewed the manuscript. Since there is a time commitment involved and accountability to the writing process from initial discussion to final preparation of manuscript, honoraria ought to be listed in the acknowledgments. Honorary authorship depends on the journal.

Making Writing a Regular Work Habit

Good work habits are important. As a graduate student, I was responsible for attending classes, meeting with my dissertation supervisor, participating in several doctoral student activities, setting up appointments for research interviews, setting up house at the campus library, writing up the dissertation findings, and attending national conferences for networking and coalition building with other graduate students and colleagues. When I became a faculty member, I needed to engage in similar activities: scheduling classes; meeting and advising graduate students; serving on various department, college, community, and university-wide committees; preparing for two or three annual professional conferences; conducting research; and publishing for tenure and promotion purposes. With those responsibilities, combined with personal commitments, it became quite challenging to schedule time for scholarly activity. I decided to seek a more balanced schedule by setting aside several regular weekly "appointments with myself" for scholarly activity by minimizing committee memberships (as a doctoral student) and as a faculty member.

In the role of faculty, I made a decision to set aside two days a week to write at home rather than on campus. It is always important to create a quiet place to undertake scholarly activity. This usually means a place where no students or colleagues can interrupt, the telephone does not ring, and there are few other distractions. As Witt (1995) indicates, "For some people it is a home office, for others, a study carrel . . . few of us can isolate ourselves in our offices: too many students, friendly colleagues, and other distractions" (para. 29).

Pruning, Paring Down, and Prioritizing the Dissertation Content

Selecting core findings from my dissertation was challenging. My dissertation was a three-hundred-plus-page monster. With all the analyses and all the detail, the simple take-home message was hard for even me to find. Based on the literature (Clay, 2007; Skinner & Policoff, 1994; Smigel & Ross, 1970; Witt, 1995) and my experiences as a writer, today I encourage my students to figure out the five most important points in their dissertation. Revising the dissertation for a journal publication requires more than cutting and pasting a dissertation. It demands careful selecting and rewriting, as well as the difficult task of figuring out the most important points in the dissertation in order of importance. The APA manual (2004) requires using active voice, including only the most significant references for the literature review, and avoiding excessive reporting.

Reviewers and editorial boards can quickly spot an article submitted as an entire section of a dissertation, usually because of the extensive length of the article and lack of concise content. I recall asking a colleague to read with an eye toward journal style to point out which sections could be pared and which passages were unclear. The feedback taught me that I needed to avoid incorporating every piece of information from my dissertation into the article and instead include the most salient findings and strive for readability. For me, this meant learning to hit the delete key not only for repetitious or wordy sections but also for material that may be fluff and inappropriate. Throughout the paring-down process, I quickly learned that throwing out every third sentence was not the solution. Instead I learned that it may well be that no sentence is preserved. Graduate students are trained to write dissertations and tend to endlessly search the literature and write something like a dissertation when writing a manuscript (Chamberlain, 1999; Pollard, 2005).

Pollard (2005) identified several helpful strategies that have proven valuable in helping writers pare down their dissertations to manageable size. First, it is critical to define a few succinct points from the dissertation. No more than five should be the focus of the manuscript. If more are necessary to include in the manuscript, then it may be necessary to carve the dissertation into several different manuscripts. Azar (2006) emphasizes that "even after editing, dissertations revised for publication tend to be too long, with wordy, passive sentences, and lots of formatting errors, including flip-flopping between 'I' and 'we' and mistakes with references" (para. 20). Even a well-conceptualized study can be rejected for publication due to poor organization of the material, an inept writing style, or inappropriate use of language.

Final Reflections

Theoretical and empirical manuscripts are increasingly necessary to support the development of the extant body of knowledge. Helping graduate students and junior faculty develop an understanding of the writing for publication mandates—whether transforming a dissertation into a published article or a book or writing up other research from scratch—and the skills to be successfully involved in the process is an increasing necessity. Without such efforts, writing will never be more than perish avoidance for the largest percentage of faculty and a nonentity for graduate students who choose not to write past the point of meeting the requirement for the degree. Practitioners also need to develop an understanding of the process and be supportive of it. Professional practice depends on a solid research foundation.

The best way to learn about the types of manuscripts that journals are likely to publish is by volunteering to be on the review board of a journal. Participating in the peer review process, as a member of a journal's board or as an occasional reviewer for conference proposals, is service that is listed on the résumé. According to Pollard (2005), "Graduate students and faculty members do not have to be experts in everything the journal publishes; manuscripts always go to more than one reviewer and editors understand if a graduate student or faculty member replies that she/he is not qualified to review a particular manuscript or comment on a particular aspect of a manuscript" (para. 33). Journal editors appreciate a longer list of people willing to review manuscripts because standing review boards get overworked or sometimes become dull and uninterested.

In summary, the process of paring down a dissertation for a published manuscript takes time, patience, and a solid understanding of the writing and publishing processes. Graduate students and junior faculty alike often struggle with the initial steps mainly because they are trained to write dissertations for a specific audience (the committee) and not for journals, which have a different audience. Individuals will offer an array of reasons and excuses for not writing their dissertation for publication: they lack enough time, other graduate students or faculty members are not engaged in the publishing process, the dissertation is not good enough, they find the writing process daunting, or their current position does not require the dissertation to be published. However, perhaps the deeper reason is a personal awareness of deficient writing skills and a fear of rejection. The self-confidence to be a successful writer requires some risk taking and developing a work plan. The competition for publication is intense, carving a dissertation into publishable articles may seem anticlimactic, and the amount of work to convert can seem overwhelming (Henson, 1999), but the good news is there are specific steps that emerging scholars can take to help demystify the process and increase their odds of getting articles from their dissertation published in journals and books.

References

American Psychological Association. (2004). Summary report of journal operations, 2003. *American Psychologist, 59*(5), 471–472.

Azar, B. (2006). Publish your dissertation. *gradPSYCH: The Magazine of the American Psychological Association of Graduate Students, 4*(6). Retrieved July 10, 2008, from http://gradpsych.apags .org/mar06/dissertation.html

Becker, H. (1986). *Writing for social scientists: How to start and finish your thesis, book, or article.* Chicago: University of Chicago Press.

Bolker, J. (1998). *Writing your dissertation in fifteen minutes a day: A guide to starting, revising and finishing your doctoral thesis.* New York: Holt.

Brogan, K. S., & Brewer, R. (2003). *Writer's market.* Cincinnati, OH: Writers Digest Books.

Chamberlain, J. (1999). Unpublished? Try your dissertation. Faculty and journal editors offer tips on transforming doctoral research into a journal article. *APA Monitor Online, 30*(11). Retrieved June 26, 2008, from http://www.apa.org/monitor/dec99/ed1.html

Clay, R. A. (2007). Writing well: Good writing begins with knowing your audience well. *gradPSYCH: The Magazine of the American Psychological Association of Graduate Students, 5*(2). Retrieved June 29, 2008, from http://gradpsych.apags.org/mar07/writing.html

Cone, J., & Foster, S. (1993). *Dissertations and theses from start to finish.* Washington, DC: APA Books.

Day, R. A. (1994). *How to write and publish a scientific paper* (4th ed.). Phoenix, AZ: Oryx Press.

Fisk, D. W., & Fogg, L. (1990). But the reviewers are making different criticisms of my paper. *American Psychologist, 45*(5), 591–598.

Harman, E. (2003). *The thesis and the book: A guide for first-time academic authors* (2nd ed.). Toronto: University of Toronto Press.

Henson, K. T. (1999). *Writing for professional publication: Keys to academic and business success.* Needham Heights, MA: Allyn & Bacon.

Jalongo, M. R. (n.d.). Defending your dissertation: Advice from a doctoral program director and journal editor. In *Intellectual Entrepreneurship: "Educating Citizen Scholars": A cross-disciplinary consortium.* University of Texas at Austin. Retrieved July 15, 2008, from https://webspace.utexas.edu/cherwitz/www/ie/m_jalongo.html

McGuire, F. A. (1986). Reflections on the peer review process in journal publication. *Physical Activity Quarterly, 3,* 285–288.

Muirhead, B. (n.d.). Writing for academic publication. *USDLA Journal, 16*(12). Retrieved July 18, 2008, from http://www.usdla.org/html/journal/DEC02_Issue/article06.html

Pollard, R. Q., Jr. (2005). From dissertation to journal article: A useful method for planning and writing any manuscript. *Internet Journal of Mental Health, 2*(2). Retrieved June 27, 2008, from http://www.ispub.com/ostia/index.php?xmlFilePath=journals/ijmh/vol2n2/writing.xml

Pyrczak, F., & Bruce, R. R. (2005). *Writing empirical research reports: A basic guide for students of the social and behavioral sciences* (5th ed.). Glendale, CA: Pyrczak Publishing.

Ray, D. S. (2002). *Freelance article writing: Tips for establishing and maintaining good relationships with magazine editors.* TECHWR-L. Retrieved July 22, 2008, from http://www.raycomm.com/techwhirl/employmentarticles/happyeditor.html

Selvin, H. C., & Wilson, E. K. (1984). On sharpening sociologists prose. *Sociological Quarterly, 25,* 205–222.

Skinner, J., & Policoff, S. P. (1994). Writer's block—and what to do about it. *Writer, 107*(11), 21–24.

Smigel, E. D., & Ross, H. L. (1970). Factors in the editorial decision. *American Sociologist, 5,* 19–21.

Strunk, W. (1999). *The elements of style* (4th ed.). Needham Heights, MA: Allyn & Bacon.

Witt, P. A. (1995). *Writing for publication: Rationale, process and pitfalls.* Retrieved July 26, 2008, from http://www.rpts.tamu.edu/Faculty/Witt/wittpub8.htm

PART TWO

IMPROVING WRITING TECHNIQUES

CHAPTER 7

WRITING WITH AUTHORITY

Pitfalls and Pit Stops

Erwin H. Epstein

This chapter is about several impediments that emerging scholars regularly face in achieving a posture of authority in their style of writing and pursuit of publication. Good writing lends authority to the author's research. New authors too often fail to gain readers' confidence, and reduced confidence diminishes the chance that publishers will accept an author's work. I base my views on long years of mentoring graduate students and processing manuscripts as editor for ten years of the *Comparative Education Review*, the official journal of the Comparative and International Education Society.

Think of pitfalls and pit stops, the metaphors in this chapter's title, as episodes that new scholars often experience on their journey toward publication. My *American Heritage Dictionary* (2001, p. 642) defines *pitfall* as "a concealed hole in the ground that serves as a trap" and *pit stop* as "a rest stop during a trip." The purpose of this chapter is, first, to make new scholars aware of the most common stylistic pitfalls that they will likely encounter along the way and, second, to describe the pit stops they should make during their writing journey to reflect back on their work so as to avoid the pitfalls.

Avoiding pitfalls and making pit stops at appropriate moments are measures that go beyond the basics of proper syntax. Yet they are crucial to achieving scholarly publication.

Pitfalls

I find that the most common stylistic mistakes that new scholars make—the pitfalls that lie in wait—fall into three categories: verbosity, ambiguity, and what I call unsubstantiality or what others might wish to call unsustainability (see Chapter Four, this volume, for discussion on evidence). These categories often overlap, and scholars who are susceptible to one quite often are susceptible to the others as well. Falling into the pit of any of these obscures the author's meaning and arouses doubts about her or his legitimacy as a scholar.

An author who falls repeatedly into one or more of these pits, however meritorious the research may be, reduces the chance of being a published scholar. I illustrate each of these pitfalls with examples inspired by initial drafts of manuscripts submitted to the *Comparative Education Review* that I edited and by graduate student papers.

Verbosity

New scholars commonly make the mistake of thinking that the more words used to express a thought, the more cogent that thought will be. To be sure, too few words used to convey the thought will give rise to stilted prose. Good writers strive for a right balance between these extremes. However, more often than not, emergent scholars err on the side of wordiness, thinking that more words will yield a greater semblance of legitimacy to their work. In fact, excessive verbiage dampens the meanings the author wishes to convey.

I show, as an example, the original version of an excerpt and then the tracked edited version. I then explain why the edited version is superior to the original.

The Original Version. The excerpt that follows might seem reasonably well written at first glance. Close inspection, however, reveals redundancies and unnecessary verbiage:

> In this paper we re-examine the link between academic competition and adolescent suicide. We are not the first to question this relationship. Other scholars have stated that the link between academic competition and high rates of adolescent suicide appear to have their origin in data from the 1950s—a time when adolescent suicide ratios were quite high in many East Asian countries. However, as we will show, these efforts to "debunk" the myth of high suicide rates have had little impact. We argue that misperceptions about Japanese adolescent suicides continue to appear in the popular and academic

literature for several reasons: 1) many researchers still assume that aggregate rates of adolescent suicide in East Asian nations are high; 2) previous works which attempted to "debunk" the myth of high rates of suicide or to critique the link between adolescent suicide and academic competition did not address the difference between an effect on aggregate rates and effects in individual cases of suicide; 3) previous work did not fully discuss the degree to which cultural values in East Asia might affect the reporting of adolescent suicides linked to academic pressure; and 4) previous works did not provide alternative causal models to replace the implicit model of academic competition = higher rates of adolescent suicide.

The Tracked Edited Version. The original version contains 213 words; the tracked version, shown in Figure 7.1, has only 90 words—fewer than half the original. Yet it is much clearer, and the author's argumentation is much more cogent.

FIGURE 7.1.   THE TRACKED EDITED VERSION.

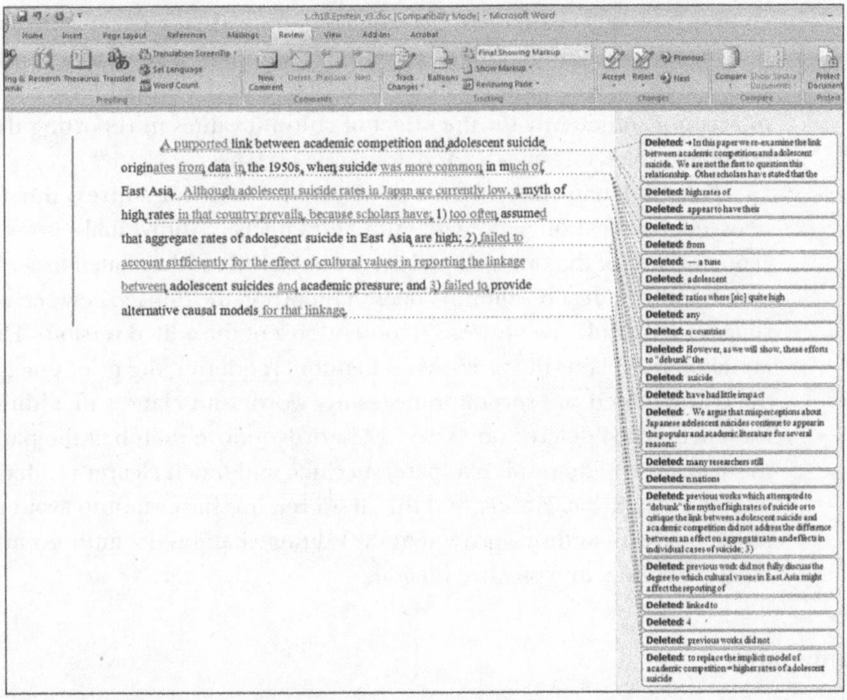

Used with permission from Microsoft.

Let us now look closely at some of this editing magic. The first step I took in the original was to delete the first two sentences of the paragraph: "In this paper, we re-examine the link between academic competition and adolescent suicide. We are not the first to question this relationship." These deleted sentences contain the same idea that is embodied in the sentences that follow them and are therefore superfluous. The sentences that follow are more detailed, reveal more information, and are more germane to the argument the author wishes to make.

Another deleted sentence repeated an idea the author expressed in a previous sentence: "We argue that misperceptions about Japanese adolescent suicides continue to appear in the popular and academic literature for several reasons." The earlier sentence, regarding a prevailing myth about high suicide rates, is more consistent with the author's argument. The contention that misperceptions exist about Japanese adolescent suicides yields no more information than the author gave in the earlier sentence about a prevailing myth regarding the same behavior.

I then deleted one of the four explanations the author enumerated for the myth about adolescent suicides in Japan: "2) previous works which attempted to 'debunk' the myth of high rates of suicide or to critique the link between adolescent suicide and academic competition did not address the difference between an effect on aggregate rates and effects in individual cases of suicide." Notice that the author's contention is addressed by the contention that follows (contention 3 in the original draft is now contention 2 in the edited version): "2) failed to account sufficiently for the effect of cultural values in reporting the linkage between adolescent suicides and academic pressure."

The explanation for why previous works "did not address the difference between an effect on aggregate rates and effects in individual cases of suicide" (contention 2 of the original version) is precisely that "they failed to account sufficiently for the effect of cultural values in reporting the linkage between adolescent suicides and academic pressure" (contention 2 of the edited version). Hence, one contention explains the previous contention, rendering the prior one gratuitous.

I also edited out several unnecessary words and clauses in addition to the sentences that I deleted and saved 123 words—more than half the paragraph—in the process. The result is a spare, succinct, and much clearer rendering of the author's own ideas. Having said this, however, it is important to avoid cutting so much out of an author's prose that the editing changes the author's meaning or creates a stilted, inexpressive version.

Ambiguity

The most common instance of ambiguity is arguably the use of passive voice—for example: "After a series of debates, it was determined that a standardized national curriculum provides students with a well-rounded education." This contention lacks a source. That is, the author leaves unknown precisely who determined that a standardized national curriculum provides students with a well-rounded education. It is as if standardized national curricula mysteriously inspire well-roundedness, needing no human intervention, which is certainly contrary to the author's intent. The use of passive voice ("it was determined") is inconsistent with proper norms of scholarly discourse, which require that authors be specific in revealing the source or sources in linkages between cause ("a standardized national curriculum") and effect ("a well-rounded education").

The use of nonsequiturs also makes for ambiguity. Often a poor choice of words creates a nonsequitur, as in the following example:

> The epistemological debate over the curriculum of teacher education refers to changing conceptions of teaching, learning, and underlying assumptions about the nature of knowledge. Constructivism has become part of this debate because it advocates giving teachers strategies that will help them reflect upon transforming their instructional style.

Here the order of the clauses and the use of the word *because* in the second sentence obscure the reason that constructivism has become part of the debate. That is, it is not so much "because it advocates" but rather it is *by advocating* giving teachers strategies that constructivism has become part of the debate. Thus, a more logical second sentence would be, "By advocating giving teachers strategies that will help them reflect on transforming their instructional style, constructivism has become part of this debate."

Often writers aggregate too many elements in a single sentence and obscure a simple intent in doing so. Consider the following sentence:

> Because the past is a road map to the present, it is my intention to analyze the role of education as a reform effort in supporting a national agenda from the two earlier periods to shed light on current educational reform efforts in Armenia.

The sentence jams together too many elements, and they are not properly sequenced. These elements are as follows: (1) the past is a road map to the present, (2) analyze a role, (3) education as a reform effort, (4) supporting a national agenda, (5) two earlier periods, (6) shed light on, (7) current educational reform efforts, and (8) Armenia. We can combine some of these elements to eliminate, or at least reduce, both verbosity and ambiguity. Here is the final edited version:

> I intend to set a platform for understanding current educational reform as part of the Armenian national agenda by analyzing reform in two earlier periods.

The result, a reduction of the original wording by more than 40 percent, is a far more direct and uncluttered version of the author's intent. The original text is not only verbose but, due to the way the author structured the order of clauses, ambiguous in both intent and meaning. Consider that the author began with an unnecessary axiom ("Because the past is a road map to the present") and then continued with too many words to describe intent ("it is my intention"). The author then followed that with too many words to describe the approach ("analyze the role of education as a reform effort in supporting a national agenda from the two earlier periods to shed light on"). On top of that, the awkward order of clauses obscured the author's thought. The original sentence is an example of wordiness reducing clarity and of ambiguity compounding verbosity.

Unsubstantiality

The failure to ground, that is, to substantiate or sustain arguments through proper reasoning or the use of proper sources, is the third major pitfall. Consider the following sentence:

> This dissertation tests the relationship between language and economic earning potential by examining the English proficiency of those entering high- and low-paying careers in Puerto Rico's workforce.

The sentence is neither verbose nor ambiguous. However, it misrepresents the author's real intent. What the author wishes to do is to test the effect of English proficiency on Puerto Rican students' selection of higher or lower income career paths, which is not the same as testing proficiency against actual entry to high- and low-paying careers. The focus on actual entry into a career would require different variables and a different methodology from a focus on selection of a career path. The author is unprepared to pursue her expressed intent with the methodological tools that she proposes to use. She has confused the nature of effect, essentially misidentifying the supposed effect of an effect for a hypothesized effect and, by so doing, set a fatal trap for herself.

The tendency to engage in oversimplification and gross generalization is another common instance of unsubstantiality. Consider the following excerpt, which represents the author's intention to provide background to an empirical investigation:

> While most Puerto Ricans saw the advantages of learning English, they by and large opposed English language mandates. They feared that the teaching of core subjects in English would retard pupils' overall progress. As a result,

Puerto Rico reacted by implementing Spanish as the medium of instruction in all subjects other than English.

Here the difficulty goes beyond the issue of a failure to furnish evidence for an argument. Even if the author had cited a source as evidence, the generalization is so sweeping that the cited source is dubious and insufficient to support the author's claim, rendering the reliability of the author herself as suspect.

Specifically, the author confuses a policy with what "most Puerto Ricans" feared. The author contends, "Puerto Rico reacted," when in fact she knows only that a policy implemented "Spanish as the medium of instruction." Connecting a generalized public reaction (fear) to actual policy is highly dubious, especially when the author fails to show evidence for the generalization. It would be extremely difficult, even with proper sourcing, to connect a generalized reaction with a policy developed by officials who may or may not be responding to a public mood.

New scholars commonly misuse sources. Perhaps the most frequent misuse of a source is to cite without giving sufficient detail about the nature of the source. The purpose of citing sources is twofold: to acknowledge the origin of claims and ideas and to establish the authority of the author doing the citing. Often writers address only the first of these and ignore the second. To do so, however, leaves the reader with no means by which to judge the authenticity of the source and, for that matter, the legitimacy of the author. It is as if the author is telling the reader to have faith in her or him that the sources cited are legitimate, a highly presumptuous posture that diminishes the scrupulous reader's confidence in the author's work.

In referencing Web sites in particular, new writers often leave out important details, especially dates and authorship. Indicating the date on which an author accesses a URL is no substitute for showing the date of the accessed publication.

Authenticity of a source applies to more than sufficiency of detail, as the following excerpt illustrates:

> The University of Puerto Rico has historically tried to facilitate English competency by making English courses practical in nature, inviting English speaking visiting professors and stocking over 60,000 volumes of English books and periodicals (Dessing, 1947, 95).

Lack of detail in this instance is not what is mainly at issue. Rather, it is that the author is using a sixty-year-old source (Dessing) to describe a contemporary condition. Does the author wish us to believe that the University of Puerto Rico has the same need today to invite English-speaking visiting professors? That university most assuredly has progressed beyond its collection of sixty thousand volumes of English books and periodicals that it had more than sixty years ago. Such use of outdated sources leaves the author's claim unsubstantiated, seriously undermining the reader's confidence in her.

How then should the author use sources? The answer depends on the nature of the source and the purpose the author has in citing it. If the author wishes merely to show that sources exist to advance a particular idea or fact, then details about the nature of those sources are unnecessary. Then, too, such detail is unnecessary if the author uses a well-known, commonly trusted source as evidence for a contention. If, however, the author intends to use a source that is crucial for advancing a particular idea or fact, or plans to use a source that is not widely acclaimed to substantiate an argument, he or she should furnish details about the source—its conceptual framework and methodology—and not merely reference it.

In building a theoretical framework in support of a proposition or hypothesis, authors commonly rely on previous studies to show work that has already been done on a given topic and also work that still needs to be done. In doing so, unless the previous research is so widely recognized by most scholars in the field, it is not enough merely to reference those studies. Rather, for the author to legitimize her or his own work, he or she should describe the purpose and methods used in the prior work that support her or his theoretical platform.

Finally, writers frequently misuse quotations. New authors often quote secondary sources (ordinarily material on which the author has not performed an original analysis) as a crutch with which to obscure the absence of original thought. By contrast, primary sources are virgin material, much more academically amenable to quotation. As a rule of thumb, authors should limit quotations to primary sources or to writings that are so pithy and well articulated that no convenient alternative way of expressing the thought exists.

Pit Stops

Verbosity, ambiguity, and unsubstantiality are pitfalls of style that reduce the author's posture of authority. The best way to avoid these is to make appropriate pit stops along the journey to publication. Pit stops are essentially reflections that authors take to shore up their work.

Revising

It is easy to come away from reading a well-written essay thinking that the author is a flawless writer. Almost certainly, however, the author achieved this "perfect" product by exerting painful effort. I remember seeing the edits that Abraham Lincoln made on the initial draft of his Gettysburg Address, one of the greatest literary achievements in American history. Lincoln had made so many corrections and adjustments that the final version hardly resembled that early draft. Revising is an essential key to effective writing.

An author writes as he or she thinks. In writing an initial draft, the author sets down immediate ideas. Yet ideas comprise complex connections of thoughts that easily shift as they are set down on paper (see Lakoff, 2008). Consider that I changed the wording and order of the previous sentence three times before it came out as it did. Magnify the revisions on that sentence by the changes I made on all the other sentences in this chapter, and you will have a sense of the effort I took to produce it. No matter how perfect the writing looks to the reader, no writer is perfect. The best writers revise, often constantly as they write, and then again and again as they proof the whole. It is never an easy process.

Revising well takes practice. Unpracticed new authors ordinarily are inept revisers. Being so close to their own work, they have a hard time seeing its flaws. Learning to spot the common pitfalls of style, which takes experience, and being willing to subject one's work to repeated proofing are essential to good writing. As emerging authors learn by experience to judge their own writing, they can eventually become independently accomplished writers. In the process, however, it is essential that they subject their work to the scrutiny of an independent reviewer—preferably a more experienced writer, but at least someone who can exercise dispassionate judgment—before they send it out to a publisher.

Contextualizing

Another pit stop is to reflect on the nature of the language in which one is writing. English is not an easy language for a writer because its norms vary extensively over time and place. Yet because of that variability, I find English highly expressive. Study the origin of English, and you will see that it is a mélange of other languages. Indeed, Mark Abley (2008) titles his book *The Prodigal Tongue* and refers to English as the "Wal-Mart of languages" (p. 78). It, after all, defies tariffs, ignores borders, and costs nothing to use. It appropriates, as needed, other languages to bring nuance and precise tone to thought. I often marvel, for example, at the number of Yiddish terms English has co-opted as it draws on the pungency of expression of that dying language.

The variability that allows great nuance also makes English a chameleon of languages. To be sure, all widely spoken languages vary by place: Peninsular Spanish is rather different from Latin American Spanish, Brazilian Portuguese is rather different from the Portuguese of Portugal, Haitian French is rather different from that spoken in France, and so on. Yet no language is as widespread as English (though Mandarin Chinese is spoken by more people), and in each place where it is spoken, it takes on a contour of its own. Add to this the many changes English has experienced over time, and the mercurial character of that language becomes evident. What is slang or brutish in one era often becomes part of the conventional lexicon in another.

Consequently, writing English properly requires close attentiveness to context. English, like all other languages, has boundaries. Although no academy exists to ensure proper use for English, as L'Académie Française does for French (nor could one, I am sure, be sustained in view of its variability), norms of proper use of English do exist. The ultimate test for the legitimacy of usage is clarity. Yet clarity varies by context of place, time, and circumstance. What is clear to speakers and writers of English in New York City is not identical to what is clear to speakers and writers in Singapore or in Dublin. If transported in time, New Yorkers of the 1920s would be dumbfounded at some expressions commonly used by New Yorkers today. And authors writing for scholars must adhere to scholarly standards that would not necessarily apply to writing for the general public. What all of this means is that new authors should reflect carefully on their audience and the contextual subtleties that will affect the clarity of their prose.

Balancing

Readers lose confidence in argumentation that is one-sided. Science and social science are all about issues. An issue, as a concern or question, always has two sides. Forming a persuasive conceptual framework for a scholarly work is a matter of fully setting out an issue or set of issues. And, indeed, the degree to which a question has two sides is the extent to which it really is an issue.

Some emerging scholars approach their topic as if it did not have more than one side. When this is the case, it is as if the writer wears blinders and is oblivious to her or his biases, leading almost certainly to a preformed judgment or conclusion. Commonly such imbalance results from knowing more about the literature on one side of the issue than the other side. Astute readers will discern the author's lack of balanced argumentation and quickly lose confidence in the author's judgment. A necessary pit stop, therefore, is for the author to reflect on the extent to which he or she conscientiously strives to achieve balance in argumentation.

Modeling

A final pit stop is to consider the types of models that are appropriate to use in writing. We all use models of writing to discern effective techniques. Students often approach me to inquire about using theses or dissertations completed by former students as models to help in developing proper style, format, and depth in their own work. I discourage them from doing so. Rather, I tell them that the best models are works published after undergoing rigorous scrutiny by established journals and publishers. To be sure, theses and dissertations undergo scholarly review. Yet such review rarely is equal to the rigor exercised by a reputable journal or academic publishing house.

A student who uses models other than publications that have gone through rigorous scrutiny invites trouble. Indeed, by the time a student reaches the thesis or dissertation stage, he or she should have already discovered what constitutes a proper model, having gone through a program of reading the important literature in the field. Certainly the emerging scholar should have reached the stage of identifying appropriate models by the time he or she embarks on the journey toward publication.

Conclusion

For emerging scholars to become publishing scholars takes more than good research and correct syntax. They must earn readers' confidence in their work by establishing authority over the subject matter they address. To do so requires avoiding pitfalls in writing. I have pointed out three of the most common of these: verbosity, ambiguity, and unsubstantiality.

New authors, if they are to avoid the pitfalls, must be aware of them and able to recognize them when reading the work of others. They also need to reflect constantly on their writing by proofing and revising, contextualizing, balancing, and identifying proper models. Establishing authority in writing is an essential key to gaining admission to the world of scholarly publishing.

References

Abley, M. (2008). *The prodigal tongue.* Boston: Houghton Mifflin.

American Heritage Dictionary. (2001). Boston: Houghton Mifflin.

Lakoff, G. (2008). *The political mind: Why you can't understand 21st-century American politics with an 18th-century brain.* New York: Viking.

CHAPTER 8

FINDING VOICE

Appreciating Audience

Monica Lee

Ever since I can remember, I have had problems with writing. When I first went to school, I found it hard to read and write, and people treated me as if I was a bit thick. It soon became clear that I could answer questions in class and that I had good verbal skills, so people treated me as if I was being awkward. At that time, all children in the United Kingdom were given an exam (called the 11+) that in part measured nonverbal intelligence. Normally the results are secret, but it was my misfortune that I got an unusually high score, and so the school was notified, as were my parents. Together they decided that I was deliberately making errors and wasting my God-given gifts (my parents and the school were religious), and so I was labeled as consistently disruptive and blasphemous. One example of the many punishments I had at school was to stand outside Sister Superior's office on a Monday (all day, missing lunch and play times) if I made a spelling mistake in the previous week. I stood there every Monday for two full years, which did wonders for my education. Both the school and my parents commented on how stubborn I was and how, even after so much punishment, I just would not see the error of my ways. I learned to bitterly hate school and, particularly, writing.

As you might have realized, I had dyslexia at a time before such things were generally recognized. I still am mildly dyslexic, especially when I am tired, but computers and spelling checkers help me tremendously. How I more or less got over my hatred of education is another story. Though I was delighted and flattered to be asked to write this chapter, I do not consider myself to be any form of expert on voice or on writing. What expertise I do have has been achieved through trying to master the problems I face in using my voice.

A problem I faced in writing this chapter was brought on by the realization that what I write here will be examined in the context of the work, which forces an extra level of reflection into my words. I address this later, but first I examine what is meant by an authoritative voice and some of the issues around adopting it. I then focus on working with others' voices and recognizing the importance of the audience, before looking at ways of strengthening the voice. Despite arguing that one's voice is individual and cannot be copied from others, this chapter finishes with a toolbox of techniques that might help.

Authenticity

Many argue that voice is integral to good writing (Zinsser, 1990). It reminds the reader of the author's self—that there is a real person involved—and is about communication, experience, and authenticity. Our experiences play an enormous part in defining who we are, and the authenticity of our voice is borne in them (Vasilyuk, 1991). There is power in asserting the personal, and writing from experience catches the reader in a way that third-party accounts struggle to match. A characteristic of good writing is a voice that draws us in and engages us as readers. "Writing with no voice is dead, mechanical, faceless. It lacks any sound. Writing with no voice may be saying something true, important, or new; it may be logically organized; it may even be a work of genius. But it is as though the words came through some kind of mixer rather than being uttered by a person" (Elbow, 1981, p. 287).

At the other extreme, we can write with so much personality and feeling that it has little resonance with the reader and so leads to the literary equivalent of the monologue. The use of voice is not about surfacing emotion or personal experience, but about the meaning conveyed by these facets of self to others. Finding voice is a communicative act. As Derrida (1987, p. 113) says, "No matter what I say, before all else I am seeking to produce effects." Similarly, Raymond (1993, p. 478) says, "The important question for writers—students and professional scholars alike—is not whether an authorial *I* is allowed, but whether it is earned and whether it is effective." Finding the voice is also about finding the audience.

The authentic voice, the me in the writing, is often described as the authorial *I* and contrasted with the academic voice, from which the authorial *I* is omitted. I explore the academic voice in more depth in the next section, but it is worth noting here that choice of voice is about much more than whether to use the word *I*.

Moss and Walters (1993) argue that what is today referred to as academic voice is actually the reinforcement of white, patriarchal, heterosexual institutionalism and that students are tamed to bleach their writing and speech of markers that reveal their native regional and social dialect, especially if these dialects are considered nonstandard by society at large. Similarly, Kirsch (1994) suggests that omitting the authorial *I* is a rhetorical strategy that can be (and has been) used to turn opinions into truth, to silence women and other marginalized groups, and to trivialize their concerns, arguing that the use of an authorial *I* (or lack thereof) has social, moral, and political consequences for which the author bears responsibility. Raymond (1993) also suggests that the suppression of the authorial *I* is a rhetorical ploy—one that gives the appearance of objectivity but is based on the faulty notion that any such objectivity exists. The existence of objectivity is a paradigmatic question that highlights the role of the researcher in relation to his or her writing. Indeed, the position of seeing and saying that we adopt in our narrative constructs us as researchers and constructs our research projects (Hatch, 1996). Therefore, to choose to adopt a particular voice is a political act and is about class and social mobility. It is also a statement about one's approach to knowledge and research. Becoming aware of one's own ideological standpoint in relation to others is therefore a necessary part of finding voice.

Academic Voice

Academic voice is the language of academia; it is linked to social mobility and social class (Moss & Walters, 2008). It is intolerant toward, and excludes, those who cannot and do not wish to adopt it (Wittig, 1992). However, for academics and those who hope to become academics, this scholarly language is the tool of their trade, often portrayed as difficult to read, complicated, or pompous, as in this example:

Twinkle, Twinkle, Little Star	Academic Version
Twinkle, twinkle, little star	Scintillate, scintillate globule aurific
How I wonder what you are	Fair would I fathom thy nature specific
Up above, the sky so bright	Loftily poised in the ether capacious
Like a diamond in the night	Strongly resembling a gem carbonaceous
Twinkle, twinkle, little star	Scintillate, scintillate globule aurific
How I wonder what you are	Fair would I fathom thy nature specific

Some people do use complicated structures, long and unusual words, and the third person to assert their authority, hide themselves, intimidate, impress, imitate, or even indicate how intelligent they are, but in doing so, they usually indicate the opposite. Intelligent writing is about clarity, simplicity, and appropriateness.

The academic culture values analytical skills, independent critical thinking, an orientation toward ideas, and an ability to rise above the personal and the communal. Academic style is clear, concise, unambiguous, and accurate; it is factual and backed up by evidence.

A quick search of the Web gives so much advice on how to adopt an academic voice—the rules to follow and the pitfalls to avoid—that it is easy to lose the reasons behind this voice. It is a voice of clarity and generality that rises above individual concerns, a voice that weighs up alternatives in a dispassionate way. Use of academic voice fosters and supports the culture of academe, and adoption of the voice is a sign that students are becoming part of the academic community. Elbow (2007, p. 181) suggests that developing the academic voice in the teaching of academic writing through firm adherence to "strict meaning and logic alone" can be constructive, as it removes the student's personal experiences and visceral reactions in relation to academic arguments and scholarly research.

The sort of texts I value are those that take me through the argument, laying out the area, presenting the ideas clearly from all sides in a way that leaves me well informed and able to accept the author's conclusions because they are clearly the best that can be made—not because I have been bullied or misled into accepting the author's point of view or feel that something has been withheld, either deliberately or through inability. In other words, the texts treat me as a thinking adult who is engaged in a journey of cognitive exploration. They provide me with an authoritative view of that which I am exploring.

The rules of academic voice help foster this, but are neither necessary nor sufficient for it. Formal academic writing might need to be adopted for a particular purpose, but it need not be stiff or artificial. It can be grammatically correct, clear, and succinct with a logical, flowing structure; demonstrate a clear understanding of subject matter; show an ability to analyze and evaluate information for relevance, accuracy, and authority; and still contain individual voice. The authoritative voice that we are searching for is a meld of the formal and the authentic, and it is through this meld that we add power and meaning to our writing.

The Voice of Authority

One of my intentions in starting this chapter with a brief personal account was to engage readers' interest through the anecdote. Another was to establish my authority to talk on the subject, albeit from a personal perspective. For me, evidencing *authority* is one of the keys to evidencing voice; voice encompasses the sense of oneself as the author, or the authorial self (Clark & Ivanic, 1997). Claiming authorship is to claim ownership and responsibility for the text; it is to assert one's natural right to shape the text and determine the path and outcome of the argument. In starting as I did, I was not trying to assert that I am an authority in the field, but I have asserted rights of ownership through experience, and thus of authority.

Both the use of the personal and the use of the impersonal can lend authority, and both can destroy authority when badly used. The personal can become emotion-led diatribe—making statements of self and of personal views that are unsupported and essentially meaningless to anyone other than the person making them. The formal can be essentially correct but so boring that it is hard to progress beyond the first page, right through to unclear argument and chaotic structure, errors of grammar and word use, unclear ownership and attribution, culminating in failed attempts to impress.

In academic writing, first-person use is often discouraged, as it is not considered a voice of authority, particularly in more quantitative work. The "need to always 'back up' assertions with evidence is a distinct characteristic of academic persuasive writing" (Read, Francis, & Robson, 2001, p. 389). Although qualitative work also requires supporting evidence, it looks to critical incidents rather than the statistical norm, and thus is generally more accepting of more personal forms of authority. Even so, it can be that taking the *I* out of a piece of writing can actually introduce a stronger sense of self into a piece of writing than by writing in first person. By removing the first person, a writer leaves room for a reader to get closer to what the writer is saying without using the writer as the mediator between the two. For example, as qualitative research becomes more popular, higher-level students are often encouraged to evidence themselves within the writing, which can lead to a host of, "I can accept . . . ," "I take up the following positions . . . ," "I have argued that . . . ," "I suggest that . . . ," and so on, to the extent that the wording implies that it is the writer's opinion that will sway the reader. It is hard for students to stand back and stop seeing the thesis as part of themselves, but at some stage they need to act and write about it as if it were birthed and had a life of its own, using, for example, "This thesis adopts the following positions." The work needs to carry a sense of inevitability about it such that the ideas and analyses lead logically from one to the other. Using the authorial *I* as a source is a necessary recognition of ownership, but reminding the reader of the author's presence as writer, can cut through that sense of inevitability and embodiment.

The voice of authority is about being sure of both oneself and of the field and being able to convey that surety. Although I do provide a brief tool kit at the end of this chapter, as if there are techniques that can be applied to all situations, my intended message is that the authoritative voice comes from and builds on individual qualities. I have pondered elsewhere (Lee, 1995) on the dilemmas associated with attempting to develop an individual style or approach through the application of a generic tool kit. As a partial resolution to this tension, the next sections of the chapter explore some of the reasons behind clarifying voice, looking at why and how the culture behind the academic voice can come through the writing in a deeper fashion than just by deciding whether to use the authorial *I*.

Knowing the Field

Perhaps the most obvious key to being an authority is to know the field. This means lots of reading and making sense of what others have written in the area. Unfortunately, this is not a static exercise, as both the field and one's understanding change as the writing progresses. I have explored this cyclical process in relation to developing the research question (Lee, 2001), but it is wider than that—all my understanding has an imminent quality. As E. M. Forster (1956, p. 101) wrote, "How do I know what I think until I see what I say?" I therefore want to emphasize the "becoming" nature of knowing and understanding (Lee, 2004), and thus of writing, so in the sections that follow, remember that the process of writing is all much, much messier than appears here.

The reading I refer to is not just about content. It is about the methods used; the things that are valued (and not valued); how the main positions are presented and the key terms defined; what use is made of structure headings and subheadings; how paragraphs are organized and links to other sections and ideas are made; the sorts of words that are used and the specific meanings behind those words; how (and if) illustrations and diagrams are used; how sources are evidenced and referenced; how other people's voices are presented; topics and developments that are of recent interest; and the particular publication outlets and the formats that are adopted for those publications: in other words, to know the discourses of the discipline.

Knowing the field also implies that one has enough ideas and information to be able to say something. That central core of what to say needs to be both located in existing knowledge and producing something new, thereby mirroring the dialectics of the authorial voice. Readers need to be led from a position of knowledge and safety along a clear path of exploration to the new place that the writer owns. This simple sentence implies a lot.

Whatever messy processes have gone on beforehand, in the finished piece of writing the author needs to know and to signal explicitly where the newly created text is located within the field and the level of knowledge that readers will need to be able to follow the argument. They will need to be able to signpost the path in a way that gives readers the feeling they could explore elsewhere, all the avenues are covered, and reasons are given why other paths are not explored, but that the current direction is the obvious one to follow. Readers need to feel that their guide knows the way and really has marked out and owns the end point. This is all about structure, clarity, and ownership, which I address in the following sections.

Structure and Clarity

I have problems with structure and envy people who can dictate text from start to finish without deviation, hesitation, or repetition. I, like all other humans, think in patterns, not in sequential tracks. Many people do not seem to be particularly aware of their more basic pattern of thoughts and accept the logical output that they are conscious of as their thought (Lee & Flatau, 1995). Perhaps because of my dyslexia, I am unusually aware of the interconnected, multidimensional, almost visual nature of my thoughts and understanding. The first problem I face when writing (long before any words get put onto paper) is getting this multidimensional mess of concepts into a logical order.

I have developed various strategies, all of which help a bit. Mind maps, diagrams, and cards help clarify the links among the concepts, and sometimes vocalizing what I want to write helps order the concepts and links. Talking into a tape recorder and transcribing it, talking to friends, or even talking to myself (when no one is listening) acts as the intermediary stage between serial and linear conceptualization. When all else fails, I go and do something entirely different—have a cup of tea, perhaps—and let my unconscious brain work it out without my interference. It is by these processes that I come to have a sense of what I might want to say and how I might want to get there, and it is the *I* in this that is really important. In doing this, *I* am carving out the path through the network of possibilities—developing ownership of the area.

This first draft normally has a strong individual voice; it has a semblance of linear structure and provides a basis from which clarity can be plucked. It becomes apparent what the line of thought might be, how the argument might develop, where the gaps are, and what sorts of conclusions are developing. It is mainly at this stage that I break the text into segments, provide headings, and mold the overall structure. When dealing with more complicated lines of thought, I also provide a hidden heading (to be removed at a later stage) for each paragraph in order to try to ensure I keep on topic and sidestep the repetition and associated pitfalls. Later drafts create signposts (not milestones) to the different sections; I make sure that I know what fits where and that readers can follow this. This sounds quite simple but actually takes me a long time for writing and rewriting and lots of rearranging. These processes lead me to a rough text that I feel I own.

I and the Other

In writing like this, I will have referred to others on the way, as I locate what I am saying and develop my ideas, but I try to ensure that this is a matter of referring to them, not deferring. This is about the vexed relationship between the authorial *I* and the other. As noted above, the academic culture values independent thinking backed up by evidence. Therefore, under normal circumstances, a unique voice in academic writing is impossible precisely because of the way the writers' own texts and ideas necessarily intertwine with other people's texts and ideas. As an aside, I wonder whether some of the few unique thinkers who have arisen over the years are as such because they have stood separately from others. For most of us, however, the task is to build on and work within existing fields of inquiry rather than create our own. Other people's ideas are presented in their own words and structures, and we need to reiterate an idea in whole or part, possibly in comparison with others, either directly or indirectly, without losing control of the main theme and without plagiarizing. Maintaining the authorial *I* is more about remaining in the driver's seat than taking full ownership of the contents.

Maintaining the authorial *I* also requires maintaining a critical and evaluative attitude toward the other, and this is one area where a writer's uncertainty of the field can really show. As Penrose and Geisler (1994) argue, students will be reluctant to take a critical attitude toward sources and to write with authority if they "see all texts (except their own) as containing 'the truth,' rather than as authored and subject to interpretation and criticism" (p. 516). This can be very obvious, to the extent that sources are presented in full and without any critical analysis, but textual clues about the relationship between *I* and other can be much more subtle. Other writers are given precedence when they are cited at the start of the sentence, for example, "Hatch (2001) argues . . . ," or less so, at the end, for example, "as shown in Hatch (2001)," whereas a bald citation, such as "(Hatch, 2001)" places the focus on the idea rather than the author.

The majority of in-text citations in academic writing are paraphrases of some kind. It is partially through paraphrasing that the writer can show the reader the relationship between other people's work and his or her own line of thought. Sometimes it is difficult to judge what needs to be attributed to another author and what does not. While at its simplest, paraphrasing is defined as translating the work of others into one's own words, in practice it includes things like summarizing, interpreting, and adapting others' research. It also includes using other authors' examples or quoting facts from another author's charts or graphs. It can be difficult to keep these separate, increasingly so as the writer becomes immersed in the ideas of others. Degrees are awarded and careers founded on the ownership of ideas, and it is particularly important to be able to clarify for readers exactly what the writer's contribution to the field is. The use of attributed quotes from the work of others helps to avoid problems of appropriation or plagiarism. The borrowed authority of others in the field in quotes from renowned sources can strengthen the work. If the author's intention is to cast doubt on or present a counterargument to a particular point, then the quote provides clarity that might be missing if the argument were to be paraphrased. In essence, a quote gives voice to the other. Too many quotes and the writer gets lost in the cacophony of voices; too few and the work becomes an unsubstantiated monologue.

A good piece of academic text needs to be well researched and written in a way that seamlessly draws together the work of relevant experts in the field as part of developing the central arguments, and incorporates and cites these sources without the authorial *I* either intruding or disappearing. Exactly the same principle holds for the analysis, interpretation, and reporting of empirical sources. Emphasizing others' voices is particularly important in the reporting of qualitative empirical evidence, and such reporting makes several different contributions to the development of the research argument. Self/other dilemmas associated with researcher as participant in qualitative work hold true throughout the process of writing, as well as the research itself, such that the resolution of these dilemmas in the writing is part of the research.

This strength of the authorial *I* helps to delineate the contribution made, but its nature also varies with the audience. As is explicit in this chapter and throughout the rest of this book, writing has a purpose and effect, and in order to know what these might be, authors need to know themselves and their audience—easily said and hard to do. For example, as all journal editors know, writing a topical editorial when it is unlikely to appear in print for another six months or so makes one wish for time travel so as to avoid awkward juxtapositions and irrelevance. Similarly, the nature of the authorial *I* in a book chapter is different from that of a book or a paper in a journal and very different from the requirements of authoring a Ph.D. dissertation. This leads me to my final message: all is contextual, so it really helps if you know your audience.

Authorial Reflections

One tension that has arisen in writing this chapter is the contrast between the need to produce a clear, flowing description of the writing process and the knowledge of how messy it really is. There needs to be clarity and structure in the outcome, but the process is iterative and can be anything but clear at the start. I have also implied by omission that the development of each piece of writing follows a similar and reasonably predictable path. In my experience, this is not the case. Everything I have written has presented different challenges and has developed in different ways. Despite what I wrote at the start of this chapter, I have even, on a couple of occasions, just sat down and written a nearly final draft, with little pain and few cups of tea. That has not been the case here.

I have found this chapter particularly hard to write because of its reflexive nature. I have been unusually aware of what I am saying and how I am saying it, to the extent that it has been hard to let my words flow. I have tried to address the needs of the audience and pull you along with me, but it is hard to know what your needs might be. I am fighting what I perhaps wrongly suppose to be a need for a tool kit: asserting that the voice of *authority* can come only from self; it cannot be applied prepackaged. I have tried to build understanding and emphasize the need to review, evaluate, and ask critical questions of oneself and one's sources, but I still provide a tool kit at the end.

I have also tried to provide examples of what I am talking about within the text, though I have not always highlighted them. This is partly because I assume that you will be reading this with a critical eye, evaluating how I say what I say and wondering whether it will work for you. It is also because if you are not already doing this, then you need to start. For example, what effect does this section have on you in comparison to one that has a more academic tone, such as the last paragraph in the "Authenticity" section above? Which is easier to read? Which carries more authority? Of what form? How are the different effects achieved?

Another thing that has distinguished this chapter from other pieces I have written is the plethora of source material available on the Web. Almost every academic institution across the world has handouts and advice available to students and anyone else who searches their site. This has presented its own problem: I have been swamped with information, most of it anecdotal and poorly sourced. The task has been one of sorting, picking, and choosing my way through the morass. The following, and final, section is the result of that sorting. Very little is my own; it is borrowed from across the world. I retain the authorial *I* insofar as I have collated it and discarded hundreds of pages of other suggestions, but I hereby resign as author. I leave you with the wish that you take what you can from the tool kit, but develop your own, unique writing voice.

Tools of the Trade: A Tool Kit

I was working on the proof of one of my poems all the morning, and took out a comma. In the afternoon I put it back again. (attributed to Oscar Wilde)

1. Read extensively to understand the field and its conventions.
2. Remind yourself that if you know your field, your voice will speak out with legitimate authority (every thesis author is a world authority on his or her chosen topic).
3. Look at the explicit and implicit criteria for your publication outlet, and keep them in mind throughout.
4. Start writing as soon as you can in the knowledge that you will need many revisions.
5. Remember that analyzing and writing, particularly if qualitative data are involved, always takes longer than you expect.
6. Try different forms of writing: notes, personal reflections, mind maps.
7. Let your ideas flow freely at the start, and then impose a structure on them.
8. Negotiate a voice that is appropriate to the genre and situation but also lively, unique, and engaging to readers. Writers can project a strong personal voice without using the first person, and they can write in the first person without writing personally.
9. Questions to ask in developing the authorial *I:*
   • Do my personal views on this subject significantly influence my approach to it?
   • Should I acknowledge my own personal investment in this topic?
   • Is my natural inclination to phrase certain sentences in the first person?
   • Do my personal experiences offer strong or relevant support for my argument?
   • What is an appropriate tone to take with regard to a certain topic?
   • Where should I use the authorial *I* or invoke my own personal experience as a form of authority?
10. The introduction to any paper sets its tone. If the voice is very formal, readers will read the rest of the piece with that in mind. Similarly, if the voice of the opening paragraph is very casual, readers will judge the rest of the paper as more casual, despite a shift of voice toward formality. Be aware of this, and set the tone for the paper carefully within the first page or so. This will allow you much more leeway in voice throughout the rest of the paper.
11. Carefully choose a title. Well-chosen titles should serve at least three purposes: to (1) capture the reader's attention, (2) convey a sense of the entire work, and (3) draw attention to the author's authority.
12. Realize that subheads, like titles, are advance organizers. They should be regarded as signposts, not milestones. They are not merely markers between sections; they also prepare readers for what lies ahead. They may simply be one-word summaries of the next section (for example, "Conclusion"), but, better, they also give a sense of the argument in the ensuing section (for example, "Notes Toward a Theory of Schooling").

13. Seek clarity. Writing is a link between your own understanding and your ability to make others understand what you mean. It is your responsibility to capture, synthesize, or sum up what has emerged from the argument.
14. Make sure that your readers know whether they are reading directly from the original source or indirectly, filtered through your understanding and reiteration of the original.
15. If and when you break with tradition, make sure that you can justify this decision.
16. When in doubt, refer to some good reference books on writing, such as Williams (1994) and Truss (2003).
17. Make sure you get someone new to what you are writing to proofread your work. (This chapter was proofread by Graham Lee, who is much better at spelling and grammar than I am.)
18. Use a formal academic style, which includes these components:
    - Has a clear structure. It is evident to readers from the introduction that the writer has organized his or her thoughts and knows what he or she wants to communicate.
    - Has fewer clauses per sentence than spoken English but more words per phrase.
    - Has more nouns (often abstract ones) than spoken English and fewer verbs. Uses the passive voice, for example, "Many things can be done in order to . . ."
    - Makes less use of coordination (joining clauses with *and* or *but*) and greater use of subordination (joining clauses with words such as *while, because, subsequently*) than spoken English.
    - Almost always uses the third person (*he, she, it, they*), rarely uses first person (*I, we*), and never uses second person (*you*).
    - Avoids direct questions; contractions (*do not* is used rather than *don't*); phrasal verbs (for example, *look into,* preferring single-word, often polysyllabic verbs, such as *investigate*); and clichés, redundant words, or colloquialisms.
    - Uses linguistic hedges (*probably, in most cases, seems, might be, appears to*) to qualify generalizations.
    - Avoids *always* and *every,* replacing them with *often* and *many* or *much,* for example.
    - Uses formal vocabulary, for example, *discuss* rather than *talk about,* and uses *there, it,* or *one* as a subject ("There is a serious risk of . . . ," "It is very difficult to . . . ," "One may ask whether . . ."
    - Ensures that grammar is accurate, ideas link together smoothly, and a full range of grammatical structures is employed, such as relative clauses.
    - Employs correct referencing in both in-text references and bibliographical lists.

References

Clark, R., & Ivanic, R. (1997). *The politics of writing.* London: Routledge.

Derrida, J. (1987). *The post card: From Socrates to Freud and beyond* (Alan Bass, Trans.). Chicago: University of Chicago Press.

Elbow, P. (1981). *Writing with power: Techniques for mastering the writing process.* New York: Oxford University Press.

Elbow, P. (2007). Reconsiderations: Voice in writing again: Embracing contraries. *College English, 70*(2), 168–188.

Forster, E. M. (1956). *Aspects of the novel.* N.p.: Harvest Books.

Hatch, M. J. (1996). The role of the researcher: An analysis of narrative position in organisation theory. *Journal of Management Inquiry, 5*(4), 359–374.

Kirsch, G. (Oct. 1994). The politics of I-dropping. *College Composition and Communication, 45*(3), 381–383.

Lee, M. M. (1995). Working with freedom of choice in Central Europe. *Management Learning, 26*(2), 215–230.

Lee, M. M. (2001). On seizing the moment as the research question emerges. In J. Stewart, J. McGoldrick, & S. Watson (Eds.), *Understanding research into HRD* (pp. 18–40). London: Routledge.

Lee, M. M. (2004). A refusal to define HRD. In J. Woodall, J. Stewart, & M. Lee (Eds.), *New frontiers in human resource development* (pp. 27–40). London: Routledge.

Lee, M. M., & Flatau, M. (1995). Seriova Logika v paralelnom svete (Serial logic in a parallel world). In M. Mitzla (Ed.), *Predpoklady Zavadzania ISO 9000 Na Slovensku* (pp. 11–33). Temecula, CA: IBIS Publishing.

Moss, B. J., & Walters, K. (1993). Rethinking diversity: Axes of difference in the writing classroom. In L. Odell (Ed.), *Theory and practice in the teaching of writing: Rethinking the discipline* (pp. 132–185). Carbondale: Southern Illinois Press.

Penrose, A. M., & Geisler, C. (1994). Reading and writing without authority. *College Composition and Communication, 45,* 505–520.

Raymond, J. C. (1993). I-dropping and androgyny: The authorial I in scholarly writing. *College Composition and Communication 44*(4), 478–483.

Read, B., Francis, B., & Robson, J. (2001). "Playing safe": Undergraduate essay writing and the presentation of the student "Voice." *British Journal of Sociology of Education, 22*(3), 387–399.

Truss, L. (2003). *Eats, shoots and leaves.* London: Profile Books.

Vasilyuk, F. (1991). *The psychology of experiencing: The resolution of life's critical situations.* Hemel Hempstead, UK: Harvester Wheatsheaf.

Williams, J. M. (1994). *Style: Ten lessons in clarity and grace* (4th ed.). New York: HarperCollins.

Wittig, M. (1992). *The straight mind and other essays.* Boston: Beacon Press.

Zinsser, W. (1990). *On writing well* (4th ed.). New York: HarperCollins.

CHAPTER 9

CREATING A WHOLE FROM THE PARTS

Qualities of Good Writing

Andrea D. Ellinger, Baiyin Yang

Writing quality is often a reflection of the clarity of the author's thoughts. Overly vague ideas invariably lead to confused writing or the lack of any writing.

J. O. SUMMERS (2001)

Engaging in the process of conducting robust empirical research and writing up that research for academic publication are time-consuming and challenging tasks. Our fond hope with this chapter is that we can share our experiences as researchers, writers, reviewers, and editors for academic journals to help readers avoid the pitfalls associated with why manuscripts may not be sent out for review, may be rejected, or require substantive revision. To do this, we begin by considering what we mean by research. Although a variety of definitions exist for *research*, scholars generally agree that research is a systematic process of inquiry that generates new knowledge and understanding (Merriam & Simpson, 1995; Swanson & Holton, 2005). A more elaborated definition, by Gall, Gall, and Borg (2007), suggests that research is "a form of inquiry in which (1) key concepts and procedures are carefully defined in such a way that the inquiry can be replicated and possibly refuted, (2) controls are in place to minimize error bias, (3) the generalizability limits of the study's results are made explicit, and (4) the results of the study are interpreted in terms of what they contribute to the cumulative body of knowledge about the object of inquiry" (p. 35).

Although Gall et al. (2007) have acknowledged that their definition has a "postpositivist slant" (p. 35), they contend that "many, if not most, constructivist and qualitative researchers share the same concerns (e.g., control for error and bias), although they think about them differently" (p. 35). We particularly resonate with this definition because it embraces the concern for robust, rigorous methodological approaches and suggests that research should contribute to a cumulative body of knowledge.

Research serves many functions. It may be descriptive of natural or social phenomena, may involve prediction, might be designed to improve practice by focusing on the effectiveness of interventions, or be done to provide explanation (Gall et al., 2007). Ultimately the dissemination of empirical research is often a primary mission of many research-intensive institutions of higher education and an important aspect of an academic career. Yet the relatively low acceptance rates by many journals suggest a need to improve on the quality of research manuscripts produced and submitted (Summers, 2001). Acceptance rates typically average around 10 to 20 percent, which suggests that 80 to 90 percent of the submissions are rejected. Scholars typically agree that the reasons for rejection often include research questions that are not particularly interesting, the lack of contribution to the literature, poorly developed conceptual frameworks, methodological issues, and lack of clarity in writing (Kilduff, 2007; Rocco, 2003; Summers, 2001). We therefore consider some of these issues with the intent of helping readers to improve their chances for getting published.

Communicating the Compelling Problem

According to Merriam and Simpson (1995), researchable problems can come from a variety of sources: from practice or current social and political issues, for example, or the literature may have highlighted previous empirical research or a specific theory. Ultimately a researchable problem is something that "perplexes and challenges the mind" when there is a gap in the literature on the topic associated with the problem (Merriam & Simpson, 1995, p. 16). More recently, some scholars have been calling for more serious attention on problems that "serve people's well-being" (Hostetler, 2005, p. 16). Unfortunately, the lack of a compelling articulation of the problem is often a fundamental reason that manuscripts require significant revision or are rejected.

Many scholars use the visual image of an inverted pyramid or a funnel to describe how the compelling problem can be effectively communicated. Typically the top portion of the funnel provides an articulation of the phenomenon of interest and why it is important, and an executive synthesis of the relevant literature helps to illustrate what is currently known about the phenomenon. Ultimately a narrowing of the funnel begins to occur that then considers what is not known about the phenomenon relative to the specific problem being given attention. Then the actual gap in the empirical literature is highlighted and reflects the narrowing of the funnel. At the bottom base of the funnel, it should become very clear that an important problem requires further research because the problem associated with the phenomenon and the lack of empirical attention that has been given to it demands more research. This typically results in the articulation of a statement on the purpose of the study that clarifies the intentionality of the research. Journal manuscripts typically embed this material in an initial "Introduction" section that concludes with a concisely stated purpose statement associated with the study. To address the intentions of the study, various sections in the manuscript typically follow that include a comprehensive review of the literature, attention to describing the theoretical or conceptual framework underpinning the research, the research questions or hypotheses that guided the inquiry, a detailed articulation of the design and implementation of the study, presentation of the results, and the implications of the study's findings for practice and for conducting future research.

We have seen firsthand that many authors do not adequately describe the problem in a way that suggests it is indeed compelling. Often on reading a manuscript, we might consider the introductory section and wonder what the problem is, why it truly is important, and what the gap in the research actually is that warrants empirical attention. More often than not, we might ask authors to support opinion-based statements with citations that lend credibility to the argument being made and to situate the argument within the scholarly literature. The ability to craft a well-developed, clear, and compelling problem is often a direct result of an in-depth understanding of the literature (see Chapter Ten, this volume).

The Literature Review

Reviewing the literature is a critical step in the process of conceiving the problem, understanding and communicating the importance of the problem to readers, and demonstrating the gaps that support the rationale for the need for the study. We believe that the review of literature must reflect a comprehensive immersion in the literature that demonstrates an extensive knowledge of the phenomenon being studied. A thorough review of the literature establishes the relevant domains that must be examined in support of the study, as well as presents, analyzes, and critiques the existing literature so that the compelling need for the study is evident. Similarly, Boote and Beile (2005) have acknowledged that "a substantive, thorough, sophisticated literature review is a precondition for doing substantive, thorough, sophisticated research" (p. 3).

The literature review serves many purposes. According to Merriam (1998), the literature review provides a foundation for building knowledge; shows how the proposed study will advance, refine, or revise what is currently known about the phenomenon of interest; helps to conceptualize the study; and provides guidance about the methodology being used (since prior research will have elaborated on the questions posed, the samples, and the design and analytical approaches used). Similarly, Boote and Beile suggest that literature reviews also set the broad context of the study and critically examine the claims made in prior research. According to Torraco (2005), a literature review is not a data dump, but rather " 'tells a story' by critically analyzing the literature and arriving at specific conclusions about it" (p. 361).

More often than not, many authors simply summarize the existing literature instead of providing a critique and synthesis of it. They often do not consider all of the relevant domains of literature related to the phenomenon that must be examined given the nature of the problem to be studied. Nor do they describe the search terms used and the databases they searched to derive the literature for the review. Such information helps readers better understand the scope, boundaries, comprehensiveness, and depth of the search process. Well-written literature reviews present an outline of the relevant literature that needs to be discussed relative to the problem in a logical, sequenced, and organized manner (see Chapter 11, this volume).

The Role of a Theoretical or Conceptual Framework

Many manuscripts are rejected because they lack a conceptual or theoretical framework (Merriam & Simpson, 1995). There is often confusion about what such frameworks refer to, but Merriam and Simpson suggest that such frameworks refer to "the same thing—and that 'thing' is the underlying structure, orientation, and viewpoint of your research study" (p. 24). To better understand what is meant by a theoretical framework, we consider the role of theory in research.

Theory plays a critical role in research by providing a foundation for the research to be meaningful. A theory is a set of interrelated constructs, definitions, and propositions that present a rational view of phenomena by explaining or predicting relationships among those elements. The role of theory in research is to provide a rational explanation of the interrelationships among constructs, definitions, and propositions and the explanation of existing conditions or prediction of future outcomes in natural phenomena. Kerlinger (1979) has clearly articulated the relationship between theory and research: "The purpose of science is theory" (p. 15). Therefore, the fundamental purpose of science is to build theoretical explanations of reality, and such explanations are created and verified by research. Research often generates and confirms theory, or the development of new theory may be the outcome of research when a grounded theory design is applied.

Theory is essential when conducting research and plays different roles in quantitative and qualitative research. A scholar who is designing a quantitative research study normally applies a deductive logic where the selected theory guides the research inquiry and the research tests the theory. Creswell (1994) has defined quantitative research as "an inquiry into a social or human problem, based on testing a theory composed of variables, measured with numbers, and analyzed with statistical procedures, in order to determine whether the predictive generalizations of the theory hold true" (p. 2). In contrast, qualitative research often applies an inductive logic, and theory generally emerges from the research. This is particularly applicable when grounded theory is used to inductively derive theory from the data. Qualitative approaches can also apply theory deductively when the theory can be used to inform the development of the interview protocol or aid in the analysis of data. Merriam (1998) has described theory as growing from speculation of qualitative data and of value in research as it provides theoretically grounded explanations of phenomena observed in a holistic context.

Although the terms, theoretical framework, and conceptual framework are often used interchangeably and may refer to "the same thing" (Merriam & Simpson, 1995, p. 24), we differentiate them here. Creswell (1994) has described the theoretical framework of a study as dependent on the researcher's worldview and culminating in a selection of a qualitative or a quantitative paradigm. A theoretical framework can be viewed as a set of theoretical assumptions that explain the relationships among a set of phenomena. However, a conceptual framework normally does not rise to the level of a theoretical framework, at least at the level of substantive theory. A theoretical framework is built on a supportable premise or the extension of such premise through a logical path of reported research and clear reasoning. In contrast, a conceptual framework does not often reach the same level of sophistication. Depending on the nature of the research, it may be that an empirical study uses a well-articulated conceptual framework to serve as the backbone that integrates various constructs and propositions in a meaningful way that can serve as a guide to the research being conducted. Often conceptual frameworks present visual depictions of the relationships between constructs and the research questions or hypotheses that emanate from such a depiction.

Ultimately theoretical and conceptual frameworks typically reflect the assumptions and worldviews that the author is making about the phenomenon to be studied. From our perspective, there are many theories that can be used to frame research problems. Some theories may specify the relationships proposed to exist between constructs and may present a unique viewpoint from which to examine a problem and ultimately analyze it. Theories can be used deductively or can be generated inductively depending on the type of research problem being considered. When theories are used deductively, they are generally tested or modified in the research process. When theory is generated inductively as an outcome of the research inquiry, it is often a result of the lack of theory on the specific phenomenon or the inadequacy of existing theory.

The Method Section

Admittedly, as many scholars contend, it is difficult, if not impossible, to perfectly replicate research in the social sciences. However, a hallmark of quality research is that it provides all of the details so that other researchers can attempt to "replicate" the study to determine if findings are consistent, or refutable.

From a qualitative perspective, Rocco (2003) has previously shared her detailed observations about the problem areas identified in qualitative manuscripts submitted to *Human Resource Development Quarterly*. Although our intent is not to be overly redundant, we wish to address some of the problems that we have witnessed in quantitative, qualitative, and mixed-method designs.

Often authors do not adequately indicate the type of research design that they have chosen and the rationale and logic for their choices. For example, an author may indicate that a quantitative design has been chosen, but then we wonder, *What type of a quantitative design?* Has the author used a descriptive research design? A causal-comparative research design? A correlational design, or some type of an experimental design? And then we wonder why that particular design choice was made.

Next, authors typically do not elaborate on the type of design choice. For example, if an experimental design was used, we would like to know what type it was. In terms of qualitative research, Rocco has acknowledged that many authors simply suggest that they conducted "a qualitative study," but, as she asserts, "Qualitative is not a type of study, and qualitative inquiry does not have a unified theoretical orientation" (p. 343). Patton (2002) has described eleven types of qualitative methods, so we would then want to know what type of qualitative approach the author used. Authors often neglect these details. In terms of mixed-method approaches, authors often neglect to describe the specific approach they used and often do not help readers understand how each phase of the mixed design was conducted.

Another source of frustration concerns the sampling approach used. Often the logic of the sampling process is lacking in quantitative and qualitative studies. From a quantitative perspective, it is important to understand the population from which the sample was drawn (or if it is a population sample), and then how that sample was drawn since one of the purposes of a quantitative paradigm is to generalize from a sample to a broader population. Within a qualitative paradigm, although the intention is not to generalize, understanding who the participants were, why they were selected, and how they were selected is equally critical.

Other areas that often lack sufficient detail in quantitative studies include information associated with measures being used or the development of the measures for instrumentation purposes. It is necessary to understand where measures being used for the study have been previously used and the issues associated with reliability and validity from past studies. Measures that have been adapted or translated should be explained so that readers understand how adaptations may influence the study or how translation and back-translation processes may have an impact on the efficacy of the study. Finally, sufficient information concerning data analysis is often lacking in manuscripts, particularly within qualitative manuscripts, along with attention to issues associated with reliability and validity from quantitative and qualitative perspectives.

Many tools and checklists exist (see, for example, Creswell, 1994, 2007) for authors to use to ensure that they provide extensive detail in a logical and well-sequenced manner in the Method section to overcome many of these problems. (For additional insights on qualitative, quantitative, and mixed methods, refer respectively to Chapters Twelve, Thirteen, and Fourteen, this volume.)

Discussion of Findings

Summers (2001) has acknowledged, "All well-written manuscripts have three characteristics in common: (1) an introduction that 'sells' the study; (2) tight logic, clarity, and conciseness throughout all sections; and (3) a creative and insightful Discussion and Conclusions section" (p. 410). From our perspective, the Discussion section serves a specific purpose. All too often, authors mix and comingle the presentation of the findings of the study and the discussion about the findings, which can become confusing for readers. Our suggestion is that authors consider their research questions or hypotheses, and then develop a logical sequencing of articulating the findings without interpretation. Authors need to consider the use of tables and other visual tools that can help readers grasp the essence of the findings so that readers can then better understand them in relation to the existing literature. It is then the author's responsibility to discuss the findings in the Discussion section with regard to the previous literature and theory reviewed in the manuscript.

We often suggest that the manuscript author provide a brief summary of the findings and then logically consider the findings in relation to the literature previously reviewed. Do the findings from the study support prior literature? Do the findings extend prior literature in unique ways? Do the findings refute and disconfirm prior literature? Do the findings add new knowledge? These are fundamental questions that the Discussion section should consider. It is this section that enables the author to develop a comprehensive synthesis of his or her findings in relation to the existing literature so that he or she can explain and situate the contributions to the cumulative base of literature. Too often, authors simply repeat the findings, make a few observations about them, and then move on to speculate how the findings can be useful to readers. Since such research has been conceived based on existing literature and the gaps, deficiencies, and potential controversies associated with it, this section becomes a critical catalyst for articulating the unique contributions that the study has made to the cumulative base of knowledge on the phenomenon.

Another often neglected element that can be located as a summary tool in the Discussion section, or presented as a separate section following the Discussion section, is the Limitations section. Often authors gloss over the limitations associated with their study, but limitations help readers to better understand the limits of the study. Limitations are often associated with the sampling approaches used, the data collection and analysis methods, and the concept of generalizability, among others. It is important to acknowledge elements that have limited the study in scope, design, or in terms of generalizability so that other authors can carefully interpret the meaningfulness and usefulness of the findings given the limitations. Limitations can also be helpful in considering ways to further research the phenomenon and often are used to develop ideas that can be communicated to readers in terms of future research endeavors.

Conclusions and Implications for Practice and Future Research

This final section in manuscripts often serves to summarize the contributions that the study has made to the literature and then helps readers to consider how the findings can be useful to practitioners. The author also uses it to present an agenda of future research ideas that can enable other researchers to continue the stream of research on the phenomenon; in this way, deeper and more illuminating insights can be generated that continue to contribute the cumulative base of knowledge. Often, however, authors give minimal attention to how the findings can improve practice or shape future research directions on the phenomenon.

We suggest that authors consider to whom the findings would be useful and the ways in which the findings would be useful, which might involve the improvement of practice, promote the use of specific interventions, or influence policy in some way. We also hope that authors consider how the findings may enrich theory and theory building on the phenomenon. Finally, we suggest that authors give sufficient attention to providing a direction for future research. Often such directions involve studies that include different samples, varied research contexts and settings, or use of alternative methods of data collection and analysis or suggest that different research paradigms be considered.

Summary

The work of scholarly writing is thought and time intensive and requires careful attention to details associated with form and structure, logic and sequencing, and organization of the manuscript given the specifications of the publishing outlet being targeted. Not only should authors give explicit attention to the areas we have addressed, which are often considered reasons for rejection or substantive revisions, they should consider the content of the manuscript from a readability perspective that includes attention to grammar, spelling, and punctuation. It is very important that authors carefully consider the publication outlets they are targeting and become educated about the journal's mission, scope, publishing requirements, submission, and formatting guidelines. It is also critical to review past journal issues so that they see examples of well-structured, logically sequenced, and accurately formatted manuscripts, which can help them with their own writing process. A review of past published articles also ensures that they will embed relevant empirical research published in the targeted journal as a part of the comprehensive literature review that they have conducted in support of their research manuscript being targeted for the journal.

Finally, writing for publication in many instances is not a solitary effort, and engaging collaborators and mentors who can coauthor or advise, review initial drafts, provide feedback, raise issues and concerns, as well as serve as a set of critical eyes are important considerations for strengthening the final submission for review.

We hope that this chapter has focused necessary attention on the problems and pitfalls that prevent manuscripts from being sent out for review so that authors can be proactive and preemptive in these specific areas to avoid such mishaps. Ultimately the overall goal has been to help authors consider ways to strengthen and improve the quality of writing for publication so that they can improve their chances of having their manuscripts sent out for review, obtain thoughtful and constructive feedback from reviewers, and have the revised manuscript published so that it can contribute to the cumulative base of knowledge. Getting to the acceptance stage in the manuscript review process is the desired outcome of good-quality writing for publication. Chapter Eighteen in this volume, along with Agarwal, Echambadi, Franco, and Sarkar's (2006) guidance from reviewer comments, are valuable sources of information for these next steps.

References

Agarwal, R., Echambadi, R., Franco, A. P., & Sarkar, M. B. (2006). Reap rewards: Maximizing benefits from reviewer comments. *Academy of Management Journal, 49*(2), 191–196.

Boote, D. N., & Beile, P. (2005). Scholars before researchers: On the centrality of the dissertation literature review in research preparation. *Educational Researcher, 34*(5), 3–15.

Creswell, J. W. (1994). *Research design: Qualitative and quantitative approaches.* Thousand Oaks, CA: Sage.

Creswell, J. W. (2007). *Qualitative inquiry and research design: Choosing among the five approaches* (2nd ed.). Thousand Oaks, CA: Sage.

Gall, M. D., Gall, J. P., & Borg, W. R. (2007). *Educational research: An introduction* (8th ed.). Boston: Pearson Education.

Hostetler, K. (2005). What is "good" education research? *Educational Researcher, 34*(6), 16–21.

Kerlinger, F. N. (1979). *Behavioral research: A conceptual approach.* Austin, TX: Holt McDougal.

Kilduff, M. (2007). Editor's comments: The top ten reasons why your paper might not be sent out for review. *Academy of Management Review, 32*(3), 700–702.

Merriam, S. B. (1998). *Qualitative research and case study applications in education.* San Francisco: Jossey-Bass.

Merriam, S. B., & Simpson, E. L. (1995). *A guide to research for educators and trainers of adults* (2nd ed.). Malabar, FL: Krieger.

Patton, M. Q. (2002). *Qualitative research and evaluation methods* (3rd ed.). Thousand Oaks, CA: Sage.

Rocco, T. S. (2003). Shaping the future: Writing up the method on qualitative studies. *Human Resource Development Quarterly, 14*(3), 343–349.

Swanson, R. A., & Holton, E. F. III (Eds.). (2005). *Research in organizations: Foundations and methods of inquiry.* San Francisco: Berrett-Koehler.

Summers, J. O. (2001). Guidelines for conducting research and publishing in marketing: From conceptualization through the review process. *Journal of the Academy of Marketing Science, 29*(4), 405–415.

Torraco, R. J. (2005). Writing integrative literature reviews: Guidelines and examples. *Human Resource Development Review, 4*(3), 356–367.

CHAPTER 10

DEVELOPING A RESEARCH PROBLEM AND PURPOSE STATEMENT

Ronald L. Jacobs

Stating the problem is fundamental to all forms of inquiry. Unfortunately, understanding what constitutes a research problem and how to articulate a problem statement clearly is an often overlooked aspect of the research process. That awareness came most strikingly to me when I was serving in various editorial roles, particularly as the associate editor and editor of *Human Resource Development Quarterly*. I often asked questions such as the following as feedback to authors: Of what value was using a complicated data analysis technique when the manuscript did not include a basis for the conceptual framework in the first place? Of what value was providing the purpose statement when no other information was given to support the intent of the study?

How to communicate the research problem demands more than good writing skills alone, though this is an essential competency. For many emerging scholars, constructing the problem statement often presents an intellectual challenge of a new sort, apart from designing the study and analyzing the data.

This chapter has four purposes. First, it discusses the role of the problem and the problem statement in doing research. Second, it discusses the various bases for deriving problems for doing research. Third, it presents a four-part logical system, or syllogism, for constructing problem statements. Finally, it discusses the implications for researchers and the field on placing greater attention on the problem statement.

Role of the Research Problem

All forms of systematic activity—research, evaluation, or development—may be considered as actions in response to problems. Although they differ in their respective goals, they all share a common need for a well-conceived statement of the problem, though this aspect is sometimes ignored or made to seem more of an intuitive process compared to other parts of the process. Problem statements serve an especially critical foundational role for research in that they communicate formally the reason for engaging in the study (Jacobs, 1997a).

Nearly all research handbooks advise that stating the problem is either the first or among the first steps of the research process. Merriam and Simpson (1995) identify five steps to the research process, with identifying a concern or problem as the first step. Hershey, Jacobs-Lawson, and Wilson (2006) use the interesting metaphor of a research script to describe a sort of personalized action plan for researchers. The formulation of the problem and research questions actually comes about as part of the third element of the process. Ary, Cheser Jacobs, Razavieh, and Sorenson (2005) discuss at some length the nature and sources of problems that need to be considered when doing educational research. Swanson and Holton (2005) propose a process of framing research in organizations, including making a problem decision, though they do not delineate this aspect well.

Emphasizing problem statements is often associated with a logical positivistic perspective of inquiry—that is, viewing research primarily as a systematic process, known as the scientific method, which basically starts with stating the problem and conceptual frameworks, then conducting the study and deriving meaning from the results based on this information. Alternatively, adherents to a grounded theory view inquiry as a means to allow theory to emerge from the results, suggesting a reversal, more or less, of the steps associated with the scientific method (Stebbins, 2001). In following a grounded theory approach, the precise problem may not be known at the outset of the study, though there might be a general hunch that a problem situation exists, which is often stated at the start. As a result, any formal problem statements become an outcome of the study, after the results have been generated and broad groups of concepts, as derived from the results, have been analyzed to generate an explanatory theory (Glaser & Strauss, 1967). Research problems can then be proposed as a means to begin testing the theory in subsequent research activities.

The intent of this discussion is not to invoke an epistemological debate about the relative merits of one approach to inquiry or another. Nor is the discussion meant to distinguish necessarily how a problem statement might differ for doing quantitative versus qualitative research. Rather, the point here is that problem statements play a crucial role in ensuring the logic of the study, regardless of the researcher's individual perspective on doing research and the methodology used. In any of these situations, problem statements play the same crucial role of communicating information about the study to others.

Research problems do not exist in nature just waiting to be plucked out by some observant researcher (Guba, 1978). Instead, they are artificial entities that come together only through the intense efforts of the researcher, who has identified a gap in information or understanding within a topic. In general, the information that forms the problem statement must be first induced from the literature, framed around certain theoretical understandings, and articulated in a way that clearly represents the interests of the researcher. Thus, problem statements differ from a topic of interest. That is, a researcher might express an interest in, say, workplace learning for doing a study. However, that information tells us virtually nothing about the research problem to be studied within the broad topic of workplace learning. Problem statements encompass more than merely narrowing a broad topic of interest into something more specific. These statements require an understanding of the discontinuities that exist when more than one phenomenon is examined at the same time.

In general, problem statements describe a gap in sets of information that, when examined carefully, results in a call for action or resolution. There are usually three major functions of problem statements. First, problem statements establish the existence of two or more factors that, by their interactions, produce a perplexing or troublesome state that yields an undesirable consequence. Kerlinger and Lee (1999) states that research problems represent the relationships between two or more variables at odds with each other. Often both factors that are being considered can be shown to be true at the same time, which results in an intellectual tension between two opposing true statements and provide the basis to formulate the problem. For instance, consider that the following statements about human resource development practice are both true and, at the same time, begin to frame the perplexing situation required of a problem:

- HRD professionals consistently profess the value of using a systems approach to develop training programs.
- In actual practice, HRD professionals seldom use all aspects of the systems approach to develop training programs.

The need to resolve two points of fact that are in opposition to each other, such as the ones presented above, forms the intellectual basis for doing research.

The second function of problem statements is to justify the usefulness of the information that might be gained by investigating the problem. That is, given that a perplexing or troubling situation exists, the following question might be asked: Many such perplexing situations exist in human affairs, so why is this one of any particular importance? The basis of this response could be drawn from a range of reasons. For instance, the importance for understanding the above two statements might rest with the need for organizations to make effective use of their resources, and the systems approach is better suited to ensure that this occurs. Thus, based on this justification, understanding how these two statements could both be true helps the researcher build the case for why these opposing statements deserve attention.

It is important to note that different types of activity—research, development, or evaluation—differ in the justification used for the problem statement. Research seeks to resolve the disparate sets of information through the generation of new knowledge and the introduction of theory. Development seeks to resolve the disparity through the implementation of solutions to address the problem. And evaluation seeks to resolve the disparity by determining the extent to which solutions have been effective in addressing the problem. Distinguishing among these activities is especially critical when considering the differences between research and evaluation.

Finally, the problem statement presents the purpose of the study to address the troubling or perplexing situation, that is, what the researcher has planned in response to the existence of the opposing factors. Given that the researcher can select among options, there is an element of subjectivity in the context of the literature in what factors precisely are used to frame the problem and what goals are set for the study. Thus, in the presence of the same information, researchers may in fact identify entirely different problems.

Deriving Problem Statements

Problem statements do not exist in nature, but need to be identified and framed through the researcher's efforts. How a research problem is identified is a matter of intense interest for many because no one intellectual process seems to fit best for all individuals and situations. Several authors suggest that researchers should use some combination of sources of information to derive the problem statement (for example, Merriam & Simpson, 1995). Unfortunately, how one should actually undertake to derive a problem statement from the various sources of information has received limited attention.

The process seldom generalizes in a specific sense since the steps inevitably feature numerous false starts, disappointments, and even moments of discovery and insight, some of which are purely serendipitous in nature. However, on personal reflection and observation of others, I propose the following general process that researchers typically use to derive problem statements:

1. Identify a topic of scholarly interest.
2. Develop expertise on the topic and its supporting bodies of knowledge through the literature and experience.
3. Induce potential research problems through a process of continuously analyzing and synthesizing the information.
4. Confirm the truth of a research problem through the literature, discussion, and peer review.
5. Construct a formal problem statement to ensure the logic of the research problem and communicate the problem to others.

As stated, the proposed process may differ based on the situation and individuals involved. However, any process should generally begin with the researcher developing expertise about the topic and conclude with the formal stating of the problem statement.

The following sections discuss the various ways of gaining in-depth knowledge about a topic of scholarly interest.

Literature Reviews

Perhaps the most common recommendation is that potential research problems can be found by conducting a thorough review of the scholarly literature of the topic (Hart, 1998). Having in-depth knowledge of a topic provides a foundational basis for using the other sources. The review should reveal what research questions have already been asked, which of those questions have been resolved and which remain open to further research, and what other research questions might still need to be asked as new insights are gained.

As stated, knowing the literature seems a logical first step in identifying a research problem. However, taking this approach alone rarely seems to provide the level of understanding to generate meaningful problem statements. More likely is that information from the literature review should be combined with other sources information.

Personal Experience

The adage often goes that nothing can replace the value of personal experience. In most instances, personal experience represents the insights gained about a topic or situation when observing the phenomenon of interest firsthand or when engaged in some level of professional practice related to the topic. Indeed, in far too many instances, researchers unfortunately carry out extensive research agendas all the while having limited, if any, contact with the phenomenon of interest.

Several years ago, I introduced the notion of partnership research as a means to bring researchers closer in contact to practice settings (Jacobs, 1997b). The underlying principle was that if the research was ultimately intended to have an impact on practice, then the research questions should be developed using insights gained through some level of involvement in practice or at least intimate contact with the practice setting. Based on this understanding, partnership research is defined as deriving research from practice. To accomplish this, researchers should consider first gaining some close-up understanding of the topic through practice, since practice is often the best way to achieve any depth of true understanding (Van de Ven & Johnson, 2006). Drawing from personal experience does not negate the need to rely on the scholarly literature. In fact, the scholarly literature provides a frame from which the observant practitioner or researcher can tease out what problems might be of some importance.

Researchers often feel frustrated when attempting to derive meaningful research problems on a topic without much grounding in practice. For instance, many researchers now express an interest in studying Web-based training as it is being used in organizations. At first glance, this focus represents an important topic for the human resource development field, but to make such research truly worthwhile, it seems necessary for researchers to have gained some firsthand experience in designing or managing this training approach. Unfortunately, many researchers express a scholarly interest in studying such topics, but are limited in their perspectives since they have few practical experiences to buttress their scholarly interest.

Discussions with Others

A third perspective on deriving research problems is to reach out to others for their opinions, such as peer researchers who may be at the same stage or who may have developed insights about potential research problems from their own experiences. Unfortunately, researchers mistakenly believe that the process of identifying a research problem should be a relatively solitary ordeal. As a result, too many close down from their usual social contacts as they engage in this stage of the research process. The result can be undue levels of frustration and anxiety.

Research Agendas

Finally, research problems can come from established research agendas. For instance, a small group of researchers may have established a line of research from which individual researchers might be able to identify a research problem. Following the research agenda of others has both advantages and disadvantages. One advantage is that new research problems are the logical result of each previous study. In that sense, research both answers questions and surfaces new questions for attention. Thus, the researcher may have some options within the scope of the agenda and, in addition, might feel a sense of belonging to a larger research effort.

From these various sources of information, the following question might be asked: How does the researcher induce a research problem from the mass of information about a topic? In response, it seems critical for the researcher to engage in a continuous cycle of reflection involving analysis and synthesis to derive meaning from the information. The following six interrelated forms suggest how sets of information might be considered in relationship with each other.

Provocative Exception. The provocative exception occurs when a consistent and accepted conclusion is contradicted by the appearance of a new finding. Detecting such exceptions requires close scrutiny of a topic, which might reveal some subtle change in understanding over time. Provocative exceptions seldom stand out as monumental events in the literature and are immediately recognized as such. Rather, researchers need to analyze the literature carefully and seize on even the most subtle discrepancies to determine whether the exception should be considered the new orthodoxy or should be considered an exception worth investigating further.

An example of provocative exception might be seen in the literature on mentoring. One line of mentoring research has consistently shown that mentors and mentees show higher levels of interpersonal attraction toward each other when they are matched by age, gender, and race, among other personal factors (McManus & Russell, 1997). However, taken from a different perspective, some studies have shown that when individuals are asked to identify the individual who has mentored them and has been most influential in their development, there is no apparent pattern in the matching of personal characteristics. Indeed, Cushnie (1999) found in a qualitative study that all seven African American women supervisors named Caucasian men as being most helpful in their professional development, even when other women were available to mentor them. In this example, the research and commonsense logic both suggest the importance of matching individuals to ensure effective mentoring results. However, some other studies suggest that other factors may be as important, if not more so.

Contradictory Evidence. Related to the provocative exception is when contradictory evidence can be shown across findings at the same time. In this instance, each set of results is compelling in its own right, but when viewed from a higher level of abstraction, the contradictions begin to appear. That is, the researcher needs to analyze the findings from each stream of research, then begin to synthesize across the related streams to uncover how they may differ.

For example, influential studies of the HRD field, such as the annual survey of the workplace learning and performance industry conducted by ASTD (*State of the Industry Report: ASTD's Annual Review of Trends in Workplace Learning and Performance*, 2008) have related the percentage of training hours and delivery methods. The results have generally shown that instructor-led training has the highest percentage of learning hours, with technology-driven delivery approaches steadily gaining in use over the years. Respondents of these studies are likely to be HRD professionals in the participating organizations.

At the same time, when employees across occupations have been asked how they learned how to do their jobs, such as salespersons, engineers, and teachers, they consistently report that they learned their jobs in the context of performing their jobs, and seldom, if ever, mention classroom training or Web-based training (Churchill, Ford, & Walker, 1985; Connor, 1983). Although these results do not directly contradict each other, they do show that learning in the workplace can be viewed differently depending on which group is selected as the respondents of the study.

Knowledge Void. It is difficult to believe that a knowledge void exists today to any extent on any topic. The volume of research being conducted and reported must certainly be the highest ever. In addition, this does not even consider the unprecedented availability of research from related fields. For instance, a doctoral researcher sought to study the HRD function in organizations within the context of service quality management. Such an approach had not been done within the HRD literature, but such an approach is quite common within the operations management literature. Thus, the researcher used the theoretical framework and literature from this related field in the study (Mafi, 2000).

Another perspective on the knowledge void is to ask why some result was actually found in a study, when some other result was expected or intended. Clearly this discrepancy occurs in many studies and provides an especially fertile ground for generating new research problems. For instance, Benjamin Bloom (1984) published a meta-analysis of studies investigating the effectiveness of mastery learning approaches. He reported a somewhat startling result that mastery learning had improved researcher outcomes by one standard deviation overall, but had not achieved the two-standard-deviation improvement that he felt was necessary to prove the efficacy of mastery learning. Instead, face-to-face tutoring approaches had consistently achieved these more ambitious outcomes. How to explain these discrepancies gave rise to a new generation of research on the topic.

Action-Knowledge Conflict. The action-knowledge conflict focuses on when individuals' professional behaviors differ from their espoused behaviors. In this instance, the research problem could seek to identify if such a gap actually exists within a specific situation or topic, the issues that contribute to the gap, and the constraints that prevent individuals from behaving in professional situations as they might wish otherwise.

Perhaps the most common example is that HRD practitioners generally agree about the critical importance of thoroughly evaluating their training programs. However, in spite of such espoused beliefs, training evaluation activities in practice are rarely shown to occur to the same extent and with the same level of fervor and commitment.

Methodological Conflict. The use of one or another research methodology may also help provide a source for a research problem. Although there are numerous ways that researchers can manage bias or undue influence in their studies, the research methodology itself becomes a source of influence, though it is unlikely the researcher ever thought of it in this way.

For instance, one could argue that much of what we know about professional practice comes from survey research that asks respondents to complete an instrument of some kind. Indeed, the development of Web-based platforms makes this approach all the more efficient to administer and the results to analyze. At the same time, some of the most insightful understandings about the vagaries of professional practice come from the direct questioning of respondents using open-ended questions or specifically formatted questions such as the critical incident technique.

Qualitative research does not owe its existence simply to serve as an alternate approach to quantitative research, as might be suggested by the above example. Each research or paradigm has its own legitimate place in its own right for facilitating our understanding of phenomena. However, when certain topics have been predominantly investigated using one method or another, then that occurrence opens the obvious question about whether the results might differ if another method was used.

Theoretical Conflict. It is possible that the same phenomenon may be explained through more than one theoretical model, and such a discrepancy might provide an opportunity for studying the explanatory power of one theory over the other. For instance, examining learning theories based on behavioral or cognitive theories has provided many researchers with a clear contrast from which to study and explain specific instructional approaches. Does learner interaction lead to higher learning outcomes because it affords individuals an opportunity to reflect on the relevance of the content or because of the perceived value of the consequence that follows the response?

Constructing Problem Statements

Problem statements typically have four major components that communicate the basis of the study or the perplexing or troublesome situation, and the general action that will be taken in the situation. Taken together, problem statements represent a system of argument, or a conditional syllogism, that is based on information recognized as being true in a particular sense. Truthful information is derived from the scholarly literature of the field, reliable sources from the general or professional literature, or commonly accepted views of the field from respected individuals. In this sense, truth is relative based on the level of confidence that a community of scholars places in its various scholarly and practitioner-based outlets of communication.

Problem statements are certainly not built from the personal opinions of the individual researcher or conclusions made from spurious sources of information that may have an inherent predisposition or prejudice about a topic. In this sense, research problem statements can be constructed to appear to be logically valid, but they may not actually be true in the manner that truth is defined here. Viewing problem statements in this way highlights the need to differentiate the quality of the scholarly sources in a field, including conference proceedings, journals, and professional texts. In general, the most "truthful" scholarly sources are those that have undergone the most rigorous review processes. Given the nature of truth, the four components of problem statements are presented.

Principal Proposition

These are the collective of statements that can be considered as being true or generally accepted as factual. The principal proposition represents a discussion that establishes for the reader what information is generally considered as being beyond question. Consider the following statement, which can be considered as being true:

> Historical records suggest that central Ohio typically has a relatively
> mild winter weather pattern. As a result, over the years, local newspapers
> have reported few disruptions on daily life caused by the weather.

Principal propositions are intended to establish a baseline of acceptable fact. Of course, such statements in themselves may be subject to scrutiny by readers.

Who conducted the analysis of the historical and newspaper records? How does a mild weather pattern differ from a severe weather pattern? What actually constitutes a disruption of daily life as described here? Regardless, given that the assertion is supported by public sources of information with some credibility, there is at least the beginning assumption that the statement has some level of truthfulness.

Interacting Proposition

The interacting proposition is arguably the most important part of the problem statement. In effect, the interacting proposition and the discussion that supports it serve to contradict, show exceptions to, or cast some degree of doubt on the principal proposition. The form of the interacting propositional statement almost always starts with a connecting adverb, such as, *however, although,* or *but.* The importance of using such words in this way suggests they should be used sparingly otherwise in the report, so that readers are clear about the location of the interacting proposition in the problem statement.

Following the general example, consider the following interacting proposition:

> However, the past five winters in central Ohio have been especially harsh, with temperatures ranging well below the daily averages. As a result, most schools have been closed more days than their allotted number.

As stated, the interacting proposition provides a contrast to the principal proposition. Thus, the interacting proposition is especially sensitive to being supported by the scholarly literature or in combination with a credible professional source. One cannot simply report that a contradiction exists to the principal proposition on the basis of the researcher's personal opinion or a source that is less than credible, such as reporting the opinion of another observer. Indeed, the problem statement depends in large part on whether the interacting proposition is constructed in a way that is sufficiently convincing to informed readers. And the most convincing support comes from either the scholarly literature or some other respected professional outlet.

Speculative Proposition

The speculative proposition juxtaposes the previous two sets of information, which are both offered as being true, and suggests why it might be important to resolve the contradiction that they seemingly have caused. The research problem is formed by the gap of knowledge that exists between the two factual statements. Such occurrences form the crux of scientific investigation, that is, how we intend to resolve the two contradictory independent statements. As such, the speculative proposition might be considered in the form of a statement of principle—for example:

> If central Ohio has had relatively mild winters in the past based on historical information, and if the recent winter weather pattern suggests a new weather pattern, which may have detrimental affects on daily life, then more must be known about the most current winter weather patterns of central Ohio.

Explicative Statement

Finally, the problem statement should conclude with a culminating statement that states how the gap will be resolved in the form of the actions that the researcher intends to undertake. Simply put, the explicative statement is the statement of the purpose of the research study. Many researchers mistakenly view the explicative statement as the problem statement itself. As a result, in the section of the dissertation, research report, or journal article labeled "Problem Statement," the author will simply provide the purpose of the research study.

In fact, the explicative statement serves to complete the cycle of logic that the researcher has generated:

> The purpose of this study is to investigate the recent winter weather pattern and its affects on daily life in central Ohio.

From this approach, it becomes apparent that problem statements are not actually singular statements. Instead, they represent a series of statements that should form a logical flow of understanding. Fitting the various pieces of the problem statement into a logical whole requires perseverance because the researcher often needs to engage in an iterative writing and revising process. Few writing attempts are successful the first time to communicate the problem statement clearly and concisely.

The following excerpts present the core statements of the problem statement adapted from a journal article by Osman-Gani and Jacobs (1996, p. 30):

Principal proposition:

Studies have shown that managers in multi-national enterprises (MNEs) confront issues of national culture in their daily activities. For instance, policies set by senior managers in one country may in fact represent the cultural assumptions of that country only and, as a result, may differ from the assumptions held by managers who reside in another country and who are expected to carry out the policies. Such differences in national culture may affect the behaviors of the managers and by extension the effectiveness of the policies.

Interacting proposition:

While a range of management behaviors have been studied related to national culture, there have been few if any studies focusing on how human resource development might differ based on national culture. Human resource development has been shown to be a critical factor in determining organizational success.

Speculative proposition:

If national cultural may affect the way in which managers carry out organizational policies and by extension the effectiveness of those policies, and if no studies have been conducted on how human resource development might differ based on national culture, which is a critical aspect in determining organizational success, then more should be known about how managers in a multinational enterprise differ in their perceptions of human resource development.

Explicative statement:

The purpose of this study was to determine whether managers in a multinational enterprise differed in their perceptions of selected human resource development practices in their organization. In addition, if such differences were found, the study sought to determine whether managers' perceptions could be clustered by the countries in which they resided.

In many instances, journal articles may not actually present the components in the same sequence. Instead, authors may decide to present the explicative statement first and then present the remaining components to support the research problem. In a sense, the logical progression of the problem statement is intentionally inverted. As a former journal editor, I have helped numerous emerging scholars revise their manuscripts for publication and have advised this approach for two reasons. First, placing the explicative statement toward the beginning helps the author to focus immediately on what information to include in the manuscript. This issue often arises when the author faces the challenge of converting a dissertation to a manuscript format, requiring that the information be reorganized into a form more suitable for a journal with specific format and length constraints.

Second, placing the explicative statement toward the beginning of the manuscript helps demarcate the explicit intent of the manuscript. I have found this to be helpful in both empirical and theoretical manuscripts. The following excerpt is from an article proposing a conceptual framework (Jacobs & Park, 2009):

> There is common agreement about the critical importance of workplace learning in organizations (Jacobs, 2003; Lohman, 2005; Clarke, 2005). As such, the topic has received much attention among human resource development scholars and practitioners alike, mostly focusing on two major components: formal training and informal learning. In effect, these components have become the defining features of workplace learning. This article proposes a conceptual framework of workplace learning that is comprised of the interaction of three variables: 1) the location of the learning; 2) the extent of planning that has been invested in developing and delivering the learning experiences; and, 3) the role of the trainer, facilitator, or others during the learning process. The need for the proposed framework stems from two concerns. First, formal training and informal learning represent incompatible levels of discourse, making it difficult to have a cohesive understanding of workplace learning. Second, definitions of workplace learning appear to exclude a large segment of HRD practice, particularly when formal training programs occur in the work setting [p. 133].

Regardless of the order, the components of the problem statement should be developed in their core form first, that is, a statement that represents the central theme for each component. This approach allows the researcher to better scrutinize the logic and receive constructive feedback from others for improvement. Constructing problem statements is a formative process. The first drafts rarely are acceptable, but they serve an important function in helping to progressively sharpen the logic and illuminate the various options. Issues with problem statements tend to fall in one or more of the following categories:

- Fails to establish the existence of the problem. For example, the problem statement contains only the explicative statement: "The purpose of the study was . . ."
- Explains every problem in the same way, using the same principal proposition as boilerplate for all interacting propositions.
- Neglects to show any history of the problem. That is, the principal proposition does not provide sufficient context.
- Lacks support to show how the interacting proposition is related to the principal proposition.

- Has limited meaning outside the personal experience of the researcher, even though the problem statement may appear to be logical.
- Projects the principal proposition and interacting proposition at too high a level of abstraction. That is, the problem statement appears to be overly ambitious or too broad in its perspective.
- Presents information that is logical, but the problem statement may have limited importance to the field or information from the literature is not accurately portrayed.
- Presents a set of statements representing the problem statement components, but the flow of logic remains uncertain or is disconnected.

Implications of the Problem Statement

The central point made at the beginning of this chapter is that the research problem is fundamental to good research. Otherwise the research could not be considered as an intellectual activity governed by system thinking. These often-stated critical comments about some studies illustrate this point: "A method in search of a problem," "The researcher knew what he wanted to do, but forgot to tell anyone else," and "Interesting results, but what does it all mean?" These types of comments plague too many research studies.

Developing research problems requires a sort of intellectual discipline that differs from other aspects of the research process. It requires that the researcher possess deep knowledge of the scholarly literature of interest, all the while holding on to some sense of what he or she would like to do. My observation is that many emerging researchers may not be able to readily articulate their research problem, but they are able to recognize it when they finally work out the appropriate logic. At some point, there comes a realization that the problem existed all along and that it just needed to be "discovered" through successful analysis and synthesis. There is a need to peel away the extraneous clutter of understandings to reveal the researcher's core scholarly interest. Engaging in this process may be as demanding as any aspect of the research process and in the process helps avoid the common criticisms directed at many studies.

Attention to the research problem carries with it benefits beyond the immediate study. Figure 10.1 suggests how the various components of the problem statement—the principal proposition, the interacting proposition, the speculative proposition, and the explicative statement—can be generalized to guide the change process, research studies, development projects, and evaluation projects. Each professional activity may be guided by a different set of requirements, such as those for change projects designed to improve, innovate, or transform.

FIGURE 10.1. RELATIONSHIP BETWEEN THE PROBLEM STATEMENT AND PROFESSIONAL ACTIONS.

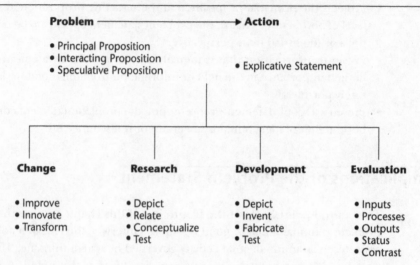

However, the basis for doing the professional activity should be guided by a logical presentation of the problem beforehand.

Conclusion

This chapter argues for the need to take greater care in conceptualizing and articulating problem statements. Meeting this challenge often differs from the more common tasks of selecting and using the correct research methods and data analysis techniques. Researchers realize that constructing problem statements in fact is an especially intellectually demanding process that requires a range of analytical skills. But such intense efforts at the start are almost always rewarded by greater clarity of the research intent and, by extension, increased meaningfulness of the results. How to ensure the integrity of this aspect of the research process remains a challenge for both emerging and experienced researchers alike.

References

Ary, D., Cheser Jacobs, L. C., Razavieh, A., & Sorenson, C. K. (2005). *Introduction to research in education.* Florence, KY: Wadsworth.

Bloom, B. (1984). The 2-sigma problem: The search for methods of group instruction as effective as one-on-one tutoring. *Educational Researcher, 13*(6), 4–16.

Churchill, G. A., Ford, N. M., & Walker, O. C. (1985). *Sales force management: Planning, implementation, and control.* Homewood, IL: Irwin.

Connor, J. (1983). *On-the-job training.* Boston: International Human Resources Development Corporation.

Cushnie, M. (1999). *African-American women first-line supervisors: A qualitative study of their career development process.* Unpublished doctoral dissertation, Ohio State University, Columbus.

Glaser, R., & Strauss, A. (1967). *The discovery of grounded theory: Strategies of qualitative research.* London: Weidenfeld and Nicholson.

Guba, E. (1978). *Toward a methodology of naturalistic inquiry in educational evaluation.* Los Angeles: Center for the Study of Evaluation, UCLA Graduate School of Education, University of California.

Hart, C. (1998). *Doing a literature review: Releasing the social science research imagination.* Thousand Oaks, CA: Sage.

Hershey, D. A., Jacobs-Lawson, J. M., & Wilson, T. L. (2006). Research as a script. In F. T. Leong & J. Austin (Eds.), *The psychology research handbook: A guide for graduate researchers and research assistants* (pp. 3–22). Thousand Oaks, CA: Sage.

Jacobs, R. (1997a). HRD is not the research problem. *Human Resource Development Quarterly, 8*(1), 1–3.

Jacobs, R. (1997b). Partnerships for integrating HRD research and practice. In R. Swanson & E. Holton (Eds.), *Human resource development research handbook: Linking research and practice* (pp. 47–61). San Francisco: Berrett-Koehler.

Jacobs, R., & Park, Y. (2009). A proposed conceptual framework of workplace learning: Implications for theory development and research in human resource development. *Human Resource Development Review, 8*(2), 133–150.

Kerlinger, F. N., & Lee, H. (1999). *Foundations of behavior research* (4th ed.). Belmont, CA: Wadsworth.

Mafi, S. (2000). *Testing the appropriateness of the gap service-management model to the human resource development function in organizations.* Unpublished doctoral dissertation, Ohio State University, Columbus.

McManus, S. E., & Russell, J. (1997). New directions for mentoring research: An examination of related constructs. *Journal of Vocational Behavior, 51*(1), 145–161.

Merriam, S. M., & Simpson, E. (1995). *A guide to research for educators and trainers of adults.* Malabar, FL: Kreiger.

Osman-Gani, A. A., & Jacobs, R. L. (1996). Differences in perceptions of human resource development across countries: An exploratory study of managers in a multinational enterprise. *Journal of Transnational Management Development, 2*(3), 21–29.

State of the Industry Report: ASTD's annual review of trends in workplace learning and performance. (2008). Alexandria, VA: ASTD.

Stebbins, R. A. (2001). *Exploratory research in the social sciences.* Thousand Oaks, CA: Sage.

Swanson, R. A., & Holton, E. F. (2005). *Research in organizations: Foundations and methods of inquiry.* San Francisco: Berrett-Koehler.

Van de Ven, A., & Johnson, P. E. (2006). Knowledge for theory and practice. *Academy of Management Review, 31*(4), 802–821.

PART THREE

PREPARING SCHOLARLY MANUSCRIPTS

CHAPTER 11

WRITING A LITERATURE REVIEW

Susan Imel

A literature review can be part of a larger study or freestanding as a research effort in its own right. Novice scholars may be most familiar with the literature review that is part of a larger study and may not realize that stand-alone reviews are also considered a form of research (Torraco, 2005). Both types of review are developed using similar processes but have different emphases. A widely held assumption seems to exist that preparing a literature review is a transparent process, and thus little or no attention is given to this aspect of preparing researchers and scholars.

As a part of a larger study, the literature review provides the foundation for the study. Unfortunately, the neglect of the review has led to many reviews, which are part of a larger study, being "only thinly disguised annotated bibliographies" (Hart, 1998, p. 1) rather than demonstrating an understanding of the research that has preceded and led to the study (Boote & Penny, 2005). Michael Moore (2004), editor of the *American Journal of Distance Education*, echoes this sentiment when he attributes low acceptance rates for the journal to "the propensity of many authors . . . to underestimate the importance of the literature review that *must* precede any presentation of data" (p. 127).

As a type of scholarly publication, freestanding literature reviews have been largely overlooked, but they are "no less rigorous or easier to write than other types of research articles" (Torraco, 2005, p. 356). Freestanding literature reviews can indicate a direction for future research in an area by pointing out gaps, highlighting central or unresolved issues, bridging related or disparate areas, or providing new perspectives on the topic (Cooper, 1985; Russell, 2005; Torraco,

2005). Novice scholars seeking publication opportunities might consider how the literature review for their dissertations could be developed as a freestanding article. Manglitz (2003) represents one example of how the literature base from a dissertation study was used as the basis for a scholarly publication.

The purpose of this chapter is to demystify the literature review process, whether the review is part of a larger study or a stand-alone effort. It begins by defining literature reviews. The majority of the second section is concerned with strategies for thinking about how to construct a review but also includes a discussion of finding and selecting the literature for the review. The third section deals with scholarly analysis of the literature in preparation for writing the review. The final section on writing makes suggestions for constructing a quality review and points out some common pitfalls that occur in writing reviews.

Defining Literature Reviews

A number of different terms have been used to describe literature reviews including *literature review, research review, integrative review*, and *research synthesis* (Cooper, 1998; Torraco, 2005). (*Meta-analysis*, another term used to describe literature reviews, is a specialized form of synthesis that uses quantitative procedures to "statistically combine the results of studies" [Cooper, 1998, p. 3]. Meta-analysis will not be covered in this chapter; readers seeking additional information on the meta-analysis process can consult Cooper, 1998.) Definitions for these terms may differ in emphasis but generally include two common elements: coverage or review of a body of literature and integration and synthesis of what has already been done in the literature. A good starting point in defining literature reviews is from Cooper (1988): "First a literature review uses as its database reports of primary or original scholarship and does not report new primary scholarship itself. The primary reports used in the literature may be verbal, but in the vast majority of cases reports are written documents. The types of scholarship may be empirical, theoretical, critical/analytic, or methodological in nature. Second, a literature review seeks to describe, summarize, evaluate, clarify and/or integrate the content of primary reports" (p. 107).

This definition introduces the idea that a variety of materials can be included in a literature review, and it also suggests that something is done to that material. In a quality literature review, the "something" that is done to the literature should include synthesis or integrative work that provides a new perspective on the topic (Boote & Penny, 2005; Torraco, 2005), resulting in a review that is more than the sum of the parts. A quality literature review should not just reflect or replicate previous research and writing on the topic under review, but should lead to new productive work (Lather, 1999) and represent knowledge construction on the part of the writer. Ward (1983) points out that as a process, synthesis shares similarities with other research processes such as the development of the problem statement and research hypotheses but that the "synthesis process is focused on creating new forms of knowledge," while the other processes are focused on design (p. 26).

Unfortunately, many literature reviews may admirably cover the literature but fail in terms of providing any insights into the literature. These reviews are mostly "a simple enumeration of 'who said what,' a regurgitation of names and ideas" (Montuori, 2005, p. 374). A literature review that is part of a larger project should provide the foundation for the research based on what has been done previously. Freestanding reviews should integrate the literature in such a way as to produce "new frameworks and perspectives on the topic" (Torraco, 2005, p. 356).

Developing a literature review requires much more than understanding what one is. Quality literature reviews have structure and form. An understanding of that structure can help in the development process.

Preliminary Work: Building the Foundation

Some preliminary work prior to starting the review can provide a foundation for what is to follow. This stage of the literature review process can be thought of as similar to planning the methodology section for a research study; a literature review that is part of a larger study can be thought of as a mini-research project. Questions at this stage might include: "What is the review designed to accomplish?" "What type of sources will be included?" "How will the review be structured?" and "What are effective ways of locating and selecting sources to be included in the review?" Writers of freestanding reviews might also ask, "Do I have a perspective I wish to share, and, if so, how will I support that perspective?" Some tools for structuring a review and suggestions for locating and selecting materials follow.

Tools for Structuring Reviews

Novices may find the process of writing a literature review overwhelming because they do not understand that reviews have structure. Cooper's taxonomy (1985, 1988, 2003), based on an extensive analysis of freestanding literature reviews in the fields of psychology and education, is a helpful tool for planning for the structure of a review. It addresses many of the questions that are part of the review's methodology. The taxonomy contains six identifying characteristics, each divided into categories that further define the characteristic. It not only provides a method of analyzing how a review is structured or organized but it can also be used as a tool to guide the development of a review, whether part of a larger study or freestanding.

The six characteristics in the typology are focus, goal, perspective, coverage, organization, and audience. For novices, the characteristics of focus, coverage, and organization may be most useful in the planning that precedes the development of a review. The characteristic of goal plays a secondary role, because the goal for most reviews is integration or synthesis. I discuss these characteristics separately but important relationships exist among them, and the completed review should have internal consistency (Cooper, 1985, 1988).

The characteristic of focus refers to the type of literature included in the review: reports of research outcomes, research methods, theoretical literature, or practical or applied literature. Most scholarly reviews focus on research outcomes or theoretical literature or a combination of the two. This characteristic helps novices think about what types of literature will be central to their review. For some reviews, the focus will always be reports of previous research studies, but for others, the choice about what to include may be tied to other aspects of the review, such as overall goal or purpose. A review by Smith (2008) included only very specific types of literature related to competency studies due to the review's purpose.

How much literature to actually include—coverage—is another aspect to consider during the planning stage. The taxonomy suggests four possible categories: comprehensive or exhaustive, comprehensive with selective citation, representative, and central or pivotal. Although a decision about the exact nature of the coverage will probably not be made during planning, considering choices is important. Coverage for a review that is part of a larger study will probably fall into the category of comprehensive with selective citation; that is, the reviewer will consider all the possible sources but not include everything in the review. A reviewer might say, for example, that all the relevant literature was retrieved and examined in some way but only those pieces that met certain stated criteria were included. In freestanding reviews, however, certain parameters may be established that will enable the coverage to be comprehensive. Decisions about coverage should be made with the understanding that "each decision alters the character of the set [of literature] as a whole and could also therefore alter the net conclusions drawn from the set" (Kennedy, 2007, p. 139). How and why decisions about coverage were made should be shared as part of the discussion of methods.

Thinking about how the review will be organized is another important part of the preplanning. Again, as with coverage, it is too early to make a definitive decision, but knowledge that a review should have an organizational structure can guide the process as it unfolds and also help in the organization of the sources prior to any analysis. The taxonomy suggests three categories for structure: historical or chronological, conceptual or thematic, and methodological. Nearly all literature reviews are structured around major themes or concepts that emerge as the author examines and reviews the literature. Some reviews then use a chronological organization to discuss the literature within the major themes that have been identified and used to structure the review. During the review process, Bruce (1994) suggests identifying major categories and sub-categories as early as possible because they can always be revised. She also advocates the use of concept maps as a way of identifying these themes or categories. The initial examination of the literature under consideration for the review may begin to reveal major concepts or themes.

The characteristic of goal is probably of secondary importance at this stage of planning because the goal for most reviews will be synthesis or integration, a defining characteristic of literature reviews. It is the work of integration or synthesis that results in new perspectives on the topic through the reviewer's knowledge construction (Montuori, 2005; Torraco, 2005). The taxonomy has major categories for goal: integration, including generalization, conflict resolution, and bridging disparate bodies of literature; criticism in which each piece reviewed is examined using a rubric or predetermined set of criteria; and identification of central issues. The categories and subcategories for goal described in the taxonomy are certainly not exhaustive. Although the major goal of most reviews falls within the integration category, as part of the integration, they may achieve other aims, such as the identification of central issues and gaps in the literature.

Perspective and audience, the other taxonomy characteristics, are important for freestanding reviews and should be considered in conjunction with potential publication outlets. Writers of review articles should take the time to familiarize themselves with potential journals prior to writing the review article to determine the major audience and the type of articles accepted. The audience is generally the readership of the journal to which a review is being submitted. Does the journal seem to appeal to a scholarly audience, or does it serve practitioners? Perspective or point of view about the material reviewed can range from neutral to advocacy of a position. Before writing an espousal review, reviewers should become familiar with what is accepted practice for that journal and its audience. Some journals have sections that encourage submissions of pieces of this nature.

Using the taxonomy to examine freestanding published reviews has been a helpful exercise for novices struggling to develop their own reviews. Despite its age, "Mentors and Protégés: A Critical Review of the Literature," an article by Sharan Merriam (1983), has proven to be an excellent tool for this exercise. Merriam clearly describes her focus by telling readers that two types of literature were selected: that which "seriously analyzed or conceptualized the phenomenon of mentoring" (which would be theoretical using the taxonomy categories) and that which "presented the results of data-based research studies" (pp. 161–162). In addition, the article delineates how the literature for the review was retrieved and selected, enabling readers to understand that the coverage was probably comprehensive with selective citation, since criteria were established for the type of literature that would be included. Furthermore, a quick scan of the article reveals that it is organized by themes found in the literature on mentoring. Finally, at the end of each thematic section, Merriam includes a summary or synthesis of the material covered and concludes the article with four overall criticisms of the mentoring literature, which extends the synthesis work and highlights central issues. Another published review that has been useful for the exercise of applying the taxonomy is "Practical Training in Evaluation" by Michael Trevisan (2004). Trevisan focuses on practice-based literature related to teaching or training in evaluation. Because of how he frames the criteria for inclusion of articles, his coverage is exhaustive. Like Merriam, he clearly describes what he is doing and how he located his sources.

In many freestanding reviews, the discussion of goals, focus, and coverage is included in a method section. Rocco, Stein, and Lee (2003) is a particularly good example of how this can be handled. In an article about writing integrative reviews, Torraco (2005) provides helpful suggestions about developing the methodology section of a review. By applying the taxonomy to published reviews, novices can see how they can adapt it to construct a methodology for their own review.

Strategies for Identifying and Selecting Resources

Whether the topic under development is new or one that is being continued or enlarged from previous work, some basic principles apply to the process of identifying and selecting resources for the review. One of the common pitfalls in finding information is overdependence on a single strategy. The Internet and Google have changed how information is located and accessed, but relying solely on these sources is shortsighted. Multiple strategies, including database searching, personal contact, Web searching, and even manually scanning contents of relevant journals, should be used to locate materials for a review. Any parameters established for the review in the categories of focus and coverage may also determine what strategies are used. It may be helpful to think of categories of strategies: formal, such as those used to retrieve the published literature; informal, involving personal contact with colleagues and other scholars working in the area of the review; and secondary, using citation indexes, bibliographies, and bibliographic databases (Cooper, 1998).

Materials in electronic research databases such as Academic Search Premier, PsycINFO, and Business Source Complete can be retrieved using a number of search strategies: key word, subject terms, author, title, date, and so forth. Most research databases use what is known as a controlled vocabulary (subject terms) to index items. For novices, the controlled vocabulary may be indistinguishable from the database itself; in other words, they do not recognize its existence and do not use it in retrieving materials, relying instead on searching using keywords (Klaus, 2000). Subject terms used to index materials are a much more effective and efficient way to locate items than key words. Information professionals such as reference librarians can help identify the relevant subject terms. They are familiar with a number of research databases and the controlled vocabulary used to index items, understand how materials can best be retrieved, and assist with developing effective search strategies. Most large libraries have virtual reference services that allow questions to be submitted electronically.

Pursuing a large number of contacts and actively gathering and receiving information from diverse sources will result in the most satisfactory search process (Palmer, 1991). The completed review should also include information about how the material was located. If sources other than electronic databases were used, that should be noted. Wanstreet (2006), for example, says that she consulted with two reference librarians as part of the process for selecting potential journal sources for use in her review.

After locating potential sources for the review, the task of selecting the best sources begins. Again, the preliminary parameters established in the initial planning stages are helpful in this step. For example, if the focus of the review is to be on research studies, then only sources that report research will be selected for further consideration. Furthermore, if the coverage is not going to be exhaustive, then some further winnowing can take place by scanning abstracts using criteria such as author, authority of the source, publication date, or other knowledge about the topic. In some cases, the goal of the review will determine the selection criteria, as in Smith (2008). Care should be taken not to eliminate foundational studies that are considered pivotal in the development of the topic. Such studies, sometimes referred to as seminal, may not appear in search results of electronic sources and may also need to be retrieved manually. Once a preliminary selection of materials is made, the scholarly analysis phase of the review process begins.

Scholarly Analysis of Selected Sources

Scholarly or critical analysis of the sources selected is the part of the review process that provides synthesis and constructs new knowledge. It results in a review that is more than "mirroring" of what has been done previously (Lather,

1999, p. 3). Failure of the reviewer to engage critically and systematically with the sources will likely result in a review that is little more than an annotated bibliography or listing of sources. Although analysis of sources can be a time-consuming process, it results in high-quality reviews that make significant contributions to the field's understanding of a topic. Some suggestions on how to manage this process follow.

For novices, critical analysis may seem to be a daunting task. They may feel that they cannot critique so-called expert knowledge (Brookfield, 1993), but with some practice and experience, they can achieve a scholarly analysis. To assist in the task of critical analysis, Brookfield (1993) poses a series of questions that may be helpful. The questions, which are designed for practitioners, give suggestions about critical analysis in areas such as methodology, communication, and experiential.

Before the material selected for review is read in detail and critically analyzed, sources should be scanned and sorted. At this stage, the work with the sources should serve to familiarize the reviewer with the material selected. Then a method of tracking each piece of literature to be included should be developed. Bibliographical software programs such as EndNote and Biblioscape can be helpful for this purpose, and many university libraries now provide access to RefWorks, a Web-based program designed to help manage research projects. Word processing software can also be used for this purpose.

Once a system for tracking sources is in place, the next task is developing a systematic means of analyzing each source. One method that has proven effective is the chart method, where each individual source is charted according to predetermined categories. Tables 11.1 and 11.2 provide examples of charts that can be used, respectively, in analyzing research studies and theoretical literature. A completed chart is shown in Table 11.3. The developer of this chart used a hybrid version of the research and theoretical charts to enable her to track both types of literature on the same chart.

Charts are only one method of analyzing sources. Another method suggested by the University of Toronto (http://www.utoronto.ca/writing/litrev.html) is a series of questions that the reviewer can ask about each source; the questions cover research, theoretical, and popular literature. The list expands the categories on the charts shown in Tables 11.1 and 11.2 to include questions about the relationship between the theoretical and research perspectives, structure of the argument, contribution to the understanding of the problem, author's research orientation, and so forth. The list is lengthy, but using it can provide a thorough analysis of each source, and the questions could be converted into a chart. Regardless of method selected for the analysis, the most important thing is to view each piece reviewed through the same lens.

TABLE 11.1. LITERATURE ANALYSIS CHART
FOR RESEARCH ARTICLES.

Citation information					
Purpose (Has author formulated a problem or issue?)					
Subjects					
Methodology					
Design and analysis					
Conclusions and results					
Implications					
Weaknesses (could use questions in Brookfield, 1993, to assess)					
Strengths (could use questions in Brookfield, 1993, to assess)					
Other (for example, Has relevant literature been evaluated? Contribution?)					

TABLE 11.2. LITERATURE ANALYSIS CHART
FOR THEORETICAL ARTICLES.

Citation information					
Purpose (Has author formulated a problem or issue?)					
Theoretical framework (theorists cited)					
Conclusions					
Implications					
Weaknesses[a] (could use questions in Brookfield, 1993, to assess)					
Strengths[a] (could use questions in Brookfield, 1993, to assess)					
Other notes such as contribution to development of literature base					

[a]Consider how the author has formulated the problem or issue.

TABLE 11.3. COMPLETED LITERATURE ANALYSIS HYBRID CHART.

Citation	Shapiro, J., Hollingshead, J., & Morrison, H. (2002). Primary care resident, faculty, and patient views of barriers to cultural competence, and the skills needed to overcome them. Medical Education, 36, 749–759.	Kripalani, S., Bussey-Jones, J., Katz, M. G., & Genao, I. (2006). A prescription for cultural competence in medical education. Journal of General Internal Medicine, 21, 1116–1120.	Rosen, J., Spatz, E., Gaaserud, A., Abramovitch, H., Wenger, N., et al. (2004). A new approach to developing cross-cultural communication skills. Medical Teacher, 26(2), 126–132.	Derosa, N., & Kochurka, K. (2006). Implement culturally competent healthcare in your workplace. Nursing Management, 37(10), 18–26.
Purpose	Literature has very little info on perception of barriers to achieve culturally competent communication for residents, faculty, and patients. Study aims to address this issue	Not all cultural competence education is effective in improving attitudes and skills of health professions; authors propose elements to improve education	Most cross-cultural training for medical students consists of lectures on topic during preclinical years rather than training in clinical years; purpose: to give students awareness, attitude, and knowledge plus communication skills	To outline a six-step approach to delivering culturally competent care to an increasingly diverse patient population
Subjects	Faculty and residents who come from socioeconomic and diverse backgrounds; patients who fall below federal poverty line		32 third-year medical students from Ben Gurion University	
Methodology	Focus groups: 5 faculty groups, 3 resident groups, 2 patient groups. Questions revolved around perceptions of effective cross-cultural communication and the barriers to it		1.5-day workshop included: intro to cross-cultural medicine issues, video on using interpreters, intro of CHAT (Cultural and Health Belief Assessment tool), actors used—students do mock interviews with patients—4 each, students devise treatment and prevention plans for each patient	Design/analysis
Design/analysis	Initial debriefing session with facilitators to look for emerging themes; verbatim transcripts made, content analysis initially descriptive and then interpretive		Students did self-evaluations at end of workshop; students surveyed before workshop and 6 weeks following workshop to assess attitudes in cross-cultural communication in 7 content areas, computed means for each pre/post-survey	

Theoretical framework		Gives general overview of 3 approaches to teaching cultural competency: knowledge based, attitude based, skills based Mentions Berlin and Fowkes LEARN guidelines, Kleinman's questions, RISK framework, and diffusion of innovations theory	The author's evaluation survey was based on work of Kleinman and the revised developmental model of ethnosensitivity by Borkan and Neher	Includes Fowkes's LEARN guidelines; mentions Kleinman's questions; includes Narayan's elements of a cultural assessment; refers to preserve-accommodate-restructure framework—not clear which author this is
Conclusions/results	Residents more language focused than faculty, patients defined competence in more generic terms than culture specific; residents and patients more likely to use person-blame models when talking of barriers; all 3 groups focused on providers for solutions	Authors conclude by calling for a more active approach to cultural competence that is integrated across all levels of medical education	Students showed a significant improvement in 5 of 8 areas measured. Authors deem workshops can be an effective, feasible, interesting, and entertaining way to hone cross-cultural skills, though note mastering cross-cultural skills cannot be achieved in a single workshop	Respect for patients must include respect for their cultural beliefs, values, and practices
Implications	Need to realize many residents are skeptical of cross-cultural training, suggests courses taught by physicians who are respected by residents and focus on generic skills of patient-centered communication	An integrated approach to cultural competence training is more likely to yield long-term outcomes rather than isolated workshops	With increasing diversity of the population, medical schools must equip students with skills needed to practice in multiethnic environment—the current depth of cross-cultural courses is insufficient and timing of courses (preclinical) suboptimal-acquisition of cross-cultural skills is continuous process	If you acknowledge the patient and family are the experts about their cultural norms and see yourself as becoming, rather than being, culturally competent, you'll achieve the most effective outcomes possible in working with patients

(Continued)

TABLE 11.3. (CONTINUED)

Weaknesses	Excluded patients who couldn't speak English because no interpreters (authors do list this as limitation); only had 2 patient focus groups out of 10 total groups; had patient focus groups in clinic—wonder about their comfort in this setting	Article describes current state of cultural competence education and its problems (lack of consensus on how to teach, limited outcome measures), but doesn't give information about their teaching experiences in the area; article would have been better if they included more examples of successful practices/programs	No background given on students (including ethnicity); did not discuss how many students attended until Results section; got poor survey response rate at end of workshop, should have been able to get >75% in my opinion	Authors could use more examples of best practices to illustrate suggestions—very few are given; authors state, "Six steps have been named that meet the cultural needs and expectations of patients." It's not clear if they are the authors of these steps. Very few people are cited in the article.
Strengths	Gave good background details of participants; tried to get high percentage of residents/faculties from each site; questions used included; key points illustrated well; good details and analysis of focus group sessions given	Encourages use of educational methods that correspond to principles of adult learning; 69 references listed so obviously did a fairly good search of the literature; article easy to read—gives clear ideas of how to improve culturally competent training	Points out that students attending workshops were doing rotations at hospital at same time—could have affected survey results not related to workshop; authors speculate about areas that did not improve	Easy to read for layperson; key ideas/examples pulled out into boxes for quick referral; good examples given of differences in nonverbal communication and questions to ask in a cultural assessment
Other	Adversarial undercurrents in groups noted—suggest importance of compassion and humility in field	Authors emphasize need for outcomes-based research to determine value of their strategies and others used in cc training	Authors note there is currently no standardized rating scale for defining essential components of an effective medical interview	

Source: Troyer (2007). Used by permission.

Charts developed in the analysis stage can be incorporated into the finished product. Examples of published literature reviews that include analysis charts are Trevison (2004); Gould, Kelly, White, and Chidgey (2004); Smith (2008); and Wanstreet (2006). Examining charts in published literature reviews can provide additional understanding about effective literature analysis. Systematic analysis of literature sources does not replace careful reading, critique of methods used, an understanding of the theoretical underpinnings of the topic, and other factors that go into critical analysis, but without it, novices may find it difficult to achieve synthesis in the review.

Writing the Review

Once the literature is systematically analyzed, the review itself can be drafted. Following some suggestions for moving from the literature analysis stage to the writing itself, the section concludes with some elements of a quality review.

From Analysis to Writing

How to turn the material from the analysis into a seamless review may seem like an overwhelming task. The challenge is to turn notes on individual sources into a review organized in a way that provides insights into the topic under review. The following questions adapted from Merriam and Simpson (1995) and Hart (1998) can be helpful in converting the information from the analysis into a narrative review and can be used in reviewing and organizing the analysis material:

- What are the major theories related to the topic?
- Who are the major contributors to the development of the topic, and what is significant about their work?
- Are there identifiable periods in which significant work was done?
- Have there been major points of departure from the conventional wisdom on the topic, and if so, when did these occur?
- Has the topic been politicized in the literature, and if so, how?
- Does a structure and organization for the topic emerge from the literature reviewed?
- Can differing points of view about the topic be identified?
- What current research is being conducted on the topic?
- What is unique or significant about the literature being reviewed?

Once the drafting of the review begins, the focus should be on the literature, not the topic. After the introduction and discussion of methods or strategies used in developing the review, the focus needs to shift to how the topic is treated in the literature under review. It is not uncommon for novices to forget this and veer off into discussing the topic rather than the literature. Phrases such as "according to the literature . . . ," "the literature under review . . . ," and "the literature selected for analysis . . ." help cue readers that the focus is on the literature and how the topic is treated in the literature, as well as help focus reviewers on the literature.

The following lead sentence from a review paper is a good example of keeping the major focus on the literature while also including information about the topic: "In the literature selected for this analysis, the topic of beginning teacher needs is treated such that teacher retention and effectiveness are tied to opportunities for professional collaboration and accountability. While these are common characteristics of the articles evaluated, the authors approach the topic in various ways" (Narishkin, 2005, p. 1).

In the summary or concluding section of the review, any observations made should be derived from the analysis of the literature, not the topic. Here, comments can address questions such as, "What is missing?" "Where are any strengths and weaknesses?" "What gaps are there in research?" and "What comments or critique can be made about the body of literature reviewed?" If the review is being conducted as part of a larger study, this section should include comments about how the literature reviewed supports the need for the proposed study.

Assessing the Quality of a Review

Discussions of criteria for judging reviews are included in Boote and Penny (2005), Hart (1999), and Cooper (1985). How the review is organized is an important quality criterion. Well-organized reviews provide reader cues (for example, "The limited empirical literature being reviewed revealed . . .") and give an indication of what literature is covered (for example, research outcomes, theoretical, date parameters). The organization stems from the literature under review, and a rationale is provided for coverage, organizational scheme, and other elements of the methodology. The review contains strong lead sentences or organizing paragraphs and summaries of the literature

Also important is writing style. The review should be written in a clear and coherent style that avoids the use of jargon, and it should follow the scholarly conventions of its intended audience. If appropriate, the review should reflect the writer's voice. Citations should be used appropriately. Any claims made should be substantiated by the literature, and any conclusions drawn should be based on evidence from the literature reviewed.

Finally, a review should have internal consistency in terms of what it intends to do. Do the elements such as goal, type of literature included, and coverage of that literature form a logical whole? And does the review address the criteria established in the methodology section or introduction? That is, does the reviewer accomplish what he or she set out to do (Cooper, 1985)?

Conclusion

This chapter has focused on the process for writing a literature review. The stages presented here are meant to demonstrate that some order or logic can be brought to the literature review process, but developing a literature review is not a linear process. The process itself moves back and forth among the various stages and should include reflection at each stage, always asking questions about the selected approach. Finally, developing a literature review is both an art and a science. The chapter has focused primarily on the science or instrumental side by presenting a systematic way of thinking about how a review is constructed and suggesting strategies that can be used in its development. Developing a quality literature review demands artistry at all stages, including how decisions are made about the overall goals, focus, and coverage for the review; how search strategies are developed and sources located and selected; how the material is analyzed; and finally how the review itself is presented. Creativity at each of these stages will result in a higher-quality review.

References

Boote, D. N., & Penny, B. (2005). Scholars before researchers: On the centrality of the dissertation literature review in research preparation. *Educational Researcher, 34*(6), 3–15.

Brookfield, S. (1993). Breaking the code: Engaging practitioners in critical analysis of adult education literature. *Studies in the Education of Adults, 25*(1), 64–92.

Bruce, C. S. (1994). Research students' early experiences of the dissertation literature review. *Studies in Higher Education, 19*(2), 217–229.

Cooper, H. M. (1985). *A taxonomy of literature reviews.* Paper presented at the Annual Meeting of the American Educational Research Association, Chicago. (ERIC Document Reproduction Service No. ED 254541)

Cooper, N. M. (1988). Organizing knowledge syntheses: A taxonomy of literature reviews. *Knowledge in Society, 1*(1), 105–126.

Cooper, H. (1998). *Synthesizing research: A guide for literature reviews* (3rd ed.). Thousand Oaks, CA: Sage.

Cooper, H. M. (2003). Editorial. *Psychological Bulletin, 129*(1), 3–9.

Gould, D., Kelly, D., White, I., & Chidgey, J. (2004). Training needs analysis. A literature review and reappraisal. *International Journal of Nursing Studies, 41*, 471–486.

Hart, C. (1998). *Doing a literature review.* Thousand Oaks, CA: Sage.

Kennedy, M. M. (2007). Defining a literature. *Educational Researcher, 36*(3), 139–147.

Klaus, H. (2000). Understanding scholarly and professional communication: Thesauri and database searching. In C. Bruce & P. Candy (Eds.), *Information literacy around the world* (pp. 209–222). Wagga Wagga, New South Wales: Centre for Information Studies.

Lather, P. (1999). To be of use: The work of reviewing. *Review of Educational Research, 69*(1), 2–7.

Manglitz, E. (2003). Challenging white privilege in adult education: A critical review of the literature. *Adult Education Quarterly, 53*(2), 119–134.

Merriam, S. B. (1983). Mentors and protégés: A critical review of the literature. *Adult Education Quarterly, 33*(1), 161–173.

Merriam, S. B., & Simpson, E. L. (1995). *A guide to research for educators and trainers of adults* (2nd ed.). Malabar, FL: Krieger.

Montuori, A. (2005). Literature review as creative inquiry: Reframing scholarship as a creative process. *Journal of Transformative Education, 3*(4), 374–393.

Moore, M. (2004). Editorial. *American Journal of Distance Education, 18*(3), 127–130.

Narishkin, A. S. (2005). *Short critical review: Beginning teacher needs.* Unpublished paper, University of Missouri–St. Louis.

Palmer, J. (1991). Scientists and information: I. Using cluster analysis to identify information style. *Journal of Documentation, 47*(2), 105–129.

Rocco, T. S., Stein, D., & Lee, C. (2003). An exploratory examination of the literature on age and HRD policy development. *Human Resource Development Review, 2*(2), 155–180.

Russell, C. L. (2005). An overview of the integrative research review. Retrieved January 12, 2009, from http://findarticles.com/p/articles/mi_qa4117/is_200503/ai_n13476203

Smith, T. F. (2008). Methods in identifying exemplary performance: A review of the literature and implications for HRD. *Human Resource Development Review, 7*(4), 443–468.

Torraco, R. J. (2005). Writing integrative literature reviews: Guidelines and examples. *Human Resource Development Review, 4*(3), 356–367.

Trevisan, M. S. (2004). Practical training in evaluation: A review of the literature. *American Journal of Evaluation, 25*(2), 255–274.

Troyer, J. (2007). [Literature analysis hybrid chart developed as assignment for literature review class]. Unpublished.

Wanstreet, C. E. (2006). Interaction in online learning environments: A review of the literature. *Quarterly Review of Distance Education, 7*(4), 399–411.

Ward, S. A. (1983). Knowledge structure and knowledge synthesis. In S. A. Ward & L. J. Reed (Eds.), *Knowledge structure and use: Implications for synthesis and interpretation* (pp. 19–44). Philadelphia: Temple University.

CHAPTER 12

INCREASING THE ODDS OF PUBLISHING
A QUALITATIVE MANUSCRIPT

Tonette S. Rocco, Maria S. Plakhotnik

We have served journals in several capacities as qualitative methods editor, assistant editor, editor, managing editor, reviewer, and editorial board members. We have reviewed manuscripts reporting qualitative studies that were poorly organized, contained an inadequate theoretical or conceptual framework, and presented insufficient detail about the research design. These difficulties contributed to an insufficient connection between framework, purpose, research questions, findings, and implications. Merriam and Simpson (1995) point out that a standard format of manuscript organization provides a ready-made outline for the researcher so that the researcher can get on with the work of writing up a study. The purpose of this chapter is to present a model that will guide emerging scholars in the development of a logical and coherent manuscript reporting qualitative empirical studies.

This chapter is based on a hope and a caution. The hope is that the model presented here has integrated the literature of qualitative inquiry in a way that is not prescriptive but is instead informative as a guide or technique for organizing a manuscript. Readers are cautioned that the suggestions we offer represent one among other equally valid presentation formats (Creswell, 2003; Ellis & Bochner, 1996; Merriam & Simpson, 1995). Authors who are preparing a manuscript for submission should also be guided by journal guidelines and organization of similar articles in that journal. In addition, organizing decisions should be

FIGURE 12.1. MAIN SECTIONS AND SUBSECTIONS OF A QUALITATIVE EMPIRICAL MANUSCRIPT.

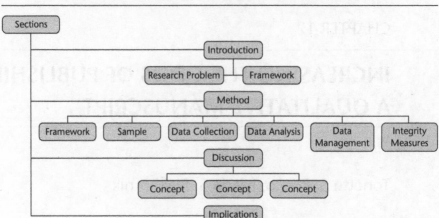

informed by the inquiry literature supporting the method and articles published using the method.

The main sections and subsections of a qualitative empirical manuscript model are illustrated in Figure 12.1. The model presents the four main sections: introduction, method, discussion, and implications. Under each main section, the corresponding subsections are listed. In this chapter, each main section is discussed in the order used in Figure 12.1 and illustrated with a model (see Figures 12.2, 12.3, 12.4, and 12.5). Figure 12.2, on the introduction, has two subsections: the research problem and a framework based in the literature. Figure 12.3, on the method, includes subsections on the conceptual framework for the method, sample, data collection, data analysis, data management, and integrity measures. Figure 12.4, on discussion, contains the logic and flow of the presentation, analysis, and meaning of the data and the relationship of the presentation to the conceptual framework, which is represented on the model as several concepts. Figure 12.5, on implications, has subsections for implications for practice, research, and policy.

Introduction

The purpose of the introduction section is to "set the stage for the entire study" (Creswell, 2003, p. 73). The introduction is divided into two subsections: the research problem and a literature review or a framework (Figure 12.2). A clear

FIGURE 12.2. INTRODUCTION.

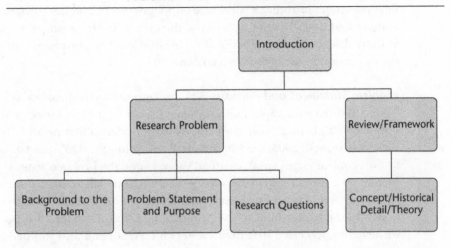

and succinct research problem subsection has three components: the background to the problem, the problem statement that ends with the purpose statement, and research questions. The research problem subsection is followed by a framework or review of the literature.

Research Problem

The research problem subsection guides the reader from the background to a problem, through to the specific problem that the study is set to address, to research questions that guide the study.

Background to the Problem. The research problem opens with a background to the problem written in one to three paragraphs that situates the study in a broader context, for example, historical, national, or international. Because the background opens the manuscript, it should also "hook the reader" (Hacker, 1998, p. 34), provoking interest and making the study relevant or important to the reader. To hook the reader, background can include staggering statistics, paradoxical or unusual facts, a surprising analogy, a quote, or other tools that engage the reader.

The background to the problem section often starts with a researcher's narrative or experiences or a story (Creswell, 2003). For example, Parrish and Taylor (2007) conducted oral history interviews to explore women's learning during the Catholic Worker Movement of the 1930s and 1940s. They opened the introduction with an account of a 1926 protest in New York City's harbor. The next paragraph introduces Nina, one of the protesters, and her story, including a quote that describes her account of the events. In the third paragraph, the authors discuss the founders of the Catholic Worker Movement and situate the movement in the broader social context.

Problem Statement and Purpose.   The background to the problem is followed by one to three paragraphs that formulate the actual problem statement, which illuminates a phenomenon, concept, issue, or dilemma that needs to be investigated (Creswell, 2003; see Chapter Ten, this volume). While the background to the problem might speak to broad social issues, the problem statement itself focuses on a specific gap in knowledge that the study will address. For example, in a phenomenological study, Kormanik (2008) explored stalled careers of white males. In the background to the problem, he briefly described a bigger issue: white males perceived that their careers hit a dead end and stopped advancing while their colleagues from minority groups continued to climb the career ladder. Furthermore, in the problem statement, Kormanik identified a specific problem that his study would address. He said that the lack of empirical evidence of this phenomenon, coupled with the fact that white males represent the majority of the U.S. workforce, created a problem that affects both employees and organization and, hence, necessitated study.

The problem statement is followed by the study's purpose. The problem statement and the purpose statement are separate components of a manuscript with different functions and should not be confused. A problem statement identifies a gap in knowledge about an issue or phenomenon; a purpose statement points to "what needs to be done" to address the gap (Merriam & Simpson, 2000, p. 19). The problem statement reflects the researcher's theoretical traditions and intended audience (Patton, 2002). For example, Kormanik (2008) uses phrases like "human capital retention or development," "stalled careers," and "workplace" (p. 51), signaling a theoretical tradition based in human capital theory and organization development. The problem statement also determines research design, analysis, and presentation of results (Patton, 2002). For example, Kormanik (2008) in his opening sentence uses "the White male backlash phenomenon" (p. 51), providing a clue early on that the study would use a phenomenological research design.

The purpose statement is considered "the most important statement in an entire research study" (Creswell, 2003, p. 87) and the first step in a study design (Patton, 2002). A good purpose statement in a qualitative study starts with a signaling phrase, for example, "The purpose of this study is . . . ," and sets out the phenomenon, research design, participants, and context (Creswell, 2003). Kormanik's (2008) purpose "is to describe the experience of middle-aged White males who perceive themselves as having a stalled career and identify its impact on the workplace" (p. 51). In this example the participants, middle-aged white males, and the context, the workplace, are named.

Research Questions. The purpose is further "refined" (Creswell, 2003, p. 88) into research questions. Creswell (2003) suggests formulating two types of questions: a central question and several related subquestions. The central question mirrors the purpose statement in a question format: "How do middle-aged White males who perceive themselves as having a stalled career experience this work transition?" (Kormanik, 2008, p. 51). Subquestions should flow from the central question and represent aspects of that question. For example, Kormanik (2008) could have had subquestions about the impact of stalled careers on the workplace or the influence of the perception of a stalled career on productivity or organizational commitment.

There is no formula to determine the number of questions needed in a qualitative study. Too many questions might lead to a loss of focus in a study, impeding the researcher's ability to see links among the results and integrate the findings (Miles & Huberman, 1994). Too few questions might limit the researcher's ability to address the study's purpose. Therefore, Creswell (2003) suggests using one or two central questions and five to seven subquestions. Miles and Huberman (1994) do not recommend using more than a dozen questions. Not all authors place research questions after the purpose; sometimes they appear just before method or early in the method. Wherever the research questions are placed, the relationship of the research questions to the purpose and problem must be evident.

Review or Framework

The introduction section also includes a subsection that presents a review of relevant empirical, theoretical, and conceptual works in the form of a literature review, a conceptual framework, or a theoretical framework (see Rocco & Plakhotnik, 2009, for a discussion of the distinctions). Frameworks share five functions: (1) to build a foundation, (2) to demonstrate how a study advances knowledge, (3) to conceptualize the study, (4) to assess research design and instrumentation, and (5) to provide a reference point for interpretation of findings (Merriam & Simpson, 2000). All five functions may not necessarily be fulfilled by the framework or review in every manuscript, but often they are, and the functions would be the same whether the form used is a literature review, theoretical framework, or conceptual framework. Regardless of the qualitative research method being used, a manuscript must contain an overview of the relevant literature.

The author must demonstrate the importance of the study by defining the main ideas and the network of relationships among them (Becker, 1998), which builds a foundation. Building a foundation requires using previous work to demonstrate linkages, illustrate trends, and provide an overview of a theory, concept, or literature. The framework is used to present existing knowledge, build a case that clearly shows the gap in what is known, demonstrate the need for the study, and clarify what the study will address. Conceptualizing a study occurs by describing previous studies, defining terms, and clarifying assumptions and limitations while citing relevant work to build a rationale for a study (Merriam & Simpson, 2000). Another function is to provide support for the research design and any instruments used in a study. A case is also made in support of the method that the researcher believes is appropriate and illustrates, citing relevant literature, why other methods are not appropriate.

The last function of the framework is to provide a reference point. The framework becomes a reference point when the other sections are connected to the framework, creating continuity and making the manuscript seamless. The literature used in the framework needs to be integrated into the discussion and implication sections to make meaningful connections and illustrate cohesion between the problem, the purpose, and the findings. For example, Alfred (2007) researched factors that hindered the transition to work and economic development of African American women who were former welfare recipients. The conceptual framework had two sections: "race and the politics of welfare reform" (p. 295) and "traditional views of women's economic dependency" (p. 296). The first part of the discussion section connected the findings with the traditional views of women's economic dependency (personal and structural) reviewed in the conceptual framework. Alfred argued that women's economic development should not be viewed as depending on either personal or structural constraints. Rather, both views should be considered in order to understand women's economic dependency. To discuss how personal or structural constraints are integrated, Alfred focused on the issues of discrimination and labor market conditions, which were contained in the first part of the conceptual framework. In the implications section, Alfred again returned to the conceptual framework, suggesting that the intersection of race, class, and gender in terms of the politics of welfare reform and women's development have been ignored in the adult education literature (to learn more about literature reviews, see Chapter Eleven, this volume).

Traditionally the framework appears after the research questions and before the method, as shown in Figures 12.1 and 12.2. However, sometimes it is necessary to merge the background to the problem with the framework in order to build the case for the problem, gradually narrowing the focus to develop a problem statement concluding with the purpose. In this instance, the background to the problem and framework are followed by the problem statement, research questions, and then the method. Some manuscripts do not have a background to the problem and instead begin with the problem statement and purpose, followed by the framework that supports the problem. In other manuscripts, the problem statement flows from the framework, which then helps to gradually refine and narrow the topic to an identifiable gap. The gap becomes the problem statement and is followed by the method (Merriam & Simpson, 2000).

Method

The purpose of the method section is to provide a rationale for and detailed description of the research design. Generally this description should take between one and four pages. The method section is divided into six subsections: (1) conceptual framework, (2) sample, (3) data collection, (4) data analysis, (5) integrity measures, and (6) data management (Figure 12.3).

The organization of the method section depends on the author's presentation logic. This might be chronological, describing the steps in the order in which they occurred, or by components, such as sample, data collection, data analysis, and data management. Organization is not as important as the systematic description of the procedures, techniques, and tools used. The central problem in manuscripts across disciplines is an inadequate discussion of the conceptual framework supporting the method and a limited description of the actual procedures, techniques, and tools used (Pratt, 2000). McKercher, Law, Weber, Song,

FIGURE 12.3. METHOD.

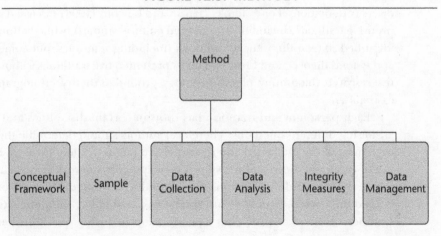

and Hsu (2007) reported that almost three-quarters of manuscript submissions in the field of hospitality and tourism were rejected due to deficiencies in research methods. An adequate and logical presentation of the research design corrects these deficiencies.

Conceptual Framework

Just as the manuscript has a framework built on literature, theory, or concepts, so does the method section. The conceptual framework supporting a method is necessary to provide the foundation for the method and does this by drawing on two types of literature. There are scholars who seek to understand and develop the epistemology, philosophy, and methodology behind the method (Creswell, 2003), while other scholars share advice on the tools and techniques to conduct the method. For example, Glaser and Strauss (1967) present the epistemology, philosophy, and methodology for grounded theory in their classic book, while Strauss and Corbin (1998) describe the actual techniques for data collection and analysis when using grounded theory. When a researcher is conducting a grounded theory study, concepts found in both books would be part of the conceptual framework.

Authors need to provide a rationale for design decisions and to ground the rationale in the extensive body of qualitative inquiry literature concerned with the specific type of method used. Many method sections and abstracts describe the study simply as "a qualitative study," citing only textbooks to support this position. Instead, the method section should clearly name the method used—for example, "a case study." *Qualitative* is not a type of method or technique, and qualitative inquiry does not have a unified theoretical or philosophical orientation. Some researchers maintain it is a paradigm or a way to see the world encompassing diverse orientations. For example, Denzin and Lincoln (1994) discussed six interpretive paradigms (including Marxist and cultural studies), while Patton (2002) identified sixteen theoretical traditions (including semiotics, phenomenology, and systems theory), and Creswell (1998) presented five traditions within qualitative research (biography, phenomenology, grounded theory, ethnography, and case study).

Each paradigm and tradition has roots in certain disciplines and aims at answering different questions. Therefore, authors should determine the appropriateness of the qualitative interpretative paradigm or theoretical tradition to the research questions and the study's conceptual framework (Creswell, 2003). Researchers should also demonstrate an understanding of the basic concepts behind the chosen qualitative interpretative paradigm or theoretical tradition (method) instead of providing a justification for using qualitative methods generically. Data collection and analysis procedures should flow from the chosen theoretical tradition.

Sample

In qualitative empirical studies, samples can be composed of people, behaviors, events, or processes (Marshall & Rossman, 1995). Patton (2002) refers to eleven types of samples, while Onwuegbuzie and Leech (2007) identify twenty-two sampling schemes. Regardless of what sampling approach is used, researchers need to provide information on their sampling decisions. "A good description of the sampling process is necessary to develop the reader's confidence that decisions were informed and well reasoned" (Rocco, 2003, p. 344). The type of sample should be named, and the rationale for the type of sample needs to be articulated. For example, the process and criteria used to select critical cases or a stratified random sample need to be discussed; demographic information about the participants should be included. Furthermore, although Patton (2002) clearly stated, "There are no rules for sample size in qualitative inquiry" (p. 244), this does not mean that no information is necessary on the size of the sample or rationale for the sample size used. Different qualitative methods suggest different sample sizes. For example, for an in-depth and detailed exploration of the essence of people's experiences with a phenomenon, phenomenological studies usually use a small sample size, such as six to ten (Morse, 2000) or six to twelve participants (Guest, Bunce, & Johnson, 2006).

The sampling information and rationale should relate to the research problem, purpose, and research questions (Morse, 2000; Onwuegbuzie & Leech, 2007). This information increases the reader's ability to understand the relationship of the participants, the data being discussed, and the usefulness of the findings to other situations and contexts. "Sampling is crucial for later analysis. . . . Your choices—whom to look at or talk with, where, when, about what, and why—all place limits on the conclusions you draw, and how confident you and others feel about them" (Miles & Huberman, 1994, p. 27). For instance, one study used a combined sample of current students and members of a professional organization. Details were lacking on the work experience of the students and the educational background of the professionals, whether the roles overlapped (students were professionals and professionals were students), or other characteristics each group possessed (work experience, educational level, age) that could influence the findings. If the students were traditional first-year undergraduates, their work-based experiences would be limited compared to nontraditional graduate students pursuing an M.B.A. Issues that could have been addressed were how the groups' experiences, demographics, and data collection tools influenced the findings.

In fact, what some consider simple demographic characteristics are considered by others to make distinctive respondents (see Gubrium & Holstein, 2001). The distinctiveness of the respondents is felt to affect data collection in terms of interviewer bias, relationship to respondents, the data that can be collected, and data analysis.

Data Collection

Qualitative data are collected from participants and others, observations and fieldwork, and documents (Patton, 2002). Data can be people focused or structure focused, as in projects, programs, and organizations, or oriented toward time (such as a critical incident) or geography (Patton, 2002). In the research design section, several questions concerning data collection must be addressed. For example, do data collection decisions clearly flow from the conceptual framework? Is the relationship between theory or perspective (for example, critical, feminist, or Afrocentric) and the particular method of data collection articulated? If a research instrument, such as an interview schedule or database for content analysis, was used, what is the relationship of the instrument to theory and the central research question? How was the instrument constructed? Was the instrument revised after a pilot test, expert review, or peer review of the instrument? How?

When discussing data collection from participants, it is insufficient to report, "Interviews were conducted." Wengraf (2001) discusses lightly, moderately, and heavily structured depth interviews. For each type of interview, specific design decisions need to be made (see Gubrium & Holstein, 2002). Different types of interviews can affect the relationship of the respondent to the interviewer and produce different types of data, changing the nature of the findings (Kvale, 1996; Rubin & Rubin, 1995; Wengraf, 2001).

Details on data collection tools should include item development, number of items, item topics, and design changes (if any) made after beginning the process. In some cases, reporting the instrument items, categories, or a sampling of items may help the reader understand the process. Details should also be provided on the actual data collection process: instrument distribution, interview time, location, and audio or video recording tools.

Data Analysis

In simple terms, to analyze data means "to draw valid meaning" from data (Miles & Huberman, 1994, p. 1) that consist of data reduction, data display, and conclusion drawing and verification. Data reduction occurs when coding data chunks, clustering, memoing, searching for themes, simplifying data into categories, and comparing the themes and categories. Data display "is an organized, compressed assembly of information that permits conclusion drawing and action" (Miles & Huberman, 1994, p. 11). Types of data displays include outlines, matrices, graphs, charts, and networks. During conclusion drawing and verification, the researcher makes decisions about which patterns, explanations, configurations, and propositions observed from the beginning of the data collection process have meaning in terms of the conceptual framework and the practical implications to the field (Miles & Huberman, 1994). Verification of these conclusions should occur throughout the process. More formal approaches include asking colleagues to review the conclusions, replicating the study with another data set, or returning to the literature (Miles & Huberman, 1994). Researchers need to report on the steps involved in how data were reduced, analyzed, and interpreted and provide a rationale for specific data analysis tools or methods. The decisions need to be grounded in the inquiry literature.

Integrity Measures

Integrity measures include the methods a researcher uses to verify plausibility or to diminish interference, contamination, or degradation of any part of the research process in order to strengthen the process. Verification is important because "the data have to be *tested* for their plausibility, their sturdiness, their 'confirmability'—that is, their *validity*." Without this step, "we are left with interesting stories . . . of unknown truth and utility" (Miles & Huberman, 1994, p. 11). Integrity might be described in terms of generalizability. However, the issue of generalizability is a philosophical one (Donmoyer, 1990). It might be useful to talk about generalizability in conducting basic research. Basic research "is knowledge for the sake of knowledge" and is in search of "formulating and testing theoretical constructs and propositions that ideally generalize across time and space" (Patton, 2002, p. 215). However, many social science disciplines are oriented toward applied research, which is interested in the application of basic theory "to real-world problems and experiences" and "research findings typically are limited to a specific time, place, and condition" (Patton, 2002, p. 217). Therefore, other standards might be more useful for the applied fields.

Quality and credibility might be better standards for ensuring the integrity of a study's design. Patton (2002) has five sets of criteria for determining the quality and credibility of qualitative research designs. Examples of one set, traditional scientific research criteria, include objectivity, validity, systematic rigor, triangulation, reliability, and generalizability. An example of another set, social construction criteria, includes subjectivity, trustworthiness, authenticity, triangulation, reflexivity, praxis, particularity, *verstehen*, and contributions to dialogue. Regardless of the criteria used, the author should explain the process and procedures used to meet the standard (Patton, 2002).

Triangulation is frequently mentioned in manuscripts as a way to establish integrity without explanation. The purpose of triangulation is to strengthen a study by using multiple forms of data, multiple researchers, multiple perspectives or theories, or multiple methods (Denzin, 1978). When multiple forms of data that have been analyzed separately and the results from each analysis are compared to the others, triangulation has occurred. There is not one right way to establish the trustworthiness of the study. However, no matter what standard is used, the author must describe the steps taken and the rationale for the steps. This description might be in a form of several sentences within the data analysis or collection descriptions or a separate subsection within the methods section.

Data Management

Data management issues are commonly discussed in sample, data collection, and data analysis subsections by the addition of a word or phrase, or they could be in a separate subsection. Data management concerns that should be addressed include answers to the following questions: How were data stored? Were interviews completely transcribed, or were decisions made to eliminate some words or phrases or to paraphrase during transcription? How were other forms of data treated? Other information might be necessary depending on the research design and actual procedures.

Discussion

The purpose of a good discussion section in an empirical qualitative study is to present the results and interpretation of the analysis of the data. The model for this section uses the word *concept* as a placeholder for the various ways this section can be organized (see Figures 12.1 and 12.4). For instance, the discussion section can use the research questions, themes, categories, and inferences as subheadings, or it can be organized by concepts presented in the introduction, usually found in the framework. As a rule of thumb, three to five subheadings divide the material discussed.

Under the heading "discussion," an advanced organizer is useful to guide the reader. This advanced organizer should include information on how the section will be divided (research questions, themes, categories, or inferences), how to understand data presentation (how participants are identified), and any other information that will help the reader. The discussion section is organized by

FIGURE 12.4. MAIN SECTION: DISCUSSION.

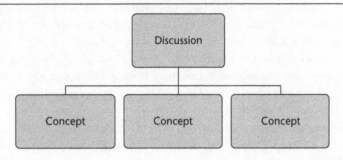

research questions, with the data presented and discussed in terms of a response to each question. When themes, categories, and inferences divide the section, defining the theme, category, or inference at the beginning of each section will increase readers' understanding. This definition or explanation can include other literature or the author's interpretation, or both. When the discussion section is organized by concepts that were introduced in the introduction, the concept should be again defined and discussed at the beginning of the subsection.

After beginning with a definition or general discussion of the organizing concept, the data are used to support the remaining discussion. There are no standard rules on how many data to use but enough should be included to provide evidence for readers that the response provided is sound. Data can be presented thematically as cases or reconstructed cases, as stories, or in other forms. If cases or stories are presented intact, they should be followed by an examination of the case or story in terms of the conceptual framework of the study. Wolcott (1994) suggests considering each detail in terms of relevance and sufficiency. Are the data relevant to the account, theme, model, or emergent theory being discussed? Are the data presented sufficient to support the analyst's contention that a theme, model, or emergent theory exists? Are the data treated consistently throughout the discussion in terms of writing style and technical considerations? If data chunks are attributed to certain participants by a pseudonym, is this done each time? In addition, is the discussion of data through comparison to the literature done in a similar fashion throughout? Also, data do not stand alone. The meaning that readers should take from the data should be introduced prior to the data. After the data have been presented, a transition is needed to the next idea or chunk of data.

Relevant literature is included and organized to build on and support the stated purpose of the paper; clarify, explain, or support the data; and illuminate the data's meaning. The interaction between the presentation of the data and the existing literature provides new insights, raises unexplored issues, and clarifies further research needs. In fact, "Qualitative evidence and qualitative data are not necessarily the same thing. . . . Data may be merely information" (Lincoln, 2002, p. 5). The researcher's paradigm, epistemology, and the method used must inform interpretation of data to qualify it as evidence. Lincoln (2002) clarifies this issue: "Evidence . . . is data brought to bear on specific questions, theories or experiences. Evidence is data with a purpose. . . . Evidence represents data to which have been added a layer—or multiple layers—of interpretation and rhetorical strategy" (p. 5). From the interpretation and rhetorical strategies, theory building can take place through exploration and explanation of the interpretation and rhetorical strategies used to turn data into evidence. The conceptual framework from which research questions are posed helps determine what constitutes evidence. It is not enough to say data are qualitative or to write that grounded theory emerged from a study. The relationship of the emergent theory to existing conceptual frameworks must be made. As Wolcott (1994) writes, "Analysis rests, ultimately, on agreed-upon knowledge, the recognition of mutually recognized properties or standards" (p. 25).

"With qualitative data one can preserve chronological flow, see precisely which events led to which consequences, and derive fruitful explanations" (Miles & Huberman, 1994, p. 1). Discovering new integrations, generating new or revised conceptual frameworks, nurturing emergent theory or models: all these and more are possible. These possibilities are lost on readers when data presentation and interpretation are given little thought. Even when the writer is using grounded theory methods (Glaser & Strauss, 1967; Strauss & Corbin, 1998), the relationship between the emergent theory or model and the existing literature should be discussed. The reader needs information provided by the researcher to understand the study's importance to the field to make a judgment as to whether successful analysis, presentation, and interpretation have occurred.

Implications

The purpose of the implications section is for the author to respond to the So What? question. The response to that question is usually organized as implications for practice, research, and policy (see Figure 12.5). Other implications might include teaching, learning, or other fields. This section may or may not be divided into subsections.

To respond to the So What? question, researchers make connections to practice, research, and policy. So what does this presentation, analysis, and interpretation of empirical data contribute to the field? What meaning can be derived from this work for practitioners, scholars, and policymakers? Answering these questions

FIGURE 12.5. IMPLICATIONS.

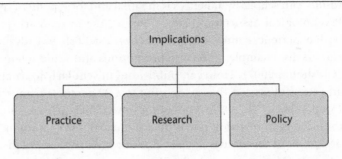

might be troublesome for both experienced and novice researchers. For example, McKercher et al. (2007) found that inability to answer the So What? question is the second top deficiency in manuscripts submitted in the field of hospitality and tourism.

In the subsection on implications for practice, the researcher should explain to readers how the findings could be used in the field. In the subsection on implications for research, the researcher suggests lines of inquiry to be pursued that further the findings from the study or answer questions raised by the study. For the subsection on policy implications, the researcher would suggest changes in organizational policies and procedures at whatever level is appropriate to the study.

The So What? question can be addressed through a figure or model illustrating the relationships between the concepts presented in the discussion section and practice, research, and policymaking to be sure that the relationships illustrated in the model are discussed in the text. Another option is to organize the implications around concepts presented in the introduction and discussion sections. Stein, Rocco, and Goldenetz (2000), in a case study of aging workers, used a table to organize policy development issues. The left column presented the themes (remaining, retiring, and returning) from the discussion section, and the top row contained concepts from the introduction section (training and development, career development, organizational development). Each cell held a policy issue. The cells could have held further research questions or even suggestions for practice.

Concluding Thoughts

"Research is central to the development of any field of study" (Merriam & Simpson, 2000, p. 1). To contribute to a field of study, research needs to be presented at conferences or meetings and, ultimately, published in peer-reviewed journals to reach wider national and international audiences. Sharing research results with scholarly audiences is the final and focal point of research (American Psychological Association, 2001). Publishing in scholarly journals also helps both experienced and novice researchers establish and advance their academic careers, for example, to receive promotions and achieve tenure-track positions (Chisholm, 2007). However, publishing in scholarly journals is a challenging and stressful process due to high (up to a 90 percent) manuscript rejection rate (McKercher et al., 2007). One of the core deficiencies in submissions that lead to such a high rejection rate is poor manuscript organization. Specifically, poor organization contributes to up to one-third (34 percent) of the manuscript rejection rate (McKercher et al., 2007).

By mentoring our students, novice scholars, and practitioner-researchers to know the language of publication, conduct rigorous research, and report their findings in an organized manuscript, we can make a difference together. For any field concerned with theory development (Lynham, 2000), with practice informing theory and theory informing practice (Jacobs, 1997; Jarvis, 1999), it is important to teach emerging scholars how to engage the field through publication.

References

Alfred, M. V. (2007). Welfare reform and black women's economic dependency. *Adult Education Quarterly, 57*(4), 293–311.

American Psychological Association. (2001). *Publication manual of the American Psychological Association* (5th ed.). Washington, DC: Author.

Becker, H. S. (1998). *Tricks of the trade: How to think about your research while you're doing it.* Chicago: University of Chicago Press.

Chisholm, K. (2007). Strategies for publishing in scholarly HRD journals. *Human Resource Development Quarterly, 18*(1), 139–147.

Creswell, J. W. (1998). *Qualitative inquiry and research design: Choosing among five traditions.* Thousand Oaks, CA: Sage.

Creswell, J. W. (2003). *Research design: Qualitative, quantitative, and mixed methods approaches* (2nd ed.). Thousand Oaks, CA: Sage.

Denzin, N. K. (1978). *The research act: A theoretical introduction to sociological methods* (2nd ed.). New York: McGraw-Hill.

Denzin, N. K., & Lincoln, Y. S. (1994). Introduction: The discipline and practice of qualitative research. In N. K. Denzin & Y. S. Lincoln (Eds.), *Handbook of qualitative research* (pp. 1–29). Thousand Oaks, CA: Sage.

Donmoyer, R. (1990). Generalizability and the single-case study. In E. W. Eisner & A. Peshkin (Eds.), *Qualitative inquiry in education: The continuing debate* (pp. 175–200). New York: Teachers College Press.

Ellis, C., & Bochner, A. P. (Eds.). (1996). *Composing ethnography: Alternative forms of qualitative writing.* Walnut Creek, CA: AltaMira Press.

Glaser, B. G., & Strauss, A. L. (1967). *The discovery of grounded theory: Strategies for qualitative research.* New York: Aldine de Gruyter.

Gubrium, J. F., & Holstein, J. A. (Eds.). (2001). *Handbook of interview research: Context and method.* Thousand Oaks, CA: Sage.

Guest, G., Bunce, A., & Johnson, L. (2006). How many interviews are enough? An experiment with data saturation and variability. *Field Methods, 18*(1), 59–82.

Hacker, D. (1998). *The Bedford handbook: Instructor's annotated edition* (5th ed.). Boston: Bedford Books.

Jacobs, R. (1997). HRD partnerships for integrating HRD research and practice. In R. A. Swanson & E. F. Holton (Eds.), *Human resource development research handbook: Linking research to practice* (pp. 47–64). San Francisco: Berrett-Koehler.

Jarvis, P. (1999). *The practitioner-researcher: Developing theory from practice.* San Francisco: Jossey-Bass.

Kormanik, M. B. (2008). The stalled career: Addressing an organizational undiscussable. *Advances in Human Resource Development, 10*(1), 50–69.

Kvale, S. (1996). *InterViews: An introduction to qualitative research interviewing.* Thousand Oaks, CA: Sage.

Lincoln, Y. S. (2002, November). *On the nature of qualitative evidence.* Paper presented at the Association for the Study of Higher Education, Sacramento, CA.

Lynham, S. A. (2000). Theory building in the human resource development profession. *Human Resource Development Quarterly, 11*(2), 159–178.

Marshall, C., & Rossman, G. B. (1995). *Designing qualitative research* (2nd ed.). Thousand Oaks, CA: Sage.

McKercher, B., Law, B., Weber, K., Song, H., & Hsu, C. (2007). Why referees reject manuscripts. *Journal of Hospitality and Tourism Research, 31*(4), 455–470.

Merriam, S. B., & Simpson, E. L. (1995). *A guide to research for educators and trainers of adults.* Malabar, FL: Krieger.

Merriam, S. B., & Simpson, E. L. (2000). *A guide to research for educators and trainers of adults* (Updated 2nd ed.). Malabar, FL: Krieger.

Miles, M. B., & Huberman, A. M. (1994). *An expanded sourcebook: Qualitative data analysis* (2nd ed.). Thousand Oaks, CA: Sage.

Morse, J. M. (2000). Determining sample size. *Qualitative Health Research, 10*(3), 3–5.

Onwuegbuzie, A. J., & Leech, N. L. (2007). A call for qualitative power analysis. *Quality and Quantity, 41,* 105–121.

Parrish, M. M., & Taylor, E. W. (2007). Seeking authenticity: Women and learning in the Catholic Worker Movement. *Adult Education Quarterly, 57*(3), 221–247.

Patton, M. Q. (2002). *Qualitative research and evaluation methods* (3rd ed.). Thousand Oaks, CA: Sage.

Pratt, M. G. (2000). *Some thoughts on publishing qualitative research.* Research Methods Forum. Retrieved February 6, 2003, from http://www.aom.pace.edu/rmd/pratt_files/pratt.htm

Rocco, T. S. (2003). Forum. Shaping the future: Writing up the method on qualitative studies. *Human Resource Development Quarterly, 14*(3), 343–350.

Rocco, T. S., & Plakhotnik, M. S. (2009). Instructor's corner: Literature reviews, conceptual frameworks, and theoretical frameworks: Terms, functions, and distinctions. *Human Resource Development Review, 8*(1), 120–130.

Rubin, H. J., & Rubin, I. S. (1995). *Qualitative interviewing: The art of hearing data.* Thousand Oaks, CA: Sage.

Stein, D., Rocco, T. S., & Goldenetz, K. A. (2000). Age and the university workplace: A case study of remaining, retiring, or retaining older workers. *Human Resource Development Quarterly, 11*(1), 61–80.

Strauss, A., & Corbin, J. (1998). *Basics of qualitative research: Grounded theory procedures and techniques* (2nd ed.). Thousand Oaks, CA: Sage.

Wengraf, T. (2001). *Qualitative research interviewing: Biographic narrative and semi-structured methods.* Thousand Oaks, CA: Sage.

Wolcott, H. F. (1994). *Transforming qualitative data: Description, analysis, and interpretation.* Thousand Oaks, CA: Sage.

CHAPTER 13

INCREASING THE LIKELIHOOD OF PUBLISHING QUANTITATIVE MANUSCRIPTS

Isadore Newman, Carole Newman

Good quantitative research has three basic characteristics regardless of the topic: consistency among the components, a logical trail of evidence, and transparency, which is a clear presentation of how the data were selected, collected, coded, analyzed, and interpreted. The thread that ties these characteristics together is consistency, which ensures that the warrants provide reasonable or adequate evidence and the conclusions are justifiable and make sense to readers.

This chapter provides helpful guidelines for the development of quantitative studies that are likely to lead to publication. The emphasis is on the importance of having consistency among the title, the purpose, the problem, and the research hypotheses of the study being described. There must also be consistency among these elements and the research design, the statistical analyses, and the discussion, conclusions, and implications. We provide a brief discussion of the major components as they relate to what should be considered when submitting a quantitative research article to a scholarly journal. The title, purpose, problem, general hypotheses, research design, sources of data, operational definitions, sampling procedures, measurement, analyses, results, and the discussion, conclusions, and implications must be carefully considered and checked for consistency.

Framing Your Article for Review

This section presents a discussion of the importance of consistency of the title, purpose, and problem.

Title

A clearly written title provides the researcher and readers with the frame of the study. It can also be very helpful to people who are searching or reviewing the research literature. The title should be written first, and as the study develops, it may be rewritten many times to reflect adjustments or refinements that have been made in the study. Frequently it is also one of the last pieces rewritten as the researcher considers if the final version of the title provides the most appropriate lens for preparing readers to view the study. A well-written title also serves as an advanced organizer for readers and can be thought of as a summary of the summary, in that it conceptualizes and captures the essence of the manuscript.

Titles are not written in stone; they must remain flexible and open to change as needed. As the concept of the manuscript becomes better defined, the title needs to reflect any research modifications that occur during the project's development. The author needs to review the guidelines of the journals being considered for submission to make sure the journal requirements for titles and headings are followed. Following these guidelines is crucial in the acceptance process.

Purpose

The purpose deals with the why of the study, answering the "So what?" question and explaining the importance of the study. Sometimes the term *purpose* is used interchangeably when discussing the study's need or significance. This discussion is usually connected to relevant literature, demonstrating analytical thinking about the previous research and using the literature to build arguments and warrants for the research being submitted for publication. A well-presented literature base also adds credibility to the researcher by letting the reviewers know that the researcher is familiar with the topic, the work that has been done in the field, and what else should be done. The literature review gets expanded in the section that is often entitled "Introduction/Background of the Study."

A good literature review should include the primary sources, classic studies, and the most current and relevant work. A strong recommendation is that the researcher takes the time to read the primary sources that support the need for the current research. In a similar manner, the author can use theories to support the research by linking the theory to the research questions and the need. If someone asks, "Why is it worthwhile to do this study?" the purpose statement is the answer. If a compelling answer cannot be provided, the study probably should be abandoned or reconceptualized before it is carried out and submitted for publication. In simple terms, the purpose explains why the study is needed.

The *why* can be explained based on empirical arguments or theoretical needs. It should be made clear how the study makes a contribution to the field. An example of types of purposes can be found in Newman, Ridenour, Newman, and DeMarco (2003), which presents at least nine purposes for doing research: (1) improving prediction; (2) increasing the knowledge base; (3) having a social, organizational, or institutional impact; (4) measuring change or improvement; (5) helping others understand complex phenomena; (6) testing and evaluating new ideas and theories; (7) generating new hypotheses and theories; (8) informing multiple stakeholders; and (9) understanding past events.

The following statement of purpose was constructed to justify the need for the development of a rating scale to measure the quality of literacy in preschool classroom environments (Lindemer, 2006): "At the time of this study there were minimal or no validity estimates reported on [scales] that had good psychometric estimates [to assess preschool literacy environments]." Obviously, this is a statement of a need that existed in the field of early literacy development and presents a reason that this study will add to the body of knowledge. Lindemer also offers an additional statement of the need for her research: "The quality of preschool literacy instruction is crucial to children's later academic success." She explains, "There is a need to provide quality literacy experiences. . . . Preschool is a vital time for literacy learning. . . . Preschool literacy development is complex and requires knowledgeable educators in order to foster optimal literacy development." Lindemer then references Hallahan and Kauffman (2005), as support for her contention that it is important to look at the learning environment to improve students' learning. She does this by referencing Hallahan and Kauffman (2005): "Often problems in achievement are directed at a child, regarding his or her lack of learning instead of focusing on the implications of the learning environment (Lindemer, 2006, p. 7).

This is an example of how one researcher justified the need for her study, was able to use recent literature to support her argument, and was able to answer the question of why the study was needed. More specifically, she demonstrated why there was a need for the development of a reliable and valid instrument to measure preschool literacy environments. As the example demonstrates, the *why* should be supported with relevant literature that helps to make the case for the need to conduct the research.

Problem

The problem explains *what* the researcher will do to carry out the study. It follows the purpose and therefore tells what is going to be done to address the identified need. To some extent, it presents the objectives of the study.

To continue with the example, Lindemer (2006) indicates the problem was "to develop an evaluation scale that measures the quality of the literacy environment in preschool center-based programs . . . and gather validity estimates for this scale. The types of validity estimates include: content, expert judge and concurrent validity." This is an example of the problem of her study. It informs readers *what* she will be doing to address the stated need and is consistent with the purpose and title: "The Development of a Rating Scale to Measure the Quality of Preschool Literacy Environments: A Validity Study."

The process is iterative. The researcher must look at the purpose and the problem and make sure they align. Then the researcher should go back to the title and make sure the purpose and problem are reflected in the title. In some cases, the title may change, or the purpose or problem may change. The key is consistency among the title, purpose, problem, and research hypotheses.

Research Method

In this section we present a discussion of the various elements needed in a well-developed method section of a manuscript.

General Research Hypotheses

The research hypotheses directly follow from the problem and should clearly reflect the statement of the problem. For example, if the problem statement says, "This study will investigate the difference between males and females on self-efficacy" (that is, what the study is going to do), the general research hypothesis might say, "There is a difference between males and females on self-efficacy." This becomes expanded in the design section, where there is the potential to list a number of specific research hypotheses that assess the general question and are tied to the specific statistical techniques. For example, specific research questions tied to the general question might add statements such as, "independent of age," "independent of education," "independent of years in school," and so on. Once again, the consistency of the title, purpose, problem, and the research hypotheses is necessary for good research.

Research Design

The research design follows from the problem and the research hypotheses. It takes into consideration the unit of analyses, why and to whom you want to generalize, subjects, context, location, and so on, and also considers data collection procedures, sampling procedures, coding issues, instrumentation, and analyses.

A good strategy when considering what the research design should be is to begin by determining if the research hypothesis reflects a causal or relational question. If it is causal, the researcher needs to consider using true experimental designs or sometimes quasi-experimental designs. If the research study is investigating independent variables that cannot be manipulated, then relational questions are the only ones that can be investigated. The researcher must decide what type of design is most capable of reflecting the purpose of the study and answering the research questions.

We believe a good way to conceptualize the design that will be used is by looking at Campbell and Stanley's (1963) classification of research designs, which presents the strengths and weaknesses of each in terms of the design's internal and external validity. It is virtually always preferential to have the gold standard, a true experimental design, but this is very difficult to achieve in an applied setting that usually has many variables not under the control of the researcher.

The next preferable type of design is quasi-experimental; some approach true experimental design, and some designs are very weak. Determining the strength of the design requires identifying the threats to internal and external validity as related to the study and explaining why it was the most preferable design choice given the specific circumstances.

If at all possible, we strongly suggest avoiding the use of preexperimental designs, which are very weak and are probably less likely to get published. These designs have virtually no internal validity, so no causal statements can be made about the research findings.

The final type of design is ex post facto, which has an independent variable (predictor variable, sometimes called an assigned variable or attribute) that cannot be manipulated. Common examples of these variables are gender, race, socioeconomic status, IQ, ability levels, attitude, and demographics. These variables sometimes reflect the most interesting and important questions for social science researchers. However, since the independent variable cannot be manipulated, one cannot legitimately assume causation and can make statements only about relationships among the variables, especially within a single study.

There are three types of ex post facto research: ex post facto research without hypotheses (the weakest in terms of internal validity), ex post facto research with hypotheses, and ex post facto research with alternative hypotheses (generally considered to be the strongest of the three). We strongly recommend that researchers use this third type, which has hypotheses and alternative hypotheses, because it attempts to control for some of the confounding alternative explanations, such as effects due to gender, ethnicity, or socioeconomic status. Reviewers tend to consider research that has taken into consideration alternative explanations, especially when based on good logic, theory, or research data, to be much more desirable than just the reporting of simple correlations.

Controlling for the possible alternative explanations makes the analyses and the logic of the warrants being used to support the conclusions much more transparent. For example, in a study attempting to explore the relationship between self-efficacy and achievement, an alternative explanation might be that ethnicity or gender is confounded with self-efficacy; this confounding may be the rival hypothesis that the researcher needs to investigate and attempt to control.

A second example is that student involvement accounts for a significant amount of unique variance in predicting achievement when controlling for ethnicity, SAT scores, and gender. This hypothesis controls for the alternative explanation that student achievement is not uniquely due to involvement, but can be attributed to ethnicity, SAT scores, or gender, or some combination of these.

Several methods can be used to attempt to control for rival or alternative hypotheses. In the first example, the researcher can covary ethnicity and gender to determine if self-efficacy accounts for a significant amount of variance in achievement when holding the two variables constant. Another approach could be blocking on gender and ethnicity, or one could use propensity analyses to statistically attempt to equate groups, approximating what exists in a true experimental design. These three approaches, and others, are attempts to control for alternative explanations. A good strategy to help the researcher decide which variables to control for is to rely on a review of the relevant literature or theories to identify the variables that may produce confounding or alternative explanations. To improve the likelihood of publication, avoid the use of ex post facto research that has no hypotheses or no tests of alternative hypotheses.

Sources of Data

In this section, the researcher identifies the types of data and the unit of analyses that will be used in the study, making sure they are appropriate for the problem and the research questions. The researcher needs to clearly indicate the characteristics of the population, how well the sample is representative of that population, a description of where the data will be collected (schools, public records, or online, for example), and how the data are being collected: by survey, interview, observations, documentation, or something else. Time schedules for data collection and who is doing the collecting, and what training will be provided for data collectors, also need to be detailed. Whenever possible, it is always a good idea to pilot data collection to determine if the procedures designed for the research project are sufficient to gather the necessary information.

Operational Definitions

It is highly desirable and necessary to define the independent (predictor variables) and dependent variables (criterion or outcome variables) in operational terms. That is, the variables need to be defined in terms of how they are being measured or assessed. This serves to clarify for reviewers and the readers what is being conceptualized and increases the likelihood that all readers will interpret the study from a similar frame and using common definitions.

An example of why operational definitions are needed can be understood by examining a hypothesis that states, "There is a relationship between intelligence and grade point average." Before a reader could appropriately interpret any findings related to this hypothesis, he or she would first have to know how intelligence is operationally defined. If it is based on teacher judgment, there would potentially be an entirely different relationship than if intelligence was being defined by scores on a standardized IQ test such as the Stanford-Binet or the WISC. Yet another relationship could potentially exist if intelligence is defined by ratings on a nonverbal IQ test, and still other relationships can exist depending on how grade point average (GPA) is operationally defined. For instance, does the GPA include nonacademic performance such as attendance, attitude, extracurricular activities, and participation, among others? As this example demonstrates, it is critical to operationally define how the variables under investigation will be measured in order to decrease potential misunderstandings of what it means when data results suggest that a relationship exists. To increase clarity and the accurate interpretation of research results, the hypothesis should state that there is a relationship between intelligence, as measured by such and such, and GPA, as measured by such and such. In an article, this information is generally provided in the design and methods section.

Sampling Procedures

Sampling procedures need to be described in detail to inform readers of how and why the specific sample was selected. These procedures can have a direct effect on the generalizations and the causal interpretations that can be made. Sampling procedures can be classified into two major broad categories: probabilistic and nonprobabilistic. All probabilistic sampling uses some type of random procedure, such as simple random sampling or stratified random sampling, and these procedures should be described in detail. Some examples of nonprobabilistic procedures are purposive sampling, convenience sampling, quota sampling, and sometimes cluster sampling. Some of the weaknesses of the nonprobabilistic sampling can be lessened by replication of the research study and subsequent sampling (Kerlinger, 1986; Kerlinger & Lee, 2000; Newman & McNeil, 1998).

Measurement and Instrumentation

All studies that have measurement or assessment components should report the reliability and validity estimates for all instruments used. No test or instrument can be said to be reliable or valid, only that there are estimates of the instrument's reliability and validity (from good to poor), generally reported by some sort of correlation coefficient. As a rule of thumb, the minimum acceptable reliability score when making group predictions is approximately .65 ($r = .65$). For individual predictions, the rule of thumb is that the reliability estimate should be .8 or higher ($r = .8$). Also, a general rule of thumb is that the validity coefficient will not exceed the square root of the reliability coefficient. In educational and psychological research, the validity coefficients of most instruments generally do not exceed $r = .4–.6$. In educational and psychological research, when the N (number of subjects) is large (more than three hundred), a validity estimate that falls within this range is considered to be high.

Since we can only estimate the reliability and validity of research instruments, the more estimates we have, the more comfortable we are with the accuracy of the estimate. It needs to be remembered that reliability and validity studies are specific to each research project. They are related to the specific subjects, location, data collection procedures, time, and other parameters of the research.

Types of reliability that should be considered are test-retest, equivalent forms, and internal consistency. Types of validity include face, expert judge, content or logical validity, concurrent validity, and construct validity. It is desirable to have more than one type of reliability and validity for a research study (Newman, Newman, Brown, & McNeely, 2006; Kerlinger, 1986; Johnson & Christensen, 2000).

Analyses

The type of analyses being used must be consistent with the purpose and the problem and must report appropriate evidence that is defensible and will support or disconfirm the hypotheses while taking into consideration alternative explanations. Reviewers generally find it valuable to have the researcher identify the underlying assumptions of the reported analyses, how the assumptions were checked, and what, if anything, was done to correct for any violations. This tends to produce a halo effect because the researcher appears to be both familiar with the analyses and careful in their use. Some of the assumptions and corrections that should be reported or checked include a description of the distribution, the accuracy of data entry and how missing data are handled, outliers and multivariate outliers, multicollinearity, normality and multivariate normality, linearity, and homogeneity.

It is always desirable to report descriptive statistics such as frequencies, means, standard deviations, and simple correlations. If an inferential statistic is being used, one should defend the appropriateness of that particular test or tests (F-test, t-test, chi square, or multivariate tests). When using inferential statistics, researchers should be sure to identify the appropriate concerns for violations of assumptions.

Researchers using inferential statistics should identify the alpha level as well as the actual p value. Along with the alpha level, they should also identify directionality and explain the rationale for using a one- or two-tailed test. We also suggest that a power analysis is highly desirable for obtaining an estimate of a Type II error and the effect size or an interval estimate. In terms of the analyses, we also strongly recommend an estimate of replicability. This is infrequently done but is always perceived as desirable. Unfortunately, replicability gets confused with statistical significance, and although the two are related, they are not the same.

Statistical significance gives an estimate of the probability that a result is not due to chance at some specified alpha level. For example, if the alpha level is .05, we can say that we are 95 percent confident that a significant result is not due to chance, or we could say that only five times in one hundred would a difference as large as one found exist in a sample when there is no difference in the population. This does not mean that if we found significance at the .05 level and if we took one hundred samples that 95 percent of those samples would also be found to be significant. Actually (depending on the N size), if we took one hundred samples, only 50 percent of them would be significant at the .05 level (Walker, 2006; Newman et al., 2006; Posavac, 2002; Greenwald, Gonzalez, Harris, & Guthrie, 1996). Replicability would provide an estimate of how many of the one hundred samples would be likely to be significant.

To increase the likelihood of getting published, we recommend that researchers use the most appropriate cutting-edge statistical techniques. Looking at the most prestigious research journals that have recently published articles on similar topics can be helpful for identifying these techniques. When appropriate, methods such as multiple regression analysis, multivariate regression analysis, multivariate analysis of variance, multivariate analysis of covariance, multiple discriminant analysis, multidimensional scaling, structural equation modeling, hierarchical linear modeling, log-linear analyses, propensity analysis, and network analysis, among others, should be considered for data analysis. These types of procedures tend to produce a halo effect on reviewers. Also, reviewers tend to prefer multiple methods when they are used appropriately. However, it is important to make sure that whatever methods are used, the use is well justified.

Presenting and Interpreting Findings

In this section, we discuss how to write up results, interpretation of findings, and the implications.

Results

The results section is written very mechanically. The best way of thinking about this is to develop the tables necessary to report the results and then write a paragraph or two describing each of the tables. Examples of tables that are generally needed include descriptive tables of both the sample and outcomes, and inferential tables, such as tables of analysis of variance, regression analyses, and multivariate analyses. (See the most current American Psychological Association manual for illustrations of how these tables can be organized; APA, 2010).

Tables should be constructed for each appropriate hypothesis and should report information such as the following: tests of significance, effect size, significance or nonsignificance, p value, degrees of freedom, corrections for multiple comparisons, sample size, power estimates, replicability estimates if possible, and partial regression weights or beta weights.

Researchers need to examine, study, and analyze published articles in the journal that will receive the submission to see how that journal formats the tables and figures. This information can then be used as a template to prepare the data presentation in a manner that is more likely to be well received. However, if the journal's format used does not facilitate readers' understanding of the findings, consider modifying that format or using another acceptable format that better communicates the results.

It is also important to look for and present patterns in data. This facilitates the communications of the findings to readers who may not be as familiar with the implications that can be drawn from these patterns. The emphasis should be on the clarity of presenting the research findings.

Discussion, Conclusions, and Implications

In this final section, the researcher needs to provide a clear summary of the major findings of the research hypotheses and connect these results to the purpose and problem of the study. The conclusions provided should be grounded in the relevant research literature and in the warrants presented and may include possible reasons that certain hypotheses were found to be nonsignificant. This section should also discuss the delimitations (the scope of the study), the limitations (the weaknesses of the study), and generalizations that can be made. The generalizations obviously will be dependent on the representativeness of the sample and the logic and internal validity of the design. Threats to the internal validity should be suggested as alternative explanations to the findings that need to be considered.

Another component of this section should be the implications that can be drawn from the findings. These should be tied to theory, the literature, and potential practice and should deal with the purpose of doing the study, previously presented as the why or the need. Although the conclusions are directly based on and do not go past the research findings (the objective data and results), the implications go beyond the conclusions and require the researcher to imply what the findings might mean. For example, in the conclusions section, the researcher may state, "The research strongly supports the theoretical position of . . . ," or ". . . hypotheses were supported." Or it may state, "The research disconfirms the predictions of the theory." The implications statement would then require the researcher to suggest how these findings may be important to the field, the practice, and the practitioner, as well as provide suggestions of the research that needs to follow. The conclusions are therefore directly related to the data, while the implications go past the data but are logically tied to the findings. Finally, the discussion, conclusions, and implications section needs to reflect and be consistent with the purpose and problem presented in the first sections.

Ethical Standards in Collecting and Reporting Data

Finally, the researcher is responsible for adhering to ethical standards in data collection and reporting. The American Educational Research Association (2005) has published these standards and has made them available online. Virtually no journal will consider a manuscript for publication unless there is indication that these standards have been followed (see http://www.aera.net/aboutaera/?id=222). These standards include concerns about consent agreements, data collection and reporting, and conflict of interest, as well as other issues (American Educational Research Association, 2006; APA Publications and Communications Board Working Group on Journal Article Reporting Standards, 2008).

Conclusion

Good quantitative research asks a question, tells how the question will be answered, and then answers the question using warrants that are consistent and transparent. This logical flow will increase the likelihood that a manuscript will be published.

References

American Educational Research Association. (2005). *Ethical standards of the American Educational Research Association.* Washington, DC: Author.

American Educational Research Association. (2006). Standards for reporting on empirical social science research in AERA publications. *Educational Researcher, 35*(6), 33–40.

American Psychological Association. (2010). *Publication manual of the American Psychological Association* (6th ed.). Washington, DC: Author.

APA Publications and Communications Board Working Group on Journal Article Reporting Standards. (2008). Reporting standards for research in psychology: Why do we need them? What might they be? *American Psychologist, 63,* 839–851.

Campbell, D., & Stanley, J. (1963). *Experimental and quasi-experimental designs for research.* Skokie, IL: Rand McNally.

Greenwald, A. G., Gonzalez, R., Harris, R. J., & Guthrie, D. (1996). Effect sizes and *p* values: What should be reported and what should be replicated? *Psychophysiology, 33*(2), 175–183.

Hallahan, D. P., & Kauffman, J. M. (2005). Exceptional learners: Introduction to special education (10th ed.). Needham Heights, MA: Allyn & Bacon.

Johnson, B., & Christensen, L. (2000). *Educational research: Quantitative and qualitative approaches.* Needham Heights, MA: Allyn and Bacon.

Kerlinger, F. N. (1986). *Foundations of behavioral research.* Fort Worth, TX: Harcourt.

Kerlinger, F. N., & Lee, H. (2000). *Foundations of behavioral research* (4th ed.). Fort Worth, TX: Harcourt.

Lindemer, C. L. (2006). *The development of a rating scale to measure the quality of preschool literacy environments: A validity study.* Unpublished doctoral dissertation, University of Akron, Akron, Ohio.

Newman, I., & McNeil, K. (1998). *Conducting survey research in the social sciences.* Lanham, MD: University Press of America.

Newman, I., Newman, C., Brown, R., & McNeeley, S. (2006). *Conceptual statistics for beginners* (3rd ed.). Lanham, MD: University Press of America.

Newman, I., Ridenour, C., Newman, C., & DeMarco, G., Jr. (2003). A typology of research purposes and its relationship to mixed methods. In A. Tashakkori & C. Teddlie (Eds.), *The handbook of mixed methods in social and behavioral research* (pp. 166–188). Thousand Oaks, CA: Sage.

Posavac, E. J. (2002). Using *p* values to estimate the probability of statistically significant replications. *Journal of Understanding Statistics, 1*(2), 101–112.

Walker, D. A. (2006). The statistically significant exact replication method: A programming and conceptual extension. *Mid-Western Educational Researcher, 19*(4), 7–11.

CHAPTER 14

WRITING RESEARCH ARTICLES USING MIXED METHODS

Methodological Considerations to Help You Get Published

Isadore Newman, David Newman, Carole Newman

Any good refereed research that is publishable requires logical and methodological consistency that is transparent to readers and has strong, logical warrants that are clearly connected to the conclusions. Strategies that the researcher used to address these considerations are generally presented in the method section of the research report or article.

Writing the methods section is often easier when the research is clearly quantitative (Campbell & Stanley, 1963) or qualitative. It generally becomes more complicated when mixed methods are used because the researcher must understand and explain why the specific quantitative and qualitative procedures were selected, how they were carried out, and how they were integrated to provide the additional information and insights that can be gleaned only when both are used.

For example, in discussing quantitative methods, the researcher must describe the design, why it is appropriate for the study, its strength and weaknesses in terms of internal and external validity, the instrumentation, sampling techniques, and the data analyses, with the appropriate assumptions (as described in Chapter

Special thanks go to Carolyn Ridenour and Tonette Rocco for their careful reading and suggestions that improved this chapter.

Thirteen, this volume). Similarly, the researcher also must write a component on the qualitative methods used that deals with the types of sampling techniques, type of qualitative study (case study or ethnographic, for example), and why it is most appropriate for the investigation. The article also must describe the data collecting procedures and how the data will be analyzed (see Chapter Twelve, this volume). The legitimation techniques for both the qualitative-quantitative sections need to be considered and described. In addition, the researcher has to make inferences explaining how the qualitative-quantitative methods inform each other, which are referred to in the four general design types presented in this chapter as meta inferences. A meta inference is the judgment a researcher makes about the data that is based on the results of more than one study. In mixed methods, the researcher is being informed by both the qualitative and quantitative aspects of the research and is then able to make meta inferences from the careful consideration of the information provided by both.

Regardless of which design is used, consideration must be given to which of the legitimating techniques are necessary and appropriate for that particular study. The techniques selected are specific to the study, not to the type of design used. This is analogous to Campbell and Stanley's (1963) discussion of approximately twenty general research design types. They indicate that the designs they presented are examples of an infinite number of designs, and for each, one has to ask the same questions about internal and external validity (legitimation considerations). These techniques are guideposts or questions that the researcher needs to ask when planning any study. They are not specific to any one design; they are applicable to all research. The questions are there to help sensitize the researcher to what needs to be considered when planning research.

The legitimating techniques presented in this chapter are in essence a checklist (similar to Campbell and Stanley's internal and external validity checklist) to guide the researcher's thought process, so he or she can ask, "Should I collect these types of data?" "Can I control for these things?" This laundry list of topics is what we believe should be taught in a research course so a novice can decide whether to use specific data collection or verification methods and how to do so. It is also what a reviewer looks for in the methods section to determine if a submitted research manuscript meets acceptable academic or scholarly standards.

We are not suggesting that all of the strategies presented in this chapter should be incorporated in any one study. We are recommending that writers should reflect on which techniques are appropriate to the purpose of the study, determine what they would like the reader to be able to infer, and determine if the resources are available to do what is needed to improve the trustworthiness of the article. If the resources are not available but the researcher believes that one or more of the techniques should be used, this can be stated in the manuscript as a limitation of the study, and this topic can be suggested for future research. Again, the suggested legitimation techniques are there to help the researcher reflect on and become sensitized to considerations that are important in mixed methods. Using these techniques makes the methodological section more transparent to the reviewer and the intended audience by presenting a clear description of what the author did to increase the integrity of the study.

Purpose of This Chapter

Mixed methodology is an integrated approach that has increased in use and desirability over the past twenty years. This is evidenced from the number of articles, books, and journals dedicated to using mixed methods (Tashakkori & Newman, 2010). In fact, the largest and fastest Special Interest Group (SIG) of the American Educational Research Association (AERA) is the Mixed Methods SIG. Because of this increased acceptance of using mixed methodology, mixed methods researchers have a better chance of getting published today than they did just a few years ago.

However, just saying a study is using mixed methods is not sufficient. Reviewers look for the presentation of a clear structure in the methods section to explain how the qualitative and quantitative methods are being used and integrated. The primary objective of this chapter is to present the concepts that will facilitate the development of a mixed methods section of a research article: examples of research designs, legitimation techniques that help to estimate the trustworthiness (credibility) of the research, and how all of this must be consistent and aligned with the purpose of the research.

Despite its increased use, neither the AERA (2006) nor the American Psychological Association (APA) (APA Publications and Communications Board Working Group on Journal Article Reporting Standards, 2008) suggests standards for publication of mixed methods research. However, several authors in the mixed research field provide some useful guidelines (Tashakkori & Teddlie, 2003; Creswell & Plano Clark, 2006; Onwuegbuzie & Johnson, 2008). The current position on mixed methods is not to deal with qualitative and quantitative methods as a dichotomy, but to view them as existing on a continuum (Tashakkori & Teddlie, 1998; Newman & Benz, 1998; Ridenour & Newman, 2008).

This chapter does not present an argument for qualitative, quantitative, or mixed methods, nor does it discuss the underlying assumptions of each. Rather, the intent is to present a pragmatic set of techniques and procedures that will facilitate the development of a strong methods section, which will improve the likelihood of publication.

We emphasize how to improve the trustworthiness of the research as presented in the methods section through the use of a variety of legitimation techniques and design considerations that increase the credibility of the research. The credibility is dependent on the legitimation of the selected qualitative and quantitative methods and the appropriate integration of both. Therefore, this chapter presents a rather extensive list of techniques that add to the legitimacy, credibility, and trustworthiness required for both the qualitative and quantitative research components. Not all of these elements are used in all research, but the more that are appropriately included, the stronger is the integrity of the research design and the conclusions that can be drawn from the data.

It is also critical to remember that in mixed methods research, as in all other research, there must be alignment between the purpose, problem, research questions, and methods that best reflect the questions of interest (Newman, Ridenour, Newman, & DeMarco, 2003; Chapter Thirteen, this volume). When the purpose of a study requires the use of both qualitative and quantitative data to answer the research questions, appropriate methods from each paradigm collect the data, which are then integrated through meta inferences drawn from the gathered information to reach a conclusion. Without logical alignment throughout the research process, the researcher will not be able to provide a convincing argument that the research is trustworthy and suitable for publication.

Philosophical Assumptions Underlying Research Methodologies

There are different assumptions that underlie quantitative and qualitative research designs. Generally the underlying philosophical assumption associated with qualitative research is constructivism (also referred to interpretivism or naturalism). This philosophy is based on the assumption that the interpretation of observations is dependent on the values and interests of the investigator. The underlying philosophical assumption often associated with quantitative research is positivism or postpositivism (Newman & Benz, 1998; Ridenour & Newman, 2008). Positivism assumes that research is based on the scientific methods employed in the hard sciences and it is a method to get at the "truth." It consists of hypotheses testing and assumes that there is an objective reality that can be estimated. Postpositivism is a revision of positivism in that it acknowledges that one cannot measure things with absolute certainty. While the intent is still to get an objective estimate of reality (truth), it recognizes that there is always some measurement error. These different philosophies are generally viewed as being diametrically opposed. This view is especially true when comparing constructivism, which tends to be inductive, to positivism, which is more likely to use deductive techniques. Mixed methods designs frequently assume pragmatism (Tashakkori & Teddlie, 2008; Onwuegbuzie & Johnson, 2008) or postpositivism (Newman & Benz, 1998; Ridenour & Newman, 2008) as the philosophical framework. Since the designs have different philosophical underpinnings, researchers need to be cautious about the underlying assumptions they make about the data selected, the techniques used to collect the data, and the inferences they want to make based on the data. Here too there needs to be consistency among the research questions, the underlying philosophical assumptions, and the techniques employed, regardless of whether the research is quantitative, qualitative, or mixed (see Chapter Thirteen, this volume). Keeping all of these considerations in mind can get quite complicated.

Typology of Purpose

A good mixed methods research project requires that the qualitative and quantitative legitimacy components listed in Figure 14.1 are incorporated whenever appropriate to help in addressing the intended purpose of the research. Mixed methods researchers are integrative in that they use the methodologies that best help them answer the questions of interest. Newman et al. (2003) developed a typology of ten broad research purposes that are not independent of each other:

- Prediction
- Adding to the knowledge base (which includes confirming and replication)
- Having a personal, social, institutional, or organizational impact that includes such things as setting policy, improving practices, and influencing change
- Measuring change
- Understanding complex phenomena
- Testing new ideas, including testing hypotheses or new innovations
- Generating ideas, which include generating theory and exploring henomena
- Informing constituencies
- Examining the past
- Other

According to Newman et al. (2003), the research design has to consider and reflect the purpose of the research. The purpose for doing the research also dictates the research questions, and these questions dictate the methodology in the context of the purpose. A mixed research project must have questions that are an outgrowth of the purpose and require both qualitative and quantitative procedures to more fully understand the phenomena under investigation.

The types of data necessary to answer mixed methods questions are generated from both paradigms and therefore require both qualitative and quantitative types of analyses. However, to be truly mixed methods, these qualitative and quantitative procedures need to be carried out in a manner that has credibility and will inform the results produced by the other, and not in isolation from each other. This consistency between the components of a research study and the thoughtful integration of research findings is an important element that reviewers look for when evaluating the scholarliness of research for publication.

Mixed Method Designs

Careful consideration must be given when selecting the most appropriate design. The design must align with the research purposes and be best able to answer the research questions of interest. *Handbook of Mixed Methods in Social and Behavioral Research* (Tashakkori & Teddlie, 2003) identifies approximately thirty-five mixed methods designs. An article by Tashakkori & Newman (2010) presents a four-category conceptualization of these designs, indicating how they can be broadly grouped and summarized. These design groupings are based on earlier work by Tashakkori, Brown, and Borghasie (2009). The categories of design are

- *Parallel mixed methods design.* This represents a research design that has two independent phases—one qualitative and one quantitative. Each phase is carried out separately, and at the conclusion of the research, meta inferences based on the findings of both studies are developed to facilitate answering of the research questions.
- *Sequential mixed methods design.* In this design the research question emerges from the findings of Phase 1 of the project. The initial phase can be either qualitative or quantitative. These findings are then used to inform Phase 2. Based on the findings from each phase, a meta interpretation is inferred at the end. Meta interpretations, like meta inferences, are based on careful consideration of the results from multiple studies.
- *Conversion mixed methods design.* In this design, there are multiple purposes and research questions. A data set is used to provide findings from which new questions may emerge. One could begin with qualitative data that may then be quantified and reanalyzed as quantitative data, or one could begin with quantitative data that would be reanalyzed qualitatively. At the conclusion of the project, the researcher does a meta analysis of the two sets of findings. Again,

the term *meta* refers to using multiple sources. Therefore, a meta analysis analyzes the results from multiple studies. These analyses yield information from the multiple sources of data that can be consistent or inconsistent. Inconsistent information can also be valuable and provide additional insights that one would not get from a single study. These insights would then be interpreted through meta interpretations and meta inferences, and implications would be drawn.

- *Fully integrated mixed method design.* This category tends to be the most sophisticated and complicated. It generally addresses multiple purposes and multiple questions. This design is iterative in that the analyses of each phase lead to inferences that may produce new questions, data, and further analyses that are qualitative or quantitative in nature. Finally, a meta analysis of all of the results is conducted based on all of the data.

These designs have at least two characteristics in common: each uses both qualitative and quantitative data and analyses, and more importantly, each integrates the findings using a meta analysis conceptualization. A thoughtful and appropriate integration of the findings is essential when concluding a mixed methods investigation and when presenting the manuscript for publication.

Legitimation Techniques

A reader who is evaluating mixed methods research considers the legitimation techniques used. As previously noted, these techniques need to be specific to the particular study, and the researcher must consider each for its appropriateness to the study. Although not all of these strategies are incorporated in one investigation, most published articles describe an array of appropriate legitimation strategies that are reported in detail in the method section.

Newman and Benz (1998) and Ridenour and Newman (2007) summarize the techniques that need to be incorporated to estimate the legitimacy of a research project. The legitimation strategies presented in Figure 14.1 represent issues of both internal and external validity that the researcher needs to consider. The qualitative elements are heavily based on the work of Guba and Lincoln (1989), and the quantitative concepts are heavily based on the work of Campbell and Stanley (1963). The components listed assist both the researcher and readers to reflect on the strength and credibility of the findings. This helps to estimate the truth value, which is sometimes referred to as the trustworthiness of the research. The methods section of an article should make explicit which legitimation strategies have been incorporated in research and how they add to the integrity of the work.

Figure 14.1 provides two lists summarizing legitimation considerations that are used when planning qualitative and quantitative research. Missing in this figure are the mixed method research designs that integrate both methods using meta inferences. These designs have been presented in the preceding section.

Definitions of Qualitative Legitimation Considerations

Reflexivity. The researcher identifies the degree of potential bias in the characteristics of the data, in part, through a process of self-critique. The researcher adopts an attitude of transparency, understanding that his or her position relative to what is being studied is not a neutral one. Researchers are open and make public their own biases in constructing meaning from the data. For example, they describe their experiences and relationships with study participants, discussing how these experiences might have helped shape their research report. It is accepted that

FIGURE 14.1. QUALITATIVE AND QUANTITATIVE LEGITIMATION TECHNIQUES.

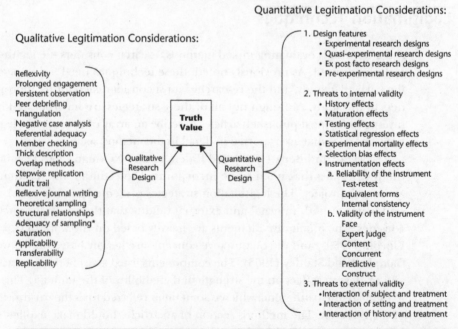

*Adequacy of sampling considerations is important for both qualitative and quantitative research.

all data are biased to some extent, but the researcher needs to make public that potential for bias. If the data are based on observation, one way to help mitigate that bias is to have more than one observer or use training to achieve consistency between coders of data, for example.

Prolonged Engagement. The assumption is that the data were collected over a long enough time period to capture the entire event, taking into consideration the cultural and historical context.

Persistent Observation. This deals with observing to determine if the behavior that is being investigated is a unique or consistent occurrence.

Peer Debriefing. The researcher engages other professionals to obtain their perspectives on the researcher's perception of what was experienced or observed.

Triangulation. The researcher obtains multiple sources of data to check for consistency. This is similar to the concept of reliability in quantitative research and, in some cases, the concept of validity. It is recognized that some sources of data may be more important than others in understanding phenomena. Denzin (1978) uses the concepts of data triangulation, theory triangulation, and methodological triangulation. (These are self-explanatory.) There is also within-group or study triangulation and between-group triangulation.

Negative Case Analysis. This is a type of sequential analysis that forms hypotheses, taking into consideration all of the data, including deviant cases. That is, it analyzes deviant cases to expand explanations (hypotheses) of the existing data.

Referential Adequacy. This relates to having enough supportive material (for example, observations, documentation, and interviews) to document the inferences being made about the data.

Member Checking. Members of the groups from which the data are obtained are consulted to determine if there is agreement between the researcher's interpretation of what was said or observed and his or her interpretation of the same data. This may be done formally (through a scheduled interview, for example) or informally as opportunities present themselves.

Thick Description. To help the readers evaluate the transferability of the findings, the researcher provides a detailed description of the data or phenomenon. The thick descriptors are used as a means for estimating external validity, so that the readers can determine for themselves if the findings are transferable to other contexts. This includes an emic perspective, which requires the inclusion of the participants' perspectives, and any additional social or cultural information.

Overlap Methods. Sometimes called methodological triangulation (Brown, 2005), this is a type of triangulation in which the researcher plans methods to create overlap when collecting different types of data (such as observational, interview, and survey) to answer the same research questions. Therefore, it is considered to be a cross-validating procedure.

Stepwise Replication. When there is more than one study within a study, a type of meta analysis is used to collect and analyze data. For example, men may be investigated to determine how they respond to a particular phenomenon, and then women may also be studied related to the same phenomenon. This could then be followed up by a comparison of men and women in specific age ranges. It may be that no differences are found between the sexes in a particular age group, but differences may exist in other age groups.

Audit Trail. It is very important to present enough detail, information, and documentation about the research study so that an independent researcher can attempt to replicate the methods used and the findings. An audit trail can be used to estimate the quality of the research.

Reflexive Journal Writing. The purpose of maintaining a journal throughout the investigative process is to provide researchers with opportunities to reflect on their thoughts, thus providing additional insight into potential biases that may affect the interpretation of the data. This process attempts to control for potential biases by identifying and considering them when writing up the research findings.

Theoretical Sampling. This is a powerful technique to aid in the development of theory (Patton, 1990; Charmaz, 1983; Glaser & Strauss, 1967). The researcher decides what data are necessary or desirable to collect to further the development of his or her theory, based on what he or she had already done in the study. This is sometimes referred as soft hypothesis testing (Newman & Benz, 1998).

Structural Relationships. This is the logical consistency among different sources of data. It is achieved by interweaving the information from the different data sources, which frequently come from different perspectives, to support the underlying emerging meaning.

Adequacy of Sampling. Appropriate sampling is an extremely important consideration in both qualitative and quantitative research. The sample and sampling techniques must be consistent with the purposes of the research. Without this alignment, any inferences made from an analysis of the data would be questionable. Rocco and Plakhotonik (see Chapter Twelve, this volume) indicate that a sample has to relate to the research problem, the purpose, and the research question. How well it relates is the basic criterion for judging the adequacy of the sample. As Sandelowski (2007) indicated, "A common misconception about sampling in qualitative research is that numbers are unimportant in ensuring the adequacy of a sampling strategy" (p. 181). She contends that without an adequate sample, any conclusions drawn from the data would be suspect.

In mixed methods research, as in qualitative and quantitative research, the investigator must use informed judgment, experience, and insight in selecting a sample that is defensible for the research purposes. Patton (2002) identified eleven sampling techniques. Newman and McNeil (1998) identified two broad categories of sampling: probabilistic (which requires some random sampling procedure) and nonprobabilistic (such as purposive, criterion, quota, systematic, or cluster). They state that virtually all sampling techniques can be classified as a subset of these two categories.

Saturation. This asks the question, "How many interviews are enough?" Although there are no clear guidelines, the researcher stops interviewing when no new themes emerge from the data. This frequently occurs with between six and twelve interviews (Guest, Bunce, & Johnson, 2006). Saturation also assumes that the sample is adequate for the purpose of the research. (See the previous description of *adequacy of sampling*.)

Applicability. This occurs when the findings from one sample are applied to another based on the similarity of the deep descriptors of both samples. It is the willingness to go beyond the original sample, to generalize, from one sample to another. This is not a statistical decision but a logical, descriptive one.

Transferability. In qualitative research, the results theoretically are not generalized in the same way as they are in quantitative studies. Transferability is based on the reader's comfort in assuming that the findings in one situation can be applied to another. It is context related. To the extent that an argument can be made that the data are not dependent on the specific context, then one can assume that it is transferable. The researcher is obligated to provide thick description of the site, the informants, and all characteristics of the data and the process of the study so that the audience is able to judge whether the meaning of the results might (*might!*) apply to his or her situation. For example, the reader may assume that the results of reinforcing or rewarding a student are independent of the student's teacher, class, or school, and therefore the results are transferable to other teachers, classes, and schools. Polkinghorne (1991) distinguishes two types of generalizability: statistical and aggregate. Qualitative research deals with an aggregate concept of generalizability, which is based on deep descriptors, not statistical assumptions.

Replicability. This is a type of consistency. It is the probability that results obtained in the original study will be predictive of what will occur in similar research.

Definitions of Quantitative Legitimation Considerations

Design Features. There are four basic quantitative research designs: true experimental, quasi-experimental, ex post facto, and preexperimental. These four can be further classified into two broad types: experimental and ex post facto.

All of the experimental designs have independent variables (for example, the researcher decides who gets the treatment) that the researcher can manipulate. Ex post facto designs have independent variables that the researcher cannot manipulate. These include independent variables that have already occurred or attribute variables, such as age, gender, race, height, or socioeconomic status.

The purpose of the research design is to control for variance in such a way as to increase the ability of the researcher to assume the independent variable affected the dependent variable. The four designs that follow allow the researcher to have a differential level of confidence in assuming a "causal" relationship or link between the independent and dependent variable. That is, to the extent that the design has internal validity (controls for alternative explanations), one can assume causation (Campbell & Stanley, 1963; Kerlinger & Lee, 2000; Newman, Newman, Brown, & McNeely, 2006):

- *True experimental designs.* These designs, the gold standard of quantitative research, have a number of unique characteristics that require control that is often difficult to achieve in a real-world setting. Three of these characteristics are an independent variable that the researcher manipulates (such as who gets the treatment), control over scheduling, and the ability to randomly assign the subjects to at least two treatment groups. Campbell and Stanley (1963) and Newman et al. (2006) present examples of true experimental designs. A design is considered a true experiment to the extent it controls for all threats to internal validity. (See *internal validity* below.)

- *Quasi-experimental designs.* These designs are most likely to be found in natural settings because it is often difficult or even impossible to meet all of the requirements for a true experimental design. They can range from having high estimates of internal validity to having low estimates, depending on how much control the design has over the phenomenon being investigated (Campbell & Stanley, 1963; Newman et al., 2006).
- *Preexperimental designs.* In these designs, the researcher has control over the independent variable (that is what makes it experimental); however, they have very weak internal validity because there are strong alternative explanations other than the treatment effect that are plausible for explaining the variability in the outcome. This type of research is the least likely of the experimental designs, and probably all of the other designs, to get published.
- *Ex post facto designs.* In these designs, none of the independent variables of interest can be manipulated. They have already occurred or they are all attributes. Since the independent variable cannot be manipulated, no statement of causal relationships or impact can be made. Instead, the researcher reports the level of relationship (correlation) between variables.

There are three types of ex post facto research (Kerlinger & Lee, 2000; Newman et al., 2006). The first type looks at relationships without hypotheses. It is just exploratory or descriptive. It is the weakest ex post facto research design and has the weakest internal validity. Its major value is descriptive or heuristic. Ex post facto research with hypotheses is considered to be superior and has a better chance of being published than does the ex post facto research without hypotheses. It is perceived to be as good as the hypotheses are credible.

The most sophisticated type of ex post facto research has hypotheses and controls for viable alternative explanations of the research outcomes. This design frequently uses analysis of covariance techniques to control for age, gender, race, socioeconomic status, experience, and so forth as alternative explanations. Sometimes one can classify path analysis and structural equation modeling in this category. This design is the most likely of the three types of ex post facto research to be published.

Threats to Internal Validity. There are at least seven major threats to the internal validity of an investigation: history, maturation, testing, statistical regression, experimental mortality, selection bias, and instrumentation. Each of these affects the ability of the researcher to legitimately assume "causation," and therefore affect the trustworthiness of the research. The researcher attempts to control for as many of these threats as possible, thereby increasing the likelihood of producing publishable results.

History Effects. Any extraneous event, other than treatment, that can influence the outcome is a history effect. The longer the span between the treatment and assessment, the more vulnerable the research is to a contaminating effect due to history.

Maturation Effects. This is similar to a history effect, but it occurs internal to the organism. Examples are getting older and tiring over the span of the treatment.

Testing Effects. The very nature of pretesting may sensitize a subject to what is going to be posttested, thereby causing a posttest change that can be attributed to something other than the treatment.

Statistical Regression Effect. When a group pretest scores are extremely high or extremely low, the posttest results will tend to regress (move) toward the mean. That is, if one selects a group that has extremely low pretest scores, the group would tend to gain (regress toward to the mean) when posttested, and the statistical regression can be misinterpreted as being due to a treatment effect. An extremely high pretest group will also tend to regress toward the mean, and therefore may have lower posttest scores that could also be misinterpreted as being due to treatment.

Experimental Mortality Effect. This is a differential loss of subjects between testing. This may be due to illness, mobility, or any number of other situations, and it can drastically affect the perceived effectiveness of the treatment.

Selection Bias Effect. When subjects are not equivalently assigned to two or more comparison groups, a selection bias has occurred. For example, if one treatment gets predominantly men assigned to it and the other gets predominantly women, any difference found may be due to sex and not to treatment.

Instrumentation Effect. The psychometric properties of the assessment instrument can have an instrumentation effect. These can include mechanical or electronic instruments that need calibration or can be affected by prolonged use. It is important to control for any differential effect between a pre- and posttest that may be due not to the treatment but to the unreliability of the assessment instrument.

A number of important reliability and validity concerns must be considered when selecting an instrument. Instruments that have higher estimates of reliability and validity add to the trustworthiness of the research and enhance the credibility of the findings. A rule of thumb is that the minimum reliability of an instrument being used for group prediction is about 0.7. For individual prediction,

0.8 or higher is generally considered to be the minimum. What is acceptable for validity estimates varies by the type of validity. For example, estimates of face, content, and expert judge validity require approximately 80 percent agreement. For predictive validity, an estimate of approximately 0.4 is needed. There are no rules of thumb for judging the adequacy of construct validity. It is based on logical judgment. (This is a very qualitative decision.) In most instances, research without adequate estimates of reliability and validity will not be accepted for publication.

Following is a brief summary of the reliability and validity considerations that influence judgments about the integrity of quantitative research. It is important that a researcher seriously consider these issues in planning and carrying out the study.

Reliability is generally defined as the consistency of the measurement instrument. This implies that the testing instrument would produce the same or a very similar result every time it is used. Generally reliability is estimated with correlational techniques. The most frequently used are

- *Test-retest reliability.* One frequently used estimate of reliability is test-retest, which estimates the stability of the instrument over time. The major shortcoming frequently cited for this approach is that a subject may recall what was initially asked and therefore improve his or her performance on a posttest. This effect would decrease the reliability of the instrument. Another concern is the length of time between testing: too short or too long may have an effect on the reliability of the instrument.
- *Equivalent form reliability.* This approach controls for the influence of the subject's recall. It is based on the assumption that the researcher has two equivalent forms of a test measuring the same underlying construct.
- *Internal consistency.* The most frequently used estimate of reliability is internal consistency. This estimate does not require two testings. It correlates the items within the same set on an instrument to obtain an estimate of how well all of the items are measuring the same underlying construct. Kuder-Richardson formula 20 (KR 20) is conceptually the average of all possible split-half correlations between every item and the overall test. Cronbach's alpha is probably the most frequently used estimate of internal consistency. It is the general case of KR 20.

There are at least five important aspects that can influence the reliability of an instrument (Newman et al., 2006): increasing the number of items, using objective methods of scoring, measuring only one concept in any test or subscale, equivalency of item difficulty, and having standardized procedures for test administration.

The validity of the instrument is probably the most important psycho-metric characteristic of an instrument. When an instrument measures what it says it intends to measure, it is considered to be valid. There are at least six broad categories of validity:

- *Face validity.* This is estimated by the extent that the respondent perceives the test as measuring what it purports to measure. It is the least accurate form of validity.
- *Expert judge validity.* This is similar to face validity except that it is the perceptions of expert judges who report the test is measuring what it claims to be measuring. This also includes interjudge agreement and is as trustworthy as the expertise of the judges.
- *Content validity.* This is also referred to as definitional validity and logical validity. Most frequently, it is estimated by using methods that demonstrate how representative the items are of the content that the test purports to measure.
- *Concurrent validity.* An estimate of concurrent validity is frequently obtained by correlating one test with another test that has already established good validity estimates. Another type of concurrent validity is referred to as known group or discriminant validity. This is estimated by determining how well an instrument differentiates, as predicted, between known groups.
- *Predictive validity.* When an instrument is used to predict a future outcome, it is useful to be able to estimate how accurately it can predict that outcome. To the extent that it does, it has predictive validity. The major difference between predictive and concurrent validity has to do with time. Concurrent validity correlates two events at the same time. Predictive validity is a correlation between a current estimate and a future prediction. Sometimes concurrent and predictive validity are grouped together and are referred to as criterion validity, empirical validity, or statistical validity.
- *Construct validity.* This has been defined as a conglomeration of all of the other types of validity. Sometimes factor analysis is used to estimate the construct validity of an instrument. Generally there is not one criterion that is sufficient as an acceptable measure of a construct; rather, a series of criteria is used.

Threats to External Validity. External validity is defined as the extent to which a study is generalizable to other people, groups, or situations. For generalizability, one has to consider not only the adequacy of the sample, but also the interaction between the subjects and the treatment, the setting and the treatment, the history and the treatment, and even the subjects and the setting. An example of interaction between the subject and the treatment would be if a researcher finds that a treatment had a positive effect on the all white male subjects in a study.

Those results should not be generalized to females or to subjects of different races. An example of interaction between the subject and setting would be if a person sitting for the bar exam to become licensed as an attorney is adversely affected by a testing environment that was in disarray due to recent flooding. The results of this exam may not be reflective of scores that would be obtained in a setting without disruption. In order to be able to generalize, a researcher has to ask how similar is the situation he or she wants to generalize from to the situation he or she wants to generalize to. This is not really much different from examining each situation through the lens of deep descriptors.

Conclusion

This chapter presented a discussion of the many elements a researcher must consider when planning a mixed methods research project that he or she wants to be able to submit for publication. One important consideration is the need for consistency between the purposes for conducting research, the questions of interest, and the design and methods selected to answer those questions (Newman et al., 2003). This consistency is essential for all high-quality research. When properly aligned, these elements best facilitate the generation of findings that have the highest truth value (legitimacy and quality) and are most likely to contribute to the intended body of knowledge. The authors also presented the philosophy underlying mixed method designs, four broad design categories, and several legitimation strategies. Using this as a template will help the researcher to consider each element when planning and conducting mixed methods research and in preparing an article that will be suitable for submission to and publication in scholarly journal.

References

American Educational Research Association. (2006). Standards for reporting on empirical social science research in AERA publications. *Educational Researcher, 35*(6), 33–40.

APA Publications and Communications Board Working Group on Journal Article Reporting Standards. (2008). Reporting standards for research in psychology: Why do we need them? What might they be? *American Psychologist, 63,* 839–851.

Brown, J. D. (2005). Statistics Corner: Questions and answers about language testing statistics: Characteristics of sound qualitative research. *Shiken: JALT Testing and Evaluation SIG Newsletter, 9*(2), 31–33.

Campbell, D. T., & Stanley, J. C. (1963). *Experimental and quasi-experimental designs for research.* Skokie, IL: Rand McNally.

Charmaz, K. (1983). Grounded theory method: An explication and interpretation. In R. Emerson (Ed.) *Contemporary field research* (pp. 109–126). New York: Little, Brown.

Creswell, J., & Plano Clark, V. (2006). *Designing and conducting mixed methods research.* Thousand Oaks, CA: Sage.

Denzin, N. K. (1978). *The research act: A theoretical introduction to sociological methods.* New York: McGraw-Hill.

Glaser, B. G., & Strauss, A. L. (1967). *The discovery of grounded theory: Strategies for qualitative research.* Chicago: Aldine.

Guba, E., & Lincoln, Y. (1989). *Fourth generation evaluation.* Thousand Oaks, CA: Sage.

Guest, G., Bunce, A., & Johnson, L. (2006). How many interviews are enough? An experiment with data saturation and variability. *Field Methods, 18*(1), 59–82.

Kerlinger, F. N., & Lee, H. (2000). *Foundations of behavioral research* (4th ed.). Fort Worth, TX: Harcourt.

Newman, I., & Benz, C. (1998). *Qualitative-quantitative research methodology: An interactive continuum.* Carbondale: Southern Illinois University Press.

Newman, I., & McNeil, K. (1998). *Conducting survey research in the social sciences.* Lanham, MD: University Press of America.

Newman, I., Newman, C., Brown, R., & McNeely, S. (2006). *Conceptual statistics for beginners* (3rd ed.). Lanham, MD: University Press of America.

Newman, I., Ridenour, C. S., Newman, C., & DeMarco, G.M.P. (2003). A typology of research purposes and its relationship to mixed methods. In A. Tashakkori & C. Teddlie (Eds.), *Handbook of mixed methods in social and behavioral research* (pp. 167–188). Thousand Oaks, CA: Sage.

Onwuegbuzie, A. J., & Johnson, R. B. (2008). Mixed research. In R. B. Johnson & L. B. Christensen (Eds.), *Educational research: Quantitative, qualitative, and mixed approaches* (3rd ed., pp. 439–459). Thousand Oaks, CA: Sage.

Patton, M. Q. (1990). *Qualitative evaluation and research methods* (2nd ed.). Thousand Oaks, CA: Sage.

Patton, M. Q. (2002). *Qualitative research and evaluation methods* (3rd ed.). Thousand Oaks, CA: Sage.

Polkinghorne, D. E. (1991). *Generalization and qualitative research: Issues of external validity.* Paper presented at the American Educational Research Association annual meeting, Chicago.

Ridenour, C., & Newman, I. (2008). *Mixed methods research: Exploring the interactive continuum.* Carbondale: Southern Illinois University Press.

Sandelowski, M. (2007). Sample size in qualitative research. *Research in Nursing and Health, 18*(20), 179–183.

Tashakkori, A., Brown, L. M., & Borghese, P. (2009). Integrated methods for studying a systemic conceptualization of stress and coping. In K. Collins, A. J. Onwuegbuzie, & Q. G. Jiao (Eds.), *Toward a broader understanding of stress and coping: Mixed methods approaches.* Kyogle, Australia: New Age Publishing.

Tashakkori, A., & Newman, I. (2010). Mixed methods: Integrating quantitative and qualitative approaches to research. In E. Baker, P. Peterson, and B. McGaw (Eds.), *The encyclopedia of international education* (3rd ed.). New York: Elsevier.

Tashakkori, A., & Teddlie, C. (1998). *Mixed methodology: Combining qualitative and quantitative approaches.* Thousand Oaks, CA: Sage.

Tashakkori, A., & Teddlie, C. (Eds.). (2003). *Handbook of mixed methods in social and behavioral research.* Thousand Oaks, CA: Sage.

Tashakkori, A., & Teddlie, C. (2008). Quality of inferences in mixed methods research. In M. Bergman (Ed.), *Advances in mixed methods research: Theories and applications.* Thousand Oaks, CA: Sage.

CHAPTER 15

WRITING THEORY, CONCEPTUAL, AND POSITION ARTICLES FOR PUBLICATION

Gary N. McLean

Not all research is based on data, whether quantitative or qualitative. An important area of publication that helps challenge existing knowledge and pushes us to new understandings occurs from the development of new theories or refinement of existing theories. In a somewhat less structured and more informal way, conceptual and opinion articles can also make an impact on the core beliefs, values, and assumptions of a field. This chapter explores each type of article, with definitions and examples of each type.

Unlike many of the other chapters in this book, the three types of articles examined in this chapter do not have a rigid or even suggested format. Problem statements, for example, are often not found in such articles. Although each type of article includes a component that references the existing literature, how that literature is used may be very different from the ways in which it is used in other articles. Furthermore, there are not clear distinctions among the three types of articles discussed in this chapter. This will be frustrating to some who have difficulty with such ambiguity. Nevertheless, the lack of such rigidity is also freeing as it allows greater creativity in the writing of such articles.

Theory Articles

The goal of theory is to help us understand more fully the phenomena that are critical to a concept under investigation. After defining theory and indicating why theory is important, this section offers suggestions for developing a theory article and an example.

Definitions

Lynham (2000) defined theory building as "the purposeful process or recurring cycle by which coherent descriptions, explanations, and representations of observed or experienced phenomena are generated, verified, and refined" (p. 161). According to Gioia and Pitre (1990), theory is "a coherent description, explanation and representation of observed or experienced phenomena" (p. 587). The definitions provided by WordNet Search (n.d.) expand this concept:

- A well-substantiated explanation of some aspect of the natural world; an organized system of accepted knowledge that applies in a variety of circumstances to explain a specific set of phenomena
- A tentative insight into the natural world; a concept that is not yet verified but that if true would explain certain facts or phenomena

Based on these definitions, a theory is not necessarily a fact that can be observed and measured consistently; it is a best guess at the time, based on "observation, experimentation, and reasoning" ("Is Evolution Only a Theory?" n.d.), as to how a phenomenon can be explained. Theories may be improved and developed over time. An important reason for publishing a proposed theory in a refereed journal is that it is then subjected to peer review and is available for other scholars to critique ("Is Evolution Only a Theory?" n.d.). This process discriminates good theory from bad theory or theory that is not yet fully developed.

Why a Theory Is Important

No field can exist without either home-grown or imported theories from other fields. Through theories, we gain greater understanding of the phenomena of the field that are essential to its study. As we conduct research in a field, theory provides a focus for identifying the research variables of importance and helps in explaining the findings of that research and making recommendations for practice and future research. Hypotheses used in conducting such research emerge from the theories currently in place in a field. Theories, by building on the past, create even broader understanding of phenomena being studied, therefore, creating cyclical, continuous growth in understanding the field.

Thus, theory is foundational to everything that is subsequently studied in a field. Writing about theory provides the building block that is essential for all other writing in a field.

Suggestions for Theory Article Development

A number of authors have suggested a formal approach to the development of a theory. A summary of these approaches is provided after general suggestions for writing a theory article are provided.

The complexity of suggesting an approach to writing a theory article, and the potential overlap with several other types of articles contained in this book, is underscored by reviewing the scope of articles requested, for example, by *Human Resource Development Review*, the theory journal for the Academy of HRD:

> Such papers may include syntheses of existing bodies of theory, new substantive theories, exploratory conceptual models, taxonomies and typology developed as foundations for theory, treatises in formal theory construction, papers on the history of theory, critique of theory that includes alternative research propositions, metatheory, and integrative literature reviews with strong theoretical implications. Papers addressing foundations of HRD might address philosophies of HRD, historical foundations, definitions of the field, conceptual organization of the field, and ethical foundations [Torraco, 2005b].

Based on this wide scope of potential approaches to a theory article and based on the ambiguity that exists among different types of articles, it is not possible to prescribe one approach to writing a theory article. A review of theory articles across a wide spectrum of HRD-related journals that publish theory confirms that there is no set format for such articles.

In spite of the wide range of approaches and paradigms used in developing theory, Lynham (2002b) proposed a useful, though broad, list of steps to take in writing a theory article:

- Conceptual development
- Operationalization
- Application
- Confirmation or disconfirmation
- Continuous refinement and development (of the theory) [p. 229]

An article focused on theory would therefore usually address the first four points, but not necessarily in order.

Those who are interested in writing about theory must have a wide understanding of what has been written previously on the topic of interest. This is possible only if one reads broadly in the field and outside the field. This requires not just a literature review at the time of the writing; rather, an author must read on an ongoing basis related to phenomena of interest to the author. Ongoing reading helps to shape the direction that an author will pursue in developing a theory. So authors who are considering writing about theory should subscribe to an extensive array of journals containing articles related to the phenomenon or will be disciplined to read from those journals regularly online or in the library. Because so many fields overlap today, it is not enough to read journals only in one's field. Rather, reading of journals across a broad scope of fields is necessary.

When Thor Heyerdahl (1950) was trying to solve the problem of how migrations occurred across the Pacific Ocean, he realized that part of the problem with previous hypotheses was the way the problem was being approached. He concluded that the problem was that scientists and researchers tend to be "specialists, the whole lot of them, and they don't believe in a method of work which cuts into every field of science, from botany to archaeology. They limit their own scope in order to be able to dig in the depths with more concentration for details. Modern research demands that every special branch shall dig in its own hole. It's not usual for anyone to sort out what comes up out of the holes and try to put it all together" (p. 31). So he decided that the solution to "the problems of the Pacific without throwing light on them from all sides was, it seemed to me, like doing a puzzle and only using the pieces of one color" (p. 32).

Although not all theories have this overarching goal of bringing together all of the elements of a theory ("the pieces of the puzzle"), many do. This can be done successfully only if one has a broad-scope understanding of what has been written about the phenomenon from multiple fields.

The literature review across this broad scope of fields should be integrated (Torraco, 2005b). This portion of the article should be interesting, lively, and internally interactive. Because the purpose of this review is to lead up to the proposed theory, it is important to draw the lessons learned from the literature as they apply to the theory (see Chapter Eleven, this volume).

As potential authors read the literature on theory and think about its implications to the evolving theory, they must allow their intuition to interact with that literature to see where it might lead them in developing their ideas. Some authors have suggested that it is important to bracket one's previous understandings or biases about the subject in order to come to the concept with a new perspective. (See Gearing, 2004, for a discussion of the differences in perspectives that exist in what bracketing means.) The goal is to be able to look beyond what is already understood today but still within the context of what is understood about the phenomenon under review.

Having allowed intuition, experience, observations, reasoning, and the concepts that emerge from literature to contribute to the development of the theory, authors must not overlook the world of practice. Integrating these sources into a theory is critical for a theory that will be useful moving forward (see Figure 15.1).

Writing a theory article requires the author to take a risk. Developing or evolving theory often requires challenging existing theory. Sometimes colleagues will have spent a lifetime researching a particular direction regarding the phenomenon, and they may not be prepared to hear a new perspective. Not all people are excited about change and new directions in their field.

Once an author has developed a theory, it is time to put it to the test—a major difference between a theory article and a conceptual article. Is it consistent with what we know from earlier research? Can the theory be supported empirically, either quantitatively or qualitatively, by observation or measurement? What more do we need to know in order to move the theory forward?

Finally, based on this further testing, the author must be prepared to change that theory or perspective based on whatever new knowledge emerges. This may be the most difficult of tasks for those who choose to research in the theory area. They have to be prepared to give up what they may have defended heartily and move to a new, and better-supported, perspective.

Torraco (2005a) offered "guidelines for developing good theory":

- The theorist should have substantial knowledge about the two domains for theory building.
- The theory should be based on the clear specification of the problem or need for theory building.

FIGURE 15.1. SOURCES OF INPUT INTO THEORY DEVELOPMENT.

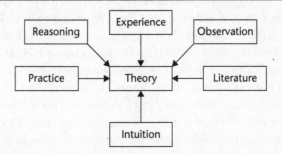

- The research should demonstrate explicitly the logic and theoretical reasoning used by the theorist to link the research problem with the theoretical outcome (e.g., the theory or model).
- The work should propose and discuss research propositions, questions, or hypotheses for further theoretical and empirical study of the phenomenon modeled by the theory [p. 364].

He explicated further the first point above, explaining the two domains:

- Knowledge of the elements of theory and of the process of developing new theoretical knowledge (i.e., knowledge of theory building)
- Deep conceptual understanding and practical knowledge (knowledge from experience) of the phenomenon or topic to be modeled by the theory [p. 369]

Those looking for more extensive advice on writing theory articles are referred to two excellent and detailed resources: an issue of *Advances in Developing Human Resources* (Lynham, 2002b) and a chapter in an edited book, *Research in Organizations* (Torraco, 2005a). In particular, Torraco provides an excellent table outlining theory-building methodologies and the values, assumptions, strengths, and limitations of each for quantitative, qualitative, and mixed-methods approaches, including several specific types of approaches under each.

Examples

As an example, consider that many articles have been written on the evolving theory of national human resource development (NHRD), a concept in which HRD principles address societal issues as well and are being applied more broadly than in traditional organizations, such as in communities, nations, and regions. In the opening article of *Advances in Developing Human Resources,* McLean (2004) conceptualized the meaning of NHRD based on previous research on the concept and then developed the operationalization and implementation of the concept through thirteen case studies. This process indicated, as Cho and McLean (2004) concluded, that there appeared to be at least five tentative models for NHRD. Lynham, Paprock, and Cunningham (2006) extended the exploration into the theory of NHRD with a focus on NHRD solely on transitioning societies. Wang and Swanson (2008a), taking exception to the broadening definition of human resource development, critiqued the concept of NHRD as being inadequately based on good theory and used an economics paradigm to refute the theories and models that were evolving. To this charge, McLean, Lynham, Azevedo, Lawrence, and Nafukho (2008) responded, point by point, to the argument that

Wang and Swanson made (2008a). With particular reference to the case that the theory on NHRD has been poorly developed, McLean et al. (2008) stated:

> Until the construct of NHRD is better understood (through increasingly deeper and *thicker* description), the development of a complete, bounded, and stable theoretical framework (if even possible) and its readiness for testing and evidence-based verification (from, for example, a post-/positivist perspective), would understandably be inappropriate from a constructivist perspective [p. 245].

Several other arguments were posited to support the appropriate immaturity of the construct of NHRD at this time and, thus, its immature theory development. To this claim, Wang and Swanson (2008b), in a rejoinder, highlighted areas of similarities and suggested a framework for additional research. This series of articles is an excellent example of the continuous evolution phase of theory that Lynham (2002b) suggested.

We still have a long way to go to have a well-developed NHRD theory, but the iteration outlined here indicates the process through which a solid, mature theory of NHRD will develop.

Conceptual Articles

Most of the literature suggests that conceptual writing is a necessary component of theory writing (Egan, 2002). In fact, Lynham (2002b) specified conceptualization as the first step in developing a theory. Although a conceptual article is similar in many respects to a theory article, it is more abstract and not yet proven, whereas a good article on theory will contain evidence that the theory has been tested and is concrete in its application. Generally a concept is more focused than a theory, as it is often a component of a theory. It also bridges to opinion articles, because such conceptual articles may also include well-informed opinions. As with much other research, there are not clear lines between these types of articles, resulting in overlapping components and approaches.

Definitions

Collins English Electronic Dictionary (Concept, 2008) has defined concept as

1. an idea, especially an abstract idea. . . .
2. in philosophy, a general idea or notion that corresponds to some class of entities and that consists of the characteristic or essential features of the class

Torraco (2005a) defined concepts as "the elements of theory that are common to all research methods" (p. 352).

Suggestions for Article Development

Because the concept of writing a conceptual article is not as well established as the other two types included in this chapter, it is more difficult to offer specific suggestions in writing such an article. Nevertheless, three are important:

1. Keeping in mind the narrow focus of a concept, write solely on that concept. Do not pull in extraneous ideas.
2. Take advantage of the foundations that others have established, and build on them. Use your own observations and experiences as you seek to extend a concept that others have established.
3. As you present your concept, be clear and concrete in indicating how the concept can be applied in a practice setting.

Lynham (2002a) suggested that conceptual thinking and writing are the first steps in the theory development process and posited that the first step is to identify "the units of the theory, also known as the concepts of the theory" (p. 245). She described these concepts as "the things or variables whose interactions constitute the subject matter, or phenomenon, that is the attention of the theory" (p. 245). The next step is "to specify how the units interact and relate to one another, which is accomplished by stipulating the laws of interaction that pertains to the units of the theory" (p. 245). It is also critical to identify the boundaries of the concept and the systems under which the concept can be applied.

Because conceptualization is only the first step of theory development, a conceptual paper will not proceed beyond the operational stage as a theory paper does. If an article goes beyond this to look at its application and confirmation or deconfirmation, then the author should write a theory article rather than a conceptual article.

Examples

Building on the work of Watkins and Marsick (1996), who built on the work of others on the concept of the learning organization, Tolbert, McLean, and Myers (2002) developed the concept of a global learning organization. It integrated concepts from the learning organization literature and literature on globalization, added their own experiences, and developed their concept of the global learning organization. It is not comprehensive enough to be considered a theory; they did not propose interactions or variables or test them at the time the article was published. Yet they went beyond writing an opinion piece by drawing on established theories and research.

Opinion Articles

Opinion articles are seldom refereed, though they are usually reviewed by an editor who may require revisions. Such articles may be published as editorials, as articles in nonrefereed sections of a journal (which may be labeled "Forum"), as letters to the editor, and even as book reviews (see Chapter Sixteen, this volume). Such articles are very different from those that usually fit into refereed journals such as those described in the bulk of this book. Generally the purpose of an opinion article is to convince or persuade others to accept the author's perspective, perhaps also leading to a change in their behavior, either personally or institutionally.

Definitions

Opinion (n.d.) has been defined as

1. A belief not based on absolute certainty or positive knowledge but on what seems true, valid, or probable to one's own mind; judgment
2. An evaluation, impression, or estimation of the quality or worth of a person or thing
3. The formal judgment of an expert on a matter in which advice is sought

An opinion article may also be called a *position paper* or *position article*.

Suggestions for Article Development

Writing opinion pieces can be fun; it gives the author a chance to be truly creative and express something of deep interest or value to him or her. At the same time, they can be tricky to write. Just as the author holds a deep opinion, others probably hold an alternative or even opposing position. They may want to submit a rebuttal article, and the opinion author then may become enmeshed in a very public debate or even argument. So potential authors need to think very carefully about the reason for writing such an article before submitting it. They also need to be prepared for what may be public humiliation or public acclaim—or perhaps both. Suggestions for writing such an article follow.

- Avoid personal attacks. Such attacks usually alienate readers, not just those you may be attacking. Keep the focus of the article on the ideas that are important to you. If you are critiquing others' ideas, be sure you focus your criticisms on their ideas and not on them.

- Avoid making overgeneralizations. Because these may be easily refuted, they weaken an argument or position. Furthermore, they may suggest that you do not have better arguments. Keep your argument focused, and stick as close to facts as you can.

- Avoid being too vague, which can lead to misinterpretation of your position.

- Keep the article relatively short, perhaps only two or three pages when published. You increase the possibility of your article being read when readers can get your point fairly quickly.

- Humor, or at least a light touch, will also keep the readers interested. It also helps to make something that is deep and serious more likely to be read and may also influence others' thinking. Being too serious may antagonize readers or bore them. Some topics, of course, may require a serious approach.

One way to get a sense for how a good opinion piece is written is to study opinion pieces that have appeared in reputable magazines such as *Fast Company* and the *New Yorker*. Reading and studying such examples will help improve the ability to write such articles.

A good idea before submitting such an article is to have people who are disinterested in the focus of the article read it. They can give feedback on whether it contains vague comments or too much emotion and has made personal attacks. They can generally help authors understand where they may have missed the mark and if the argument is weak.

Examples

As a former editor of a number of journals, I have extensive experience in writing opinion pieces, primarily as editorials. Two of my most interesting articles to write, and that provided me with the greatest fun, were written for *Human Resource Development International* and published in nonrefereed sections of the journal.

One example was stimulated by a visit to a Leonardo da Vinci museum exhibit. I have long been puzzled by the emphasis on developing a narrow research agenda on the part of many academic institutions. It is well known, however, that da Vinci was a genius who had a broad scope of excellence across many fields: anatomy, art, architecture, design, and others. This led to my article entitled: "Tenure Denied! Not Ready for Promotion! No Merit Pay Increase! Poor Leonardo da Vinci!" (McLean, 2007).

Another example is an exchange of articles between Richard Swanson and me over the foundational areas that support human resource development. I first wrote a critique of Swanson's (1995) three-legged stool model, in which the stool of HRD is supported by the legs of psychology, economics, and systems theory. I titled my critique: "HRD: A Three-Legged Stool, an Octopus, or a Centipede?" (McLean, 1998). Swanson (1999) responded with a defense of the model, to which I also responded in an article entitled: "Get the Drill, Glue, and More Legs" (McLean, 1999).

What I have found to be so interesting is that these nonrefereed pieces (along with many others) have generated much more interest and feedback than all of my refereed pieces.

Submission Outlets

Every author struggles to find an appropriate outlet for his or her work. There is no one right place to submit an article. Almost any journal will accept the three types of articles discussed in this chapter, although some journals focus primarily on theory and conceptual articles (for guidance on finding these, see Chapter Two, this volume). Answering the following questions will help in making a decision on where to submit theory, concept, or opinion articles:

1. Do I want to publish in a journal that is primarily theoretical and conceptual, or do I want to include it in a journal with broader inclusion of article types?
2. What audience do I want to influence?
3. What is my purpose for writing this article? If you are writing for promotion and tenure purposes, you may have to target different journals than if you are simply trying to influence your field. Some institutions, for example, have established tiers of journals (A, B, C, D), and top-tier journals are given more credit than low-tier journals. If you are in an institution that gives, say, Social Science Citation Index journals higher credit, you may wish to go to http://scientific.thomson.com/mjl to identify *SSCI*-listed journals.
4. What journals are interested in the content matter of my article?
5. What journals do I most often cite in my article?
6. Do I want fast turnaround, or am I willing to wait longer? Some journals take very long for the referee process; others are much faster.
7. Where do leaders in my field publish?

No matter which journal you choose for submitting your article, always review its guidelines in detail and examine past issues. Also, you may wish to seek out an established author in your field, who may be willing to help you think through options for submission.

Conclusion

Every type of article, including the three discussed in this chapter (theory, conceptual, opinion), requires a particular approach by the author. The three focused on here move from formal and fact-based to informal and personally influenced.

One of the joys of this book is that it highlights many different approaches to writing. There is surely an approach here that meets the needs and interests of all authors.

References

Cho, E., & McLean, G. N. (2004). What we discovered about NHRD and what it means for HRD. *Advances in Developing Human Resources, 6*(3), 382–393.

Concept. (2008). *Collins English electronic dictionary* (digital ed.). New York: HarperCollins Publishers.

Egan, T. E. (2002). Grounded theory research and theory building. *Advances in Developing Human Resources, 4,* 277–295.

Gearing, R. E. (2004). Bracketing in research: A typology. *Qualitative Health Research, 14,* 1429–1452.

Gioia, D. A., & Pitre, E. (1990). Multiparadigm perspectives in theory building. *Academy of Management Review, 15,* 584–602.

Heyerdahl, T. (1950). *Kon-Tiki: Across the Pacific by raft.* New York: Grolier.

Human Resource Development Theory. (n.d.). Aims and scope. Retrieved June 26, 2009, from www.sagepub.com/journalsProdAims.nav?prodId=Journal201506

Is evolution only a theory? (n.d.). Retrieved January 12, 2009, from http://www.fsteiger.com/theory.html

Lynham, S. A. (2000). Theory building in the human resource development profession. *Human Resource Development Quarterly, 11,* 159–178.

Lynham, S. A. (2002a). Quantitative research and theory building: Dubin's method. *Advances in Developing Human Resources, 4,* 242–276.

Lynham, S. A. (Ed.). (2002b). Theory building in applied disciplines. *Advances in Developing Human Resources, 4.*

Lynham, S. A., Paprock, K. E., & Cunningham, P. W. (Eds.). (2006). National human resource development in transitioning societies in the developing world. *Advances in Developing Human Resources, 8*(1).

McLean, G. N. (1998). HRD: A three-legged stool, an octopus, or a centipede? *Human Resource Development International, 1*(4), 375–377.

McLean, G. N. (1999). Get the drill, glue, and more legs. *Human Resource Development International, 2*(1), 6–7.

McLean, G. N. (2004). National human resource development: What in the world is it? *Advances in Developing Human Resources, 6,* 269–275.

McLean, G. N. (2007). Tenure denied! Not ready for promotion! No merit pay increase! Poor Leonardo da Vinci! *Human Resource Development International, 10*(3), 351–354.

McLean, G. N., Lynham, S. A., Azevedo, R. E., Lawrence, J.E.S., & Nafukho, F. (2008). A response to Wang and Swanson's (2008) article on national HRD and theory development. *Human Resource Development Review, 7*(2), 241–258.

Opinion. (n.d.) Retrieved October 14, 2010, from www.yourdictionary.com/opinion

Swanson, R. A. (1995). Human resource development: Performance is the key. *Human Resource Development Quarterly, 6*(2), 207–213.

Swanson, R. A. (1999). HRD theory, real or imagined? *Human Resource Development International, 2*(1), 2–5.

Tolbert, A. S., McLean, G. N., & Myers, R. C. (2002). Creating the global learning organization (GLO). *International Journal of Intercultural Relations, 26,* 463–472.

Torraco, R. J. (2005a). Theory development research methods. In R. A. Swanson & E. F. Holton III (Eds.), *Research in organizations* (pp. 351–374). San Francisco: Berrett-Koehler.

Torraco, R. J. (2005b). Writing integrative literature reviews: Guidelines and examples. *Human Resource Development Review, 4,* 356–367.

Wang, G., & Swanson, R. A. (2008a). The idea of national HRD: An analysis based on economic and theory development methodology. *Human Resource Development Review, 7,* 79–106.

Wang, G., & Swanson, R. A. (2008b). Economics and human resource development: A rejoinder. *Human Resource Development Review, 7,* 358–362.

Watkins, K. E., & Marsick, V. J. (Eds.). (1996). *In action: Creating the learning organization.* Alexandria, VA: American Society for Training and Development.

WordNet Search. (n.d.). Theory. Retrieved January 12, 2009, from www.cogxci.princeton .edu/cgi-bin/webwn2.1

CHAPTER 16

CREATING AND PUBLISHING NONREFEREED MANUSCRIPTS

How to Write Editorials and Book Reviews

Tim Hatcher, Kimberly S. McDonald

This chapter addresses how to think about, design, and write nonrefereed publications such as editorials and book reviews for scholarly outlets. General guidance and ethical concerns when writing nonrefereed manuscripts are included, followed by more detailed discussions of editorials and book reviews. *Nonrefereed* means that the manuscript is not blind-reviewed by the author's peers or an expert editorial team of peers. It may, however, include a review by the editor, managing editor, and an editorial staff but is still not considered peer or blind reviewed.

Nonrefereed publications are important in any discipline or profession for a variety of reasons. For example, research-based social science writing falls short in providing prompt and usable responses to contemporary social problems. Peer-refereed manuscripts go through a time-consuming review process. In some cases, the time from submittal to print can be a year or longer. In the meantime, urgent social problems go unaddressed and unresolved by the academic community that may be in an excellent position to address them. Manuscripts that do not need a blind review can appear in print quickly and be available to the scholarly and practitioner community long before a refereed manuscript can. For example, a score of editorials and other nonrefereed publications came out almost immediately after the 2001 Enron ethics scandal and collapse, long before any empirically based manuscripts were finally published.

In addition, nonrefereed publications provide writers the opportunity to express an opinion, be creative, and create a conversation or dialogue with readers. In other words, they offer the chance to write in a different format from the typical peer-reviewed empirically based research report. As the American Psychological Association (2010) makes clear in its *Publication Manual,* "Just as a disciplined scientific investigation contributes to the growth and development of a field, so too does carefully crafted writing contribute to the value of . . . literature (p. 31). Although "scientific prose and creative writing [may] serve different purposes" (p. 32), nonrefereed writing can and should offer authors a venue for creativity. For example, the creativity involved in placing I, self, and personality into nonrefereed writing, especially for experienced scholarly writers, can rejuvenate and recover what is suppressed in traditional scholarly writing (Simon, 1996; Thompson, 1998).

Luckily, there are outlets in scholarly publications, including many refereed journals, for creative expression and timely dissemination of information. Three common forms of nonrefereed publications are book reviews, editorials, and perspective pieces. Reviews of books and other forms of media are found in many scholarly journals. For example, both *Human Resource Development Quarterly (HRDQ)* and *Business Communication Quarterly* publish these types of reviews. Editorials, which often introduce a journal issue, typically offer an opinion regarding an issue facing the discipline. The third type of publication is referred to as a perspective manuscript. For example, *Human Resource Development International (HRDI)* publishes nonrefereed articles on practice, research in progress, interviews with researchers or practitioners, and position papers on a human resource development–related issue. These kinds of manuscripts are in not-peer-reviewed sections of journals and are included in this perspective category. *HRDQ* has a Forum section that publishes similar types of articles. For example, in one Forum column, Mensch and Rahschulte (2008) advocated for learner autonomy in developing military leaders. This article stated a position that HRD scholars and practitioners needed to read about but was not based on empirical data or evidence, and therefore was not applicable to a blind review process. Table 16.1 offers a summary of criteria to distinguish among these three forms of nonrefereed publications.

This chapter provides general guidelines for writing nonrefereed manuscripts, as well as specific recommendations for writing editorials and book reviews. The information and guidelines offered for writing book reviews apply to all forms of media a writer might be critiquing. The third category of nonrefereed manuscripts, forum or perspective articles, tends to be much broader in scope and purpose. When writing a perspective piece, the writer may use similar approaches to those employed when writing editorials and reviews.

TABLE 16.1. TYPES OF NONREFEREED PUBLICATIONS.

Criteria	Book Reviews	Editorials	Forum/Perspectives
Purpose	Critique contemporary books in the discipline Critique other forms of media (for example, software, instructional media)	Introduce and comment on current issues affecting the discipline Persuade or present an opinion regarding a topic	Provide preliminary findings on research in progress Present a point of view on an issue or a topic Introduce new topics in the discipline React to previously published reports and articles
Author	Some expertise as a practitioner or scholar in subject matter of the book or medium	Usually experienced practitioners or scholars	Broad array of potential authors, including graduate students, researchers, and experienced practitioners
Format and structure	Usually brief (approximately 1,000–1,500 words), with few or no references	Brief (approximately 500–750 words), with few or no references	Length depends on publication (typically anywhere from 1,000–4,000 words), with some references

Guidance for Writing Nonrefereed Manuscripts

Gene Fowler, the American dramatist, is credited with saying "Writing is easy: All you do is sit staring at a blank sheet of paper until drops of blood form on your forehead." Demystifying nonrefereed writing may not require drawing blood, but it does take motivation, creativity, following directions, and paying attention to some simple guidelines.

Nonrefereed scholarly manuscripts should meet the editorial goals and objectives of the targeted publication. For example, the guidelines of the *Journal of European Industrial Training* (2008) state that all manuscripts submitted should focus on "research and practice in training . . . primarily on activity in Europe." Guidelines for the Forum, the nonrefereed section of the *Human Resource Development Quarterly* (2009), state that it "provides a way to present ideas or issues related to the human resource development field, differing perspectives on specific topics, and reactions to previously published articles . . . the forum section is meant to encourage open discourse among scholars, who may not necessarily share the same point of view on a topic. The field as a whole should be enlivened by the varying opinions presented in forum articles."

If specific guidance is not readily available in a journal or related Web site, the writer should contact the editor directly with questions about publishing nonrefereed manuscripts. The editor may recommend following the published guidelines for refereed articles. The guidelines are typically located in the back section of the hard copies of journals and on the journal's, publisher's, or sponsor's Web sites.

Ethical Issues in Nonrefereed Publications

As with any other writing and publishing, authors, reviewers, and editors of nonrefereed manuscripts confront confidentiality, plagiarism, and other ethical issues. It is beyond the scope of this chapter to offer an in-depth discussion of every ethical issue and concern that an author may face when creating and publishing a nonrefereed manuscript.

Nonrefereed manuscripts may not involve people as research subjects or fall within the strict guidelines established by federal regulations such as the U.S. Code of Federal Regulations, Title 45, Public Welfare issued by the Department of Health and Human Services, Part 46, Protection of Human Subjects, or those required by most universities such as review by an Institutional Review Board (IRB). However, they should still consider journal-specific guidelines, plagiarism, and conflicts of interest.

Editors of scholarly publications likely make little distinction between a refereed and nonrefereed manuscript when it comes to ethics. In most cases, editors encourage scholarly integrity by making ethical and publishing guidelines clear and easily accessible.

Most journals publish guidelines for authors. For example, *HRDQ* lists its guidelines for authors in each hard-copy volume and on the publisher's Web site. Publishing guidelines might not address specific ethical issues. Nevertheless, it is still the author's responsibility to be familiar with publishing guidelines, codes of conduct, or applicable ethics guidelines in developing the manuscript and before submitting it to a scholarly journal.

Journal editors and readers have a right to expect that submitted manuscripts are the author's own work and not plagiarized and that the author quotes someone else's work properly. Avoiding plagiarism includes giving due credit to others' work. For example, it is dishonest to patch together a manuscript by cutting and pasting from a variety of databases or the Internet. Authors who fail to give credit when incorporating someone else's words or images into a manuscript not only ignore common courtesy but also expose themselves and their publisher to the consequences of plagiarism.

Creativity encourages imagination and novelty in the development of each type of nonrefereed publication. This is especially applicable to the editorial, the subject of the next section. Of the many different types of nonrefereed publications, the most accessible and straightforward is the editorial. In terms of rigor and format, it offers writers flexibility and a creative outlet not found in some nonrefereed writing.

Writing the Editorial

Editorials are typically written to offer an interpretation or explain something, introduce a pressing issue of importance to the publication's readers, or provide an opinion regarding a topic. Often they are written with the intent to create a conversation or dialogue with readers. From this perspective, writing an editorial can be surprisingly demanding since many writers, particularly those writing for scholarly publications, are used to following well-known conventions and formats. Although there is no prescribed format for writing editorials, there are some recommendations to consider before beginning to compose one.

Most editorials in scholarly journals are long enough so that the writer can make an independent, substantive argument or opinion, but short enough that most people will take the time to read it. A well-written editorial offers readers an informed opinion supported by facts, solid interpretations, and rigorous persuasion. Editorial writers need many of the same skills required for any other type of good writing: organization, clarity, and correct grammar. But editorial writing also requires creativity and a unique point of view, which may not be normal practice for typical scholarly writing.

To begin, an editorial should have a central theme or single focus. This is not as simple as it may sound. The large majority of important topical issues have a multitude of variables that could be discussed and a myriad of foci. Writers ought to concentrate on issues in which they have some interest and expertise coupled with readers' interests and the journal's contexts and focus. Trying to cover too much in an editorial can dilute an argument or focus and may leave readers confused or overwhelmed by too much information or too many vague connections.

An effective editorial includes evidence and support for the particular position or argument that the writer is making. For example, in one editorial, Sambrook (2008) referenced recent research to support her contention that the discipline of HRD is being stretched beyond the limits of its traditional roles. Unsupported opinions weaken the editorial, however, which would benefit from facts, quotes, and other objective supporting materials to bolster an opinion or point of view.

Experienced editorial writers recognize that often their published editorials will evoke strong reactions from readers. In many cases, readers', peers', and others' critiques of an editorial offer less than civil responses and emotion-laden reactions that may sharply question the writer's opinions and personally attack the author. Thus, it behooves editorial writers to develop thick skins and avoid taking reader feedback or negative critiques too seriously. Conversely, editorials can elicit strong positive reactions, although they tend to educe fewer letters or other responses than negative ones.

Generally a negative editorial is easier to develop than a more positive one. Although a negative editorial may elicit stronger reactions, it may also fail to stimulate critical thinking or further debate on the subject, thus stifling potential for real dialogue or in-depth learning. Excellent editorials avoid negativity by offering readers a choice: they contain arguments for both sides of an issue or problem, often with a slight slant toward one or the other. Using this approach, the writer downplays his or her opinion (however informed it might be) by acknowledging the intelligence, logic, and values of readers. In addition, good editorialists tend to assume that readers do not necessarily readily accept the premise or the underlying principles on which the editorial is written; they may have their own assumptions and points of view that shape their interpretations.

Of course, principles, like any other moral arguments, must be supported by facts lest they become one-sided dogma. Writers should avoid being zealots. Understanding that readers will question or even oppose the editorial's arguments urges the writer to offer valid arguments while supporting any personal principles or strongly held moral values. Excessive hyperbole should not be part of a well-defined and well-written editorial.

Being a good editorial writer requires less reliance on flowery and eloquent language than on being clear, simple, and logical. If it is not easily understood, moving readers to action or to critically consider something will be difficult. Even when being critical about a person, issue, or group, the author should offer suggestions for change or dissent. The writer whose editorial produces action on the part of a reader is well on the way to becoming an excellent writer. Tom Donaldson, in his 2003 editorial in the *Academy of Management Review*, wrote that the time was right for researching and theorizing about ethics and business in society. He challenged readers to consider both "normative and empirical enquiry" and suggested taking ethics and research about ethics seriously (p. 364).

Editorials are also often written to begin or promote a dialogue regarding an issue of interest or controversy within the members of the discipline's community. As a result, a more conversational style of writing may be employed. For example, the writer may choose to shift from the typical third-person past tense to a more personal and conversation first-person present tense.

The editorial offers writers the opportunity to be creative and innovative and to develop a unique and entertaining manuscript. It also can address current and critical issues of importance to readers of scholarly publications on a timely basis. By following a few simple guidelines and being prepared for possible strong reactions from readers, authors should find writing and publishing editorials both challenging and fulfilling.

Writing the Book Review

Writing book reviews is an important activity because it informs various constituencies of the contents and the worthiness of books related to a particular field of study. Reviews of books in scholarly journals are read by book publishers, librarians, academicians, and practitioners, depending on the focus of the journal (Spink, Robins, & Schamber, 1998). Studies examining university and college faculty's perceptions of the usefulness of book reviews have found that in general, faculty, particularly those in the arts and humanities and the social sciences, find book reviews useful for both their teaching and research (Hartley, 2006; Spink, et al., 1998). In addition, some recommend it as an excellent way to start the publishing process and maintain or develop one's reasoning and analytical skills (McKinzie, 1996; Simon, 1996).

Book reviewing is not without controversy: Henige (2001) calls it an "onerous and largely thankless task" (p. 24), and Cortada (1998) laments the poor quality of many reviews. However, recommendations and guidelines regarding the development of book reviews are offered that address Cortada's quality concerns. This section of the chapter explains how to write a book review for a scholarly or a scholar/practitioner-oriented journal and addresses ethical issues specific to book reviews.

Getting Started

Journal editors select book reviewers in a variety of ways. Some journals use a team of reviewers the editors have selected, other journal editors solicit reviews of particular books from individuals they believe have the expertise to write about the work, and some have an open acceptance policy where reviews are submitted and then either the editors or a review team determine the acceptability and quality of the review. Often the information to contributors is generally available in a hard copy of the journal or on a related Web site. This information, sometimes listed under "Information for Authors," explicitly states how the book review process works. It is often a good idea to query a targeted journal editor or book review editor asking about the process, book selection, qualifications of authors, and other information. McKinzie (1996) and Simon (1996) recommend that individuals interested in reviewing send a letter along with their vitae outlining their interests and qualifications to the editor of the journal.

Before writing a review, authors should feel comfortable that they have at least a minimal level of expertise in the general subject matter of the book. For novices or junior scholars, this may require partnering with a recognized expert or senior faculty member. This expertise or collaboration ought to be sufficient for the author to be able to address these general writing guidelines about the book:

1. Describe the purpose, content, and structure of the book.
2. Identify and analyze the authors' arguments. Are they supported by reliable sources, and are they valid?
3. Identify the book's primary and secondary audiences.
4. Present and discuss the context, theoretical bases, or unique perspectives of the book.
5. Provide a critique or other critical assessment of the book.
6. Discuss the relationship of the book to a discipline and its contributions relevant to a discipline's research and practice.
7. Integrate other scholarship into the review to support one's assessment of the book.
8. Other issues as required by the specific journal or editor requirements.

Part of preparation for writing a book review might include reading published reviews to develop ideas regarding what constitutes a good review. McKinzie (1996) points out, "One can learn much about reviewing by examining the works of those who do it well" (p. 97). Hartley (2005, 2006) found that academicians identified the following four characteristics of good book reviews:

1. Incisive pinpointing of the strengths and weaknesses of the book
2. Comprehensive yet succinct
3. Providing a good assessment of theory in the field and the place of the book within it
4. Went beyond criticisms to draw conclusions of much broader importance [Hartley, 2006, p. 1200]

Hartley then identified four characteristics of poor reviews:

1. Poor writing
2. Reviewer inappropriate to the task

3. Reviews containing incorrect and/or insubstantial claims and references
4. Reviews which were all content and no critique [Hartley, 2006, p. 1200]

Once an author or the journal staff has chosen a book, it is critical for the reviewer to read the entire book before starting the review. Although this seems to be common sense, not all reviewers take the time to read the book thoroughly before reviewing it (Cortada, 1998; Henige, 2001).

Writing the Review

According to Hartley (2006), there are common elements included in book reviews regardless of the discipline in which the reviewer writes. Three major components of reviews are a description of the book's contents, a discussion of the book's intended audience, and an evaluation of the book, including a critique as applicable.

Description of the Book's Contents. This portion of the review describes the purpose of the book and provides details regarding the topics covered. Some reviewers choose to provide a brief synopsis of each chapter, while others discuss the major sections of the book. Still others do a more general summary of the entire contents of the reviewed material.

Overall, the reviewer wants to provide readers with the essential ideas presented by the author. Additional information about the author (background and qualifications, for example) is useful because readers make judgments regarding the credibility of the book. This information also helps readers understand the point of view or perspective of the author (Thomson, 1991). For example, a reviewer of a career development book highlighted that its author was an expert on not only careers but also management in general. The reviewer speculated that this broad background may explain why the author took a contextual approach in his examination of careers (Bozionelos, 2007).

Discussion of the Intended Audience. Hartley (2005) conducted a survey on book reviewing and found that both reviewers and journal referees valued reviews that offered information regarding the intended audience for the book, as well as a critique of its usefulness to that audience. For example, a review appearing in the *Academy of Management Review* clearly informs the reader of the book's audience after a brief discussion of its contents. The reviewer wrote: "This is an academic book that is unapologetically intellectual, and the prospective reader can expect a couple of things" (Knapp, 2008, p. 777), which the reviewer explained. Later, the reviewer suggested that perhaps the author was attempting to accomplish too much and that the book was "a challenge to read" (p. 778). However, he recognized that "this criticism may be unfair, because the intended audience of this book is an academic one, and more should be expected of that audience" (p. 778). Providing this type of an assessment is helpful in alerting readers of what to expect from a book and whether it will meet their needs.

An Evaluation of the Book. Ultimately an effective book review provides an assessment of the book. There are numerous items a reviewer might critique regarding a book; those most frequently discussed are the relevancy, accuracy, and currency of its contents; its structure or organization; and the author's writing style. Perhaps most important is to assess the book's significance or contribution to the field. To do this effectively, the reviewer needs to be knowledgeable on other significant research or literature in the discipline. An effective reviewer will use the work of other scholars and writers to support the arguments made as to the significance and usefulness of the book. For example, Kuchinke (2008) offers a comparison between a previous text on individual and organizational transformation and the book he is reviewing to reach the conclusion that the authors have framed action learning "as a program or an intervention, and not as a way for deep transformation" (p. 275).

A critique is more than a minimal response of "The book was informative," or "I didn't like the book"; rather, it is a personal yet rigorous analysis that illuminates the book's strengths and weaknesses and communicates the book's primary ideas. Like an editorial, a critique should follow a publication's guidelines. In cases where little or no guidance is available, a critique ought to address questions as listed in Exhibit 16.1.

Use the questions in Exhibit 16.1 creatively rather than methodically. Beware of responding verbatim, or the critique could result in a listing of disjointed and isolated responses. Organize reactions into a consistent, coherent, and holistic opinion. Critiques, positive or negative, should state and clarify your assumptions. Stated or not, assumptions underlie all critiques. In making your assumptions known, you fulfill your obligations to the author, the readers, and yourself. Examining your own assumptions enables you to expose and critique your own beliefs and understanding and ultimately discover yourself. In evaluating a book, it is important to keep the author's purpose and intention in mind. As Cortada (1998) points out, it is easy for the reviewer to focus on how he or she would have liked the book to be written rather than how it is written.

Another issue reviewers must consider is what to do about a negative assessment of the work they are reviewing. In general, readers are exposed to many more positive reviews than negative ones (Hartley, 2006). Some suggest that journal space is too precious to print bad reviews (Henige, 2001; Simon, 1996).

EXHIBIT 16.1. BOOK CRITIQUE QUESTIONS FOR REVIEWERS.

While reading the book, take notes and ask the following questions:

Does the author state a problem or purpose, make an important argument, or describe a controversy?

Is enough background or related information provided so that readers have scaffolding to understand the argument, problem, or controversy described in the book?

What assumptions underlie the author's arguments?

Why is the problem, purpose, argument, or controversy of current interest, and for whom is the book intended?

An overall analysis of the text evaluates the validity of the author's ideas, foci, or themes and asks a number of questions:

Is the purpose or problem significant, and why?

Is the problem or theme argued in a logical way?

How well are points made and supported?

To what extent did the author succeed in achieving his or her purpose or offer solutions to the problem addressed?

This analysis addresses whether the information seems to be accurate and if it was used or interpreted fairly, without undue bias. It also notes if the author has defined any new or uncommon terms used in the book.

At this point, you have more of a book report than a book review. So you next need to react to the book. Use the following guidelines to do this:

Respond to the author's views and main themes. With which do you agree or disagree? As you discuss your reasons for agreement or disagreement, take a point of view, and tie these reasons to both the author's and your own assumptions.

Also ask these questions:

Is the text valuable?

Did you learn anything from the material?

Was the text entertaining?

Were any obvious or familiar issues overlooked?

How did the text contribute to your growing knowledge of the subject matter?

Henige (2001) also explains that the required brevity of book reviews may lead to more positive reviews. As he writes, "It takes far fewer words to praise than to condemn" (p. 27). Nevertheless, negative reviews can be helpful. Recently one of us read a review of a book, primarily because the title of the book was catchy and she thought it might be interesting and useful. The negative review (which had many valid criticisms) influenced her decision not to read the book, saving her time and energy. Ultimately, in the case of a bad review, the editorial staff will make the decision whether to publish it. But most editors do want reviewers to be critical and point out the weaknesses of a book, as well as its strengths. As McKinzie (1996) writes: "Be critical. Your readers deserve your honesty" (p. 97).

Book Review Ethical Issues

Book reviewers make judgments regarding other individuals' work, and as a result, ethical issues can and will arise. Although space does not permit a lengthy discussion of these issues, it is important to briefly mention two of the most critical dilemmas writers are likely to face when reviewing a book:

- *Conflict of interests.* Reviewers should avoid evaluating a book written by a competitor or rival. According to Bloom (2002), "The reviewer should have nothing to gain or lose—from judgments rendered about the book at hand" (p. 12). A reviewer also may want to avoid reviewing a book written by a friend, close colleague, or former student. In some disciplines, this may be difficult to do. If this is the case, Bloom recommends the reviewer be explicit regarding the nature of the relationship to the editor and explain it in any subsequent written review.
- *Expertise.* Since book reviewing involves assessing the significance and quality of a work, it is critical for the reviewer to have the expertise to complete this task. A reviewer should not accept a reviewing assignment if he or she does not have the knowledge, experience, or background to do an adequate job. Bloom (2002) provides another rationale for using experts to review: "An additional but powerful reason for reviews by experts is implicit in their economical length, usually between 500–1000 words. Because experts know the codes and the disciplinary conventions that contribute to conciseness, they can thus be expected to address all of these essentials with trenchant efficiency" (p. 13).

In general, reviewers need to have the knowledge and be willing to take the time to write an effective review. They also need to be fair and honest in their assessment of the book. Good book reviews serve an important function in any discipline. Bloom (2002) writes that "reviews have the power to ensure ethical integrity, influence taste and values, and change the world" (p. 16). Gaining the necessary skills to write them well can be a rewarding endeavor.

Summary and Conclusions

This chapter has offered experienced and novice writers advice and guidance on the design, development, and publishing of nonrefereed manuscripts for scholarly journals. Locating and following journal-specific guidelines and considering the suggestions in this chapter offer authors a good start in creating publishable manuscripts. In addition, editorials in particular can provide a creative outlet for experienced scholarly authors and for inexperienced writers and others who may feel constrained or intimidated by purely scholarly writing.

Although the suggestions were focused primarily on editorials and book reviews, they are applicable to most other nonrefereed writing and could be applied to other forms of scholarly writing.

Nonrefereed writing is often overlooked or even slighted, yet it is an important part of scholarly publishing. Purists who feel that publishing editorials and book reviews is an unworthy or ineffectual endeavor should keep in mind that incentives for quality and excellence are available and quite impressive. A Pulitzer Prize for Editorial Writing has been awarded since 1917. There is also a growing need for scholars to offer responses to significant global issues and pressing social problems that more traditional scholarly writing and publishing simply cannot or should not be addressing.

References

American Psychological Association. (2010). *Publication manual of the American Psychological Association* (6th ed.). Washington, DC: Author.

Bloom, L. Z. (2002). How to talk about heartbreaking works of staggering genius—and those that are not: A guide to ethics in book reviewing. *Journal of Information Ethics, 11,* 7–18.

Bozionelos, N. (2007). [Review of the book *Managing careers: Theory and practice*]. *Academy of Management Perspectives, 21,* 110–111.

Cortada, J. W. (1998). Five ways to be a terrible book reviewer. *Journal of Scholarly Publishing, 30,* 34–37.

Donaldson, T. (2003). Editor's comments: Taking ethics seriously: A mission now more possible. *Academy of Management Review, 28*(3), 363–366.

Hartley, J. (2005). Book reviewing in the *BJET:* A survey of *BJET*'s referees' and writers' views. *British Journal of Educational Technology, 36,* 897–905.

Hartley, J. (2006). Reading and writing book reviews across the disciplines. *Journal of the American Society for Information Science and Technology, 57,* 1194–1207.

Henige, D. (2001). Reviewing reviewing. *Journal of Scholarly Publishing, 33,* 23–36.

Human Resource Development Quarterly. (2009). *20*(1). San Francisco: Jossey-Bass.

Journal of European Industrial Training. (2008). *32*(1). Bingley, UK: Emerald.

Knapp, J. R. (2008). [Review of *Discursive leadership: In conversation with leadership psychology*]. *Academy of Management Review, 33,* 776–778.

Kuchinke, K. P. (2008). [Review of *Understanding action learning*]. *Human Resource Development Quarterly, 19,* 273–276.

McKinzie, S. (1996). The noble art of reviewing: Challenges, rewards, and tricks of the trade. *College and Undergraduate Libraries, 3,* 91–99.

Mensch, K. G., & Rahschulte, T. (2008). Military leader development and autonomous learning: Responding to the growing complexity of warfare. *Human Resource Development Quarterly, 19,* 263–272.

Sambrook, S. (2008). Editorial: People, organizations and development: Is HRD being stretched? *Human Resource Development International, 11*(3), 219–222.

Simon, L. (1996). The pleasures of book reviewing. *Journal of Scholarly Publishing, 28,* 237–241.

Spink, A., Robins, D., & Schamber, L. (1998). Use of scholarly book reviews: Implications for electronic publishing and scholarly communication. *Journal of the American Society for Information Science. 49,* 364–374.

Thompson, A. (1998). How scholarly writing makes readers work. *Journal of Scholarly Publishing, 29,* 87–100.

Thomson, A. (1991, December). How to review a book. *Canadian Library Journal,* pp. 416–418.

PART FOUR

REFLECTING ON THE WRITING AND PUBLISHING PROCESS

CHAPTER 17

WHY WRITERS SHOULD ALSO BE REVIEWERS

Robert Donmoyer

When Tonette Rocco, one of this book's editors, informed me she was in the process of putting together a proposal to publish this book, I was pleased. Many years ago when I was a professor at the Ohio State University, Tonette was a student in one of my classes on research methodology and also had worked for a time with me as a graduate assistant. Although we work in somewhat different fields, I had followed Tonette's career—albeit from a distance—for a period after she graduated, and, consequently, when she contacted me about the book, I was pleased to hear that she was continuing to do scholarly work.

I was even more pleased when I was told the focus of the book Tonette and her coeditor were putting together: writing for publication. For better or worse, publishing is a prerequisite for success in the academic world, and in this era of action research, even some practitioners who are not pursuing academic careers often have important insights and information to share. I also was painfully aware, however, that many young scholars have difficulty publishing because they are not very good writers. Furthermore, I knew that writing problems can be especially acute when less-than-adept writers are tackling the less familiar genre of academic writing. The book Tonette and her coeditor were attempting to put together therefore seemed to respond to a real need, and I was eager to contribute a chapter.

I was more than a little perplexed, however, when Tonette told me the topic she and her coeditor would like me to address in my chapter: reviewing for publication. I did have some inkling of why I might have been targeted to address the topic. After all, when Tonette first knew me, I was the editor of *Educational Researcher*, a high-profile journal published by the American Educational Research Association. Before that, I edited the journal *Theory into Practice*. In both positions, I had presided over the review of manuscripts.

Later, in an e-mail exchange, Tonette confirmed that my experience in these positions had indeed been a factor in the decision to invite me to write about reviewing. She also reminded me that as my assistant in the era before I had discovered the joys of doing my own word processing, she often had typed the reviews I had written for other journals. She indicated that she was impressed by the comprehensiveness of these reviews, the thought I had put into writing them, and my obvious concern with helping authors improve their manuscripts. She even reminded me that on one occasion, an editor made his decision to publish a manuscript I had reviewed and recommended contingent on my agreeing to rework my review as a published response to the manuscript.

Tonette reminded me that she once had asked me to critique *her* work as if I were reviewing it for publication rather than as a professor reviewing the work of a graduate student. She anticipated that if I did this, she would get both more detailed and more pointed and useful feedback. I assume, given her request for me to write this chapter, my critique did not disappoint.

Even after I understood how I got the assignment to write a chapter about playing the reviewer role, I still was less than clear about what the process of reviewing had to do with mastering the academic writing process, which, after all, was the topic of the book to which I was being asked to contribute. As I thought about the matter, however, I came to realize that reviewing, when done well, has a great deal to do with becoming a better writer. In fact, I came up with five lessons that reviewing could potentially teach a writer. I discuss these five lessons in this chapter and conclude by discussing how young scholars might go about becoming reviewers.

Lesson 1: The Need to Decenter

As I began to think about the relationship between writing and reviewing, one of the first things that came to mind was a line from the poem, "To a Louse, on Seeing one on a Ladies Hat, in Church," written more than two hundred ago. After describing in great detail a bug's meanderings all over an elegantly dressed lady's hat, the Scottish poet Robert Burns concluded his poem with these words:

"O wad some power the giftie gie us, to see oursels as ithers see us!" This line from Burns's poem reminded me of what is arguably the most important skill required to become an excellent writer, especially during the self-editing phase of the writing process: being able to escape our inevitable egocentrism so we can read what we have written (or are in the process of writing) as another person is likely to read it.

An author usually knows what he or she is trying to say, and because of this—and the tacit knowledge the author brings to the writing process—he or she can fill in the details that are left out when the author translates his or her thinking into words, sentences, and paragraphs. Those who read what an author has written, however, do not necessarily share the author's tacit understanding, and even if they do, particular readers may not know that they need to invoke particular tacit knowledge to understand a particular piece of text. Consequently, writers must always be conscious not only of what they mean but of the meaning that readers may make of what they have written. They must fill in enough of the details, in other words, so that readers can make sense of the text. During the self-editing part of the writing process at least, an author must, to paraphrase Burns, read his or her writing as others will read it.

Writers also must understand that too much information can overwhelm readers. This was a lesson taught to me years ago by the wonderful scholar Michael Huberman (personal communication, May 15, 1978). During a conversation, Huberman reflected on his own development as a writer and said something like the following: "Over the years, I have become a lot less egocentric as a writer. I realize that there might be 80 or 90 pieces of literature that have impacted my thinking on what I am writing about, but I now realize that, in a particular article, I can only discuss two or three of them. Otherwise I will overwhelm and confuse the reader." Huberman went on to say that the literature that authors do not discuss in the interest of not confusing their readers is still important because it provides valuable background information that deepens authors' understanding. Huberman argued, however, that much of this tacit knowledge must remain tacit in the interest of not overwhelming readers and obscuring an author's argument in too much detail. Writing, according to Huberman, is a bit like a distillation process, and his advice seemed to be to keep things simple.

This entreaty to keep things simple (and tacit) when writing academic papers directly contradicts the earlier point about authors needing to be explicit so readers will be able to understand the author's point. This obvious contradiction suggests how tricky the business of seeing our writing as readers are likely to see it can be. When details are too limited, the reader is likely to miss the point, but when a writer provides too much information, the writer is likely to obscure his or her point and confuse readers.

There are no formulas to tell us how much of our tacit understanding must be made explicit in the text and how much must remain tacit in the interest of not overwhelming readers. Becoming a decentered writer—learning to read what we have written as others are likely to read it—can occur only through experience and practice.

Reviewing provides an opportunity to experience and practice—albeit with other writers' texts—what we must learn to do with our own writing. When we review other people's writing, in other words, we get to practice the sorts of skills we will need to invoke when, during the writing process, we take off our composer hat and temporarily put on the hat of a reviewer of our own work. When reviewers read other authors' texts that have either insufficient or too many details, they are likely to lose their way, just as other readers are likely to do. As they attempt to diagnose the problem in the interest of providing formative feedback to the writer or a justification for their publication recommendation to the editor, they will have an opportunity to analyze problems that almost certainly will at some point be problems with texts that they themselves have been composing. In short, they will be sensitized to the difficulties of either too much or too little detail and alerted to the need to eliminate such difficulties when they are doing the writing and functioning as reviewers of their own work. (Of course, when reviewers have an opportunity to critique texts that successfully manage the tension between providing too much or too little detail, they also will have an opportunity to see techniques being used that reviewers themselves can later emulate and adapt in their own writing. There will be more on this point in the discussion of modeling below.)

There is no guarantee that the critiquing skills practiced with the work of others will automatically transfer to reviewing one's own work. Still I can think of very few other ways of teaching a decentering process that requires that we think and act as if we were someone other than ourselves. In essence, decentering requires something akin to play-acting skills, and just as actors often learn how to play, say, fictitious policemen and policewomen, soldiers, or doctors on the stage or screen by working alongside real policemen or policewomen, soldiers, and doctors, writers should be able to learn how to temporarily abandon the role of text constructor and assume the role of reviewer of what they have constructed by first being actual reviewers of the work of others.

Lesson 2: The Logic of Certain Grammar Rules

Reviewing also can help with the somewhat more mundane, but no less important, matter of using correct grammar. Many grammar rules are not arbitrary or merely a matter of social convention. Frequently grammar rules and linguistic conventions have become rules and conventions precisely because they are ways of ensuring that the reader will not misunderstand the author's point. The rule that a pronoun should be close to the noun it represents and, in fact, that the pronoun represents the noun that is closest to it, for instance, is designed to eliminate the apparent ambiguity in sentences such as the following: *The wives spoke of their husbands and said that they were very romantic.* Were the wives saying that they themselves were romantic, or were they saying that their husbands were romantic? The rule about the proximity of noun and pronoun makes clear that the latter meaning is the correct one. Unfortunately, many writers who write sentences like the example often ignore the proximity rule and actually mean the opposite of what they have written. Even if these writers at some point were taught the proximity rule, they either have forgotten it or have dismissed it as unimportant.

Reviewers who must make sense of texts by authors who have ignored the proximity rule—or the many other grammatical rules designed to eliminate ambiguity—quickly understand the communication difficulties that result when writers ignore grammatical conventions. There is nothing as frustrating as having to reread a sentence or paragraph multiple times to figure out what the author was probably trying to say.

The good news here, however, is that in the process of rereading to resolve ambiguity that could have been resolved through attending to linguistic conventions, reviewers have an opportunity to see the reasons behind grammatical rules that all too often had been presented to them through a pedagogy focused on rote memorization rather than logic. Reviewing, in short, is, at the very least, an opportunity for those engaged in the reviewing process to grasp the logic behind many of the grammatical rules they were forced to memorize (or, in some cases, were never taught at all). Once the logic behind the rules is understood, writers are more likely to use linguistic conventions appropriately in their writing.

Lesson 3: Providing Feedback in Ways That Help Rather Than Hurt

A third lesson that can be learned by serving as a reviewer of other people's papers—and learning to do that job well—has as much to do with the affective as it does with the cognitive aspects of reviewing and writing. When I became a journal editor, I quickly realized that reviewers approached the job of reviewing in very different ways. One group—a group I dubbed the *good-ship-lollipop reviewers*—was invariably positive but provided little to justify their positive assessments. These reviewers made authors feel good, but they did not provide much in the way of useful formative feedback to writers. Furthermore, reviewers who indiscriminately praised writers' work created real problems for an editor when the praise was not justified and the work they lauded had to be turned down for publication.

At the other end of the continuum were reviewers I called *the ogres*. The ogres did not shy away from criticism, but their criticism could hardly be considered constructive. They were what Miller (2006) referred to as *hostile* reviewers. From their perspective, the writer had done virtually nothing right, and the critiques of what reviewers had done wrong were, more often than not, so harsh and devastating that few readers could have learned much from them and retained any sense of self-worth.

Ogres also often seemed to want an author to write a different paper from the one they had attempted to write and discuss ideas (often developed by the reviewers, themselves) that did not really seem to fit with the paper's topic or the author's purpose in writing the paper. Even when this was not the case, ogres tended to display a degree of self-centeredness that matched their self-righteousness. They did not attempt to get into the mind of the author and try to figure out what the author was attempting to do and say before unleashing their damning criticism or telling an author how to fix things.

The ogres and the good-ship-lollipop reviewers represent opposite ends of the continuum of reviewers I conjured up to make sense of my experiences as a journal editor. In between these two extremes were reviewers who neither sugarcoated problems nor provided overly severe and inappropriate critiques. To a greater or lesser degree, these middle-ground reviewers seemed to really want to help authors improve, even when their recommendation was not to publish an author's work. They made a serious attempt to try to figure out what an author was trying to say and attempted to use the author's own frame of reference in critiquing the author's work. These reviewers' criticisms were pointed yet presented in a way that there was little doubt that criticism was being offered in the spirit of helping the author improve his or her writing. Furthermore, criticism normally was accompanied by relatively concrete suggestions for improvement.

Even when offering suggestions, however, this third group of reviewers exhibited a certain degree of tentativeness and humility. "Here is something you might want to consider," they seemed to be saying to the author. "It may or may not be appropriate, and it may or may not help." Interestingly, the suggestions that were offered with this sort of subtext frequently were more on target than much of the ex cathedra advice offered by many of the reviewers I classified as ogres.

I urge anyone reading this chapter to strive to be this third type of reviewer rather than either the good-ship-lollipop or the ogre variety. If reviewers succeed in doing this, they certainly will make an editor's work easier. And although some writers may prefer a good-ship-lollipop critique of their work, such critiques seldom result in bad papers being published since no single reviewer determines the fate of a paper submitted for publication. Furthermore, a good-ship-lollipop critique provides no assistance for a writer intent on either revising the paper she or he had submitted for review or avoiding the problems that led to a nonpublication decision in future work.

The middle-ground reviewer stance is also the one required when writers review drafts of their own work. Writers most certainly must take off the rose-colored glasses when they read what they have composed if they are to see how their drafts can be improved. Ignoring problems never makes them go away, and that is certainly so when the problems occur in material an author hopes will be published.

But many authors also go to the opposite extreme and believe they can do nothing right. Actually many in this group never have the opportunity to do much reviewing of their own work because they are such perfectionists—and consequently become so blocked from producing much of anything—that they never actually produce much text to critique.

Clearly a middle-ground stance is required when reviewing one's own work, just as when reviewing the work of others. The hope is that if writers learn to adopt this stance when reviewing the work of others, they will also be able to adopt it when looking at their own work. Once again, reviewing one's own work requires a kind of play acting, and reviewing the work of others can serve as a kind of rehearsal for the self-critique part of the writing process.

Of course, there are no guarantees that the dots between reviewing and writing will connect, but it is clear that successful reviewing is as much an affective as it is a cognitive process. If we learn how to be simultaneously pointed and charitable in reviewing the work of others, some of this attitude may transfer to reviewing our own work. At the very least, reviewing the work of others from the middle-ground perspective should teach us that no writer's work is either perfect or completely hopeless. Consequently our task—whether reviewing the work of others or the work that we ourselves have produced—is to provide helpful suggestions in a way that can be heard and, once heard, incorporated in subsequent drafts.

Lesson 4: Learning Through Positive Models

Thus far my focus has been on learning from the mistakes of others and on how to provide feedback that can help correct mistakes. Those who review papers for academic journals or proposals for conference presentations, however, almost certainly will be able to see—and learn to imitate—the positive features of many of the papers they review.

Language development is not solely a matter of imitation, of course. Linguists assure us that language skills ultimately are constructed rather than merely mimicked. If this were not the case, my three-year-old grandson's name for the imaginary appliance in which he places his imaginary culinary concoctions would be a *refrigerator*, not what he calls it: a *cooler-offer*. Still, modeling provides potentially valuable input into the linguistic development process. Even for my grandson, cooler-offers will eventually become refrigerators because he will have heard others using this conventionally accepted terminology rather than his quite descriptive, but somewhat idiosyncratic, label.

Positive modeling is certainly important in learning how to write effectively. I learned how to organize and present—first orally and, eventually, in writing—a coherent, understandable, and convincing argument for a position I was trying to defend largely by watching and listening to my highly skilled intercollegiate debating partner—who later became a clerk for a U.S. Supreme Court justice and eventually a highly successful attorney—make coherent, understandable, and convincing arguments. I simply mimicked—and, of course, adapted—the techniques and strategies I had watched him use.

Not all of us have an opportunity to learn from debating partners whose skill levels are greater than our own, but young scholars can learn by reviewing the often quite skillfully constructed works of other scholars within their fields. Just how one gets to do this is the subject of the concluding section of this chapter. In the remainder of this section, my focus will be on a few examples of things that can be learned through reviewing superb models of academic writing.

A review of excellent models of academic writing can teach the use of advance organizers, summaries, and, in papers where the line of argument is relatively complex, transition paragraphs. Advance organizer paragraphs appear near the start of a paper or section and list the major points that the paper as a whole or a section of it will cover. Such paragraphs provide an intellectual itinerary for the journey that readers will take in the process of reading the paper.

Summary paragraphs appear at the end of a section or the paper as a whole and review the salient points made. If advance organizer paragraphs are analogues for a travel itinerary, summary paragraphs function as a kind of travel journal. They recap the major points made in either a particular section of a paper or in the paper as a whole.

Transition paragraphs link one section of the paper with the next and to the overall line of argument that the author is attempting to present. I should note that I have not modeled the use of transition paragraphs in this chapter because the chapter's organizational structure is relatively simple and, I hope, easy to follow. Basically a paper is a list of relatively discrete benefits that are likely to accrue to writers who take the time to be reviewers. The headings at the start of each section seemed sufficient to signal shifts from discussing one benefit to another.

The effective use of headings and subheadings, in fact, is another thing that well-written academic papers often model. In well-written papers, headings or sub-headings often function as road maps for readers. They keep the reader focused on the route (that is, the line of argument) that the writer is following to justify his or her position. In well-written papers, readers also will see a relationship between the headings used and the topics outlined in the advance organizer and summary paragraphs; the terminology used in both places, for instance, will be virtually identical.

Advance organizers, summaries, and transitional paragraphs, on the one hand, and headings and subheadings, on the other, represent ways to manage the contradiction between the need to add details so readers will understand what authors are talking about, on the one hand, and the need to limit the number of details so as not to overwhelm readers, on the other. When an article has a clear structure and readers are made aware of the structure and the relationships among the parts of the structure, more details can be added without necessarily overwhelming and confusing readers.

There are many other techniques and strategies that can be learned by reviewing excellent academic writing. Unfortunately, space limitations do not permit the explication of these techniques and strategies here. Here it must be sufficient to point out that modeling is a tried-and-true method of learning all sorts of things, and there is no reason to believe that this generalization does not apply to learning how to write. Those who function as reviewers are as likely to encounter positive examples of academic writing as they are to encounter problematic writing, and writers who are also reviewers can certainly learn through positive models just as they can learn by analyzing other scholars' writing problems.

Lesson 5: An Opportunity to Compare One's Critiques with the Critiques of Others

Finally, serving as a reviewer can provide the opportunity to compare one's assessment of a paper's strengths and weaknesses with what other reviewers have said about it. Most academic journal editors and many program chairs who preside over the proposal review process for academic conferences send out reviewers' comments (with reviewers' names omitted, of course) not only to authors but also to those who served as reviewers. This means that every reviewer has an opportunity to compare his or her critique of a paper with what other scholars who reviewed the paper wrote. This opportunity allows each reviewer to take note of points of agreement and disagreement, as well as to note both perceived problems and strengths that the reviewer did not address but others did.

This sharing of reviews, in short, is a way for the reviewer to get feedback on the feedback he or she provided to others. When reviewers once again become writers, this feedback-on-feedback also should alert them to issues that they might tend to overlook when they create their own compositions and edit their own work.

So, How Does a Scholar New to His or Her Field Become a Reviewer?

In this chapter, I have demonstrated why those who wish to become better academic writers should become reviewers of other scholars' manuscripts. But how does a scholar just starting out in his or her field go about doing this?

In most fields, it is relatively easy to be invited to review papers that have been submitted to academic journals and proposals that have been submitted to academic conferences. Often all one needs to do is go to a professional association's Web site, click on the request-for-reviewers section, and follow the procedures for applying to review. At the very least, a scholar who is just beginning an academic career is likely to be asked to review conference proposals, but I also am aware of many graduate students who have been asked to review manuscripts that have been submitted for publication in prestigious academic journals.

If the standard operating procedures outlined here do not work, young scholars can also contact editors and program chairpersons directly—either in writing (a letter or e-mail message) or face-to-face at a professional meeting—and ask about reviewing possibilities. Those who do this should be prepared to make their pitch in the form of a brief but pointed presentation. They should certainly be prepared, for instance, to quickly articulate their areas of interest and expertise. They should also have a brief résumé ready to hand out during face-to-face contact and should attach a résumé to letters and messages.

Most editors and virtually all conference program chairs are eager to find volunteer reviewers. I have never known a young scholar or even a graduate student who wanted to be a reviewer who was unable to find a situation in which to practice their reviewing skills. Indeed, my personal concern is less about providing opportunities for those who are new to a field to engage in the reviewing process and more about the vetting of those who are selected to serve as reviewers.

To minimize the quality control problem, I urge graduate faculty members who teach graduate students to incorporate into their classes opportunities for students to formally critique each other's work. I provide such opportunities in a number of the courses I teach. Students post drafts of their papers online and receive detailed written and oral feedback from me and also other members of the class.

The student who receives peer feedback has an opportunity to learn a great deal from the process, and so do the students providing the feedback. For instance, those providing feedback get to experience the ambiguity—and the frustration—that results when language is less than precise and grammatical conventions are not followed. More than once I have seen students who continually made the same grammatical mistake despite my continued efforts to correct the problem suddenly no longer exhibit the problem after they encountered their rather chronic problem in the writing of a classmate.

Students in a class situation also have an opportunity to practice providing feedback in a manner that is helpful rather than hurtful. It is difficult to be rude and inconsiderate in critiquing the work of those we know personally and encounter regularly. Familiarity also provides an incentive for not glossing over problems and instead providing the sort of feedback that will likely lead to improvement. This stance, once mastered, is normally easy to transfer to other reviewing situations, including efforts to review one's own work.

Conclusion

I am encouraging professors to build time into their syllabi for graduate students to review each other's work in an effort to improve not only students' ability to review but also their ability to write. I also have encouraged young scholars who wish to improve their writing to seek out reviewing opportunities that have the potential to teach emerging academic writers at least five things.

First, reviewing sets the stage for engaging in the decentering process that is required for writers to view what they have written as others are likely to view it. Second, reviewing has the potential to reveal the logic behind grammatical rules and conventions when reviewers must confront and deal with the ambiguity that almost always results from a writer's failure to follow the rules; once writers understand the logic behind grammatical conventions, they are more likely to remember and use these conventions in their writing.

Third, in the process of becoming a reviewer who provides helpful rather than hurtful feedback, a writer is learning how to take a stance that should help him or her effectively review his or her own work. Fourth, reviewing provides opportunities to learn from the modeling of more skilled writers and to adopt and adapt the techniques these writers have used when the reviewer once again becomes a writer. Finally, reviewing for academic journals or conferences normally permits one to compare the feedback one has given to the feedback that others have provided. This opportunity, like the other experiences young scholars have while functioning in the reviewer role, should help young scholars become more effective writers.

References

Burns, R. (1786). To a louse, on seeing one on a lady's bonnet in church. Retrieved May 6, 2009, from www.robertburns.org/works/97.shtml

Miller, C. C. (2006). From the editors: Peer review in the organizational and management sciences: Prevalence and effects of the reviewer hostility, bias, and dissensus. *Academy of Management Journal, 49*(3), 425–432.

CHAPTER 18

ADDRESSING FEEDBACK FROM
REVIEWERS AND EDITORS

Stephen D. Brookfield

If you are reading this chapter, it is probable that you have had the experience that has been a regular feature of my own professional life: submitting an article that you have painstakingly prepared and reworked multiple times, only to receive a letter from a journal editor informing you that in the editorial board's opinion, it needs significant revisions. I have published over seventy articles in refereed journals in the past thirty years and only once—I say again, only once—have I received a verdict from the particular journal concerned that the article was fit for publication with no revisions. That particular article was published over twenty years ago, so clearly time and experience do not diminish the likelihood of receiving requests for revisions. If my experience is anything like that of other authors, which I believe it is, receiving the letter containing suggestions for revision is a normal and inevitable part of the scholarly publishing rhythm. For example, in the two years previous to writing this chapter I had two submissions to the Adult Education Research Conference rejected outright, and my most recent published article went through two rounds of revisions.

From the other side of the editorial desk—that of being a reviewer and editorial board member for six scholarly journals in the United States, United Kingdom, and Australia—my experience has been the same. Each year I review up to twenty articles submitted to these journals. In the last fifteen years, I have never sent in an editorial review that did not request further revisions. More often than not, my requests are for the author to do some restructuring and rewriting of major parts of the piece. When providing feedback to authors, I try to follow the general guidelines for evaluation I provide in my book *The Skillful Teacher* (Brookfield, 2006) and to make suggestions that are clear, written in understandable language, and specific. For example, if I feel an author has omitted an important theoretical perspective, I try to give three or four specific citations (books and articles) the author can locate to read about that perspective. I also try to link any criticisms I make to specific paragraphs and specific pages. I do this because as an author, I know that the more specific the feedback is, the more helpful it is to me.

But no matter how carefully crafted the feedback is, and no matter how much the reviewer finds to praise in my article, receiving requests for revisions is always upsetting, triggering a familiar cycle of emotions. Learning to cope with these is the first learning task authors face, before they even begin to respond to specific editorial suggestions.

The Emotional Cycle of Responding to Feedback

Receiving critical feedback on a piece one has labored over prompts several typical emotional responses. The first is devastation—complete demoralization brought on by the feeling that your efforts have been for naught. You feel you have been picked on and subjected to unfair and unreasonable criticism of a kind that others are not receiving. This emotion spurs one to ask oneself "Why me? Why am I the one they have zeroed in on when other article submissions are breezing past mine and going straight into the journal?" These feelings of demoralization often mean one's sense of impostorship is likely to be heightened. Impostorship is the feeling you have that behind the mask of confidence and command that you wear as you go about your scholarly duties lies the realization that you know you are muddling through as best you can without falling flat on your face. One typical trigger of this feeling is receiving one negative evaluation and twenty-nine positive ones of your performance and remembering and taking seriously only the single negative one. The same dynamic is present in receiving negative feedback from journal editorial boards. You feel that your basic inadequacy as a writer has been discovered and revealed and that there is little point going on in the face of this clear indication that your self-doubts were justified.

Following this initial devastation eventually comes a period of recovery marked by a growing anger at the inability of reviewers to appreciate the merits of one's work. "How can this journal employ reviewers who are so obviously ill informed, obtuse, and myopic?" you ask yourself. Sometimes the anger is aimed directly at the editor in chief of the journal for picking reviewers of your piece who clearly are drastically ill qualified for the task. Along with this anger is often a loss of energy and momentum. You say to yourself, "Well, if they are too stupid to see why my piece should be published, then there's no point going further with this." There seems little point in spending more time working on a piece when you are convinced the people judging it obviously know nothing about the field that is the focus of your study.

What do you do in the face of this emotional maelstrom? It seems to me that the major task is to keep things in perspective and not to climb the inferential ladder that ends with the decision not to pursue the article any further. One thing that is helpful to remember is that receiving this kind of feedback is very typical. This is why I began the chapter with a description of how seventy-one out of my seventy-two published articles were returned to me as needing further revisions. If you know that everyone else is receiving requests for more work on their pieces, your own need to undertake this on your piece is unremarkable. The more that well-published authors like myself can go public with the inner workings of their own authorial efforts, the more it normalizes receiving feedback. To readers it may look as if my books, chapters in edited collections, and refereed journal articles flow seamlessly from my pen (or the tips of my fingers as they press my laptop keys). In fact, everything I have published has appeared in print only after my attending to several revisions that were required.

A second strategy when receiving feedback is to vow to sleep on it and not to make any immediate judgments about the future of the piece. Just as you should always sleep on a vitriolic e-mail you have written out of frustration or anger in response to someone's perceived idiocy, it is a good idea to hold off responding in any way to editorial feedback for at least a couple of days. A little bit of distance can go a long way to ensuring that any response that you give is received by the journal's editors as reasonable. Third, try to assume that the feedback has been given with the purpose of improving the article and thereby retaining the scholarly credibility of the journal. If the journal receives far more submissions than it can print, then the fact that yours has gotten to the stage of being asked for revisions, rather than being rejected out of hand, should be a mark of significant accomplishment for you, not a cause for pique or lamentation. As a reviewer, any suggestions I make to authors are to ensure that the piece falls clearly within the guidelines the journal has set for contributions, or to anticipate criticisms unfriendly readers would make of the article (and by implication the journal) and address them before publication.

Fourth, I have found it is often a good idea to shift attention temporarily to another project, giving time for the feedback to settle in. Metaphorically speaking, most of us have two or three pots boiling at the same time, and concentrating on an alternative project gives you the sense things are still moving forward there, even as you feel blocked by having your article returned. Rereading evaluative feedback after a couple of days' work on another project often helps you keep things in perspective by allowing you to do a more considered reading of the original comments. Fifth, there is nothing like talking to colleagues about feedback you have received to keep a sense of proportion. They will help you understand the comments that puzzle you or (if they too find them incomprehensible) make you feel better about your confusion. If they know the field you have addressed, they may well be able to give a different perspective on the comments and suggest approaches or resources to address the comments that would not have occurred to you.

Sixth, if the comments are genuinely confusing to both you and your colleagues, then there is nothing to stop you from writing to an editor asking for clarifications. Of course, depending on the editor's other commitments and the support she receives from her host institution, it might be quite a while before you receive a reply. But when you are demoralized at a situation, taking even the smallest step to respond to it usually makes you feel less a victim of circumstance. Finally, if you feel depressed and deflated at receiving critical commentary, it can be a salutary visceral reminder of how your own students feel when they receive less-than-stellar evaluations from you. I know that my own evaluations of students' work have become more specific, concrete, and rich with suggestions for improvements as a result of receiving feedback from journal reviewers who are vague and express reservations about my work with no pointers as to how I might address these criticisms. I have also noticed that my ability to take students' negative evaluations of my teaching less personally has improved with time. I realize this may be quite simply a function of age and experience, but I do suspect that regularly receiving criticisms of my scholarly work from journal reviewers has hardened my previously pretty thin skin.

Understanding the Reasons for Negative Feedback

Journal editors and reviewers are unconcerned with the emotional roller coaster you may be riding as you struggle to keep from being completely demoralized by suggestions for rewriting your piece. What they are concerned with is how you respond to their requests to reshape and revise the manuscript. As you consider next steps, there are several tasks you need to undertake, the first of which is to determine the reasons for any negative feedback you have received. Once you know the cause of the criticisms, you are much better placed to address them.

In some ways, the easiest feedback to receive is that which says your piece does not fall within the journal's guidelines so is considered unsuitable. As a reviewer for adult education journals on three continents, I am often struck by how many pieces I review that either do not mention adult learning or adult education at all or provide a cursory sentence or two tacked on to the opening and closing paragraphs while the bulk of the article resolutely steers clear of any other mentions. If you have submitted an article to a journal without convincing yourself, and convincing the reader, that your work is clearly within the journal's scope of interest, it should be no surprise to get feedback requiring you to demonstrate the relevance of your work for the journal's readership.

At other times it may be the form of your work, rather than its content, that is the problem. Placing a piece of qualitative research in a journal that features only statistical or experimental research is clearly pointless. Likewise, exceeding the page limit because of your attraction to long, verbatim extracts from your research will often disqualify you. Some journals have a house policy of no first-person writing, in which case an autoethnography is clearly going to receive negative feedback. Authors also sometimes create needless problems for themselves by using a citation style different from the one specified by the journal. All of these things indicate to a reviewer that you have not bothered to read the guidelines for contributors that most journals reprint in every issue, and they call your scholarly credibility into question.

More difficult are situations in which your piece has run into opposition that is more ideological, such as an article that analyzes Marxism, Queer Theory, or Afrocentrism that is returned because the reviewers regard those perspectives as discredited or insufficiently intellectual. In my own case, I have spent several years trying to place a piece on how adults learn to deal with clinical depression, using myself as a case study, with no success. Many pieces are also returned because the intent of the article is unclear to the extent that it lacks even the most cursory statement of purpose. Despite my own success in eventually placing my own pieces in refereed journals I still receive criticism to the effect that my purpose in writing an article is unclear. This is usually when I am so captivated by the topic that its inherent fascination seems to require no explicit elaboration.

More specific reasons for rejection are that an author has, in the opinion of the reviewer, misinterpreted or misunderstood central concepts, made false inferences from data, neglected to include relevant research or theory that casts important light on the problem, made factual errors in wrongly attributing events or theories, omitted potential criticisms of the work outlined in the article, or simply reproduced work that is already published. These are more easily addressed than the most damning criticism of all in my opinion: that an author's writing is incomprehensible. Short of going to a remedial writing clinic and undertaking an intensive course in academic writing, there is little one can do in the face of that particular criticism. It is particularly demoralizing when it happens in a field that prizes clarity of communication as one of the highest of all scholarly virtues.

Responding Technically to Feedback

Probably the first technical task facing an author receiving negative feedback is to try and prioritize the kind of comments received. It is important to remember that not all editorial suggestions are requirements; some are just what they say: suggestions. So at the outset, try to sort out which parts of reviewers' comments are nonnegotiable and absolutely required and which fall more into the category of "it would also be nice if . . ." Along with this task is the prioritizing of which parts of reviewers' comments to address first. In my opinion, the initial strategy should be to decide which comments are big picture comments—those that deal with the structure of the piece and call for major structural reorganization. For example, if a reviewer writes that your literature review should be drastically reduced or that a small section of the first draft should comprise the focal point of a resubmitted draft, then addressing those issues is the first order of business. I have often received feedback that has isolated one part of my work and asked me to develop it more fully, while deleting or significantly reducing much of the original paper. This is usually because the reviewer shows me where material I am elaborating on at length has already been published and which other parts of the piece explore ideas not previously documented. This kind of analysis is extremely helpful and ensures that your article has a better chance of being accepted and of having a wider impact in the field. So the first priority is to sort out the structural advice and decide how that is going to be addressed.

After the big picture, first-order, structural changes come the more detailed second-order comments. These are much more specific, having to do with subheads that need to be inserted, research that needs to be acknowledged, ideas that need to be developed or explained more fully, criticisms that need to be dealt with, contradictions that remain unrecognized, and so on. The list of specific suggestions and requests is much more likely to contain items that fit the "it would be nice to address this if you have space" category, so here you have to judge which of these should receive your attention. Sometimes you will be in the situation where one section or point that one reviewer finds problematic is lauded by another reviewer. In those situations, you can usually use much more discretion in deciding whether to respond to them. As a general rule, if more than one reviewer makes the same observation or criticism, that is a good reason for attending to it in the second draft. If the editors are doing their job properly, they will prioritize the reviewers' comments in a cover letter that sets out what is expected of you for the second draft. But sometimes editors are so overwhelmed by fitting their editorial duties into an already crowded life that they simply give you the verdict of revising and resubmitting, together with copies of the different reviewers' comments.

When deciding which parts of reviewers' comments to address first, it is often helpful to have colleagues to bounce ideas off. We are sometimes so close to our own work that changing one word, or deleting one sentence, seems to rip out a piece of our soul. In my own case, if I have labored long and hard over a paragraph or a page, if I am enormously proud of what seems to me to be a wonderfully lyrical passage, or if I have spent weeks reading and then distilling a massive amount of work into a page or two, the suggestion from a reviewer that these things be deleted is very hard to take. But it is a major mistake to assume that the length or intensity of one's effort as a writer is correlated with its perceived relevance or usefulness to a reader. I have often written articles that have required months of reading and analysis to make sure I have understood the gist of a theory correctly, only to find that the section on implications for practice that I dashed off as an afterthought, and that was based on a quick review of my experience, is the one a journal reviewer selects as the most significant aspect of the whole article. If you can call on a colleague or two to do a quick read of your article, and if they agree with the substance of the reviewer's comments, this helps you force yourself to deal with those comments. A colleague can also help you focus on which elements of the reviewers' comments he or she feels you should take most seriously.

Addressing Specific Suggestions

How to go about doing this work will in large part be determined by the suggestions themselves. What will be required from you in all instances, however, will be some kind of letter or memorandum you will provide that lists how you have addressed the suggestions asked of you and shows exactly where in the article these changes have been made. This memo or letter should take each of the items listed in the editor's review and provide specific page numbers and paragraphs that allow the editor to see how you have responded to the requests in your resubmitted manuscript. Think of your letter as a map of a redrawn electoral district in which you indicate the new elements that are now included in the district's political terrain.

One general addition that is useful to make in a resubmitted article is to strive diligently to recast the article in terms that align exactly with the journal's editorial guidelines to authors and the journal's statement of purpose. This may seem like a blindingly self-evident observation. Often, however, the author is so taken with her analysis that the implicit connection she sees between her work and the journal's remit remains just that: implicit. In the intellectual excitement one feels about a piece of work that one finds stimulating and engaging, it is sometimes hard to imagine that disinterested readers will not immediately be inspired by one's efforts. Along with making explicit the connection of the article to the journal it is also good to do the "So what?" check by asking, "Have I shown in the opening two or three paragraphs how reading this article will be beneficial to the journal's readership?" This does not mean giving an encapsulation or précis of the most important findings. What is more important is to link one's work either to enduring concerns in a field of study or to a contemporary dilemma. In adult education, for example, enduring concerns are to understand the way in which adults create meaning from new experiences, the ways in which educators balance credibility and authenticity in learners' eyes, or the reasons students drop out of programs created with them in mind. A contemporary dilemma might be how to balance a concern for the development of a learner's independence of judgment with a requirement to ensure she passes a test in which certain correct answers have been rigidly prescribed in advance. Or perhaps the prevailing scholarly paradigm in a field has been found to be seriously skewed in favor of an elite group of researchers or scholars who are drawn from a highly segmented group that rejects other epistemologies, other ways of determining knowledge and truth.

Another element that is often usefully addressed in a cover letter to the editor detailing one's changes is to make any link one can between theories, research findings, models, or concepts contained in the resubmitted article and other recent articles, papers, or books. These need not be pieces that have appeared in the journal. In fact, sometimes reviewers reject a piece precisely because it deals with ideas that have already received a lot of attention in the journal concerned. But as a general rule, any time you can link your work to recent controversies in the field concerned, you raise the chances that it will be published.

When Not to Proceed

This is the $7 trillion question: When do I judge that it is worth my putting a great deal of time into addressing reviewers' suggestions in a bid to ensure that my work will then be published? There really is no clear answer to this question. However, I do feel there are clear instances when you should probably decide not to do this and that your contact with a journal has probably run its course.

First, a clear ideological divide between the reviewers and the author is a good case for deciding to cut the cord and approach another journal. An ideological divide is much harder to breach than a methodological one if the methodological questions raised have to do with how statistical analyses are run or data interpreted. A methodological debate is usually conducted with a reasonably clear and shared understanding of what rules are at play. An ideological debate usually operates with two colliding epistemologies, so that the very grounds by which one judges knowledge to be sound or arguments to be valid are in different universes. So if you have written a piece arguing for the legitimacy of an Afrocentric analyses of adult teaching methods and a journal accepts only Eurocentric perspectives as valid, it is probably more profitable to look elsewhere for publication. If a journal privileges only qualitative case studies and regards regression analysis or experimental and control group studies as anal-compulsive and reductionist, you will waste a lot of time trying to convince the inconvincible that your approach is legitimate. If you are seriously concerned with identity politics but are dealing with a board that believes facts are facts and theories are theories regardless of the race, class, gender, or sexual orientation of the knower, you probably will not win that battle. So unless you are on a mission to reorient a whole field, which should probably be your after-tenure project, discretion is probably going to be the better part of valor. It is better to place your work where it will be judged in terms you understand rather than fight a battle to get your work accepted by people who dispute the most fundamental procedures by which you judge truth.

Second, if reviewer feedback calls for a massive structural redesign of an article, to the extent that it really is a whole new edifice being constructed from scratch, you should think long and hard about whether the time that will involve is worth it. Sometimes it will be, as when your final piece appears in a journal that is highly prestigious, widely read, and hugely influential in shaping the discourse of a field. But remember that a major restructuring of a piece means you are essentially submitting a whole new article to the board, so you should expect another testing round of reviewer suggestions. Many suggestions sent back to authors have to do with the importance of including literature and research that the reviewers judge to be important but that you have omitted from your first draft. In my experience, those are the simplest revisions to make since the reviewers usually specify which material you need to consult and include in a redrafted piece.

Finally, there are three instances in which it is fairly easy to decide that reviewer feedback means you should stop pursuing publication in a particular journal. The first is when the editors require that you cut out information that you judge is crucially significant to the arguments you are making in the paper or the research you are presenting. If you judge that removing significant data or interpretations does irreparable harm to the quality of the work, you should cut and run. Second, if following the reviewers' suggestions means that the original purpose is nullified and if you feel that your original purpose must be retained at all costs, then I advocate trying to place the article elsewhere. For example, if you have mounted a critique of what you regard as omissions, biases, poorly conducted research, or false inferences in an area of study and the reviewers ask you to turn your piece into a review of literature in which all sides in a dispute are given equal time, then I feel your original purpose has been compromised. However, I will say that there are times when, as both reviewer and as author submitting my work for review, I have been convinced that my original purpose for a piece is misconceived and that a new direction suggested by reviewers is ultimately more interesting or useful. So, as with most of the other suggestions in this chapter, there are always multiple exceptions to the rule.

Probably the easiest situation in which to decide that your time working with a particular journal has run its course is when the feedback you receive is abusive, belittling, mocking, or personal. At times in my career, I have received feedback when I have felt the suggestions made have bordered on being all of these. In these instances, the reviewer usually feels my conclusions are either blindingly obvious or seriously inaccurate. I am prepared to grant individual reviewers some latitude in this regard, since in my role as reviewer, I have read pieces that I felt committed both these faults and have said so in my review. However, the editorial note that accompanies the summary of the reviews should always be professionally courteous and clear in its instructions. There is no excuse for an editor to be anything other than respectful to you. If this is not the case, I say there is an almost overwhelming case for you to try to place your work elsewhere.

Conclusion

What every author knows, but what few journals acknowledge in their editorial guidelines, is the enduring reality of power. People like me who are on the editorial boards of journals might not get paid for our efforts, but we do wield power whether or not we choose to acknowledge that reality. We have the chance to shape what counts as acceptable scholarship in a field, to construct what Foucault (1980) called a regime of truth—the set of procedures that are applied to determine what is legitimate knowledge. However, in the world of journal publishing, power is not wholly in the hands of the editorial board (a point Foucault himself would probably make); it is also exercised by those who are positionally powerless: the authors submitting work for publication. For what would happen if authors decided to stop submitting articles for publication? The journal's stream of publishable papers would dry up, and the board members would be forced to seek contributions from students and colleagues that would not be published in other journals. Once that happens, word gets around, subscriptions decline, and the journal eventually folds.

So authors do have some power, even though it may feel as if you are subject to the arbitrary and capricious whims of a group of people who cannot decide what they want. After all, editors and publishers rely on you to keep the journal afloat. Your work is the one resource they cannot do without. Staff can be cut, turnaround time can lengthen, board members can be changed, and still the journal will go on. But should authors just decide to stop submitting pieces for publication, the journal is done for.

When you get negative feedback from reviewers, try to remember that it is not the end of the world and that from the journal's point of view, what the editors and board most hope for is that you will decide to deal with the critique and resubmit a piece. It is much more in their interest to have your work published in their pages than it is to turn it away. This is why it is usually worth at least one attempt to try to address the suggestions made. The key point is to communicate explicitly to the editor and reviewers how you are trying to respond to their concerns and how you are going about incorporating their suggestions.

References

Brookfield, S. D. (2006). *The skillful teacher: On technique, trust, and responsiveness in the classroom.* San Francisco: Jossey-Bass.

Foucault, M. (1980). *Power/knowledge: Selected interviews and other writings, 1972–1977.* New York: Pantheon Books, 1980.

CHAPTER 19

INTERNATIONAL AND CROSS-CULTURAL ISSUES IN SCHOLARLY PUBLISHING

AAhad M. Osman-Gani, Rob F. Poell

In today's interactive and interdependent global environment, the value of a scholarly publication is increasingly being judged by the exposure to and coverage of wider global issues. This is accomplished through the participation of international scholars who represent many nations and cultures (Osman-Gani & Hyder, 2008; Osman-Gani, 2000). But there are only a few of these international scholars.

We have studied the possible reasons for this underrepresentation and analyzed the relevant issues that non-English-speaking international scholars face. Authors who are not fluent English speakers are many times confused by the process and structure followed by American and other English-only scholarly publications, which can be different from publications in other languages. For example, the linear structure of a standard research paper using clear, substantive demarcations between the theoretical, methodological, results, and discussion sections is far less prevalent in non-Western cultures. Although the quality of many scholarly writings by non-English-speaking authors is high, they face enormous challenges in publishing their research in mainstream Western journals due to language, culture, and process issues. As a result, the global scholarly community, which relies mostly on English-language publications, is deprived of exposure to a significant amount of high-quality research. Efforts should be taken to recognize this problem and then to take appropriate measures to encourage and help scholars from non-English-speaking countries to publish in English-language journals and thereby reach out to a wider global audience.

This chapter addresses four particular problem areas that international authors face, loosely based on the various stages through which a research project may take shape: (1) the initial identification of a research topic, (2) the design of research studies and other methodological issues, (3) problems associated with writing in a language different from one's own, and (4) specific ethical issues. Each of the problem areas is discussed in detail in the following sections. The chapter also presents a number of recommendations to international authors as well as to journal editors.

Identification of Research Topics

A number of issues are associated with the first stage of conducting most research studies: identifying a research topic. Some topics that are locally relevant and interesting can be met by a "So what?" from editors and reviewers of Western journals. For example, a study of educational reform in the Netherlands will have to be framed in a rather specific way: providing lots of context information and decontextualized to a large extent in order to be acceptable to an American journal. Much of this required information would be assumed to be well known had the study dealt with a U.S. educational reform.

Another issue has to do with research topics that have no equivalence (yet) in mainstream American and other Western journals. It is generally very difficult for non-English-speaking authors to get local, often untranslatable, concepts published in American and other Western journals. Nonaka's concept of *ba*, meaning "space" (see Nonaka, Toyama, & Konno, 2000), and the equally Japanese notion of *kaizen*, meaning "continuous improvement" (Imai, 1986), were two exceptions, in that they did get widely published and cited internationally. On the whole, though, non-Western authors either need to come up with an often unsatisfactory direct translation of the topic or resort to using a related (but often dissimilar) better-known concept from the English language and the related literature. In both cases, local knowledge loses much of its meaning despite being potentially relevant to a wider international audience. For example, the Dutch polder model of consensus decision making is a direct translation of the Dutch term, which in English loses much of its original meaning—that those who lived in low-lying areas in the Netherlands had to work together to reclaim their land from the water and protect it.

Many non-English-speaking authors have therefore resorted to borrowing Western concepts and applying them to their local situation. One example is the French literature on *l'organisation apprenante*, a straight translation from Senge's (1990) concept of the learning organization. The problem here is that in France, organizations are not considered capable of learning, which means that many French scholars missed the whole point of using the concept. Another example is the growing empirical literature on self-directed learning in the Korean context (Cho & Kwon, 2005). Here the problem is of a more cultural nature, as the highly individualistic Western concept does not fit well with the more collectivistic Korean culture, which may be one reason that not much self-directed learning has been found in Korea.

Examples from Japan show that it can be worthwhile to take a locally relevant research topic and attempt to get it published internationally. A direct translation of the concept will be necessary to give the readers a first, if only partially correct, impression of what the topic is about. An important next step is to provide readers with an overview of how the term relates to similar but better-known concepts from the established Anglo-Saxon literature. This would then need to be followed by an account of the similarities as well as the differences between the local topic and the more established concepts.

Many of the articles published in American and other Western journals are based on research conducted in the United States or on comparative analysis with U.S. research findings (Wasti & Robert, 2004; Wasti, Poell, & Çakar, 2008). This signals to international scholars that in order to publish in top-tier journals, authors should act accordingly. This would imply studying U.S. concerns, doing comparative analyses with U.S. data, or even moving to the United States and conducting research in the U.S. context. In the end, however, what matters most to authors wanting to get published internationally is the quality of their research and the development of new knowledge that is valid across various contexts and should be useful to scholarly communities around the world. According to March (2005), "Improving scholarship is more a function of improving the quality of research within a world-view and tradition than it is of choosing a world-view" (p. 12).

Research Design and Methodological Issues

The selection of an appropriate research design is an important issue for every researcher; however, international scholars may face some specific problems. The research design that international scholars choose could be most relevant to the specific types and contexts of their research; however, that may not be appreciated by or acceptable to English-only Western journals. This could be due to reviewers' or editors' strong preference for certain research designs (for example, experimental, tightly controlled, or context independent), which international scholars may not find relevant considering their research types and contexts. Although non-English-speaking authors are interested in publishing their work in top-tier journals to reach a larger global audience, they are often not welcomed due to conflicting design expectations, and as a result, the global audience misses some significant research findings. As we know, basic research designs are generally universal, but their uses and applications can vary significantly based on the types and contexts of the research conducted in different parts of the world. Western journal editors and reviewers need to be flexible considering the topical, contextual, and other sociocultural differences.

Societal and local academic community expectations may conflict with the expectations of Western journals especially around the dimensions of conceptual-empirical and qualitative-quantitative research. Many U.S. journals emphasize quantitative, empirical work, while European journals on the whole are oriented more toward conceptual and qualitative studies. In a content analysis of 267 human resource development (HRD) research articles published between 1990 and 2003, Wasti et al. (2008) found notable differences in underlying theoretical orientations as well as methodological approaches. The U.S. HRD and mainstream management and human resource-oriented literature adhered firmly to the natural science paradigm, with significantly more empirical work and a greater concern for validity and reliability. The European literature had a greater likelihood of endorsing critical perspectives and, on the whole, more theoretical analyses. In terms of method, the natural science paradigm was not as strictly endorsed, and where it was, the concern about adhering to methodological standards imposed was not as strong as in the U.S. literature (Wasti et al., 2008).

Most Asian authors seem to follow the predominant U.S. style of focusing more on quantitative, empirical designs for getting published in American and other Western journals, for which they are appreciated and rewarded by the university administration in making promotion and tenure decisions. This is particularly due to U.S. dominance as the training ground for many Asian-based or Asian-focused researchers (White, 2002). Major Asian universities require data on the impact of faculty research: citation counts of publications and information on where their research was published. The citation counts are greatly influenced by the global readership and circulation of the journal (not necessarily the quality of the article). Some East Asian universities seek prestige by higher placement in worldwide university rankings conducted by various agencies (for example, *Times Higher Education, US News & World Report*, and the Economist Intelligence Unit). A major determinant of the prestige is indicated by the high correlation between impact factor and subjective evaluation of the quality of journals in which faculty members publish. High-impact journals seemed to have some biases toward specific types of research designs. The top-tier journals with high impact factors tend to favor deductive rather than inductive research design, which Mintzberg (2005) has severely criticized as a major limitation to good theory development (Leung, 2007; Tung, 2006). Moreover, inadequate attention was paid to international management and HRD research, and alternative research agendas and paradigms that are popular outside North America have often been shunned in the United States (Tung, 2006; Osman-Gani & Rockstuhl, 2008; Wasti et al., 2008).

Another issue that international scholars often face is in doing comprehensive meta-analysis on relevant topics. Beside the limitations of language proficiency, accessing relevant databases and important non-English research publications can be difficult. Even if access could be made to some specific non-English-language publications, translating those into English becomes another challenge considering the sociocultural interpretations of the wordings and phrases used in the texts of those publications.

A recommendation to non-Western authors wishing to get published in good-quality Western journals is to acquaint themselves with their intended outlet's standards and expectations around study design before submitting their paper or, preferably, before even beginning their research. Nevertheless, a crucial overriding concern is whether there is support for the chosen research design from related literature, which should be referred to in the paper. Moreover, the research design should clearly be appropriate to address the central research question. If there are any uncommon research design aspects, the authors should offer a justification for their use.

Another major issue that international scholars face is dealing with research methods that Western journals consider appropriate. The types and methods of academic training that non-English-speaking scholars receive in their home countries or elsewhere on various research methods is different in many cases from the requirements of many Western and other English-language journals. This puts them at a disadvantage in getting their research published. Expectations of methodological rigor are also generally different from their local-language journals as the term *rigor* is interpreted differently in different countries and cultures. The Western and other English-language journals generally focus on high research rigor (using quantitative methods) used in questionnaire design, validation, and administration, as well as on sophisticated data analysis procedures, while the local-language journals are more interested in the key findings as long as the researcher followed satisfactory methods.

Although we all agree that methodological rigor should not be compromised in developing quality research papers, the overemphasis on methodological rigor at the expense of useful content is becoming a major problem for non-Western scholars and is a significant obstacle for publishing their research in major American and other Western journals (Tung, 2006; Barney, 2005). The practical aspects of data collection through interviews, surveys, and other methods are significantly different in other nations compared to the Western (English-speaking) countries. This is mainly due to lack of proper research environments in those countries, and the lack of English-language proficiency of the field investigators. Many non-Western companies are bought by Western multinationals, and English-speaking managers take up key positions in these firms. These problems result in low response rates, incomplete responses, and inconsistencies. Because quality primary data collection is needed through extensive field studies in most social science research, the roles of survey administrators, interviewers, and data collectors become more significant. This is particularly true when Western research instruments are used in the data collection process. The wording, phrases, and illustrations used in the validated Western instruments are often difficult to translate properly due to different interpretations and cultural explanations of the wording in the local language. Even when back translations are made, these often do not provide accurate meanings of English words or phrases. Similarly, statements as well as response categories and choices mentioned in the questionnaires can confuse respondents from different cultural backgrounds because they do not seem to find appropriate response categories in their own languages. As a result, the quality and quantity of responses are often found to be below expectations by Western standards, which limits the possibilities of publishing those studies in many English-language Western journals.

The use of research methods and procedures as well as the way these are described in scientific articles are found to be standardized and strictly enforced by journal reviewers and editors without considering the societal and cultural norms of many countries. Non-English-speaking authors do not always share these same expectations. Examples are presented of the most important issues confronted by authors—for example, separating the analysis, the results, the conclusions, and the implications and providing rich enough detail about the methods used for readers to be able to replicate the study (White, 2002). The biases of editors, board members, and reviewers (most of whom are American or other Western scholars) toward certain methods can also become stumbling blocks for non-English-speaking international scholars. As of today, very few non-Western scholars are on the editorial boards of high-quality journals in HRD and related management fields. This could be due to editors' or board members' preferences toward Western scholars or lack of sufficient responses from international scholars. The issues relating to preferences for qualitative or quantitative analyses, instrument validations, translations and back translations, and so forth become significant challenges for many international non-English-speaking scholars (Noorderhaven, 2000).

A common reaction, which each of us has personally experienced, from American journal editors commenting on studies conducted outside the

United States is to ask to what extent the conclusions can be generalized to other countries. When studies are conducted based on U.S. data, the editors of the same journals assume the conclusions are generalizable beyond the United States. Sometimes they assume that the results will be valid only locally (not globally) and reject the submission. It is advisable to address this issue in the limitation section of the manuscript before submission.

Writing in a Different Language

The fact that American and other Western journals generally publish articles in a language different from that of aspiring contributors poses many problems for nonnative English authors. Even well-trained authors use English in a different way from native writers (Flowerdew, 1999), not to mention knowing all the subtleties involved in distinguishing British English from American English. Editors and reviewers can easily be put off by an article in poorly written English, even if its content and contributions may be of great value to the journal's readership. Poor use of the English language can seriously harm the chances of an article's acceptance; a manuscript might not even be sent out for review (Flowerdew, 2001).

The best strategies to deal with this problem are for non-Western authors to team up with native-English writers for their research or to have their work translated and edited by a professional agency. These solutions and opportunities, however, are not readily available to everyone. Professional translation agencies are usually very expensive, and the learning and spin-off effects bestowed on the author are relatively limited. Collaborating with native English writers can be fruitful for both parties, especially if they manage to make it a long-term commitment based on an appreciation and recognition of each another's specific areas of expertise. Participating in the international community of scholars, however, is a necessary precondition for such collaborations to come into being.

Another possible way around the problem is to study thoroughly how published articles about the topic at hand frame the problem, state the research questions, put forward the theory associated with the topic, provide an account of the methods used in the study, present the findings, and discuss the implications of the study. Then authors can use that experience of self-learning to restructure and revise the manuscript appropriately before submitting it to a reputable journal. Two risks here are that paraphrasing other articles might get dangerously close to plagiarism and that creative and innovative research might be hampered if this strategy is followed too strictly.

An obvious but longer-term approach to reducing translation problems is for scholars to engage in a number of efforts:

- Improve their English writing skills by taking classes in English academic writing.
- Submit many conference papers.
- Attend specialized preconferences focusing on their academic specialty.
- Study the feedback provided in both writing and presenting their work.
- Broaden their academic network so as to increase the chances that native English writers will team up with them for a research project.

In other words, learning by doing and learning by social interaction are prime ways for aspiring authors to improve their English and their publication record.

A recommendation in this area to journal editors is to talk to their publishers about the opportunities to offer translation services. Some journals provide prospective authors from non-English-speaking countries the option of submitting research manuscripts in their own (non-English) language. Reviewers are then sought from countries that speak the same language as well as English. If the reviewers convince the editor that the article deserves to be published in the English-language journal, the journal offers the authors the necessary translation services. This is obviously more expensive for the journal than not allowing submissions in languages other than English; however, it does open up many possibilities to attract new and relevant research from other parts of the world and its scholarly communities. It would also provide a way of doing justice to the rhetoric on globalization.

Ethical Issues

International scholars also face various ethical issues that are associated with publishing in English-language Western journals. For example, U.S. journals often ask for a statement about the ways in which approval was gained to conduct a study among organizational members (for example, human subject research approvals), which is often not an issue in other countries due to the differences in legal requirements and litigation environments. In some countries (including the United States), such approval is needed to protect journals in any future litigation, which is not the case for other countries where such legal recourse is absent or scarce. Participation in research may be regarded as consent from the subjects.

There are different interpretations of ethics in research and publications among different nations and cultures. There is no set of globally accepted ethical standards subscribed to by all institutions and agreed to by scholars from various fields in different countries. There are, however, some common denominators of ethical standards for publication. Many international scholars from non-Western nations do not have clear information about those ethical standards. Therefore, unknowingly they resort to extracting or copying large chunks of information from published texts without properly citing or placing text in quotations or paraphrasing them appropriately. Their work then comes very close to plagiarism, another major ethical issue among authors mostly from non-English-speaking countries (Wheeler, 2009).

There have been many debates about attitudes toward plagiarism among students educated outside the Western Hemisphere. Many scholars argue that plagiarism does not necessarily carry the same negative connotations across cultures (Wheeler, 2009; Bloch, 2001; Dryden, 1999; Scollon, 1995). Buranen (1999) cautioned about the possible consequences resulting from easily excusing plagiarism as a mere cultural difference by following a very simplistic definition of culture. Sowden (2005) stated that plagiarism in written exams is a culture-specific concept, and generalizations about cultural background and its influence do need to be taken seriously to avoid degenerating into stereotypes. Liu (2005) expressed problems with Sowden's arguments, particularly for indicating that plagiarism is an acceptable practice in the "Far East, especially China" (p. 234).

Rinnert and Kobayashi (2005) conducted a study comparing attitudes toward plagiarism and citation techniques between American and Japanese university students. They found Japanese students are more likely to struggle with correct citation procedures than Americans are and do not necessarily feel that acknowledging their sources is always necessary or important. In addition, 69 percent of the American students said they had received formal writing training at the university level compared to only 39 percent of the Japanese students (Wheeler, 2009).

The term *plagiarism* has been translated in Japanese as *ukeuri*, loosely defined as "second-hand account" or "echo of someone else's words." According to Rinnert and Kobayashi (2005), "It is important to understand that the terms '*ukeuri*' and 'plagiarism' are not exact translation equivalents" (p. 35). Plagiarism is not regarded as negatively in Japan and other countries as it is in the United States. Dryden (1999) mentioned that in a Japanese university, cheating on exams, rather than plagiarism, is "the cardinal sin" (p. 78).

Hence, the word *plagiarism* and its interpretations have different implications in non-Western nations. Attempts should therefore be made to identify an agreeable definition of *plagiarism* by finding appropriate terms in major languages that will eliminate the confusion and misunderstanding regarding acceptable ethical boundaries relating to plagiarism. To deal with this issue may require that journal editors and international authors take some additional responsibilities. Editors should clearly specify the requirements to international authors and may ask for a brief statement of understanding and agreeing to those principles. International authors should also identify the ethical requirements of the journal before submitting their manuscripts, and specifically ask the editors about the requirements if they do not get clear information in this regard.

Issues relating to copyright, quotation and citation, conference proceedings publication, and other matters are also different across countries and societies. The legal system and penal codes are different in various countries, especially in terms of enforcement of intellectual property rights acts and laws. Scholarly communities around the world deal with the ethical issues within their sociocultural environments through the activities of various professional societies and scholarly associations. Relevant issues could then be discussed at annual meetings and conferences of international and global professional organizations. Identifying the common denominators of scholarly ethical standards could diminish the incidences of misunderstandings and misinterpretations.

Conclusions

In order to increase contributions to the global treasure of knowledge from scholars in the non-English-speaking world, we have attempted to identify and analyze relevant issues constraining those resourceful international scholars from publishing in mainstream English-language Western publications. We have discussed a number of critical issues that might develop awareness among journal editors and board members, so that they can take appropriate measures for attracting international scholars. It should be worthwhile to tap into the knowledge and insights available internationally that could be of great importance for the global scholarly community. We have also made some recommendations to scholars and authors whose first language is not English for making extra efforts in preparing and submitting their manuscripts, thus reaching out to a wider global readership.

We hope that this chapter will trigger more discussion and result in more publications in this area. Our attempts will have been worthwhile if the analysis and discussion manage to motivate non-English-speaking international scholars to make significant efforts in submitting their manuscripts to the mainstream global journals.

References

Barney, J. B. (2005, August). *No new theory.* Paper presented at Opportunities and Challenges in Developing New Management Theory: Processes Used by Top Scholars at the Annual Meeting of the Academy of Management, Honolulu, HI.

Bloch, J. (2001). Plagiarism and the ESL student: From printed to electronic texts. In D. D. Belcher & A. Hirvela (Eds.), *Linking literacies* (pp. 209–245). Ann Arbor: University of Michigan Press.

Buranen, L. (1999). But I wasn't cheating: Plagiarism and cross-cultural mythology. In L. Buranen & A. M. Roy (Eds.), *Perspectives on plagiarism and intellectual property in a postmodern world*. Albany, NY: SUNY Press.

Cho, D., & Kwon, D. B. (2005). Self directed learning readiness as an antecedent of organizational commitment: A Korean study. *International Journal of Training and Development, 9*, 140–142.

Dryden, L. M. (1999). A distant mirror or through the looking glass? Plagiarism and intellectual property in Japanese education. In L. Buranen & A. M. Roy (Eds.), *Perspectives on plagiarism and intellectual property in a postmodern world*. Albany, NY: SUNY Press.

Flowerdew, J. (1999). Problems in writing for scholarly publication in English: The case of Hong Kong. *Journal of Second Language Writing, 8*, 243–264.

Flowerdew, J. (2001). Attitudes of journal editors to non-native speaker contributions. *TESOL Quarterly, 35*, 121–150.

Imai, M. (1986). *Kaizen: The key to Japan's competitive success.* New York: Random House.

Leung, K. (2007). The glory and tyranny of citation impact: An East Asian perspective. *Academy of Management Journal, 50*(3), 510–513.

Liu, D. (2005). Plagiarism in ESOL students: Is cultural conditioning truly the major culprit? *ELT Journal, 59*(3), 234–241.

March, J. G. (2005). Parochialism in the evolution of a research community: The case of organization studies, *Management and Organization Review, 1*(1), 5–22.

Mintzberg, H. (2005, August). Remarks at the panel: *Opportunities and challenges in developing new management theory: Processes used by top scholars.* Paper presented at the Annual meeting of the Academy of Management, Honolulu, HI.

Nonaka, I., Toyama, R., & Konno, N. (2000). SECI, *ba* and leadership: A unified model of dynamic knowledge creation. *Long Range Planning, 33*, 5–34.

Noorderhaven, N. G. (2000). Positivist, hermeneutical, and postmodern positions in the comparative management debate. In M. Maurice & A. Sorge (Eds.), *Embedding organizations* (pp. 117–137). Amsterdam: Benjamins.

Osman-Gani, A. M. (2000). Developing expatriates for the Asia-Pacific region: A comparative analysis of MNE managers from five countries across three continents. *Human Resource Development Quarterly, 11*(3), 213–235.

Osman-Gani, A. M., & Hyder, S. A. (2008). Repatriation readjustment of international managers: An empirical study of HRD interventions. *Career Development International, 13*(5), 456–475.

Osman-Gani, A. M., & Rocksthul, T. (2008). Antecedents and consequences of social network characteristics for expatriate adjustment and performance in overseas assignments: Implications for HRD. *Human Resource Development Review, 7*(1), 32–57.

Rinnert, C., & Kobayashi, H. (2005). Borrowing words and ideas: Insights from Japanese L1 writers. *Journal of Asian Pacific Communication, 15*(1), 31–56.

Scollon, R. (1995). Plagiarism and ideology: Identity in intercultural discourse. *Language in Society, 24*(1995), 1–28.

Senge, P. M. (1990). *The fifth discipline. The art and practice of the learning organization.* New York: Random House.

Sowden, C. (2005). Plagiarism and the culture of multilingual students in higher education abroad. *ELT Journal, 59*(3), 226–233.

Tung, R. L. (2006). North American research agenda and methodologies: Past imperfect, future-Limitless possibilities. *Asian Business and Management, 5,* 23–25.

Wasti, S. A., Poell, R. F., & Çakar, N. D. (2008). Oceans and notions apart? An analysis of the U.S. and European human resource development literature. *International Journal of Human Resource Management, 19*(12), 2155–2170.

Wasti, S. A., & Robert, C. A. (2004). Out of touch? An evaluation of the correspondence between academic and practitioner concerns in IHRM. In J.L.C. Cheng & M. Hitt (Eds.), *Managing multinationals in a knowledge economy: Economics, culture and human resources* (pp. 207–239). Stamford, CT: JAI Press.

Wheeler, G. (2009). Plagiarism in the Japanese universities: Truly a cultural matter? *Journal of Second Language Writing, 18*(1), 17–29.

White, S. (2002). Rigor and relevance in Asian management research: Where are we and where can we go? *Asia Pacific Journal of Management, 19,* 287–352.

CHAPTER 20

WORKING WITH COAUTHORS

Ann I. Nevin, Jacqueline S. Thousand, Richard A. Villa

Each member of our collaborative writing team has engaged in a variety of strategies to generate numerous publications. Some of our publications have been written individually, some with one or both members of this writing triad, and some with other collaborators. Collectively, from 1990 to present, the three of us have published thirty-five co-generated books, chapters, papers, refereed conference presentations, research projects, and in-service training guides and DVDs. The purpose of this chapter (which represents our thirty-sixth coauthored endeavor) is to share the processes that have enabled the three of us to continue to work, grow, and publish together for two decades.

In this chapter, we examine the dilemmas, difficulties, and benefits that occur when coauthors work together. First, we share a tale of three authors, which describes the beginning of our coauthoring journey. Second, we explain the theoretical frameworks that underlie the collaborative processes we practice. Finally, we delineate several tips for coauthors to practice so as to avoid the difficulties that vex many coauthor teams.

A Tale of Three Scholars: Beginning a Coauthoring Journey

Imagine a late autumn afternoon twenty years ago where four individuals meet in a Vermont school administrator's office. In attendance were Ann (a full professor), Phyllis (an assistant professor), Jacque (a lecturer and funded grant writer) from the University of Vermont, and Rich (the director of instructional services and staff development for the school district in which they are meeting). As they gathered around a table in the director's office at sunset, the four started to brainstorm a possible outline for a journal article. The ideas came fast and furious. So as to not lose any valuable ideas, in addition to having one person serve in the traditional role of recorder, they tape-recorded this and future meetings.

The meeting was precipitated by an invitation to Ann to contribute an article for the premier edition of a new journal on educational and psychological consultation. However, Ann noticed she had changed the paradigm that framed her previous work in school-based consultation. She invited the three others to join her to conceptualize and articulate a new approach to consultation and collaboration. She believed that each of the collaborators brought complementary skills and perspectives that would contribute to the development of a timely, provocative, and practical article on a new paradigm for school-based collaboration. At this time, she was an experienced author with over forty publications.

Ann and Phyllis had previously coauthored two books on collaborative consultation. Phyllis was expected to continue to publish in order to advance up academia's career ladder. Jacque, the lecturer and grant writer, had earned her doctorate in psychology with an emphasis on developmental disabilities. Recognized for her creativity and work ethic, Jacque coordinated the Homecoming Project, the first federally funded demonstration grant project to show that students with moderate and severe disabilities could be successfully educated in general education classrooms of their neighborhood schools. She had coauthored ten refereed journal articles (including several with Ann), three book chapters, and a journal article. Rich worked in one of the pilot schools participating in the Homecoming Project and subsequently gained recognition as one of the nation's first fully inclusive school systems. Rich and his staff relied on collaboration in planning and teaching to successfully include diverse learners in mixed-ability classrooms. Previously he had published one journal article and coauthored a refereed journal article and a book chapter with Jacque.

As the four gathered for that first meeting, they recognized clear differences in age, gender, skill, position, and power relationships among the four that might facilitate or hinder their ability to write collaboratively. For example, Ann was an instructor in a master's degree program that both Jacque and Rich had completed. Might the status difference intimidate the lecturer and director and keep them from challenging the full professor's ideas? Ann had collaborated with Phyllis on a major professional development project that resulted in the publication of two books. In what ways might their prior experiences interfere with positively interacting with Jacque and Rich, who were the less experienced coauthors? Three of the members of the team were university faculty (Ann, Jacque, and Phyllis), and

Rich was a school-based employee. How might the role differences influence the dynamics? (Note that the first meeting was held in the school district setting rather than a university office to accommodate Rich's administrative schedule.) Three of the four were women. Moreover, Jacque and Rich, wife and husband, had been married for eight years. Some married couples easily work together; others learn it is best to separate the worlds of home and work.

Fast-forward twenty years: Ann, Jacque, and Rich have continued to collaborate on coauthored research projects, refereed journal articles, and books. Phyllis, who did not continue with them, followed a different career path as a social work faculty member and subsequently established coauthor relationships with others.

While writing this chapter, Ann, Jacque, and Rich were completing three other writing projects. Twenty years ago, none of the members of the collaborative writing team who sat in the Vermont school administrator's office could have imagined that their first jointly authored journal article was just the beginning of a long and productive collaborative writing journey. During these twenty years, Ann taught at several research universities (University of California, Santa Barbara; University of Hawaii Manoa; Arizona State University; and Florida International University) where she codeveloped various innovative teacher education programs at the postgraduate, graduate, and undergraduate levels. Jacque, the former lecturer and grant writer, is now a full professor at California State University, San Marcos, who co-coordinates the special education professional preparation and master's programs. Rich, the Vermont school administrator, remained in the inclusive school district for several years until numerous requests for consultation, training, and evaluation led him to become an independent consultant. For over seventeen years, he has provided training and consultation on topics such as inclusive educational practices, co-teaching, differentiated instruction, and systems change to school systems, advocacy organizations, and governmental and nongovernmental agencies at various levels (state, national, and international).

Empirical and Theoretical Framework for Collaborative Writing

Some scholars have published opinions about how to increase faculty productivity (Gray, 1999; McDonald, 1995), models to explain the collaborative writing process (Isenberg, Jalongo, & Bromley, 1987), and methods to increase productivity such as professional development activities (Pololi, Knight, & Dunn, 2004) or behavior modification techniques (Boice, 1992). Tschannen-Moran, Firestone, Hoy, and Johnson (2000) compared highly productive and typical scholars in the field of educational administration, finding that the more productive scholars focused on research and theory while less productive scholars focused on issues. In "Too Many Co-Authors?" McDonald (1995) noted that the average number of authors of scientific papers had doubled between 1945 and 1995. Given the increasing numbers of coauthored publications, the need for research on the dynamics of coauthoring becomes an important area of exploration. Yet only a few researchers have focused on coauthorship (Isenberg et al., 1987; Gray, 1999). Isenberg et al. (1987) reported survey findings that describe motivation for coauthoring and criteria for selecting coauthors, ways for determining division of labor and allocating credit for authorship, deterrents to multiple authorship, and ethical issues. To increase scholarly productivity, Gray (1999) developed twelve strategies to become productive scholars based on her review of the literature.

We note that our coauthoring experiences had not been informed by the empirical literature. Instead, the framework for collaborative writing is based on multiple sources. One source is our firsthand experience as coauthors with one another and others, as well as our experiences as members of school-based planning teams to differentiate instruction for diverse classrooms. A second source is our reading and implementation of the literature regarding the social-psychological and creative thinking processes that promote effective communication and collaboration: cooperative group learning (Johnson & R. Johnson, 2002), adult collaboration (Villa & Thousand, 2005), group theory (Johnson & F. Johnson, 1997; Johnson & R. Johnson, 1999; Slavin, 1994), and creative thinking (Leff & Nevin, 1990; Nevin & Leff, 1990; Leff, Thousand, Nevin, & Quiocho, 2002).

In our work together, we have systematically implemented the elements of a collaborative teaming process, derived from the theoretical frameworks outlined above, so as to produce our coauthored pieces:

- An agreement among the coauthors to coordinate their work to accomplish an agreed-on writing goal
- A belief that all coauthors have unique and needed expertise
- A demonstration of parity, defined as the equal valuing of each member's input by applying a distributed functions theory of leadership where all coauthors distribute among themselves the authorship functions of research, writing, reviewing, and editing
- A collaborative teaming process that involves face-to-face interaction, positive interdependence, individual accountability, and the performance and group processing of interpersonal skills

Although we consider all of these elements to be critical to successful coauthoring, the last one, the collaborative teaming process, is the focus of this chapter. This is because when coauthors pay attention to the collaborative teaming process, the other three elements (common goal, belief in members' unique expertise, and parity by implementing the distributed functions theory of leadership) automatically are practiced. When the collaborative teaming process is implemented, common barriers and challenges to successful coauthorship can be avoided. Among these barriers and challenges are unequal perceived power differentials inherent in team membership (for example, senior-junior faculty, dissertation chair and doctoral candidate, published author and yet unpublished team member), failure to recognize contributions, coauthors who fail to do their share, writer's block, and domineering or feuding coauthors.

What follows is an overview of the dimensions of the collaborative teaming process followed by tips for translating these dimensions into action for effective professional coauthoring.

Dimensions of the Collaborative Teaming Process

Effective adult collaborative partnerships are the adult analogues of effective student cooperative learning groups (Johnson & R. Johnson, 1999). For adults and children, groups perform best when the five dimensions that define the collaborative teaming process are practiced:

- Regularly scheduled face-to-face interaction among coauthors
- Using structures and strategies to create a sense of mutual positive interdependence among the coauthors
- Attention to small group interpersonal social skills in trust building, communication, leadership distribution, creative solution finding and decision making, and conflict management
- Processing group interactions—regular assessment and discussion of how successfully the coauthors are accomplishing tasks and using interpersonal skills
- Individual accountability using methods for holding one another accountable for agreed-on responsibilities and commitments (Villa & Thousand, 2000)

Tips for becoming highly effective coauthors, shown in Exhibit 20.1, encompass strategies for activating the five dimension of the collaborative teaming process. As you read each tip, be sure to notice how the dimensions of the coauthoring process are addressed.

EXHIBIT 20.1. TIPS FOR SUCCESSFUL COAUTHORS.

Tip 1: Choose coauthors strategically: Know with whom you want or need to coauthor.

Tip 2: Clarify coauthoring goals: Know how to recognize and respect differences in goals.

Tip 3: Getting along is as important as producing: Know how to nurture a collaborative culture.

Tip 4: Agree to reflective analysis of the coauthoring process and celebrate.

Tip 5: Expect to be responsible and to be held accountable.

Tip 6: Be willing to let go of personal paradigms to create new paradigms.

Tip 1: Choose Coauthors Strategically

The first question authors need to ask in order to structure the first dimension of the collaborative teaming process—regular face-to-face interaction among coauthors—is, "Who should or must be part of the cowriting partnership?" Authors may come together for a variety of reasons. They may share a research interest, be involved in a common project, or be thrown into a writing task that needs to be accomplished for a higher purpose, such as a program quality review.

If coauthors have the luxury of selecting one another, one question to consider in the selection process is, "Who has the needed or desired content or authoring expertise to produce a written product of quality?" What is considered needed or desired expertise may differ depending on numerous variables. One variable is the developmental stage of the author's career. A coauthor who is just beginning his or her career in the professoriate may need to focus on producing peer-reviewed, blind-refereed articles for scholarly journals and thus desire the collaboration of senior faculty with a successful track record in this type of writing. A professor may have students or colleagues who are practitioners doing cutting-edge exemplary work that deserves to be shared with the profession, but who have little experience or opportunity to write. In this case, a professor and a practitioner may partner as coauthors so that the experienced writer can ask the questions and shape the story of the best practice in a way that suits the publication guidelines and demands of the selected publication venue. In summary, the idea is to balance expertise, filling in gaps, and rounding out knowledge of and skills in the content and the authoring process. In these ways, the possible intimidation factor that novice authors sometimes experience when working with more experienced authors may be mitigated by an appreciation for the mentoring and modeling offered by the more experienced authors.

Tip 2: Clarify Coauthoring Goals

One powerful way to create a sense of positive interdependence, the second dimension of the collaborative teaming process, is to clearly define shared goals. Common goals guide coauthors' actions and serve as criteria for resolving conflict and judging the partners' effectiveness. Common goals also create the tension or achievement motivation needed to get coauthors to coordinate their work. When coauthors first meet together, a critical first goal-setting step is to come to consensus about expected outcomes, time lines and due dates, division of labor inside and outside their face-to-face meetings, and how to deal with competing agendas or demands.

As part of this conversation, each coauthor needs to honestly share any individual goals. One author may have a personal goal of getting the product completed within the shortest amount of time; another may have as a goal to produce the most polished document that will have the greatest possibility of being accepted by a top internationally respected peer-reviewed journal. One author may be motivated to reach a researcher audience, while another may want to reach a practitioner audience. Goal conversations can spare coauthors from experiencing the distress that can occur when unspoken agendas, that is, hidden agendas, are not shared.

Central to the goal-setting process is an agreement among coauthors to take a win-win position. This means that everyone agrees to forward the group's goal. And it is important to each coauthor to ask for what she or he may need to achieve personal goals (for example, have time to attend to family demands, have exercise breaks, take a mandatory phone call in the middle of a work session) at the same time while recognizing that personal and group goals may appear to clash at times.

Tip 3: Getting Along Is as Important as Producing

The third dimension of the collaborative teaming process, attending to small group interpersonal social skills, is at the core of this tip for coauthors. In addition to establishing common goals, an initial step in developing coauthor relationships is to devote time to learning about one another's cultural, personal, and professional backgrounds and each member's experiences with collaborative teaming (Webb-Johnson, 2002). It helps to know that working with others can be a developmental process that requires individuals to learn, practice, and use different sets of social skills. Johnson and F. Johnson (1997) identify skill sets related to four stages of group development. The *forming* stage requires individuals to exhibit trust-building behaviors. The *functioning* stage involves coordinating and distributive leadership skills. At the *formulating* stage, coauthors apply creative problem-solving skills. Controversy management skills are activated at the *fermenting* stage. Knowing about these four group development stages and skill sets alerts coauthors to use the specific skills, as needed, to help each other get along—develop and maintain positive relationships—in order to accomplish the task of generating a written product. Note that although the stages of group development appear to be sequential, in fact, coauthors often must practice all four sets of skills as they experience all four stages in a single meeting.

When new coauthors are in the initial forming stage, each person must use communication skills that build mutual and reciprocal trust. One technique is to establish and consciously practice group norms throughout the writing process. Norms are "a group's common beliefs regarding appropriate behavior for members; they tell, in other words, how members are expected to behave. . . . All groups have norms, set either formally or informally" (Johnson & F. Johnson, 1997, p. 424). Ground rules or norms include actions such as arriving to meetings on time, knowing and using one another's preferred names, actively listening to one another, never putting down anyone or using pejorative language, and waiting to interject a comment until after the speaker has finished. By explicitly stating and committing to adhere to norms, coauthors create a sense of safety for each other to have and express different perspectives and to risk telling their truths about concerns and needs.

Once coauthors have developed trust, they can focus on the functioning stage skills of communication and distributive leadership skills that allow the coauthoring task to get done, and also further develop positive interpersonal relationships. Functioning skills include clarifying one's own views, coordinating tasks, distributing various leadership actions among all coauthors, paraphrasing the views of others, and checking for understanding of and agreement with decisions.

Skills that help coauthors proceed through the formulating stage include creative thinking and problem-solving skills that lead to new conceptualizations and solutions. Formulating skills include brainstorming, seeking additional information through questioning, thinking about and explaining out loud one's thinking and decision-making processes, asking for critical feedback, and risk taking to try out unfamiliar practices. Coauthors who activate these skills are more likely to be successful when facing expected and unexpected challenges.

The fermenting stage involves skills in constructive controversy and conflict resolution that allow coauthors to deal successfully with the controversies and conflicts that are inevitable within every team. An example of a fermenting skill is to ask for more information and underlying rationale in order to understand someone else's position. Knowing and practicing controversy and conflict management skills allow for the clashing of ideas to stimulate the integration of these ideas into new and novel conceptualizations or solutions. It also pushes teammates to a higher level of cohesiveness, since teammates learn that they not only can survive but actually thrive through conflict.

Exhibit 20.2 displays key skills related to each of the stages (forming, functioning, formulating, and fermenting) that coauthors can activate to guide reflective conversations about how they are getting along. Coauthors can also be encouraged to use Exhibit 20.2 as a self-assessment tool by asking the two-pronged question, "What stage of group development are we currently experiencing and what skill set should we be emphasizing?" Coauthors increase their productivity and enjoyment of the work when they understand and consciously practice all four sets of social skills.

EXHIBIT 20.2. CHECKLIST OF SOCIAL SKILLS ASSOCIATED WITH FOUR STAGES OF GROUP DEVELOPMENT.

Forming (Trust-Building) Skills

Use coauthors' preferred names (for example, first name, nickname, formal title).

Use affirming statements (that is, agree to a no-put-down norm).

Come to meetings on time, and stay for the entire time.

Demonstrate trustworthiness by following through on agreements.

Acknowledge coauthors for their follow-through.

Functioning (Communication and Leadership) Skills

Clarify tasks, goals, and responsibilities.

Set or call attention to time limits.

Suggest procedures on how to perform a task effectively.

Express support and acceptance verbally.

Paraphrase and clarify.

Energize the group with humor, ideas, and enthusiasm.

Describe rather than hide or discount feelings.

Formulating (Creative Solution-Finding) Skills

Summarize what coauthors have said or written.

Seek accuracy by correcting or adding to the summary.

Seek connections to other knowledge.

Ask coauthors to explain the reasoning behind their positions.

Fermenting (Constructive Controversy and Conflict Resolution) Skills

Critique ideas without criticizing coauthors.

Differentiate ideas when there is disagreement.

Integrate different ideas into a single position.

Probe by asking questions that lead to deeper understanding.

Suggest new answers and ideas.

Think of new ways to resolve differences of opinion.

We want to underscore the idea that the skills associated with the four stages of group development can be translated into roles that coauthors can take on to help the coauthoring task and build interpersonal relationships. Exhibit 20.3 offers just a few examples of roles that coauthors can create and use to foster task accomplishment or build or maintain relationships. It should be emphasized that any role can be created and practiced that helps the team to get along while working to produce their co-created work.

Tip 4: Agree to Reflective Analysis of the Coauthoring Process and Celebrate

This is the fourth dimension of the collaborative teaming process: engage in group processing. Group processing means that coauthors regularly assess how well they are engaging in productive versus unproductive work and interpersonal behaviors. The importance of this tip can best be illustrated by an incident that

---

EXHIBIT 20.3. COAUTHOR ROLES TO ACHIEVE THE TASK AND MAINTAIN POSITIVE INTERPERSONAL RELATIONSHIPS.

Roles That Facilitate Task Achievement

Timekeeper—Monitors the time, encourages coauthors to stop at agreed-on times, and alerts members when the meeting is approaching the end of the agreed-on time period: "We have five minutes left to finish."

Recorder—Writes down the decisions coauthors make and distributes copies to present and absent members within one week.

Summarizer—Summarizes outcomes of a discussion before moving on to a new topic.

Checker—Makes sure coauthors understand the discussion and decisions. "Can you explain how we arrived at this decision?"

Roles That Facilitate Maintenance of Positive Interpersonal Relationships

Encourager—Encourages coauthors to participate and carry out their roles.

Praiser—Lets coauthors know when they are using collaborative skills that have a positive impact on each other. The praiser is careful to make the praise sound and feel authentic as well as specific—for example, "Thanks, Rich, for keeping us focused on our tasks!"—rather than general—"Good job!"

Jargon buster—Lets coauthors know when they are using terms, acronyms, or abbreviations that not everyone might understand (for example, "Oops, does everyone know what that means?").

---

occurred among the coauthors of this chapter when we forgot to abide by our own advice to pause, reflect, reframe, and celebrate.

While meeting recently at a conference to work on our sixth book project, we had powered through a writing session during the morning, and instead of meeting our agreements for exercise, we continued with a quick working lunch. We were stuck, so we decided to go for a walk that was interrupted and made stressful by a phone call noting that a beloved great uncle of Rich's was hospitalized and very ill. When we came back to the writing table, Jacque began the session by asking us to pause from work and reflect not only on the work but the emotions we were experiencing. We each shared our different frustrations. Rich felt sad and distracted by the news about his uncle; Ann felt edgy and overwhelmed because her need for alone time (meditation) was not being met; and Jacque said she wanted to "jump out of her skin" because of her unmet need for exercise.

We agreed to step away from the intense writing agenda we had created; in fact, we redesigned the agenda to include time for exercise, alone time, personal connections with each other, and a "walk 'n' talk" as a group along the bay. Essentially we tabled the discussion about the content (the task) and focused instead on maintaining our personal relationship. We met our needs for exercise, meditation, and personal time. We paused to reflect and readjust our goals and the process for accomplishing the work. We engaged in a walk 'n' talk rather than continue the meeting in a hotel room. During the walk, we decided to use the "What if?" idea-jogging strategy (Leff et al., 2002). Our dialogue went something like this:

> *Question:* What if we didn't meet the due date for the manuscript?
>
> *Agreement:* We would ask for a new due date!
>
> *Question:* What if we didn't write the book?
>
> *Agreement:* This question allowed us to re-commit to finishing the book!
>
> *Question:* What if we let go of thinking that the chapter that was vexing us needed to be a separate chapter and integrated it into other chapters?

At this point, we came to a group aha! moment in which all three of us literally stopped in our tracks. We realized, "That's it; we don't need the chapter! The information is already embedded in previous chapters." The solution was that we created and submitted a book of seven rather than eight chapters. That revision was subsequently accepted by the publisher.

Tip 4, then, suggests that coauthors pause to reflect often, especially when there are differences of opinions as to where to go next or when one or more coauthor feels stuck or has a writing block. This tip suggests that coauthors notice, acknowledge, and attend to feelings as well as ideas. It suggests that coauthors remember to notice and celebrate the small as well as the large accomplishments as well as celebrate each other and the team collectively.

Tip 5: Expect to Be Responsible and to Be Held Accountable

This tip focuses on the fifth dimension of the collaborative teaming process: individual accountability. Coauthors are responsible for accomplishing many tasks and commitments, including these:

- Being on time at face-to-face meetings and telephone conference calls
- Agreeing to rotate roles that help to facilitate the meetings
- Exchanging frequent messages to report progress and check on each other's needs (e-mail messages or mail delivery of manuscript drafts, for example)
- Meeting the due dates to submit written work to each other

In other words, coauthors must honor their agreements related to division of labor (who composes the letter of transmittal, who arranges for a meeting space, who takes the lead on a particular section of writing). To facilitate the implementation of this tip, we recommend that coauthors consider and commit to the following norms prior to beginning work together:

- I expect to be responsible and live up to accepted commitments.
- I expect my coauthors to hold me accountable for my commitments.
- If I cannot meet a commitment, I will communicate this clearly and as soon as I know about my challenge.
- If a coauthor cannot meet a commitment, I (we) will refrain from blaming or shaming and, instead, renegotiate (if possible) a new time line, needed supports, or division of labor.

Methods for holding one another accountable help clarify each coauthor's responsibilities, minimize freeloading, and acknowledge each person's efforts as valued. We use the structured agenda format shown in Exhibit 20.4 as a method to help ourselves be accountable for accomplishing our commitments when in face-to-face or proxy face-to-face meetings such as phone conferences. Exhibit 20.5 shows a completed agenda from an actual face-to-face meeting at the start of one of our book projects.

As you can see by examining agenda items in both the format presented in Exhibit 20.4 and the example presented in Exhibit 20.5, the agenda structures individual accountability for meeting attendance, participation, and equitable

EXHIBIT 20.4. COAUTHOR AGENDA FORMAT.

People Present:		
Absentees:		
Others Who Need to Know:		
Roles	**This Meeting**	**Next Meeting**
Timekeeper		
Recorder		
Others		

Agenda

Agenda Items	Time Limit
1. Review agenda and positive comments	5 minutes
2.	
3.	
4. Pause for group processing of progress toward task accomplishment and use of interpersonal skills	2 minutes
5.	
6.	
7. Final group processing of task and relationship	5 minutes

Minutes of Outcomes

Action Items	Person(s) Responsible	By When?
1. Communicate outcomes to absent members and others by:		
2.		
3.		

Agenda Building for Next Meeting

Date	Time	Location

Expected Agenda Items		
1.		
2.		
3.		

EXHIBIT 20.5. COAUTHOR AGENDA FORMAT: EXAMPLE.

People present:	Anne, Rich, Jacque	
Absentees	NA	
Others Who Need to Know:	NA	
Roles	**This meeting**	**Next meeting**
Timekeeper	Anne	Rich
Recorder	Rich	Jacque
Others: Process Checker	Jacque	Anne
Agenda Items: July 25, 2–3:00 P.M.	**Time Limit**	
1. Review agenda and positive comments	5 minutes	
2. Update re status of three current writing projects	15 minutes	
3. Articulate goals: verify Table of Contents, decide division of labor and due dates for book, facilitator guide, DVD/video		
4. Build in time for other tasks such as grading papers, exercise, nature walk, errands, nutrition, fun	10 minutes	
5. Pause for group processing of progress toward task accomplishment and use of interpersonal skills	5 minutes	
6. Snack break	10 minutes	
7. Discussion and division of labor for frontmatter, section I	10 minutes	
8. Final group processing of task and relationship	5 minutes	

Minutes of Outcomes

Action Items	Person(s) Responsible	By When?
1. Distribute notes	Rich [scribed the book decisions]	Next meeting
2. Memorialize agenda	Anne [scribed the agenda]	Next meeting

(Continued)

EXHIBIT 20.5. (CONTINUED)

Agenda Building for Next Meeting

Date	Time	Location
July 26	8–10 A.M.	Rich's office

Expected Agenda Items
1. Review outcomes of July 25 meeting.
2. Complete division of labor (DOL) for Section II.
3. Confirm agendas for next meetings—12:00–2:00 (DOL Section 2 and 3); 3:30–5:30 (DOL Section 3); July 27—8:30–10:00 (DOL Section 4); 11:30–2:30 (finalize decisions); 3:00–7:00—time for individual goal achievement (biking; movie; grading papers)

distribution of work during and before meetings. It also ensures that coauthors pay attention to the other four elements of the collaborative teaming process: face-to-face interaction: who is present, late, and absent; positive interdependence: distribution of roles and time for celebration; social skill performance and attention to interpersonal relations through group processing midway and at the end of the agenda.

Tip 6: Be Willing to Let Go of Personal Paradigms to Create New Paradigms

When collaborating with others, there is always the potential for difference of opinion, debate, and controversy. Zealous adherence to pet perspectives can lead coauthors to enter seemingly endless cycles of point-counterpoint that do not advance the writing process itself. It might help to ask a question such as, "In what ways are my personal paradigms interfering with creating a new paradigm that would encompass our divergent points of view?" Our discovery of the importance of this tip occurred in 1995 when we reflected on the experiences of collaborating as members of a seven-person writing team. We wrote,

> [Those of us] who collaborated on this risky venture went into it with a healthy
> sense of our own limitations in taking on such a task. We know that the
> usefulness of the insights we offer depends on the context into which they are

applied—the individual students, families, teachers, schools, and communities involved. As we struggled to identify areas of convergence and divergence in our views, we were all struck by how difficult it is to come up with static "for all time" answers, given the clear fact that times change, thinking changes, and paradigms change, often quite rapidly [Villa et al., 1995, pp. 136–137].

Tip 6 is derived from our work with metacognitive techniques for busting what has been referred to as paradigm paralysis (Leff et al., 2002). As shown in Figure 20.1, some of the techniques include thinking of unusual ways to approach the problem, defining the goal in different ways, asking "What if" questions, and forming new mental connections.

Actions and thoughts that discourage creativity—being critical or judgmental, putting the burden of proof on others, reacting negatively by discounting or putting down, pointing out only the flaws, being domineering—can be overcome when coauthors adopt ways of thinking that add fun and flexibility to their search for new ways to write about their ideas (Adams, 2001; Osborn, 1953). Especially when confronted with the dilemma or challenge of working with someone whose ideas of the world are dissimilar to one's own, the strategies can help everyone break out of their personal paradigms.

The scenario described for tip 4, where we were stuck because of a number of issues, illustrates how we have used paradigm-busting techniques offered in Figure 20.1. For example, to define the goal in a new way, we asked "What if?" questions such as, "What if we changed the due date?" "What if we didn't write the book?" Another strategy that we tend to favor is to think of unusual or even nutty things. We notice that we can break out of paradigm paralysis when we ask each other to be as ridiculous, strange, or crazy as we can. Deliberately thinking

FIGURE 20.1. CREATIVE THINKING STRATEGIES TO CHANGE YOUR PARADIGMS.

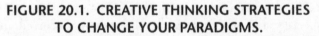

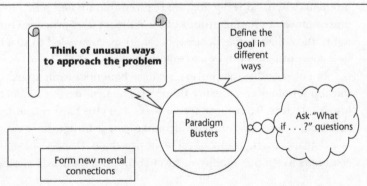

in unusual ways can generate useful ideas that depart from our old assumptions. Off-the-wall ideas can actually lead to useful feasible actions.

A creative thinking strategy called forming new mental connections consciously links what is familiar to what might be new to spark new thoughts or ways of thinking. One way to form new mental connections is to tell a personal story. This is one of Rich's favorite strategies, shared by another occasional coauthor, Alice Quiocho. Quiocho (2000) describes how, as a principal, she used the forming new mental connections strategy when she asked fifty teachers to tell stories about their students (that is, the familiar) in the positive narrative style of Kuzmekus (1996), author of *We Teach Them All: Teachers Writing About Diversity* (the unfamiliar or new). Quiocho's teachers not only learned the power of storytelling but they also created positive images of and connections with students from diverse cultures that led to new culturally responsive actions in their classrooms.

Tip 6 not only can improve coauthors' abilities to think creatively, but also can lead to greater enjoyment and appreciation of the collaborative process itself. We invite you to invent your own extraordinary creative techniques and share them with others, especially those who are new to the authoring and coauthoring process.

Discussion

In embarking on our coauthoring journey, we suspected coauthoring would be a complex and cognitively demanding process, which indeed it is. However, we were not prepared for the emotional roller coaster that emerges in such collaborative work. In any one session, we learned to expect the unexpected—to be exhilarated and confused, surprised and displeased, praised and pained—sometimes at the same time. We have experienced synergy and harmony, as well as distress and eustress (positive stress). We have learned to trust the process, especially at those moments when breakdowns occurred. In fact, those were the moments when, on reflection, we realized that we had failed to pay attention to one or more of the dimensions of the collaborative process. Once we recommitted to the collaborative process, breakdowns always led us to a breakthrough, a new conceptualization, or a new agreement.

In our coauthoring process, we have benefited from applying frameworks of social psychology and creative thinking. The first five tips for successful coauthoring are derived from those frameworks. We also have recognized the power of being able to release ourselves from known paradigms; we do not subscribe to one best approach, formula, recipe, or paradigm. Hence, our sixth tip encourages coauthors to choose, modify, or invent other frameworks. Echoing the statements we endorsed in 1995, in writing this chapter on our coauthoring journey, we emphasize that we do not pretend to have definitive answers or a corner on what is correct. The ruminations in this chapter simply represent our collective best thinking as of October 2010. They are part of a dialogue that we hope will be ongoing and include many other voices in the future, including those who read this book and this chapter.

And so our journey continues.

References

Adams, J. (2001). *Conceptual blockbusting: A guide to better ideas* (4th ed.). New York: Basic Books.

Boice, R. (1992). Combining writing block treatments: Theory and research. *Behaviour Research and Therapy, 30*(2), 107–116.

Gray, T. (1999). Publish, don't perish: Twelve steps to help scholars flourish. *Journal of Staff, Program and Organizational Development, 16*(30), 135–142.

Isenberg, J., Jalongo, M., & Bromley, K. (1987, April). *The role of collaboration in scholarly writing: A national study.* Paper presented at the annual meeting of the American Educational Research Association, Washington, DC.

Jalongo, M., & Isenberg, J. (1989). Collaborative professional writing in teacher education. *Journal of Industrial Teacher Education, 27*(1), 65–75.

Johnson, D. W., & Johnson, F. P. (1997). *Joining together: Group theory and group skills* (6th ed.). Needham Heights, MA: Allyn & Bacon.

Johnson, D. W., & Johnson, R. T. (1999). *Learning together and alone: Cooperative, competitive, and individualistic learning* (5th ed.). Needham Heights, MA: Allyn & Bacon.

Johnson, D. W., & Johnson, R. T. (2002). Ensuring diversity is positive: Cooperative community, constructive conflict, and civic values. In R. Villa, J. Thousand, & A. Nevin (Eds.), *Creativity and collaborative learning* (2nd ed., pp. 197–208). Baltimore, MD: Paul H. Brookes.

Kuzmekus, J. (1996). *We teach them all: Teachers writing about diversity.* York, ME: Stenhouse.

Leff, H., & Nevin, A. (1990). Overcoming barriers to creative and meta-thinking. *Teacher Education and Special Education, 13*(1), 36–39.

Leff, H., Thousand, J., Nevin, A., & Quiocho, A. (2002). Awareness plans for facilitating creative thinking. In J. Thousand, R. Villa, & A. Nevin (Eds.), *Creativity and collaborative learning: A practical guide for empowering students, teachers, and families in an inclusive, multicultural, and pluralistic society* (2nd ed., pp. 157–174). Baltimore, MD: Paul H. Brookes.

McDonald, K. (1995, April 28). Too many coauthors? *Chronicle of Higher Education,* pp. 35–36.

Nevin, A., & Leff, H. (1990). Is there room for playfulness in teacher education? *Teaching Exceptional Children, 22*(2), 71–73.

Osborn, A. (1953). *Applied imagination: Principles and procedures of creative thinking.* New York: Scribner.

Pololi, L., Knight, S., & Dunn, K. (2004). Innovations in education and clinical practice: Facilitating scholarly writing in academic medicine: Lessons learned from a collaborative peer mentoring program. *Journal of General Internal Medicine, 19*(1), 64–68.

Quiocho, A. (2000). Narrative as transformation. *New England Journal of Education, 3,* 30–36.

Slavin, R. (1994). *Cooperative learning, theory, research, and practice* (2nd ed.). Needham Heights, MA: Allyn & Bacon.

Tschannen-Moran, M., Firestone, W., Hoy, W., & Johnson, S. (2000). The Write Stuff: A study of productive scholars in educational administration. *Educational Administration Quarterly, 36*(3), 358–390.

Villa, R., & Thousand, J. (2000). *Restructuring for caring and effective education: Piecing the puzzle together* (2nd ed.). Baltimore, MD: Paul H. Brookes.

Villa, R., & Thousand, J. (2005). *Creating an inclusive school* (2nd ed.). Alexandria, VA: Association for Supervision and Curriculum Development.

Villa, R., Van der Klift, E., Udis, J., Thousand, J., Nevin, A., Kunc, N., et al. (1995). Questions, concerns, beliefs, and practical advice about inclusive education. In R. Villa & J. Thousand (Eds.), *Creating an inclusive school* (pp. 136–161). Alexandria, VA: Association for Supervision and Curriculum Development.

Webb-Johnson, G. C. (2002). Strategies for creating multicultural and pluralistic societies: A mind is a wonderful thing to develop. In J. S. Thousand, R. A. Villa, & A. I. Nevin (Eds.), *Creativity and collaborative learning: The practical guide to empowering students, teachers, and families* (2nd ed., pp. 55–70). Baltimore, MD: Paul H. Brookes.

CHAPTER 21

WRITING AS MENTORING

Bradley C. Courtenay, Ronald M. Cervero, John M. Dirkx

One of the most rewarding aspects of being a faculty member in higher education is helping doctoral students and less experienced faculty members develop their writing skills for completing a dissertation or, later, for publishing in books, refereed journals, and other scholarly venues. Even if students bring to the doctoral program relatively good writing ability, they still need assistance in understanding how to write in a scholarly style. The fulfillment of hearing someone exclaim he or she finally understands what it means to write in a scholarly fashion is the same regardless of initial ability. Sometimes the growth in writing ability is evident over the term of a single course, particularly if the faculty member has emphasized the importance of writing instructions for and grading of assignments. More often, growth in writing ability occurs over the entire doctoral program, and especially when a student has the opportunity to be mentored by a faculty member for an extended period of time.

Although new doctoral graduates may have completed a dissertation and, in some instances, published an article or two during their doctoral study, their scholarly writing ability may still be at an immature stage. For new graduates who end up in a university setting where research and publications are emphasized for professional advancement, scholarly writing is an essential aspect of their work. These new faculty members can benefit from a mentoring relationship focused on the development of scholarly writing. In a situation where a mentoring relationship about scholarly writing has extended beyond graduation, the mentor delights at seeing the inexperienced colleague mature in scholarly writing ability and also benefits from the knowledge generation of the mentee.

This exploration of mentoring for scholarly writing begins with our understanding of mentoring to enhance scholarly writing. Next, we examine the benefits of a mentoring relationship for the mentor and mentee, followed by information on how to establish a mentoring relationship. Once formed, mentoring relationships depend on several important elements that we cover in the next section. Over time, mentoring relationships evolve through several phases; we describe phase models and demonstrate how one model relates to scholarly writing. In the final section, we point to a few future trends in mentoring for scholarly writing.

Definition of Mentoring

Mentoring is a word used as if everyone understands its meaning. Without defining *mentoring*, annual faculty reports ask for the number and nature of mentoring activities conducted during the year. Young faculty members may be assigned a senior faculty member or a group of senior faculty members to serve as their mentors, again under the assumption that the younger and more experienced faculty members know what is meant by the term *mentor*. Students refer to faculty members who are their mentors, assuming those listening to them agree on the definition of *mentor*.

Unfortunately, the perception that there is a widely understood definition for *mentor* is incorrect. Over twenty-five years ago, Merriam (1983) conducted a comprehensive review of the literature on mentoring in three areas: adult growth and development, business and industry, and academic settings. In the introduction section, she concluded that "early in preparation of this review it became apparent that a precise definition of mentoring—at least one that all could agree upon—was not to be found" (p. 162). Today the literature on mentoring still does not provide a single universally adopted definition. Since this chapter concerns mentoring activities to develop emerging scholars as publishable authors, only definitions offered for academic settings are examined. Following on Phillips's (1979) work, Merriam (1983) concluded that in academic settings, mentoring in graduate study "is a mentor-ward involvement in which the faculty member seeks advancement for the student in order to enhance the field and the student's role in it" (p. 167). This generic definition has been qualified with attention to benefits of the mentoring relationship. For example, a University of Michigan (2006) handbook on mentoring graduate students defines "a mentoring relationship [as] a close, individualized relationship that develops over time between a graduate student and a faculty member and that includes both caring and guidance" (p. 6).

Girves, Zepeda, and Gwathmey (2005) use such phrases as "multidimensional, dynamic, reciprocal relationship" and "intentional process that is supportive, nurturing, and protective, providing . . . structured experiences to facilitate growth" (p. 453) to portray mentoring in higher education. For Johnson (2002), mentoring in the academy is not just a relationship, but "a personal relationship in which a more experienced (usually older) faculty member or professional acts as a guide, role model, teacher, and sponsor of a less experienced (usually younger) graduate student or junior professional" (p. 88). The mentor's job is to provide for the growth of the mentee through such academic responsibilities as "teaching, advising, supervising, counseling, friendship" (Johnson, 2002, p. 89). Although mentoring graduate students for developing scholarly writing ability is not listed in these or other definitions, it is often referenced as a part of advising the student in research projects or the dissertation process.

To offer a definition of *mentoring* that focuses on scholarly writing, we first had to realize that there is no set formula for graduate study for all students and faculty members. For example, in the natural sciences, most graduate students are enrolled full time, and faculty members in those fields of study generally have two to three doctoral students who could be mentees. In the social sciences, faculty members in some fields of study (for example, adult education, educational leadership, higher education) may have more than ten advisees who could be mentees. And it is likely that most of the students are enrolled part time because they are not able to put their jobs on hold for a few years. The potential large number of mentees and their part-time status is exacerbated in online doctoral programs that also require mentoring by electronic means.

A second factor we considered in arriving at a definition of *mentoring* for this chapter is the outcome: scholarly writing ability. We asked ourselves if it is necessary to mentor for scholarly writing in face-to-face meetings between the mentor and mentee. Why couldn't mentoring for developing scholarly writing occur in group settings—either a formal course or an informal meeting that could include several faculty members and several students or colleagues? This question highlights the conventional perception that mentoring is a one-to-one relationship, yet we know from the literature that students and less experienced faculty members can grow in scholarly writing ability through writing courses or regularly scheduled group meetings devoted to improved writing (Caffarella & Barnett, 2000; Nackoney, Munn, & Gallagher, 2007; Nielsen & Rocco, 2002; Rankin, 2001).

Thus, for the purpose of this chapter, *mentoring* is defined as the relationship between a faculty member (usually more experienced) and a student or colleague (usually less experienced) in which the faculty member offers opportunities and guidance for the student and colleague with a caring spirit for the purpose of developing scholarly writing ability. This definition accommodates one-to-one mentoring relationships, as well as group mentoring activities. Although not stated explicitly, the definition assumes that mentoring can happen through electronic communication and the more traditional face-to-face discussions.

Benefits of Mentoring: Mentors and Mentees

Mentoring graduate students and junior colleagues offers several benefits not just to mentees but also to mentors (Girves et al., 2005; Johnson, 2002; Nackoney et al., 2007; Tenenbaum, Crosby, & Gliner, 2001; University of Washington, 2005a, 2005b; University of Michigan, 2006, 2007; Wilde & Schau, 1991). As an example of a general benefit, mentoring "enables graduate students to acquire the body of knowledge and skills they need as well as an understanding of the way their discipline operates" (University of Michigan, 2006, p. 6). Furthermore, mentoring yields higher levels of production and involvement in the department and leads to a satisfying experience in the program of study.

Girves et al. (2005) offer a list of nine specific benefits provided by mentoring that range from "teaches specific skills," to "relates how the field or profession operates," to "exemplifies values and an approach to professional and personal life" (p. 454). After a review of the literature on the outcomes of mentoring, Johnson (2002) adds these benefits: "enhancement of confidence and professional identity," "scholarly productivity," and "dissertation success" (p. 89). A valuable contribution in Johnson's article is the list of benefits for graduates or postdoctoral mentees: "increased income," "more rapid promotion," "career 'eminence,'" "willingness to mentor others," and "increased satisfaction and achievement" (p. 89).

In the 1980s, models describing the benefits of mentoring in education began to appear. Until that time, very few empirical studies had been conducted on the benefits of mentoring in the academic setting (Wilde & Schau, 1991). The few empirical works about mentoring in educational settings indicated "that faculty mentors improve the student's employment possibilities . . . , professional skills . . . , and professional growth" (Wilde & Schau, 1991, p. 165). Seeking to fill the knowledge gap in the field of education, Wilde and Schau (1991) built on a model for mentoring in training psychologists presented by O'Neil and Wrightsman (1982). O'Neil and Wrightsman proposed an interactive model that accounted for the benefits that a mentoring relationship offers mentees and mentors, although the model emphasized benefits in general rather than benefits specifically for scholarly writing. The model included mutuality (reciprocity in feelings and values), comprehensiveness (interaction that occurred in diverse settings), and congruence (agreement about the mentoring relationship). High degrees of these components in the relationship were claimed to "produce positive and functional mentoring relationships with the outcomes of interpersonal respect, profession-alism, collegiality, and role fulfillment" (p. 167).

Wilde and Schau combined the components that O'Neil and Wrightsman (1982) found with traditional career development and designed a survey that asked mentees in the field of graduate education their perceptions about the benefits in mentoring relationships. The graduate student mentees offered four components, all confirming and expanding those proposed by O'Neil and Wrightsman: psychological and professional mutual support (sharing of mutual respect and support), comprehensiveness (the extension of the relationship beyond graduate school), mentee professional development (help with career, referring mentee to professional development activities), and research collabora-tion (coauthoring, presenting papers together, conducting research together). Embedded in the last component are benefits of mentoring for scholarly writing, such as collaborating on research, writing conference papers together, student assisting with research, and grant writing.

Surveying graduate students representing nine different academic depart-ments, Tenenbaum et al. (2001) identified three groups of benefits (referred to as "support" by the authors) in advisor-advisee relationships. The authors assumed that the advisor and student have a mentoring relationship, although they admitted that the relationship may not be, in every case, "perfect" from a mentoring standpoint. Participants identified psychosocial support (feelings of respect, empathy with feelings and concerns, and open sharing of the mentor's experiences), instrumental support (to strengthen career-related skills—how to write, how to develop research designs, how to teach more effectively), and net-working support (introducing the mentee to influential leaders in the field and colleagues at other institutions).

Turning now to the importance of mentoring specifically for scholarly writ-ing, Nackoney et al. (2007) claim that faculty members can provide instrumental support by teaching mentees "how to write for a public audience," introducing them to the scholarly community, and providing opportunities to work on col-laborative writing projects. Moreover, faculty members can offer psychosocial support to improve writing ability by sharing their experiences of failure and success in writing and publishing.

What seems evident from the literature is that there are two prominent types of benefits for mentees—one that provides psychological and social benefit and one that contributes to career development. Both forms of benefit are relevant to the use of mentoring to build scholarly writing skills. In terms of career develop-ment, benefits accrue in helping the mentee build writing skills, conceptualize and conduct research, and write grants. The instrumental types of benefits have been found to influence productivity of the mentee. Tenenbaum et al. (2001)

found "that level of instrumental help statistically predicted the student's products with the advisor" (p. 338). Psychosocial benefits are associated with the mentee's satisfaction in the mentoring relationship and the doctoral program. In one study, Haring (1999) showed that the psychosocial benefits were the most important to the mentees. In actuality, both psychosocial and instrumental benefits are likely to work together for the mentee. Feedback that builds confidence in mentees is certain to influence their writing success, and this success is sure to enhance perception of self as a scholar.

Despite the fact that mentors perceive the mentoring relationship as consuming too much of their time and potentially making the student too dependent, they engage in mentoring relationships as a consequence of several benefits to them. Consolidating the lists of benefits provided in work by Bush (1985), Girves et al. (2005), Johnson (2002), and the University of Michigan (2006) yields at least seven benefits of the mentoring relationship to the mentor:

- The emotional satisfaction of facilitating a mentee's professional growth
- The realization of one's own professional development by keeping current with new knowledge and techniques
- The establishment of a network for future collaboration in writing projects
- Assistance for current writing projects that leads to increased publication productivity
- Stimulus to one's creative energy
- Growth of the mentor's reputation through the mentee's accomplishments as a student and graduate
- The possibility of a transformation as a consequence of engaging in the mentoring act

Although these benefits were identified from faculty and graduate student relationships, they are also important for the longer-term mentoring relationships involving the faculty member and the graduate student who has become a colleague.

Forming a Mentoring Relationship

Mentoring relationships are established by invitation of the mentor or mentee or by third-party assignment, such as a department head or coordinator of graduate advisement. When initiated by the mentor or mentee, a mentoring relationship is formed by a simple request made by one member of the pair. Is one approach to creating a mentoring relationship more effective than the other? The literature on this question comes mostly from the business field and leans toward informal, voluntary pairing rather than a formal assignment (Burke, 1984; Johnson, 2002; Ragins & Cotton, 1999), although at least one study from the academic setting indicates that there is no significant difference in the success of the relationship between the two approaches. In a study of mentoring junior faculty, Boice (1992) concluded that "arbitrarily paired mentors and mentees worked as well as traditional pairs" (p. 52). However, Boice explains that the mentees in the study were faculty members who were relatively equal before the pairings. Moreover, he concludes that "the process of meeting regularly in supportive fashion is more important than the personal characteristics of the pair members" (p. 53).

Other scholars concur, arguing that the informal approach is inherently more effective. For example, Merriam (1983) concludes that "it would seem that the forced matching of mentors and protégés ignores a characteristic crucial to the more intense mentor relationships—that the two people involved are attracted to each other and wish to work together" (p. 171). Those sentiments are echoed by Johnson (2002), who maintains that in the academy, mentoring relationships should be facilitated but not assigned and that the most enduring relationships are based on "shared interests, similarity, frequent contact, and enjoyment of interaction" (p. 89).

Assuming the informal approach is adopted to initiate a mentor relationship, what criteria are important for selecting a mentor? Johnson (2002) concludes that experience, confidence, competence, and interest in mentoring are hallmarks of an outstanding mentor. One would expect a student to apply the first three in determining what faculty member to approach about a mentoring relationship, but the criterion that may hold the most promise in the selection process is the extent to which a faculty member is interested in "facilitating the personal and professional development of one or more well-selected protégés" (Johnson, 2002, p. 93). Before approaching a potential mentor, students might observe how the faculty member interacts with them and with other students. Is the faculty member friendly, forthcoming in conversations, and open to suggestions and new ideas? Does the faculty member listen? What is the faculty member's interest in and reputation as a writer? How often does the faculty member collaborate with mentees on books, book chapters, journal articles, or research papers in conference proceedings? How well known is the faculty member for being an outstanding mentor?

Elements of Successful Mentoring Relationships

What makes for a successful mentoring relationship focused on the improvement of scholarly writing? Empirical studies that provide outcomes predicting successful mentoring relationships are scarce, and studies that address mentoring and scholarly writing ability are even more limited. However, there are a few works based on anecdotal information drawn from the experiences of the authors that are in consensus about the important elements for a successful mentoring relationship (Johnson, 2002; University of Washington, 2005a, 2005b; University of Michigan, 2006, 2007). All mentoring relationships would appear to benefit from psychosocial and instrumental support. For example, Daloz (1986) suggests that mentoring has three primary functions: support, challenge, and vision. Certainly mutual respect and support contribute to healthy mentoring relationships, and providing the mentee with career-building skills is a general goal of the mentoring relationship (Wilde & Schau, 1991). But beyond these general types of support, what elements in the mentoring relationship enhance the scholarly writing ability of the mentee?

Agreement on Goals and Expectations

Misunderstanding about the purpose and outcomes of mentoring relationships often causes problems between the mentor and mentee (University of Michigan, 2006). Clarifying goals related to scholarly writing ability and expectations for the mentoring relationship can help avoid conflicts. For example, prior to meeting with the mentor, mentees can develop a list of goals that are important to their development as a scholarly writer. During the first or an early mentorship meeting, the mentor realizes what the important outcomes to the mentee are and can offer advice about the clarification and relevance of the goals and approaches for reaching them. As an illustration, some mentees might realize that they have weak scholarly writing abilities and are able to articulate only that they want to be better writers. By probing, the mentor can help the mentee identify the nature of the writing weakness and prescribe assignments for improvement.

Goals may be organized into short- and long-term outcomes as a way of helping the mentee understand that some activities take longer because they depend on the acquisition of foundational skills. One example is the goal for writing a journal article, which the mentor would suggest is a long-term goal. To reach that goal, the mentee might need to understand the parts of a research article and, more important, how an author composes the various parts of an article, that is, what constitutes acceptable writing standards for the sections of an article.

Whether goals are short or long term, they should also have deadlines. Mentees experience due dates in their courses, and they will be faced with them as scholarly writers regardless of the publication type (book, book chapter, journal article, or paper in a conference proceedings, for example). Just as deadlines for publication are often revised, mentees may also need to revise their goals and the time lines for completing them.

Expectations are the preferences about the guidelines for the mentoring relationship. Rather than operate a mentoring relationship on assumptions about guidelines, mentors and mentees need to express and agree on them. The University of Michigan (2006) mentoring handbook calls for clarifying expectations for meetings, feedback, drafts, publishing and presenting, intellectual property, and recommendation letters.

Actions and Behaviors of the Mentor

Johnson (2002) provides several guidelines for the role of the mentor in training psychologists that are relevant for most mentoring relationships. Among those that appear to be important for mentoring and scholarly writing are being aware of the developmental needs of mentees, modeling acceptable standards, and rejecting opportunities for exploitation.

Being Aware of the Mentee's Development Need. Most graduate students have no experience in scholarly writing and therefore bring to the mentoring relationship not only a desire to learn but also anxiety and insecurity at the prospects of learning a new way of writing. Too often mentors assume that the mentees know more than they actually do about scholarly writing and are puzzled at the unclear, disorganized, and illogical first draft of the first chapter of the dissertation. Mentors need to recall that their mentees have never before written a dissertation or any parts of a dissertation, such as a review of the literature. Consequently, "good mentors exude patience and provide unconditional acceptance" (Johnson, 2002, p. 93). Good mentors also determine the level of a mentee's scholarly writing expertise and work with them from that point, realizing that good scholarly writing does not happen overnight. This approach is important for conveying to the mentee that scholarly writing is not an inherent ability given to some and not others, but that with guidance and practice it can be learned.

Learning to write is often closely bound up with the mentee's personal or developmental issues, such as identity and sense of competence. At times it can become a context that evokes a number of emotional or psychosocial issues. As we mentioned earlier, mentees often feel uncertain and even anxious about their writing, especially in its early, formative stages. Or they may overestimate their level of expertise and knowledge about scholarly writing. When presented with feedback on their writing, even if it is provided in a supportive and constructive manner, they may react defensively and become upset. Mentors need to recognize the powerful emotional dynamics associated with this process and not take such reactions personally. Mentees need the psychological and sometimes physical space to work through these issues within the context of the mentor-mentee relationship.

As Daloz (1986) suggests, there are times especially in their development when they need both support and challenge. In such instances, mentors should think of their relationship with mentees as a kind of "holding environment" (Kegan, 1982; Winnicott, Shepherd, & Davis, 1989) in which mentees feel safe and supported to give voice to their fears, uncertainties, and anxieties. Mentors should help mentees recognize and express these emotions but also challenge them to work through their emotional responses.

Modeling Acceptable Standards of Scholarly Writing. When he discusses modeling, Johnson (2002) uses the qualifier *intentional* to distinguish between the circumstantial or happenstance modeling opportunities. Good mentors plan for and take advantage of opportunities to model acceptable standards for scholarly writing for their mentees. Mentees are brought into the writing of grants, research reports, or journal articles and are shown, for example, the acceptable format for a grant or a journal article or the link between recommendations and conclusions in a research report.

Rejecting Opportunities for Exploitation. There is a robust literature on the ethical implications in a mentoring relationship, and it includes discussions of the potential for exploitation (Clark, Harden, & Johnson, 2002; Johnson, 2002; Johnson & Nelson, 1999; Simon & Eby, 2003; University of Washington, 2005a, 2005b; University of Michigan, 2006, 2007). The more obvious areas of exploitation would be sexual harassment or acts of racial or cultural prejudice. But mentors can also exploit mentees by claiming a mentee's written product as their own. This potential for harm to the mentee supports the need for clarifying matters of authorship from the initiation of the relationship.

Actions and Behaviors of the Mentee

Mentees can also contribute to successful mentoring relationships that focus on the improvement of scholarly writing. The University of Michigan (2006, 2007) mentoring handbooks for faculty and students provide lists of several issues that are important for mentees in a mentoring relationship. Among the list of issues are four that contribute to the success of mentoring relationships in support of good scholarly writing: be realistic in expectations of mentors, adopt the identity of a colleague, seek and accept criticism in a professional manner, and demonstrate the mentor's advice was used.

Be Realistic in Expectations of Mentors. Mentoring is only one of several assignments for faculty members, meaning their time and energy levels should be respected.

Mentees can help on this issue by being explicit about their needs with mentors and being patient with mentors' turnaround time on drafts of scholarly writing.

Adopt the Identity of a Colleague. Inherent in the mentoring relationship is that mentees aspire to be graduates who can become mentors to others. One way of making the transition to a potential colleague is by immersing oneself in scholarly writing activities, such as a writing group that meets regularly or by preparing papers for presentation at professional conferences.

Seek and Accept Criticism in a Professional Manner. More often than not, the mentor will provide feedback on drafts of scholarly works. However, some mentors may not be as elaborative in their comments as the mentee needs. In such cases, mentees should feel free to seek out the additional information or clarification necessary for their understanding of the feedback. It is not always easy to receive feedback on and criticism of one's writing. Mentees need to recognize the close relationship between their writing and who they are as persons and that such feedback can evoke powerful emotional reactions. Mentor-mentee interactions need to be grounded in authentic relationships, and the quality of such relationships often requires self-work. It is important that mentees recognize and give voice to these emotional and psychosocial issues but that they do not act out these issues. In receiving constructive criticism, mentees need to understand that it is not personal; although they feel somewhat defensive, mentors simply wish to help mentees learn good scholarly writing, and the feedback is designed to provide the best possible draft. On some occasions, mentees may feel the feedback is unjustified or incorrect; in those instances, they should be comfortable in defending their positions or asking about the feedback in the spirit of seeking to understand its importance. These forms of interaction require an authentic relationship in which all parties recognize the complex interrelationships of skill and psychosocial development.

Demonstrate the Mentor's Advice Was Used. Mentors want to know that the mentee has used their suggestions and recommendations. When mentees resubmit previous drafts of scholarly work, it should be evident to mentors that their advice was incorporated into the document. When a mentee decides not to use the input, he or she should be prepared to justify the omission.

Phases of the Mentoring Relationship

Like most other aspects of life, the mentoring relationship changes over time, even if it lasts for only three to four years while a student is completing the doctoral degree. One of the earliest empirically derived stage models for a mentoring relationship was proposed by Kram (1986), although the participants were in business-oriented mentoring relationships. The model has four stages: initiation (the establishment of the relationship), cultivation (a diverse set of functions is provided and reaches a zenith in activity), separation (the relationship is altered by a structural event or a change made by members of the relationship), and redefinition (the relationship changes significantly and can continue indefinitely or ends). These phases were validated by Chao (1997) in an empirical examination of their relationship to mentoring outcomes.

A more recent four-phase mentoring model was developed by Zachary (2002). This model is especially relevant to this chapter in that it focuses on teachers who "formally or informally mentor graduate or undergraduate adult learners, or mentor other teachers (also adult learners)" (p. 27). Referring to the model as "the mentoring journey," Zachary advances preparing, negotiating, enabling, and coming to closure as the four phases that characterize a mentoring relationship.

According to Zachary (2002), her phases "are less bound by time definition and psychological milestones and focus more on the behaviors required to negotiate each of the stages" (p. 29). Moreover, she maintains that phases are not to be taken for granted or skipped; either action is likely to have an unwelcome outcome. A review of her explanation of the phases confirms the emphasis on the behaviors that define each. Preparing involves preparation of the mentor and the relationship. Negotiating refers to discussion and agreement on expectations, goals, content, and process. In the enabling phase, the emphasis is on the mentee's learning, with the mentor serving as nurturer. In the final phase, coming to closure, the "mentoring partners implement their exit strategy" from the mentoring relationship (p. 34). Zachary claims that closure procedures should be discussed at the negotiation phase.

How well do these four phases reflect a mentoring relationship that emphasizes the development of scholarly writing? Table 21.1 demonstrates how a mentoring relationship for scholarly writing evolves through the four phases that Kochan and Trimble (2000) and Zachary (2002) proposed. The table delineates the primary actions to be taken in each phase by the mentee and mentor. According to Kochan and Trimble (2000), the phases are not separate, isolated elements but "fluid, sometimes repeated, overlapping, and connected processes or layers. As such, they comprise a unified whole rather than being distinct, linear points on a journey that has a beginning and an end" (p. 25). The last phase marks the transition to terminate the relationship or continue it, but with modifications. Revisions are necessary because the mentee's status changes once the goals have been achieved. If the dissertation is one of the goals and it has been approved, the mentee graduates and becomes more of a colleague to the mentor.

TABLE 21.1. PHASES OF THE MENTORING RELATIONSHIP FOR SCHOLARLY WRITING.

Phase	Mentee Actions	Mentor Actions
Groundwork (Zachary's "preparing")	Decide to engage in mentoring process to improve scholarly writing Assess strengths and weaknesses of scholarly writing ability Determine scholarly writing goals for the relationship Identify potential mentors with emphasis on ability to mentor for scholarly writing	Why do I want to be a mentor for scholarly writing? What are my skills to help with scholarly writing? What are my goals for a mentoring relationship that emphasizes scholarly writing?
Warm-up (Zachary's "negotiating")	Approach potential mentors Verbalize goals for scholarly writing Select a mentor Share values and clarify goals for scholarly writing Prepare writing assignments and meeting agenda; guide meetings Share openly	Identify relationship needs and expectation Assist in preparing goals for scholarly writing Share openly
Working (Zachary's "enabling")	Share successes and failures about scholarly writing and publishing Practice desired scholarly writing skills Give and receive critical feedback about scholarly writing	Adopt a nurturing, candid, but challenging approach Share successes about scholarly writing and publishing Provide scholarly writing opportunities Introduce mentee to leading scholars in the field Coauthor scholarly works with mentee Give and receive critical feedback
Long-term status (Zachary's "coming to closure")	Discuss issues about modifying or ending relationship Implement strategies for continuing or ending relationship	Discuss issues about modifying or ending the relationship Assist in implementing strategies for continuing or ending the relationship

Source: Adapted from Kochan and Trimble (2000) and Zachary (2002).

The needs of the graduate for mentoring are different now, with emphasis on publishing articles in refereed journals, books, book chapters, or other scholarly publications.

Zachary (2002) offers specific guidelines for modifying or ending the mentoring relationship:

1. A learning conclusion (reflection on learning outcomes) and process for integrating what was learned (how to apply the learning and taking it to the next level)
2. A meaningful way to celebrate success (collaboratively planning a mutually satisfying way to celebrate)
3. A conversation focusing on redefining the relationship (talking about how the relationship is to continue; whether it moves from professional mentoring relationship to colleague, friendship, or ceases to exist at all)
4. A comfortable way of moving on (acknowledging transition and identifying ways to sever the relationship or stay in contact) [p. 36]

One difference in the mentoring relationship after the mentee transitions to colleague status is the decrease or elimination of the power difference between the mentor and mentee. In their early career years, mentees may still depend on the mentor for connecting them with important scholars and publication venues, but the overall power differential is lessened by the new status of the mentee. Mentees feel freer, more confident, and more competent to initiate research and publication projects.

Another difference in the mentoring relationship once mentees transition to new positions is the potential sources available to them. For example, if mentees end up in a research position in such organizations as state or federal government, foundations, or business and industry, they may have more resources to offer the mentoring relationship because of their access to samples for research or to financial and other forms of support to carry out research.

Future Trends

Although we have shown how the phases of a mentoring relationship include scholarly writing, they may not be appropriate for describing the needs of students and colleagues in the future. The similarities in the various phases of the mentoring relationship can give the impression that one size fits all. However, in some disciplines and fields of study, there is a high student-to-faculty ratio, and part-time study is the norm for doctoral students. In those academic areas, most students must continue to work full time and pursue the doctoral degree part time, either in traditional face-to-face classes, often in the evening or on the weekends, or in online courses that may be blended with occasional face-to-face classes or completely virtual. Another characteristic of these students is that they are practitioners who are likely to remain practitioners, rather than individuals who will enter into a research-focused career such as a university professor. Yet they too need to build scholarly writing skills, particularly for conducting and reporting on studies that will inform their decision making. Recent studies of both the Ph.D. and Ed.D. in several disciplines and fields of study point to the need for responding to part-time doctoral students and, in particular, to their interests to become scholarly writers (Carnegie Foundation for the Advancement of Teaching, 2008; Golde & Dore, 2001; Golde & Walker, 2006; Nerad, 2004; Nerad, Rudd, Morrison, & Picciano, 2007; Walker, Golde, Jones, Bueschel, & Hutchings, 2008). At the very least, these studies point to the need to recognize the increasing and multiple pressures on full-time doctoral students, such as family responsibilities and length to degree. These studies also reflect the widening need for doctoral programs that can accommodate part-time learners.

Doctoral programs can respond to these trends by being intentional about their responsibilities to mentoring students for scholarly writing. Specifically, they can

- Develop and implement policy statements regarding mentoring practices for scholarly writing. Like the University of Michigan (2006, 2007) and the University of Washington Graduate School (2005a, 2005b), faculty in doctoral programs can develop faculty and student mentoring handbooks. They can go beyond existing handbooks by including suggestions for mentoring students on scholarly writing.
- Encourage faculty in doctoral programs to be creative in how to mentor for scholarly writing. For example, one or two faculty members can be assigned mentoring in scholarly writing courses and seminars that meet monthly to accommodate the part-time student's schedule.
- Support faculty members' establishment of two mentoring groups. One would serve students committed to a career devoted to research, such as a professor or a member of a think tank, research laboratory, or research and development center. The purpose of this group would be to focus on conducting and writing research that generates knowledge for publication in scholarly books, journals, and monographs. The second group would include students who will follow a practitioner career in deputy and executive leadership positions and therefore need mentoring in collecting information and writing it in a format to enhance decision making.

- Establish mentoring groups in which members use online techniques to exchange information, drafts of papers and discuss topics related to scholarly writing, as well as the strengths and weaknesses of their written assignments.

The future knowledge that theorists and practitioners need depends on individuals who are proficient in scholarly writing. As we have demonstrated in this chapter, mentoring is one means for enhancing scholarly writing. Viewing scholarly writing as important for theorists and practitioners will increase the demand for mentoring activities in the future, opening the door to alternative mentoring techniques such as mentoring groups and mentoring by electronic means. Whether mentoring relationships proceed through the typical phases identified in this chapter is secondary to the importance of creating authentic relationships that benefit mentors and mentees alike. Authenticity is the hallmark of mentoring relationships, and if it pervades the relationship, what happens within the phases will reflect caring, learning, and the development of scholarly writing.

References

Boice, R. (1992). Lessons learned about mentoring. In M. D. Sorcinelli & A. E. Austin (Eds.), *Developing new and junior faculty* (pp. 51–61). New Directions for Teaching and Learning, no. 50. San Francisco: Jossey-Bass.

Burke, R. J. (1984). Mentors in organizations. *Group and Organizational Studies, 9,* 353–372.

Bush, J. (1985). Mentoring in graduate schools of education: Mentors' perceptions. *American Educational Research Journal, 22*(2), 257–265.

Carnegie Foundation for the Advancement of Teaching. (2008). *Carnegie Project on the Education Doctorate.* Retrieved January 23, 2008, from www.carnegiefoundation.org/programs/index.asp?key=1867

Caffarella, R. S., & Barnett, B. G. (2000). Teaching doctoral students to become scholarly writers: The importance of giving and receiving critiques. *Studies in Higher Education, 25*(1), 39–52.

Chao, G. T. (1997). Mentoring phases and outcomes. *Journal of Vocational Behavior, 51,* 15–28.

Clark, R. A., Harden, S. L., & Johnson, W. B. (2000). Mentor relationships in clinical psychology doctoral training: Results of a national survey. *Teaching of Psychology, 27*(4), 262–268.

Daloz, L. A. (1986). *Effective teaching and mentoring: Realizing the transformational power of adult learning experiences.* San Francisco: Jossey-Bass.

Girves, J. E., Zepeda, Y., & Gwathmey, J. K. (2005). Mentoring in a post-affirmative world. *Journal of Social Issues, 61*(3), 449–479.

Golde, C. M., & Dore, T. M. (2001). *At cross purposes. What the experiences of doctoral students reveal about doctoral education.* Philadelphia: Pew Charitable Trusts.

Golde, C. M., & Walker, G. (Eds.). (2006). *Envisioning the future of doctoral education: Preparing stewards of the discipline.* San Francisco: Jossey-Bass.

Haring, M. J. (1999). Foreword from the field. In C. A. Mullen & D. W. Lick (Eds.), *New directions in mentoring: Creating a culture of synergy* (pp. xi-xii). New York: Falmer Press.

Johnson, W. B. (2002). The intentional mentor: Strategies and guidelines for the practice of mentoring. *Professional Psychology: Research and Practice, 33*(1), 88–96.

Johnson, W. B., & Nelson, N. (1999). Mentor-protégé relationships in graduate training: Some ethical concerns. *Ethics and Behavior, 9*(3), 189–210.

Kegan, R. (1982). *The evolving self: Problem and process in human development.* Cambridge, MA: Harvard University Press.

Kochan, F. K., & Trimble, S. B. (2000). From mentoring to co-mentoring: Establishing collaborative relationships. *Theory into Practice, 39*(1), 20–27.

Kram, K. E. (1986). Phases of the mentor relationship. *Academy of Management Journal, 26*(4), 608–625.

Merriam, S. (1983). Mentors and protégés: A critical review of the literature. *Adult Education Quarterly, 33*(3), 161–173.

Nackoney, C. K., Munn, S. L., & Gallagher, S. J. (2007). Becoming scholarly writers: An autoethnography of three emerging scholars. In K. L. Servage & T. Fenwick (Eds.), *Learning in community: Proceedings of the Joint International Conference of the Adult Education Research Conference and the Canadian Association for Adult Education* (Vol. 2, pp. 445–450). Halifax, NS: Mount St. Vincent University.

Nerad, M. (2004). The PhD in the US: Criticism, facts and remedies. *Higher Education Policy, 17,* 183–199.

Nerad, M., Rudd, E., Morrison, E., & Picciano, J. (2007, December). *Social science PhDs—five+ years out: A national survey of PhD's in six fields. Highlights report.* Seattle: Center for Innovation and Research in Graduate Education, University of Washington.

Nielsen, S. M., & Rocco, T. S. (2002). Joining the conversation: Graduate students' perceptions of writing for publication. In J. M. Pettit (Ed.), *Proceedings of the 43rd Annual Adult Education Research Conference* (pp. 309–314). Raleigh: North Carolina State University.

O'Neal, J. M., & Wrightsman, L. S. (1982). The mentoring relationship in psychology training programs. In G. F. Sumprer & S. Walfish (Eds.), *Clinical, counseling, and community psychology: A student guide to graduate training and professional practice.* New York: Irvington.

Phillips, G. M. (1979). The peculiar intimacy of graduate study: A conservative view. *Communication Education, 28,* 339–345.

Ragins, B. R., & Cotton, J. L. (1999). Mentor functions and outcomes: A comparison of men and women in formal and informal mentoring relationships. *Journal of Applied Psychology, 84,* 529–550.

Rankin, E. (2001). *The work of writing: Insights and strategies for academics and professionals.* San Francisco: Jossey-Bass.

Simon, S. A., & Eby, L. T. (2003). A typology of negative mentoring experiences: A multidimensional scaling study. *Human Relations, 56*(9), 1083–1106.

Tenenbaum, H. R., Crosby, F. J., & Gliner, M. D. (2001). Mentoring relationships in graduate school. *Journal of Vocational Behavior, 59,* 326–341.

University of Michigan. (2006). *How to mentor graduate students.* Retrieved May 13, 2008, from http://www.rackham.unmich.edu/StudentInfo/Publications/index.html

University of Michigan. (2007). *How to get the mentoring you want.* Retrieved June 27, 2008, from http://www.rackham.umich.edu/downloads/publications/mentoring.pdf

University of Washington. Graduate School. (2005a). *Mentoring: How to mentor graduate students: A faculty guide.* Seattle: Author.

University of Washington. Graduate School. (2005b). *Mentoring: How to obtain the mentoring you need.* Seattle: Author.

Walker, G., Golde, C. M., Jones, L., Bueschel, A., & Hutchings, P. (2008). *The formation of scholars: Rethinking doctoral education for the twenty-first century.* San Francisco: Jossey-Bass

Wilde, J. B., & Schau, C. G. (1991). Mentoring in graduate schools of education: Mentees' perceptions. *Journal of Experimental Education, 59,* 165–179.

Winnicott, C., Shepherd, R., & Davis, M. (Eds.). (1989). *Psycho-analytic explorations: D. W. Winnicott.* Cambridge, MA: Harvard University Press.

Zachary, L. J. (2002). The role of teacher as mentor. In J. M. Ross-Gordon (Ed.), *Contemporary viewpoints on teaching adults effectively* (pp. 27–38). New Directions for Adult and Continuing Education, no. 93. San Francisco: Jossey-Bass.

RESOURCES: FURTHER READING FOR SCHOLARLY WRITING

Maria S. Plakhotnik, M. Brad Shuck

The additional resources listed here can help novice scholars become productive writers. We have organized these into five sections. The first section contains resources useful at the beginning of a writing for publication project, such as reasons to write for publication, making authorship decisions, and foreseeing common pressures. The second section provides resources that can guide novice scholars through the writing process, from idea to submission, including how to write an effective literature review and method section of a manuscript and how to convert a thesis or dissertation into a publication. Listings in the third section focus on two issues that writers need to consider before submitting a manuscript to a journal: how to choose the journal and how to meet the journal editor's expectations. The fourth section lists resources that can help novice writers learn about the peer review process and deal with reviewers' feedback. The final section contains resources that discuss faculty experiences with teaching writing for publication and students' experiences with learning writing for publication.

Beginning the Writing Process

Authors should weigh many decisions before attempting to put pencil to paper (or, more likely, fingers to keyboard). The listings in this section will help novice writers recognize the challenges and critical questions that they must answer as the writing process develops. The resources focuses on the perils of beginning the writing process, from the reasons to start writing (de Rond & Miller, 2005; Mee, 2007), to making decisions about authorship (Hart, 2007; Musoba, 2008), to working effectively through the pressures of completing a writing project (Beukelmans, 1999; Cho, 2004).

Reasons for Writing for Publication

Answers to the question that novice authors commonly ask, "Why should I publish?" include an increasing sense of personal accomplishment, contributing to scholarship, advancing one's career (Lawrence & Honeycutt, 2005), or sharing new techniques and approaches that may affect practice (Mayer, 2007; Mee, 2007). Each writer undertakes a writing project for a variety of reasons, many of which should be considered at the onset. Questions about motivation (Mayer, 2007; Mee, 2007) and audience (Lawrence & Honeycutt, 2005) should be answered with clarity before writing the first sentence

de Rond, M., & Miller, A. N. (2005). Publish or perish: Bane or boon of academic life? *Journal of Management Inquiry, 14*(4), 321–329.

Jaeger, R. M., & Hendricks, A. Y. (1994). The publication process in educational measurement. *Educational Measurement: Issues and Practice, 13*(1), 20–26.

Lawrence, F. C., & Honeycutt, J. (2005). Writing in higher education: More than publish or perish. *Journal of Personal Finance, 4*(4), 86–90.

Mayer, D. K. (2007). Why write? To impact patient care! *Clinical Journal of Oncology Nursing, 11*(3), 323.

Mee, C. L. (2007). You, an author? Why not? *Nursing 2007, 6.*

Rankin, E. (2001). *The work of writing: Insights and strategies for academics and professionals.* San Francisco: Jossey-Bass.

Shaw, D. V. (1994). To publish or not? *SRA Journal, 26*(2), 5–9.

Sweitzer, H. F. (2003). Multiple forms of scholarship and their implications for human service educators. *Human Service Education, 23*(1), 5–13.

Authorship

Many novice researchers write with more experienced researchers, such as their faculty. When starting a coauthored publication, researchers often face issues of authorship, such as who should be credited as an author and in what order. Examination of hypothetical (Fine & Kurdek, 1993) and real (Musoba, 2008) cases can help novice researchers deal with the many ethical dilemmas around authorship. Weighing advantages and disadvantages of coauthored publication also can help researchers plan their future research projects (Hart, 2007; Moore & Griffin, 2006).

Fine, M. A., & Kurdek, L. A. (1993). Reflections on determining authorship credit and authorship order on faculty-student collaborations. *American Psychologist, 48*(11), 1141–1147.

Hart, R. (2007). Collaboration and article quality in the literature of academic librarianship. *Journal of Academic Librarianship, 33*(2), 190–195.

Malo, T. L., Hogeboom, D. L., & McDermott, R. J. (2007). Authorship trends in the *American Journal of Health Education:* 1996–2006. *American Journal of Health Education, 38*(6), 356–362.

McClimens, A. (2008). This is my truth, tell me yours: Exploring the internal tensions within collaborative learning disability research. *British Journal of Learning Disabilities, 36,* 271–276.

Moore, M. T., & Griffin, B. W. (2006). Identification of factors that influence authorship name placement and decisions to collaborate in peer-reviewed, education-related publications. *Studies in Educational Evaluation, 32,* 125–135.

Musoba, G. D. (2008). Writing across power lines. *New Horizons in Adult Education and Human Resource Development, 22*(3/4), 60–67.

Nguyen, T., & Nguyen, T. (2006). Authorship ethics: Issues and suggested guidelines for the helping professions. *Counseling and Values, 50*(3), 208–216.

Roberts, G. A., Davis, K. S., Zanger, D., Gerrard-Morris, A., & Robinson, D. H. (2006). Top contributors to the school psychology literature: 1996–2005. *Psychology in the Schools, 43*(6), 737–743.

Ruth, D. (2008). Being an academic: Authorship, authenticity and authority. *London Review of Education, 6*(2), 99–109.

Susser, M. (9997). Authors and authorship: Reform or abolition? *American Journal of Public Health, 87*(7), 1091–1092.

Dealing with Pressures

Authors working toward the completion of a writing project often face real-life challenges that can be time-consuming to overcome and at times cause writing projects to halt altogether. This section provides resources to help prepare novice researchers to face some of these challenges, including such issues as overcoming writing blocks (Boice, 1993), being productive (Boice, 1985), and maintaining publication/life balance (Beukelmans, 1999) for native and nonnative speakers of English (Cho, 2004). Awareness of these challenges and strategies to overcome them can help writers focus on completion of their projects rather than regrets of never finalizing their ideas.

Beukelmans, D. R. (1999). Scholarly writing: Managing the competition for time and attention. *AAC Augmentative and Alternative Communication, 15,* 212–214.

Boice, R. (1985). The neglected third factor in writing: Productivity. *College Composition and Communication, 36*(4), 472–480.

Boice, R. (1993). Writing blocks and tacit knowledge. *Journal of Higher Education, 64*(1), 19–54.

Cho, S. (2004). Challenges of entering discourse communities through publishing in English: Perspectives of nonnative-speaking doctoral students in the United States of America. *Journal of Language Identity and Education, 3*(1), 47–72.

Davis, A. J., & Tschudin, V. (2007). Publishing in English-language journals. *Nursing Ethics, 14*(3), 425–430.

Writing Process: From Idea to Submission

Just like any great idea that must be moved to action, this section covers a lot of important ground for novice writers to consider. Subsections include tricks of the trade (Klinger, Scanlon & Pressley, 2005), writing literature reviews (Rocco & Plakhotnik, 2009) and method sections (Wolcott, 2008) in a manuscript, and dissertation and thesis writing and publishing (Germano, 2005). Each section provides the specifics that authors need to succeed in each area and presents some of the most widely used articles to date on the process of writing (Torraco, 2005).

Tricks of the Trade

Regardless of the level of experience in writing for publication, any writer can find some tricks of the trade in the articles listed in this section: in-depth techniques for writing in unique areas such as writing toward specific disciplines (Becker & Richards, 1986; Dixon, 2001; Jalongo, 2002), writing for academic audiences (Hiemstra & Brier, 1994; Huff, 1999; Klinger et al., 2005), and overall guidelines for good writing (Apps, 1982; Barley, 2006).

Apps, J. W. (1982). *Improving your writing skills: A learning plan for adults.* Chicago: Follett.

Barley, S. R. (2006). When I write my masterpiece: Thoughts on what makes a paper interesting. *Academy of Management Journal, 49*(1), 16–20.

Becker, H. S. (1998). *Tricks of the trade: How to think about your research while you're doing it.* Chicago: University of Chicago Press.

Becker, H. S., & Richards, P. (1986). *Writing for social scientists: How to start and finish your thesis, book, or article* (2nd ed.). Chicago: University of Chicago Press.

Booth, W. C., Colomb, G. G., & Williams, J. M. (2008). *The craft of research* (3rd ed.). Chicago: University of Chicago Press.

Casanave, C., & Vandrick, S. (Eds.). (2003). *Writing for scholarly publication: Behind the scenes in language education.* Mahwah, NJ: Erlbaum.

Dixon, N. (2001). Methodology matters: Writing for publication—A guide for new authors. *International Journal for Quality of Health Care, 13*(5), 417–421.

Dutton, J. E., & Dukerich, J. M. (2006). The relational foundation of research: An underappreciated dimension of interesting research. *Academy of Management Journal, 49*(1), 21–26.

Heitzmann, R. (2008). Writing for publication in social studies education. *Social Studies, 99*(1), 37–40.

Henson, K. T. (1995). *The art of writing for publication.* Needham Heights, MA: Allyn & Bacon.

Hiemstra, R., & Brier, E. M. (1994). *Professional writing: Processes, strategies, and tips for publishing in educational journals.* Malabar, FL: Krieger.

Huff, A. S. (1999). *Writing for scholarly publication.* Thousand Oaks, CA: Sage.

Jackson, J.F.L., Nelson, J. R., Heggins, W. III, Baatz, C. M., & Schuh, J. H. (1999). Guidelines for writing for publication: Demystifying the process. *College and University, 75*(1), 11–14.

Jalongo, M. R. (2002). *Writing for publication: A practical guide for educators.* Norwood, MA: Christopher-Gordon.

Journal of Scholarly Publishing, University of Toronto Press. Available at http://www .utpjournals.com/jsp/jsp.html

Klinger, J. K., Scanlon, D., & Pressley, M. (2005). How to publish in scholarly journals. *Educational Researcher, 34*(8), 14–20.

Mosteller, F., Nave, B., & Miech, E. J. (2004). Why we need a structured abstract in education research. *Educational Researcher, 33*(1), 29–34.

Moxley, J. M. (Ed.). (1992). *Writing and publishing for academic authors.* Lanham, MD: University Press of America.

Murray, D. M. (1986). One writer's secrets. *College Composition and Communication, 37*(2), 146–153.

Raymond, J. C. (1993). I-dropping and androgyny: The authorial I in scholarly writing. *College Composition and Communication, 44*(4), 478–483.

Schwartz, M. (1995). *Guidelines for bias-free writing.* Bloomington: Indiana University Press.

Smiles, T. L., & Short, K. G. (2006). Transforming teacher voice through writing for publication. *Teacher Education Quarterly, 33*(3), 133–147.

Wallace, M., & Wray, A. (2006). *Critical reading and writing for postgraduates.* Thousand Oaks, CA: Sage.

Williams, J. (1990). *Style: Toward clarity and grace.* Chicago: University of Chicago Press.

Witt, P. A. (1995). Writing for publication: Rationale, process, and pitfalls. *Journal of Park and Recreation Administration, 13*(1), 1–9.

Literature Reviews

A literature review is a component of any manuscript, regardless of the topic, method, or discipline. Writing a literature review can be a daunting task for a novice writer who must learn how to identify streams of literature, select databases, and set selection criteria for which articles to choose. For example, Fink (2009) discusses issues around beginning the literature review, such as where to start, where to end, and how to thread each article together to make a comprehensible argument. Torraco (2005) and Yorks (2008) provide guidelines for structuring a literature review, while Rocco and Plakhotnik (2009) differentiate among commonly used terms such as *conceptual and theoretical frameworks* and *literature reviews.* Some authors view the literature review as a creative outlet (Montuori, 2005), a means of personal and academic expression, and an exercise in scholarship (Boote & Beile, 2005).

Boote, D. N., & Beile, P. (2005). Scholars before researchers: On the centrality of the dissertation literature review in research preparation. *Educational Researcher, 34*(6), 3–15.

Cooper, H. (1998). *Synthesizing research: A guide for literature reviews* (3rd ed.). Thousand Oaks, CA: Sage.

Fink, A. (2009). *Conducting research literature reviews: From the Internet to paper* (3rd ed.). Thousand Oaks, CA: Sage.

Hart, C. (1998). *Doing a literature review: Releasing the social science research imagination.* Thousand Oaks, CA: Sage

Montuori, A. (2005). Literature review as creative inquiry: Reframing scholarship as a creative process. *Journal of Transformative Education, 3,* 374–393.

Roberts, C. M. (2004). *The dissertation journey: A practical and comprehensive guide to planning, writing, and defending your dissertation.* Thousand Oaks, CA: Corwin Press.

Rocco, T. S., & Plakhotnik, M. P. (2009). Literature reviews, conceptual frameworks, and theoretical frameworks: Terms, functions, and distinctions. *Human Resource Development Review, 8*(1), 120–130.

Torraco, R. J. (2005). Writing integrative literature reviews: Guidelines and examples. *Human Resource Development Review, 4*(3), 356–367.

Yorks, L. (2008). What we know, what we don't know, what we need to know: Integrative literature reviews are research. *Human Resource Development Review, 7*(2), 139–141.

Method Sections

Because of the critical information they communicate to the reader, the method section is one of the most important sections of any academic undertaking (Merriam & Simpson, 2000). Writers are encouraged to follow accepted practices to document techniques of mixed method (Johnson & Onwuegbuzie, 2004), qualitative (Rocco, 2003), and quantitative (Creswell, 2003) research. Careful attention should be paid to the structure, identification of steps, and transparency of the research process when writing such sections.

Bem, D. J. (2002). Writing the empirical journal article. In M. P. Zanna & J. M. Darley (Eds.), *The compleat academic: A practical guide for the beginning social scientist* (pp. 185–219). New York: Random House.

Bogdan R. C., & Biklen, S. K. (2007). *Qualitative research for education* (5th ed.). Needham, MA: Allyn & Bacon.

Bryk, A. S., & Raudenbush, S. W. (2002). *Hierarchical linear models: Applications and data analysis methods.* Thousand Oaks, CA: Sage.

Creswell, J. W. (2003). *Research design: Qualitative, quantitative, and mixed methods approaches* (2nd ed.). Thousand Oaks, CA: Sage.

Creswell, J. W., & Tashakkori, A. (2007). Editorial: Developing publishable mixed methods manuscripts. *Journal of Mixed Methods Research, 1*(2), 107–111.

Isaac, S., & Michael, W. B. (1995). *Handbook in research and evaluation: A study of principles, methods, and strategies useful in the planning, design, and evaluation of studies in education and the behavioral sciences.* San Diego, CA: EdITS.

Johnson, R. B., & Onwuegbuzie, A. J. (2004). Mixed methods research: A research paradigm whose time has come. *Educational Researcher, 33,* 14–26.

Merriam, S. B., & Simpson, E. L. (2000). *A guide to research for educators and trainers of adults* (2nd ed.). Malabar, FL: Krieger.

Rocco, T. S. (2003). Shaping the future: Writing up the method on qualitative studies. *Human Resource Development Review, 14*(3), 343–349.

Wolcott, H. F. (2008). *Writing up qualitative research* (3rd ed.). Thousand Oaks, CA: Sage.
Woods, P. (1999). *Successful writing for qualitative researchers.* London: Routledge.

Thesis and Dissertation

Many graduate and doctoral students convert their thesis or dissertation into a publication, which can be challenging (see Harman & Montagnes, 2000; Heppner & Heppner, 2003). A dissertation or thesis can become "a single scholarly article, a handful of them, a specialized monograph, a broader scholarly work, a trade book, even the seeds of two or more distinct projects that could occupy the author for decades" (Germano, 2005, p. 4). The resources listed in this section are focused on effective dissertation and thesis writing and have sections or chapters that discuss how novice writers can convert their dissertation or thesis into a publication.

Bryant, M. T. (2004). *The portable dissertation advisor.* Thousand Oaks, CA: Corwin Press. (See Chapter Seven.)

Cottrell, R. R., & McKenzie, J. F. (2005). *Health promotion and education research methods: Using the five chapter thesis/dissertation model.* Sudbury, MA: Jones & Bartlett. (See Chapter Fourteen.)

Germano, W. (2005). *From dissertation to book.* Chicago: University of Chicago Press.

Glatthorn, A. A., & Joyner, R. L. (2005). *Writing the winning thesis or dissertation: A step-by-step guide* (2nd ed.). Thousand Oaks, CA: Corwin Press. (See Part Four.)

Harman, E., & Montagnes, I. (2000). *The thesis and the book: A guide for first-time academic authors.* Toronto: University of Toronto Press.

Heppner, P. P., & Heppner, M. J. (2003). *Writing and publishing your thesis, dissertation, and research: A guide for students in the helping professions.* Florence, KY: Brooks-Cole.

Luey, B. (2007). *Revising your dissertation: Advice from leading editors.* Berkeley: University of California Press.

Madisen, D. (1992). *Successful dissertations and thesis: A guide to graduate student research from proposal to completion* (2nd ed.). San Francisco: Jossey-Bass. (See Chapter Nine.)

Piantanida, M., & Garman, N. B. (1999). *The qualitative dissertation: A guide for students and faculty.* Thousand Oaks, CA: Corwin Press.

Sternberg, D. (1981). *How to complete and survive a doctoral dissertation.* New York: St. Martin's Press.

Considerations Before Manuscript Submission

Learning about different journals in the author's field and related fields, choosing the best journal for submission of each manuscript, and following journal guidelines help researchers' work get accepted, known, and cited. This section provides resources that can help novice researchers choose the journal (Henson, 1997) and meet the journal editors' expectations (Thompson, 2005).

Choosing the Journal

Choosing the right journal is not an easy task. For example, the American Anthropological Association alone publishes twenty-two journals. Choosing a journal usually starts with reading about a journal's audience and scope and whether submissions undergo a peer review process. However, many other journal characteristics can make a difference, including citation rate, journal ranking, and circulation (Kupfersmid & Wonderly, 1994; Leung, 2007), journal acceptance rates, turnaround time (Henson, 1997), or the country where the journal is published (Faria, 2005).

Faria, J. R. (2005). Is there a trade-off between domestic and international publications? *Journal of Socio-Economics, 34,* 269–280.

Gargiulo, R., Jalongo, M. R., & Motari, J. (2001). Writing for publication in early childhood education: Survey data from editors and advice to authors. *Early Childhood Education Journal, 29*(1), 17–23.

Henson, K. T. (1997). Writing for publication: Some perennial mistakes. *Phi Delta Kappan, 78*(10), 781–784.

Judge, T. A., Cable, D. M., Colbert, A. E., & Rynes, S. L. (2007). What causes a management article to be cited: Article, author, or journal? *Academy of Management Journal, 50*(3), 491–506.

Kupfersmid, J., & Wonderly, D. M. (1994). *An author's guide to publishing better articles in better journals in the behavioral sciences.* Hoboken, NJ: Wiley.

Leung, K. (2007). The glory and tyranny of citation impact: An east Asian perspective. *Academy of Management Journal, 50*(2), 510–513.

Minton, C.A.B., Delini, F. M., & Dee, R. C. (2008). Ten years of peer-reviewed articles in counselor education: Where, what, who? *Counselor Education and Supervision, 48*(2), 133–143.

Shelley, M. C., & Schuh, J. H. (2001). Are the best higher education journals really the best? A meta-analysis of writing quality and readability. *Journal of Scholarly Publishing, 33*(1), 11–22.

Torraco, R. J. (2005). Ratings, rankings, results, and what really matters. *Human Resource Development Review, 4*(3), 3–7.

Torraco, R. J., & Yorks, L. (2007). Do practitioners compromise scholarly standards? Do scholars comprehend the rigors of practice? Can a theory journal be a viable bridge across the chasm? *Human Resource Development Review, 6*(3), 3–6.

Wellington, J., & Torgerson, C. J. (2005). Writing for publication: What counts as a "high status, eminent academic journal." *Journal of Further and Higher Education, 29*(1), 35–48.

Wicks, A. C., & Robin, D. (1996). An evaluation of journal quality: The perspective of business ethics researchers. *Business Ethics Quarterly, 6,* 359–371.

Following Editors' Expectations

Once the journal is chosen, the manuscript should be formatted and modified as needed according to the journal guidelines. These guidelines can be found on the journal Web site or in the preliminary or back pages of each issue. Often journal editors share their expectations about the types and quality of manuscripts. Following editors' advice (Plakhotnik, 2006; Yorks, 2007) also can help researchers improve their manuscripts and meet editors' expectations.

Ballenger, R., Kaser, S., Kauffman, G., Schroeder, J., & Short, K. G. (2006). Our reflection on writing for publication. *Language Arts, 83*(6), 534–543.

Burton, M. (2007). *Hits and tips on how to write for publication in academic and professional journals.* New York; Great Britain: Elsevier. Available at http://www.writingforpublication.com/pageturning_doc/page_turner.html

Craik, R. L., & Riddle, D. L. (2007). Sometimes it *is* better to read the instructions first. *Physical Therapy, 87*(4), 366–367.

Duncan, S. S. (1995). Writing for publication. *Journal of Industrial Teacher Education, 32*(2), 95–102.

Plakhotnik, M. P. (2006). Creating order from chaos: A few observations and suggestions on using APA guidelines. *New Horizons in Adult Education and Human Resource Development, 20*(4), 3–5.

Quallich, S. (2007). Fear factor: The write stuff. *Urologic Nursing, 27*(4), 275–277.

Thompson, A. M. (2005). Writing for publication in this refereed journal. *Midwifery, 21,* 190–194.

Waters, L., & Argersiner, J. L. (2009). Slow writing; or, getting off the book standard: What can journal editors do? *Journal of Scholarly Publishing, 40*(2), 129–143.

Yorks, L. (2007). Observations about submissions and publications in HRDR. *Human Resource Development Review, 6*(3), 219–221.

Peer Review Process

A peer review process is used "to assess the value of new knowledge presented in journal submissions" (Miller, 2006, p. 425). A manuscript submitted to a journal for publication is sent to several, usually three, peers who use their expertise to provide feedback to the authors. Once all reviews are complete, journal editors make a decision as to whether to accept or reject the manuscript. After the first round of reviews, up to 90 percent of manuscripts are rejected by high-ranking journals (Agarwal, Echambadi, Franco, & Sarkar, 2006; McKercher, Law, Weber, Song, & Hsu, 2007). Therefore, most authors face more than one round of reviews that can stretch for many months and sometimes a couple of years. This section provides resources to help novice scholars learn about the review process (Miller, 2006; Rynes, 2006a) and deal with reviewers' feedback (Agarwal et al., 2006; Bergh, 2006).

Learning About the Review Process

Peer review is a stressful part of the writing for publication process. Editors' decisions to reject or revise and resubmit a manuscript often discourage researchers. Presenting a manuscript at a conference or seeking peers' feedback prior to submitting a manuscript to a journal can maximize the chances of acceptance, publication, and citation (see Brown, 2005). Learning about how journals choose their reviewers (Rynes, 2006a), what aspects of the manuscript reviewers find most important (McKercher et al., 2007), and what difficulties are often identified in the review process can help novice scholars understand what happens behind the scenes of the peer review process.

Brown, L. D. (2005). The importance of circulating and presenting manuscripts: Evidence from the accounting literature. *Accounting Review, 80*(1), 55–83.

Change, J., & Lai, C. (2001). Is it worthwhile to pay referees? *Southern Economic Journal, 68*(2), 457–463.

Kumashiro, K. (2005). Thinking collaboratively about the peer-review process for journal-article publication. *Harvard Educational Review, 75*(3), 257–285.

McKercher, B., Law, B., Weber, K., Song, H., & Hsu, C. (2007). Why referees reject manuscripts. *Journal of Hospitality and Tourism Research, 31*(4), 455–470.

Miller, C. C. (2006). Peer review in the organizational and management sciences: Prevalence and effects of reviewer hostility, bias, and dissensus. *Academy of Management Journal, 49*(3), 425–431.

Runeson, G., & Loosemore, M. (1999). Gate-keepers or judges: Peer reviews in construction management. *Construction Management and Economics, 17*(4), 529–537.

Rynes, S. L. (2006a). "Getting on board" with AMJ: Balancing quality and innovation in the review process. *Academy of Management Journal, 49*(6), 1097–1102.

Tsang, E.W.K., & Frey, B. S. (2007). The as-is journal review process: Let authors own their ideas. *Academy of Management Learning & Education, 6*(1), 128–136.

Dealing with Feedback

Many researchers struggle when dealing with reviewers' feedback: up to 50 percent of revised and resubmitted manuscripts are rejected (Rynes et al., 2005). Researchers can learn from fellow authors (Agarwal et al., 2006; Seibert, 2006) and journal editors (Bergh, 2006; Rynes, 2006b) how to understand and evaluate reviewers' feedback, step back and reexamine the logic and depth of their manuscript, and make decisions about what feedback to incorporate and how.

Agarwal, R., Echambadi, R., Franco, A. M., & Sarkar, S. (2006). Reap rewards: Maximizing benefits from reviewer comments. *Academy of Management Journal, 49*(2), 191–196.

Bergh, D. D. (2006). Editing the 2004 *AMJ* best article award winner. *Academy of Management Journal, 49*(2), 197–202.

Caffarella, R. S., & Barnett, B. G. (2000). Teaching doctoral students to become scholarly writers: The importance of giving and receiving critiques. *Studies in Higher Education, 25*(1), 39–52.

Dossin, M. M. (2003). Among friends: Effective peer critiquing. *Clearing House, 76*(4), 206–207.

Golden-Biddle, K., & Locke, K. D. (2007). *Composing qualitative research* (2nd ed.). Thousand Oaks, CA: Sage.

Rynes, S. L. (2006b). Observations on "Anatomy of an R&R" and other reflections. *Academy of Management Journal, 49*(2), 208–214.

Rynes, S. L., Hillman, A., Ireland, R. D., Kirkman, B. L., Law, K. S., Miller, C. C., et al. (2005). Everything you've always wanted to know about *AMJ* (but may have been afraid to ask). *Academy of Management Journal, 48,* 732–737.

Seibert, S. E. (2006). Anatomy of an R&R: (Or, reviewers are an author's best friend). *Academy of Management Journal, 49*(2), 203–207.

The Experience of Teaching and Learning to Write for Publication

Writing is a special experience for all those who undertake the process. As the capstone section to this chapter, the publications listed here reflect on two perspectives of the writing process: the faculty who teach writing for publication and the students who learn to write for publication. For example, Belcher (2009) speaks to the personal transformation she experienced as a result of teaching writing for publication to graduate students over the course of ten years, while Nackoney, Munn, and Gallagher (2007) recall their transformation as emerging scholars. Rich with voice and meaning, these publications represent the development of the writing process from a personal standpoint.

The Experience of Teaching to Write for Publication

Many novice researchers are also novice or aspiring faculty. This section provides resources that can help novice and experienced faculty to teach writing for publication. These resources include best practices of teaching writing (Dyson & Freedman, 1990; Hernandez, 1985), teaching writing to doctoral students (Caffarella & Barnett, 1997; Nolan & Rocco, 2009; Rocco, Parsons, Bernier, & Batist, 2003), teaching to write for practitioner audiences (Carnes, Jennings, Vice, & Wiedmaier, 2001), and teaching graduate and doctoral students to peer-review and write in groups (Lee & Boud, 2003; O'Connor & Ruchala, 1998).

Barnett, B., Caffarella, R. S., & Gimmestad, M. (1998). *Teaching scholarly writing to doctoral students: Giving novice scholars a running start.* Paper presented at the American Education Research Conference, San Antonio, TX.

Belcher, W. L. (2009). Reflections on ten years of teaching writing for publication to graduate students and junior faculty. *Journal of Scholarly Publishing, 40*(2), 184–200.

Bloom, L. Z. (1981, August). *Why graduate students can't write: Implications of research on writing anxiety for graduate education.* Paper presented at the Annual Meeting of the Conference on College Composition and Communication, Dallas, TX. (ERIC Document Reproduction Service No. ED199710)

Caffarella, R. S., & Barnett, B. G. (1997, October). *Teaching doctoral students writing: Negotiating the borders between the world of practice and doctoral study.* Paper presented at the annual Convention of the University Council for Educational Administration, Orlando, FL. (ERIC Document Reproduction Service No. 415792)

Carnes, L. W., Jennings, M. S., Vice, J. P., & Wiedmaier, C. (2001). The role of the business educator in a writing-across-the-curriculum program. *Journal of Education for Business, 76*(4), 216–219.

Cohen, M., & Riel, M. (1989). The effect of distant audiences on students' writing. *American Educational Research Journal, 26*(2), 143–159.

Dyson, A. H., & Freedman, S. W. (1990). *On teaching writing: A review of the literature.* Washington, DC: Office of Educational Research and Improvement. (ERIC Document Reproduction Service No. ED 324690)

Gaillet, L. L. (1996, March). *Designing a graduate seminar in academic writing.* Paper presented at the Annual Meeting of the Conference on College Composition and Communication, Milwaukee, WI. (ERIC Document Reproduction Service No. ED402595)

Harris, M. J. (2006). Three steps to teaching abstract and critique writing. *International Journal of Teaching and Learning in Higher Education, 17*(2), 136–146.

Harris, K. R., Graham, S., & Mason, L. H. (2006). Improving the writing, knowledge, and motivation of struggling young writers: Effects of self-regulated strategy development with and without peer support. *American Educational Research Journal, 43*(2), 295–340.

Hernandez, N. (1985). *The fourth, composite "R" for graduate students: Research.* (ERIC Document Reproduction Service No. ED267671)

Jeske, J. M. (1985). *Resources for graduate instruction.* (ERIC Document Reproduction Service No. ED273975)

Kalmer, B. (2008). Rethinking doctoral publication practices: Writing from and beyond the thesis. *Studies in Higher Education, 33*(3), 283–294.

Lee, A., & Boud, D. (2003). Writing groups, change and academic identity: Research development as local practice. *Studies in Higher Education, 28*(2), 187–200.

Loux, A. K., & Stoddart, R. (1993). Denial, conflagration, pride: Three stages in the development of an advanced writing requirement. *College Composition and Communication, 45*(4), 521–534.

Nolan, R., & Rocco, T. S. (2009). Teaching graduate students in the social sciences writing for publication. *International Journal of Teaching and Learning in Higher Education, 20*(2), 267–273. Available at http://www.isetl.org/ijtlhe/

O'Connor, T. J., & Ruchala, L. V. (1998). A model for small-group writing labs in an accounting curriculum. *Issues in Accounting Education, 13*(1), 93–111.

Pfeifer, H. L., & Ferree, C. W. (2006). Tired of "reeding" bad papers? Teaching research and writing skills to criminal justice students. *Journal of Criminal Justice Education, 17*(1), 121–198.

Pollard, R.P.F., & Easter, M. (2001). Writing across curriculum: Evaluating a faculty-centered approach. *Journal of Language for International Business, 17*(2), 22–41.

Rocco, T. S., Parsons, M., Bernier, J. D., & Batist, C. (2003, October). Guiding the work of writing: Reflections on the writing process. In T. Ferro & G. Dean (Eds.), *Proceedings of the Midwest Research-to-Practice Conference in Adult, Continuing, and Community Education* (pp. 174–180). Columbus: Ohio State University.

Rose, M., & McClafferty, K. A. (2001). A call for the teaching of writing in graduate education. *Educational Researcher, 30*(2), 27–33.

Simmons, T. L. (2000). "Getting the words right": How to teach—and not to teach—writing. *National Review, 52*(17), 48–50.

Sorcinelli, M. D., & Elbow, P. (Eds.). (1997). *Writing to learn: Strategies for assigning and responding to writing across the disciplines.* New Directions for Teaching and Learning, no. 69. San Francisco: Jossey-Bass.

The Experience of Learning to Write for Publication

Depending on their backgrounds, knowledge, and skills, students can have different experiences with the same writing project (Engstrom, 1999). These experiences can either hinder the process or help move it toward completion (Lavelle & Zuercher, 2001). This section provides resources that can help novice faculty who teach writing for publication and students in their classrooms understand other students' experiences with writing. These experiences include the development of the emerging scholar's perspective (Nackoney, Munn, & Gallagher, 2007), the quest for voice (Heinrich, 2000), and some of the many strategies students use to hone their writing skills (Torrance, Thomas, & Robinson, 1994).

Engstrom, C. M. (1999). Promoting the scholarly writing of female doctoral students in higher education and student affairs graduate programs. *NASPA Journal, 36*(4), 264–277.

Heinrich, K. T. (2000). The passionate scholar: A mid-life, woman doctoral student's quest for voice. *Qualitative Studies in Education, 13*(1), 63–83.

Lavelle, E., & Zuercher, N. (2001). The writing approaches of university students. *Higher Education, 42*(3), 373–391.

Nackoney, C. K., Munn, S. L., & Gallagher, S. J. (2007). Becoming scholarly writers: An autoethnography of three emerging scholars. In L. Servage & T. Fenwick (Eds.), *Proceedings of the 48th Adult Education Research Conference* (pp. 445–450). Halifax, Nova Scotia.

Nielsen, S. M., & Rocco, T. S. (2002). Joining the conversation: Graduate students' perceptions of writing for publication. In J. M. Pettitt (Ed.), *Proceedings of the 43rd Adult Education Research Conference* (pp. 309–314). Raleigh: North Carolina State University.

Torrance, M., Thomas, G. V., & Robinson, E. J. (1992). The writing experiences of social science research students. *Studies in Higher Education, 17*(2), 155–167.

Torrance, M., Thomas, G. V., & Robinson, E. J. (1994). The writing strategies of graduate research students in the social sciences. *Higher Education, 27*(3), 379–392.

INDEX